BY THE EDITORS OF
HORIZON MAGAZINE

EDITOR
THOMAS FRONCEK

INTRODUCTORY ESSAY BY
JAMES H. BILLINGTON
Professor of History,
Princeton University

CONSULTANT
S. FREDERICK STARR
Assistant Professor of History,
Princeton University

AMERICAN HERITAGE PUBLISHING CO., INC.,
NEW YORK

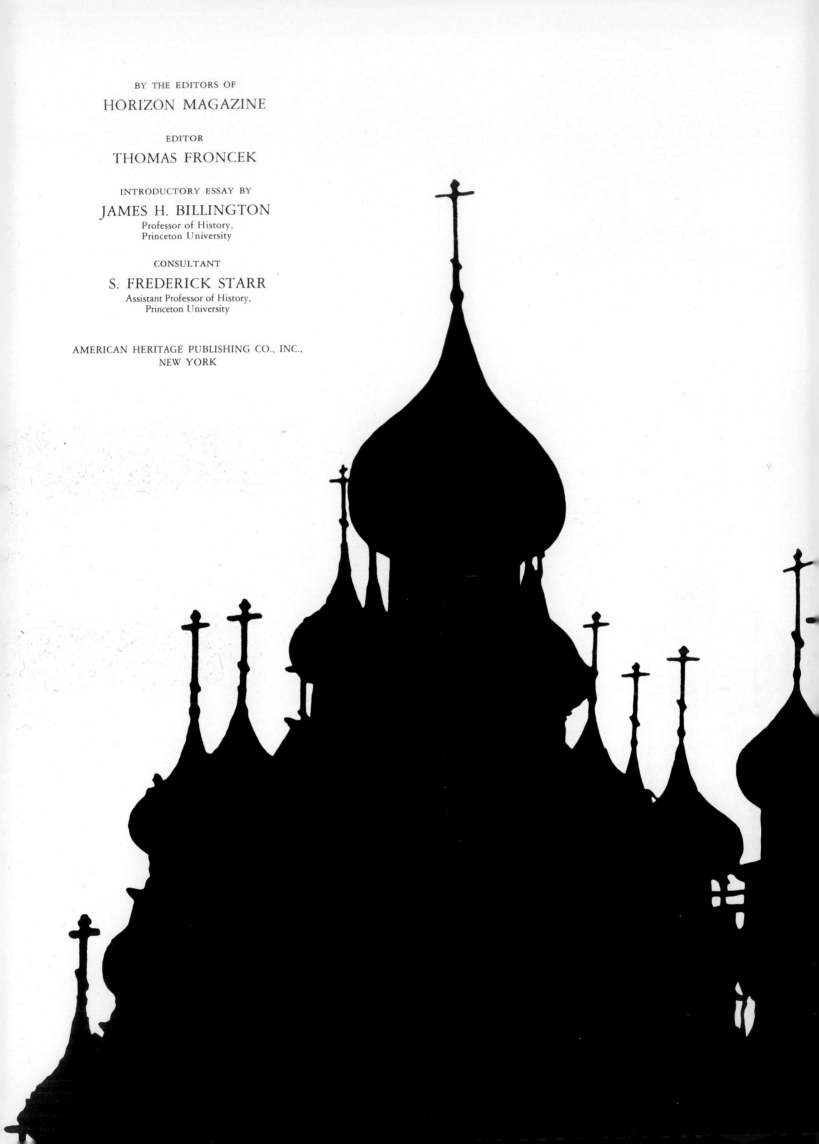

THE HORIZON BOOK OF THE
ARTS OF RUSSIA

HORIZON BOOK DIVISION

EDITORIAL DIRECTOR
Richard M. Ketchum

GENERAL EDITOR
Alvin M. Josephy, Jr.

EDITOR, HORIZON BOOKS
Wendy Buehr

Staff for this Book

EDITOR
Thomas Froncek

ART DIRECTOR
Mary Ann Joulwan

PICTURE EDITOR
Maureen Dwyer

COPY EDITOR
Brenda Bennerup

ASSOCIATE EDITORS
Virginia Bennett
Charles W. Folds

CONTRIBUTING EDITORS
Margot Brill
Mary Durant
Angela Hill
Anne Moffat

RESEARCHER
Michael Feist

EDITORIAL ASSISTANT
Roxanne Wehrhan

EUROPEAN BUREAU
Gertrudis Feliu, *Chief*

AMERICAN HERITAGE PUBLISHING CO., INC.

PRESIDENT
James Parton

EDITORIAL COMMITTEE
Joseph J. Thorndike, *Chairman*
Oliver Jensen
Alvin M. Josephy, Jr.
Richard M. Ketchum

EDITORIAL ART DIRECTOR
Murray Belsky

PUBLISHER, HORIZON MAGAZINE
Paul Gottlieb

Horizon Magazine is published quarterly by American Heritage Publishing Co., Inc., 551 Fifth Avenue, N.Y., N.Y. 10017. Printed in the United States of America. Library of Congress Catalog Card Number 70–117352. Standard Book Numbers: Regular Edition 8281–0100–0; Deluxe Edition 8281–0101–9; Boxed Edition 8281–0102–7.

Published simultaneously in Canada by Fitzhenry & Whiteside Limited.

ABOVE: *Saint George the Dragon Slayer, the patron and protector of old Muscovy, is depicted in this seventeenth-century wood carving.*

NOVOSTI

HALF-TITLE PAGE: *The Order of the White Eagle symbolized imperial Russia's might and her neighbor's fate. A Polish order, it became Russian in 1831, when Poland was conquered and made part of Russia's empire. In the order's gold and enamel badge Russia's double-headed eagle engulfs the white eagle and Maltese cross of Poland.*

COLLECTION OF MRS. MERRIWEATHER POST, HILLWOOD, WASHINGTON, D.C.

TITLE PAGE: *Looming in silhouette on Kizhi Island in Lake Onega are the wooden onion domes of the Churches of the Transfiguration (left) and the Intercession (center); at right is a wooden bell tower.*

Contents

The Spirit of Russian Art

An Essay by James H. Billington

No region in Eurasia would seem more inhospitable to artistic creation than the sixth of the world's landed surface covered by the U.S.S.R. The southern steppe offers no natural obstacles to invaders. The northern forest is perennially inflammable and unutterably cold. Both regions stretch on with an unrelieved monotony that makes the individual and his creative efforts seem insignificant, if not foredoomed to failure. Nor is there any seeming sense of relief in the eastward reach of the frontier itself. The forest leads only to the Siberian tundra with the lowest temperatures ever recorded in inhabited parts of the earth; the steppe trails off into the almost equally forbidding deserts of central Asia and Mongolia. In both directions lie wastelands without water. The great rivers of the Siberian forests—Ob, Yenisei, Lena—vanish into the Arctic ice; the lesser rivers of the Asian plain—Murgab, Tedzhen—literally disappear into the sands of Kara-kum. In the north, snow often evaporates without melting into water; in the south rain evaporates before reaching the earth.

Yet within this land, there have appeared in relatively recent and rapid succession some of the most luminous religious paintings, the most imposing architectural ensembles,

Moscow's Kremlin, the fortress seat of tsars and commissars, towers over Red Square and Lenin's tomb (the low building at center). St. Basil's Cathedral rises in the distance, at the end of the square.

and most powerful prose fiction of all time. In addition, great traditions of decorative art, satirical theater, and classical ballet were lifted to new heights of achievement far from the warmer Mediterranean and Near Eastern lands of their origin. All of this varied artistic activity combined with new economic energies at the beginning of the present century to produce a burst of innovation that shattered most of the old molds within which art had been contained in modern Russia and the West. Working together in what had formerly been independent arts, painters, writers, musicians, dancers, and even film makers began developing alternatives to past artistic convention: abstraction in painting and sculpture; chromatic and multimedial music; free-form literature and dance; method acting; and film montage. Out of this upheaval, conservative Europe and America found new models for modernity in art, and revolutionaries in and beyond Russia were briefly infected with an artistic ideal that had been lost since the Middle Ages: of a selfless, communal art whose scale is the total environment and whose aim is not the entertainment but the salvation of the human race.

If Stalin and his heirs have destroyed much of the credibility of this ideal and of the Russian legacy of creativity in the arts, much still survives in museums and memories. And this fact may provide Russia with resources for the future as well as nostalgic consolation in the present. Entire cities are often museums—imperial Petersburg encapsulated inside

7

modern Leningrad like a crown jewel in a new base metal setting; or medieval Suzdal, largely untouched by modernity and currently being restored to its former glory. These cities inspire the imagination in ways no modern city can—least of all those built by Soviet architects as they moved from monstrosity under Stalin to monotony under his successors.

Even more than the monuments, the memories of Old Russia are well preserved. For Russia is rich in oral folklore and has long experience in keeping alive aspects of past history and present aspiration that have been denied expression in the officially controlled written culture and that have only occasionally—and belatedly—been written down for a wider audience. As in its early religious art, Russia's enduring oral folklore is the anonymous and usually collective work of the Russian people themselves, more than of any individual craftsman.

The Russian people perhaps bear comparison with the American more than with any other people, despite obvious differences in cultural heritage and political development. Like America, Russia is a relatively new civilization that grew from Christian roots on the periphery of Europe to become one of the world's two great industrial superpowers. During parallel periods of expansion from the seventeenth through the nineteenth centuries, the two civilizations moved toward each other across the Northern Hemisphere, their pioneer settlements overlapping briefly in Northern California, where the old Russian Fort Ross (from *Rossia*) may still be seen fifty miles northwest of San Francisco.

Russians developed their own frontier spirit and psychology. The earliest Russian epic, *The Lay of Igor's Campaign*, is a Cowboys-and-Indians tale of a raid out of Kiev against the Polovetsian peoples of the steppe; and this tale was transposed in the nineteenth century into perhaps the most popular of Russian national operas, Alexander Borodin's *Prince Igor*. The rugged Cossacks who established military outposts on the frontier and thus carried Russian civilization down the Dnieper, the Don, and the Volga—then on into Siberia—recall the stockade settlers and freebooters of the early American West. They inspired a rich literature from Nikolai Gogol's *Taras Bulba* through Mikhail Sholokhov's epic of the Russian Revolution and Civil War, *And Quiet Flows the Don*. The schismatic Old Believers who sought refuge in the hitherto vacant wastelands of the Russian north and east recall the Mormons and other American sects who set off into forbidding virgin territory in search of freedom from religious persecution. They too inspired many Russian writers and became the all-consuming interest of Modest Mussorgsky, who made them the subject of his unfinished operatic masterpiece, the "popular musical drama" *Khovanshchina*.

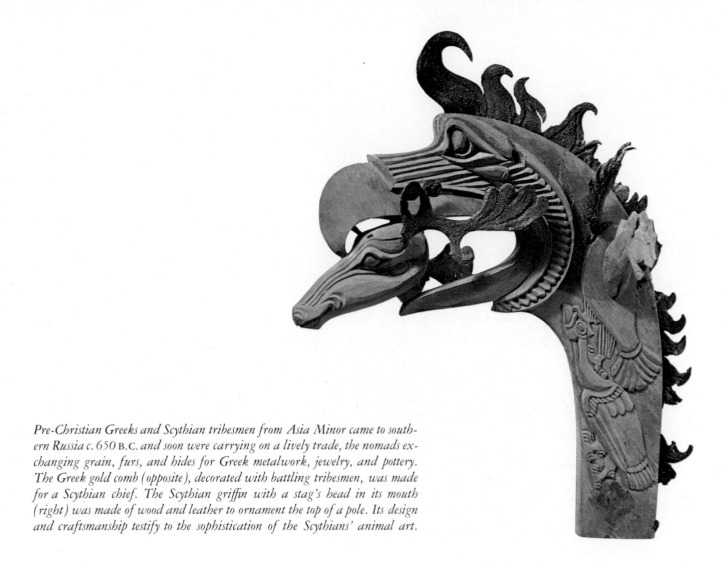

Pre-Christian Greeks and Scythian tribesmen from Asia Minor came to southern Russia c. 650 B.C. and soon were carrying on a lively trade, the nomads exchanging grain, furs, and hides for Greek metalwork, jewelry, and pottery. The Greek gold comb (opposite), decorated with battling tribesmen, was made for a Scythian chief. The Scythian griffin with a stag's head in its mouth (right) was made of wood and leather to ornament the top of a pole. Its design and craftsmanship testify to the sophistication of the Scythians' animal art.

Out of the frontier society's need for discipline amidst physical adversity, and out of the imperatives of an ascetic monasticism that championed the colonization of the Russian interior, there arose the strain of moralism and repressed or deferred sexuality that Russian culture shared with American culture. Where the pioneering settlers were not missionary monks, they were cossacks and fur traders forced to accept long periods of celibacy. Even more than the early Puritans in relatively temperate North America, Russians had to forego personal indulgence for communal survival.

Since the Russian frontier communities tended to assimilate rather than annihilate the pre-existent native communities, they were influenced in many subtle ways by the animistic, naturalistic cults that had preceded Christianity. The official Orthodox culture felt compelled to suppress the earthy impulses that had been evoked by a lustier paganism and by a life on the steppe and in the forest that was heavily dependent on the cycles of nature. The tradition of *dvoeverie*, or "duality of belief," persisted, however, and helped enable the Russians of the "silver age"—the period after the revolution of 1905 and the subsequent repeal of censorship—to produce a culture of passion, color, and sensuality that astonished the European world.

Another legacy of the pioneer spirit in both Russia and America was a passion for the practical and demonstrable, a

suspicion of the abstract and intellectual. Medieval Kiev's Prince Vladimir, who embraced Orthodox Christianity for Russia in 988, had himself been converted by the beauty of Constantinople, not by the ideas of Byzantium; and the Russian people sought to embellish this heritage, not to criticize it—to vindicate it by deeds of physical construction and conquest, not by philosophical arguments. The Moslems to the south and east were the people of the book; and Russian culture remained remarkably resistant to the assimilation of Islamic learning. Russia was equally opposed to the assimilation of philosophic thought from Western Christendom. The first printers were driven out of Moscow in the 1560's; the attempt to print corrected versions of the basic Church books precipitated a schism in the Church in the 1660's; and it was not until the reign of Catherine in the 1760's that the large-scale printing of secular books on philosophical subjects gained official approval. Not before the early nineteenth century did a vernacular version of the complete bible become widely available or a university offer a full course of instruction in the Russian language. Thus, prior to the nineteenth century, critical, intellectual activity was largely conducted in French, German, or even Latin, rather than in the august Church Slavonic which controlled the literary culture or in the vernacular used for the practical tasks of war, commerce, and administration.

Like America, Russia was and remains a multi-cultural melting pot, the conglomerate Great Russians of the central and northwestern U.S.S.R. providing only a slim majority of the population. While subduing pre-existing native populations that ranged from Eskimos in the north to desert nomads in the south, both countries drew on successive waves of emigration from Europe (though these became increasingly more important and numerous in America than in Russia during the nineteenth century). Both countries contain men of many races and creeds not always successfully integrated into the often parochial mainstream. If Russia had few blacks to persecute, it had a large Moslem population on which to visit various forms of discrimination. Fleeing Western oppression in the late Middle Ages, the Jews moved East and were gradually absorbed into the western portion of the Russian empire, which became the leading center of world Jewish culture before renewed persecution in the late nineteenth century began a new exodus, largely to America.

But for all its prejudice and provincialism, Russia like America was more often a source of refuge from old persecutions than a source of new ones. Oppressed German sects of the eighteenth century emigrated not only to the land of the Pennsylvania Dutch, but to the equally virgin lower Ukraine and Crimea newly wrested by Catherine the Great from the Mongols. Those who had opposed the successful French revolution of 1789 tended to flee to tsarist Russia, while partisans of the unsuccessful revolutions of 1848 generally fled to America. Far more than is realized, Russia as well as America offered both the space and the freedom for a fresh start to a wide variety of western Europeans. Scratch a Russian and you are likely to find not so much a Tatar (as the old saying has it), but a European who emigrated East rather than West.

Like America, Russia experienced a marked tension between the culture of its interior regions and that of its semi-European cities. Just as an American once said that Europe extends to the Alleghenies and America lies beyond, so many Russians have felt that Europe extended to the Valdai Hills (just to the east of Novgorod and Petersburg), and that Russia lay beyond. A special world of commerce and culture that was as self-contained in its own day as it is forgotten in ours grew up among the rich forests, mineral resources, and river trade routes of the Old Russian interior. A key role in developing a continent-wide civilization in Russia as in America was played by one great central river with innumerable navigable tributaries. Mother Volga, no less than old man river, dominated the imagination and controlled the commerce of a heartland culture that lay within—but pointed beyond—Europe.

"Far away above the rye there rose up a white gleaming tower with a blue onion dome upon it, close by another tower with a golden dome, then a cluster of five towers and domes together, to the left—a high, slender belfry, and still more to the left the pink walls of a monastery like the walls of a fortress with turrets along it. . . ." Thus a contemporary Russian writer describes the approach to Suzdal, one of the earliest Slavic settlements in northern Russia. Founded in the 900's, Suzdal was a flourishing city when Moscow was a hamlet; until it was overrun by the Mongols in 1238 it was a major agricultural and commercial center. A key role in the development and protection of such settlements was played by the monasteries, which served as religious havens and military outposts. Suzdal's Pokrovsky Monastery is at left.

Russians like Americans in the nineteenth century felt a special compulsion to explain who they were and how they differed from Europeans. Writers felt obliged to find meaning for an expansive but still relatively inarticulate populace that was dominated by, but no longer felt secure in, its older religious traditions. One can find American parallels for many Russian ideological preoccupations and literary personalities. The metaphysical answers that Herman Melville sought in southern seas, Fedor Dostoevsky found in the Siberian camps—after each had experienced an almost simultaneous spiritual crisis in the Europeanized parts of his native land. Ivan Turgenev and Henry James feared the intolerance and anti-aristocratic plebianism of their native lands and fled to western Europe, where they became friends. Yet their elegant fiction returns incessantly for subject matter to the lands they left behind. Maxim Gorky, like Jack London (a special favorite of Russians—even of Stalin), glorified the world of the unspoiled interior and the rough egalitarianism associated with it. Then, in the early twentieth century, from the interior of each country came a romantic figure who personified the dream of middle-class America and lower-class Russia. Scott Fitzgerald of Minnesota and Sergei Yesenin of Ryazan longed to be literary voices in touch with the new order being built in the urban centers closer to Europe. But each moved on through the

Paris that lay beyond New York and Leningrad to alcoholic despair and premature death.

The links and affinities that have been detected between Russians and Americans by such disparate observers as Alexis De Tocqueville, Nehru, and Mao Tse-tung are now based on more than geographic and psychological similarities; for, in the Soviet period, Russia resolved first to imitate and then to "overtake and surpass" American industry. More recently the two powers have extended competition into the heavens.

Beyond politics, however, stands the undoubted responsiveness of the one to anything that is authentically exuberant in the popular culture of the other—as attested by the fascination of ordinary Russians with American jazz and ordinary Americans with Moiseev dancing. It was not simply cold war curiosity that produced either the extraordinary popularity in America of the writers Boris Pasternak and Alexander Solzhenitsyn or the extraordinary curiosity in Russia about new material trends and spiritual unrest in America. Plagued by inadequate exposure and imperfect understanding, many citizens of each superpower feel a simple childlike desire, as well as a responsible adult need, to know more about the other. It is to such that this essay is addressed; for it is not an inventory or guide, but only an invitation addressed by a citizen of the one to an adventure in discovering the civilization of the other.

Russian culture is the creation of a rugged people on a ragged frontier given little respite by either nature or their fellow men. Its development has been dramatically uneven and frequently interrupted. Iron—the sinew of civilization— was widely used across southern Russia in the seventh and sixth centuries B.C., but did not penetrate large areas of northern Russia until the sixteenth and seventeenth centuries A.D. Even well into the present century much of the elaborate and imposing wooden architecture of the north was fashioned without the use of saws or even iron nails.

Recent extensive excavations have provided a rich if confusing picture of pre-Christian culture in the U.S.S.R. Animal figures from Iranian mythology were being transposed into indigenous bone and wood carvings by the late Bronze Age inhabitants of the upper Volga at the same time that the iron-bearing Scythians were producing fantastic variants of many of the same models in more sophisticated metal forms. One wishes that mute burial places contained some explanation of how the Scythians in the Crimea were able to miniaturize figures in ways that subsequent art has been unable to duplicate.

Scythian art displays clear thematic originality as well as technical virtuosity in such characteristic forms as the bird with the head of a lamb, the spiraling animals with heads interlocked in combat. But, in a general way, the sun gods and animal figures seem to reflect interaction with Persia— while many Slavic words for religious ideas and symbols suggest Persian origins. Hellenistic culture probably also affected the Scythians, particularly as they retreated from the steppe to their Crimean capital of Neapolis, in close proximity to the age-old Greek settlements of the Taurida (the Crimean Peninsula). Alexander the Great became a special hero of Slavic oral folklore and an early model for the semideified prince in Russia as elsewhere in the Byzantine world.

The Scythians were supplanted on the southern steppe by an even more obscure group of nomads, the Sarmatians, in the third century B.C. Nearly a millennium later, after many subsequent invasions and migrations, the first distinctively Russian civilization appeared. Scandinavian warrior princes, together with the indigenous eastern Slavs, established—first in Novgorod, then in Kiev—clear political and cultural hegemony over the steppe. By then, another fantastic, zoomorphic art had evolved that was either wrought in, or enameled upon, metal; and the Slavs developed the art to such perfection that a twelfth-century German monk called them the best in the world in the "precision of enamel and the uniformity of niello." Mute testimony to the apparent richness of the pre-Christian culture is provided by a gilded bracelet recently recovered from the ruins of old Ryazan, in the remote northern regions of the Kievan domain. On it is depicted a lost ritual dance being performed to the music of a wooden reed, a goatskin bagpipe, and a *gusli*, the distinctive Russian zither. This resonated stringed instrument provided evocative accompaniment to the recitation of oral epics, which were the main medium for transmitting secular lore among the early Slavs. In the nineteenth century it was placed on stage by Mikhail Glinka, the "father of Russian music," to accompany a bearded bard's recitation at the beginning of *Ruslan and Ludmila*, the opera based on a poem by Alexander Pushkin.

If the high culture of Russia from the early tenth to the early twentieth century was largely dedicated to the Christian God and controlled by a deified Christian prince, the pre-Christian sun god stands behind both of these figures; and— in a sense—his authority both preceded and succeeded theirs. There are suggestions of affinity with Scandinavian mythology with its sun god, Freyr, and its god of thunder, Thor, who closely parallels the Perun of Russian paganism (whose worship became the model in some respects for the special veneration accorded the Prophet Elijah in northern Russia).

The most festive popular holidays of early Russia were those of the summer and winter solstices (which were only gradually and imperfectly transposed into St. John's Day and Christmas). The ornately decorated Russian Easter egg, like the round holiday loaf of bread, symbolized the sun and honored the return of its light in the spring. Raised above the ships that sailed the rivers of the interior was a round wooden orb, or "sun" (of the type shown on page 111), that in later years was only occasionally replaced by a cross. Prominent among the carved wooden figures that protruded from both the prows of ships and the roofs of dwellings was the head of a horse, representing the sun god. The special Russian siren-mermaid, the *rusalka*, found a less exalted but even more frequent representation in Russian popular carving—particularly in the marvelously detailed window casings of wooden dwellings. The evil spirits of the deep had to be propitiated even on the steppe, for water was the "sister of the sun," guiding it through its subterranean labyrinth after each sunset back to the point at which it reappeared each morning.

The search for the sun became no less urgent under Christianity, as missionary zeal took Orthodox civilization far north into the lands of dark winters and unreal, irridescent summers. The characteristic Russian onion dome developed out of the native wooden architecture, its graceful upper surface providing a snow-shedding roof, while the gilding and the rounded lower edge set up on a drum captured and reflected down to the surrounding region the first and last

The traditional Madonna and Child, known in Russia as the Virgin of Tenderness, was one of the most revered subjects in Russian religious painting, and is represented here by a sixteenth-century icon, Our Lady of Yevsemanisk. The silver and gilt frame, with silver appliqué, was made for the icon in St. Petersburg in 1817.

daily rays of the slanting Northern sun. Thus, the main cupola (the "vault of heaven"), and the elaborately decorated indoor ceiling beneath it (known in wooden churches as *nebo*, or heaven), was crowned by a dome that glistened through the evergreen and ever dark forest. To the faithful the rays of light often seemed transformed back into tongues of fire from the sun itself. The contemporary novelist Solzhenitsyn has suggested that "the secret of the pacifying Russian countryside" lies in its onion-domed and tent-roofed churches and bell towers "graceful, shapely, all different," yet reaching up "high over mundane timber and thatch . . . from isolated settlements invisible to each other . . . to the same heaven."

The greatest of all surviving wooden churches in Russia, the magnificent twenty-two-domed church at Kizhi (shown on page 64), some two hundred miles northeast of Leningrad, was built on a spot near a former shrine of the pagan sun god. It is called the Church of the Transfiguration, after the mystical feast (specially honored in the Christian East) which commemorates the sudden appearance to the apostles of the blinding, sun-like "uncreated light" through the body of Christ on Mount Tabor. This church, like other monasteries throughout northern Russia, is located directly on a body of water. Thus, it is approached from the sea—usually from west to east as befits a pilgrimage and as churches are entered.

When Russian artists sought to make culture a secular celebration of their own Promethean powers at the beginning of this century, they often turned back to the old sun god, seeking like the poet Konstantin Balmont to be "like unto the sun." The revolutionary era is framed dramatically by Alexei Kruchenykh's *Victory over the Sun*—the futurist, partly electronic opera staged on the eve of World War I, with Cubist designs by the painter Kazimir Malevich—and *Mystery Bouffe*—the Communist mystery play by the poet Vladimir Mayakovsky, performed by a cast of eighty thousand on the steps of the former stock market for a Congress of the Communist International and ending with an ecstatic chorus urging the masses to "Play with the sun, roll the sun, play in the sun."

Like his ancestors the Soviet Russian continued to seek not just the sun, but renewing contact with all nature. The Russian peasant, whose forced collectivization was one of the cruelest aspects of Stalinist industrialization, had the consolation of the open field and followed the sun as did his perennial companion on the steppe, the sunflower. In the silent movie *Earth*, the outstanding product of this new, secular art medium during the bloody initial period of collectivization, the faces of little children are blended with those of sunflowers in unforgettable images framed by the fields of feather grass. These and other simple pictures of men and nature by the Ukrainian moviemaker Alexander Dovzhenko bore quiet tribute to the natural and harmonious against the

Two archangels, guiding spirits, are positioned regally on either side of a saintly figure in this eighteenth-century icon panel. In Russian iconography the divine rather than human aspect of such figures was emphasized by elongated forms and a severe frontal pose.

artificial and arrogant. The latter was symbolized by the tractor in *Earth*, which when out of gasoline is subjected to ritualistic communal peasant urination into the tank (a scene predictably deleted from subsequent Soviet versions).

The sunflower suggested to some another form of response to persecution by the powerful. Amidst the sufferings of the first Siberian colonists in the seventeenth century, their metropolitan reminded them that "even in darkest days a sunflower completes its circular course, following the sun by unchangeable love and natural inclination. . . . May our love to our sun, the will of God, be strong enough to draw us inseparably to it in days of misfortune and sorrow, even as the sunflower in dark days continues without faltering. . . ." His words acquired added poignancy when reprinted in the journal of the Moscow patriarch amidst the renewed persecutions of religion in the mid-1960's.

Nature became a symbol of fresh hope during "the thaw" (the title of Ilya Ehrenburg's weathervane novel of 1954) and the subsequent partial de-Stalinization under Khrushchev. *The Cranes are Flying* and *Clear Skies* were titles of two of this period's widely acclaimed films. Perhaps the greatest film of the era, *Shadows of Forgotten Ancestors* (titled, for American audiences, *Wild Horses of Fire*), came appropriately from the Dovzhenko studios in Kiev and provided, with surrealistic color techniques, a haunting evocation of the natural life and indigenous folk religion of an ostensibly Christian peasantry in the mountains of the western Ukraine.

The ordinary Russian continues to find renewing strength in nature whatever the cycles of thaw and frost in ideology and high politics. Perhaps the most frequently sung chorus in the U.S.S.R. today is the simple verse composed by a four-year-old boy beneath a drawing of the sun. Hailed as an example of the natural poetic genius of children by the greatest Russian children's writer of the twentieth century, Kornei Chukovsky, the verse is sung to a lilting melody by schoolchildren throughout the U.S.S.R.—often as the finale to an otherwise political festival program:

> *May there always be sunshine*
> *May there always be blue skies*
> *May there always be mama*
> *May there always be me.*

The emphasis on mother is characteristic. If the tsar was viewed as the father, Russia itself was the mother. The image of *Rus* and "the Russian land" is that of a mother in the earliest chronicles; her greatest river, the Volga, is *matushka*, or "little mother," in the first popular folk songs to be written down in the seventeenth century. The mother of Jesus was traditionally called "the God-bearer" (*Theotokos, Bogoroditsa*) in the Christian East; and the fertility as well as the virginity of Mary was emphasized in the Russian north where the earlier pagan cult of the Damp Mother Earth was partly assimilated into Orthodoxy.

Turgenev once complained that alone of all the great European literary traditions, the Russian had never produced its own distinctive pair of idealized lovers. The compassionate mother rather than the passionate lover is clearly the dominant female figure of Russian art from the early oral epics to the last movie of Sergei Eisenstein, with its eerie scene of mother weeping over son at the end of part two of *Ivan the Terrible*. Even when the woman is in fact a wife or lover, she seems drawn by the drift of the culture to assume the role of sorrowing mother in a *pietà*—as in the final scene of Maria singing an unearthly lullaby over the dying Andrei in Tchaikovsky's opera *Mazeppa*, or of Lara bending over the dead body of Doctor Zhivago. But beyond the sorrows that each woman bears individually stand the collective sufferings of Russian womanhood, which has been afflicted through foreign wars and civil convulsions with losses of husbands and children unequalled by any other nation in the twentieth century. One of the most moving moments in all war films

comes with the surge through waving wheat fields of the peasant mother to see her young soldier son for a brief, final farewell at the end of Grigory Chukhrai's *Ballad of a Soldier*.

Behind all this stands in part the subliminal hold on the Russian imagination of the most revered and reproduced of all religious objects in Russia: the icons or holy pictures of the Virgin and Child. The bringing of the prototypical Byzantine icon, the Virgin of Vladimir (shown on page 68), from Constantinople to Kiev, then north to Vladimir and Moscow traces the movement of Byzantine culture itself to new frontier outposts in the declining period of the Eastern Roman Empire. Even more than in Byzantium, the Virgin was viewed as the only sure guarantor of "indestructible walls" for a Christian city. The feast of the Protection of the Virgin was a special regional feature of Orthodox devotion in north Russia. The main cathedrals in the two cities—Vladimir and Moscow—that successively served as capitals of Russia after the eclipse of Kiev were named after the feast of the Virgin's entry into Heaven (called *uspenie*, meaning Dormition or Assumption). Left behind was the more serene Hellenic model that Kiev and Novgorod had taken over from Constantinople: a central cathedral named for Saint Sophia (Holy Wisdom).

Early artists—like the bards who composed the medieval epics—represented only that which was believed to have actually happened and had been authentically recorded by artistic witness and tradition. God the Father was not represented, because no man had seen Him, and He had revealed Himself to human perception only through the Pre-Sanctified Mother and their common Risen Son. Ineffable mysteries of the faith were symbolically represented by their historical, Old Testament anticipations. Thus, the Holy Trinity—as in Andrei Rublyov's famous icon (shown on page 83)—is depicted as the three angels who appeared to Sarah and Abraham.

The special richness of Old Russian religious painting can be seen as a kind of humanizing compensation for the remoteness and majesty of Russian worship. The word *altar*, meaning in Western churches a sacred table set apart for the re-enactment of Christ's Last Supper, was used in Church Slavonic for the entire area in which the holy sacrifice was re-enacted—the sanctuary. Since this area was closed off from the worshiping congregation, the celebration of the eucharistic mass was shrouded from the believer, who rarely shared in the communion or understood its meaning. The word for sacrament (*tainstvo*) was appropriately derived from the word for "secret"; the Last Supper known as the "secret supper"; and the word for the altar proper (*prestol*) increasingly associated with its exclusive modern meaning of "throne" rather than with its more Christian and literal meaning of "most sacred table."

The "secrets" of the Church often must have seemed as remote from the world of the ordinary Russian as did those of

The tsar's apartments inside the Moscow Kremlin were located in the Terem Palace, first built in about 1500 and enlarged and reconstructed during the seventeenth century. It is a grandly barbaric palace, a labyrinth of richly painted corridors, staircases, and vaulted chambers; and during its most sumptuous period, under Tsar Alexei Mikhailovich (1645–76), it was furnished with rich brocades, silks, and Venetian velvets, and was heated by great multicolored, faience-tiled stoves.

the State, which were also conducted behind closed doors in a sanctuary or inner fortress—known as a kremlin—within each major city. In the Moscow Kremlin the Russian tsars had their thrones and performed their rituals. But whereas their sanctuary was set off by an impassibly thick and bleakly monochromatic wall, the wall separating the priest's sanctuary from the people was a richly colored screen of icons, or an *iconostasis*, a uniquely Russian elaboration of the Byzantine art of icon painting.

This holy screen was the mediator between the remote world of the sanctuary and the congregation beyond. Marking the line which symbolically represented the boundary between heaven and earth, this many-paneled wall of holy paintings provided the faithful with an encyclopedic inventory of sacred history. From the distant Old Testament patriarchs in the top row to the popularly venerated local saints at the bottom, the nonliterate public could learn directly of the concrete, historical ways in which God had visited and redeemed His people. Looking to the East, the believer saw human bodies in transfigured heavenly form. The composure of the icons offered hope for the next world, just as their stylized arrangement on the screen provided a model for the hierarchical organization of this world.

The seventh (and, to the Orthodox, the last) Ecumenical Council of the Christian Church restored icon veneration in 787 in the midst of the iconoclastic controversy, proclaiming that while the *technique* may be that of the individual artist, the *form* of a sacred picture must follow tradition. God's intervention in history was an unmerited act of grace, a *eurema* (the Greek for windfall) of which man can record only the spiritual essence as it has been distilled through the paintings and prayers of the faithful. The artist can—and indeed should—perfect his technique, without, however, inventing subject matter and usurping the divine prerogative of *eurema*. The Slavs, who were converted to Orthodoxy in the wake of the Council's restoration of holy painting, faithfully accepted the Byzantine conception and joyfully elaborated inherited forms with the enthusiasm of new converts—and with a technique that soon became both more expressive and more abstract than that of their forebears.

Icon painting was an anonymous, usually monastic art. In at least one school of painting—the sixteenth-century Stroganov school—six separate artistic specialists were required to create an icon: one to prepare the board (northern pine having replaced southern cypress); another to compose the outline sketch of the prescribed form; one to paint the gilding and other adornments of sanctity; a painter of clothing and buildings; a fifth painter for growth and nature (a higher form of reality with symbolic moral meaning); and a final painter for the faces (the highest form of creation), in which the divine ideal attains its nearest human approximation. The head was never painted in a state of agitation or even in profile: eyes, the outer expression of inner wisdom, were bigger than lips, which were thin and devoid of sensual suggestion. Perspective was inverted to flatten the surface. There was no shadow, no inner source of light within the icon. Light came only from God behind and the sanctity that filtered through the icons (just as the Slavic word for blessed, *svyatoy,* is related to the word for light, *svet*). Icons are usually perceived not by the bright sunlight but by candlelight, the small flame being ardent if agitated like the faith of the believer praying before it.

In the rich chromatic world of Russian icons there are almost no truly dark colors, contrast being suggested by the differences in density or by the number of layers of the bright tempera paints. Dark blue, for instance, was often created by piling up layers of light blue, rather than using a deeper shade of blue paint. It is no accident that the first discovery of the glory of fully restored Russian icons at the beginning of this century coincided with the pioneering flight into Abstract Expressionism of Vasily Kandinsky. The new generation of artists found fresh inspiration not in the stereotyped classicism of the eighteenth century, nor in the stereotyped photographic realism of the nineteenth, but in the ancient icons' free play of pure line and color. For Russian icons developed to an extreme both the expressiveness and the abstractness inherent in the medium; and the Russian people were conditioned to look not for reality, but for "spiritual harmony" in art (to use the title of Kandinsky's famous essay). The tendency toward distortion and abstraction is illustrated in the penchant of the Rublyov and "northern schools" for lengthened and dematerialized bodies, and also in the favorite form of the Virgin, Our Lady of Tenderness. In the Russian elaboration of this Byzantine form, she distends her neck down to the Child beyond the point of physical possibility, while the bodies and limbs of the two figures become part of a meditative geometry of curved lines that leads the eye from one to another deep pool of pure color. The basic lines of the icons inspired many of the experimental paintings of the early twentieth-century artists Natalya Goncharova and Vladimir Tatlin; the glory of tempera colors, much of the simple purity of Kuzma Petrov-Vodkin, and perhaps some of the joyful expressiveness of Marc Chagall.

White, which contains all other colors, attained a new purity in icons. Deep white provides the tonsure and vestments of age and sanctity for prophets and saints, and the uncreated light that dazzles the disciples in icons of Christ's Transfiguration. In a thousand icons and wood carvings, Saint George rides a white, sinuous steed as he spears the dragon. This figure may have had special appeal because of the pagan association of the sun god with the image of a horse. Similarly, the curvilinear white horse is one of the last consistently recognizable objects in those crucial Kandinsky canvases of 1910 and 1911, in which he took his own—and

much of all—modern painting outside the world of recognizable reality. By 1918 the modernist flight into the abstract and spiritual had reached its zenith in the ultimate creation of Malevich's Suprematist "art of the fifth dimension," his famed "White on White."

For the modern artist as for the medieval iconographer, each color had its own spiritual significance. Nikolai Rimsky-Korsakov believed there were precise equivalents between colors and sounds. To Kandinsky, yellow had a special significance as the color of trumpets. Yellow was the color of the egg-yolk base of the icon painters' tempera, and the ochre of sunlight and autumn leaves plays a central role in many of the artistic triumphs of the Russian north: in Rublyov's Old Testament Trinity, in the bright flowers and golden-headed faces that uniquely appear in the seventeenth-century enamelwork of the far northern city of Solvychegodsk, and even a century later in the more subdued and whitish yellows that covered most of the dominant buildings of Petersburg at the height of its glory. This ornamental yellow of the Empire style provided a contrast of warmth and brightness to the cold and omnipresent dark blue of the Neva River and its tributaries; and in the snow-covered winter, wrote one citizen of Petersburg, "shadows from these yellow façades seemed so intensively dark blue that at times one could not believe that it was only a reflection and not original cobalt."

The icons that were fashioned in Old Russia added not only a richness of color to Byzantine models, but frequently a special quality of tenderness—as in the enveloping love of Mother bending toward Child. The paintings of Russia's Christian millennium can be fully understood only as signposts on a spiritual pilgrimage. Like the church without a choir, the icon without a prayer is the artificial product of a later, unbelieving age. All that the Soviet regime has kept alive of the earlier iconographic culture is the veneration of pictures of leaders, and of the sainted Lenin himself, mummified for the masses in the sepulcher on Red Square. Perhaps all that the secular modern mind—East or West—can do to recapture the importance of icons is to imagine them as pictures of departed parents or of close friends, whose presence from beyond the grave continues to be felt. In more contemporary language the saint in the icon may be described as "beautiful," in the sense of one who relates selflessly to others and thus draws others into his presence.

It was this sense of a protecting and consoling divine presence that guided Russia's pioneering civilization through the first two of its three great waves of expansion. The first was that of the tenth to the twelfth century, which brought Byzantine Christianity and artistic forms to the eastern Slavs and their partly Scandinavian military elite. The center was Kiev, "the mother of Russian cities"; the dominant silhou-

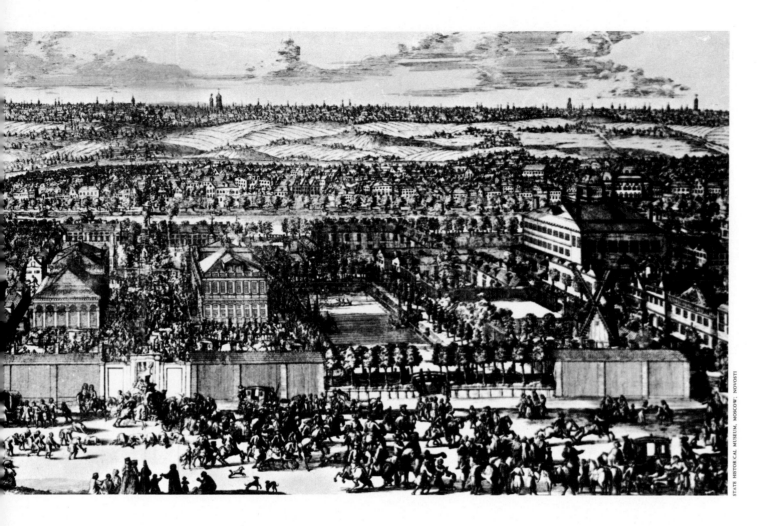

ette was that of the rounded Byzantine dome of its St. Sophia Cathedral; and the heroes were its idealized princes: Vladimir (the prototypical hero of the chronicles) and his son Yaroslav the Wise (the builder of the new Kiev in the first half of the eleventh century, who was lionized by the new vernacular authors of Byzantine-style panagyrics). The second wave was that of the fourteenth and sixteenth centuries, which extended the by-then-indigenous Orthodox civilization far beyond already established northern centers like Old Ladoga and Rostov the Great, north to the White Lake and the White Sea, and east to the farthest interior reaches of the Volga tributaries: to Perm and on into Asia.

The center of this second wave of colonization was Moscow, which had gradually risen to power after the decline of Kiev and, later, of Novgorod. As the controlling force of the Russian north, Moscow came to be called by some "the third (and final) Rome" of Christendom after "the second Rome," Constantinople, fell to the Turks in 1453. The dominant silhouette of Muscovite Russia was that of onion domes atop the swirling, gilded tent roofs of the Moscow Cathedral of the Protection of the Virgin, commonly known as St. Basil's. Moscow's heroes were the ascetic monks who provided the faith and fortitude to establish new monastic settlements from which local Finno-Ugric peoples could be converted for the glory of God, and from which local animals could be skinned for the profit of Muscovy. These rugged pioneers moved beyond Europe—some along the upper tributaries of the Dvina River through the Ural Mountains on a tortuous route known to contemporaries as *chrezkammeny*, or "passing through stone." Two particular heroes of the new literature (which was written in praise of saints rather than princes) were Saint Sergius of Radonezh, founder of the still-functioning national monastic shrine at Zagorsk in the forest just northeast of Moscow, and Saint Stephen of Perm, who converted the distant Komi peoples far to the northeast of Muscovy and gave their exotic Zyrian tongue a written alphabet, just as two Macedonian Slavs, Cyril and Methodius, had done for Russia some four hundred years earlier.

The two saints who led these remarkable waves of Russian expansion were aided by their belief that the very process of moral perfection was itself a kind of setting off in geographical space. Both heaven and hell were real places that had allegedly been seen by the sailors of Novgorod. Christianized folklore spoke repeatedly of heaven on earth near some distant "holy mountain" or "white waters"—or in the invisible city of Kitezh, which was saved by God from infidel foreign conquerors and was preserved at the bottom of a lake near the Volga, sounding forth its beckoning bells on the night of the summer solstice.

Each journey was a kind of pilgrimage. The peasant's daily return from field to hut required passing by the home of evil spirits in field, forest, and stream. His periodic jour-

Across the Neva River, glistening neoclassical façades recall the gracious splendors of eighteenth-century Petersburg: to the left, the palaces

neys to God's home, the church, required passing intact through the home of the evil one in the secular cities. A voyage to "holy lands" (a term used to describe both Jerusalem and the great domestic monasteries of Russia) required passing through "unclean lands"; and at the end of life's journey lay the fear of hell on the way to heaven—the fear of falling off the ladder or mountain, as depicted in instructive icons. The last hope of the damned was the intercession of the Virgin, who in the Orthodox legend reworked by Dostoevsky into *The Brothers Karamazov,* descended into hell to help sinners gain a reprieve from their sufferings during the annual period between Easter and Whitsuntide.

Thus, the boundaries between this world and the next became blurred in Muscovite Russia. When Ivan the Terrible conquered the Mongol stronghold at Kazan in 1552, his triumphal return to Moscow was painted by an iconographer as a journey from Sodom to the New Jerusalem, and his retinue was shown to include saints and archangels interspersed with contemporary Russian soldiers. Soaring St. Basil's, which Ivan had built on high ground in Red Square to commemorate the victory, was endowed with an asymmetrical series of spiraling towers designed to suggest the upreach of the entire city to heaven. The main chapel within the complex was dedicated to Christ's entry into Jerusalem on Palm Sunday, and became the point of departure for the annual ritual re-enactment of Palm Sunday through Red Square (shown on pages 52–53), with the tsar conducting the leading prelate of the Russian Church, who was mounted on a donkey. As the Church became rich and the faith began to fade in the sixteenth and seventeenth centuries, the "sensual hallucinatory cast of mind" attempted to shore it up with even more elaborate buildings and ritual. A climax came in the 1660's, just before the deposition of the last great patri-

arch of Moscow, Nikon, when he built (then was forced to retire into) the Monastery of the New Jerusalem near Moscow at Istra—a place of beauty where some expected the New Jerusalem would literally be realized.

Each of the first two waves of pioneering expansion was ended by violent internal conflict. The model figures of each era—the princes of Kiev and the monks of Muscovy—brought fatal division into their society. In the twelfth century, quarreling princes split Kievan Rus into minor principalities that became easy prey to physical conquest a century later, when the Mongols attacked from the East. In the seventeenth century disputatious priests from the Russian north broke with Nikon to produce a profound schism in Russian Christendom between Old and New Believers, each helping destroy the other and thus exposing Russia to cultural conquest by western Europe.

St. Petersburg, which was the symbol and center of the Westernization and secularization of Russia under Peter the Great, was also the command post for the third, imperial wave of Russian expansion in the eighteenth century. The dominant silhouette was the bleak, north European spire that rose over the military centers on either side of the Neva: the Peter and Paul Fortress and the Admiralty Building. But there were no clear and undisputed heroes for the new secular civilization. For every one who wrote classical verse to the all-conquering General Suvorov, there was another who sang folksongs praising the peasant rebel Pugachov who had taken arms against him. For every magnificent eighteenth-century architect who helped build imperial Petersburg, there was to come an equally surpassing nineteenth-century writer who would speak of the capital as artificial and perhaps doomed. Russia, which had for so

long been dominated by nomads of the steppe, was to find its culture increasingly shaped by nomads of the spirit who were never fully at home in the new Westernized cities.

But it is to the cities that one must turn for any understanding of the culture of imperial Russia. They replaced the old monasteries as the gathering place of the cultural elite, and provided the setting for the triumphs of the new secular culture in architecture, literature, and the theatrical arts.

The early Vikings had spoken of Russia as a "realm of cities"; and a German bishop of the tenth century spoke admiringly of a pagan Slavic city near the Baltic Sea with three wooden gates and a wooden temple "decorated with magnificent carvings of gods and goddesses." Kiev in the twelfth century and Moscow in the sixteenth were among the largest cities of their time anywhere in Europe. Excavations of early medieval Novgorod (the "father of Russian cities" to which the legendary Scandinavian prince Ryurik allegedly came in 862 to bring political order to the Slavs) have revealed extensive if not very informative early commercial writings on birchbark. "Great Lord Novgorod," which was linked with the Hanseatic League, poured its wealth into small, tasteful churches within the city and into great monasteries in the vast areas it colonized to the north.

But Petersburg of the eighteenth century was the first thoroughly secular city of Russia. It soon became the new center of culture as well as the new capital—offering hospitality not just to an Academy of Sciences (modeled on the German) and an Academy of Fine Arts (modeled on the French), but to rich international traditions of ballet, opera, and satirical drama. The new aristocratic culture spread beyond the court in the late eighteenth century into the somewhat broader world of masonic lodges and periodical pub-

lications. Moscow, too, began to participate in the process of Europeanization, founding in 1755 the first (and, until the early nineteenth century, the only) Russian university. But Petersburg remained the center of the new secular culture.

Peter's city was geometrically designed, and built by forced labor on a swampy, often flooded estuary located as far north as the middle of Hudson Bay. The fabled "white stone" (limestone and mortar) of Muscovy was replaced with bricks and granite. The Muscovite tradition, by which settlements developed outward concentrically around a sanctifying church-dominated kremlin, was replaced by grids of straight lines dominated by public buildings. The political, economic, and military appetites of Petersburg were not to be confined within protective walls, but moved out either in ships to the West or over wide, straight prospects and beneath triumphal arches into the imperial domains to the east and south.

Characteristic of the architecture that developed in and around the new capital under the Empresses Elizabeth and Catherine in the eighteenth century was a tendency to plan in terms of large ensembles rather than individual buildings. The flamboyant style of architecture developed by Bartolomeo Rastrelli and other Western architects in eighteenth-century Petersburg shows many links with the European baroque; and the decorative feminine frills that were soon added suggest the rococo. But the impetus toward a more worldly architecture was already being felt internally in the seventeenth century via the political reabsorption of the Ukraine, which had been developing independently to some extent under increasing Polish influence. A new three-dimensional sense of depth, an elegant interplay of red brick and white stone, and a growing preference for classical proportions and rectangular shapes—all are features of a progres-

"Darkly it looms in terrifying power:
What force of mind that brow conveys!
What mighty strength lies there concealed!
And in that horse what fire!
Whither away, thou haughty steed?
Where shall these proud hooves bear thee now?"

Thus wrote Alexander Pushkin in his "Bronze Horseman" describing the magnificent equestrian statue of Peter the Great (above), the symbol of Petersburg and of Peter's might. Commissioned by Catherine the Great, the statue is the work of the Frenchman Étienne Falconet. It was cast in bronze in 1782 and then mounted atop a massive granite block.

sion from the Muscovite style of the early seventeenth century to the classical or Empire style of the early nineteenth century.

The new Petersburg concern with creating a planned environment was a logical development: all construction had to be designed with full awareness both of natural dangers like swamp erosion, swelling pack ice, and sudden flood, and of the multiplicity of purposes—naval, commercial and ceremonial—that Peter had intended for his city.

The need to plan new cities rationally was also a requirement of the enlightenment philosophy which Catherine the Great adopted as an antidote to Muscovite superstition. The need to build such cities rapidly was a result of the difficulty of consolidating local control in newly conquered and frequently rebellious parts of her vast empire. Always in the background was the model of Petersburg, the symbol of central power and the site of the most impressive architectural ensembles.

The new cities, the provincial "Petersburgs" that grew up in the late eighteenth and early nineteenth centuries, often had imperial pretense built into their very names: from Yekaterinoslavl, or "Praise Catherine" (now Dnepropetrovsk), in the Ukraine to Sevastopol, or "August City," in the Crimea; from Vladikavkaz, or "Ruler of the Caucasus" (now Ordzhonikidze), in the newly Russian dominions in the Caucasus to Vladivostok, or "Ruler of the East," the port at the southern extremity of Russia's expanded Pacific coastline.

Among the new cosmopolitan commercial centers, the rise of Odessa in the first half of the nineteenth century was perhaps the most spectacular. Only a village at the beginning of the century, it became by 1850 the second seaport of Russia, providing a "window on the West" by the Black Sea that was almost as wide as that which Petersburg provided by the Baltic. In the early twentieth century Odessa was to produce many of Russia's most vivid storytellers (among them, Ilya Ilf, Yevgeny Petrov, and Isaac Babel) and the legendary *Odessa Mama:* the proverbial Jewish mother transposed into a folk principle of modern Russia typified by an infinite resourcefulness, an ability to solve practical problems in spite of official obfuscation and delay.

In the great palaces that sprung up outside Petersburg—Peterhof, Gatchina, Pavlovsk—the elite spent their holidays in gardens filled with statues of naked classical goddesses rather than chapels filled with draped and dematerialized paintings of biblical figures. They conversed before busts of ancient philosophers rather than icons of saints. Sculpture became the characteristic form of adornment of the new secular, imperial culture—and one of the last of the visual art media to come to flower on Russian soil.

Statuary had been too sensual for the old religious culture. Even the rich popular traditions of decorative carving in wood and bone found no effective translation into stone church architecture after the middle of the thirteenth century. Although the Orthodox Slavs had tended to replace the preexistent pagan idols with wooden images of the saints, these were so flattened and motionless as to be closer in spirit to two-dimensional painting than to bas relief, let alone sculpture.

As Western ideas intruded in the seventeenth century, Russian artists were infected by the desire to express emotion and to depict nature more realistically. This required a new medium of expression—one that was not subject to the static and abstract forms nor to the religious purposes with which the icon tradition had infected painting. At first, sculpture began to develop within a religious framework—in wooden statues and carvings of the Passion and Crucifixion of Christ (depicting human suffering with a realism unfamiliar in the idealized iconography of the East). The best surviving examples of the late seventeenth and early eighteenth centuries come from the Ural mountains; and the expressions of suffering may reflect the harsh conditions in this region, where resettled Russians labored in new mines and foundries. But the marble and metals extracted by their labors were destined for more secular uses such as the monumental statuary of Petersburg.

Peter the Great had decreed after his famous trip to the West in 1697 that the garden of his Summer Palace in Petersburg should be filled with "the fables of Aesop in figures." These statues were swept away by a flood in 1777; by that time, however, classical statuary had conquered the city, and an entire galaxy of knights, nymphs, and goddesses stared down from safer heights atop Rastrelli's newly completed Winter Palace (shown on pages 156–57). These statues perched atop two rows of columns—like those commanding the fountains at nearby Peterhof—seemed somehow defiant of both men and nature. They were to bear mute witness to repeated floods from the Neva on one side, and to revolutionary demonstrations from the Palace Square on the other.

Imperial sculpture was epitomized by the bronze equestrian statue of Peter the Great that was erected in Senate Square atop an imposing slab of natural Finnish granite. The statue was created over a twelve-year period by the French sculptor Étienne Falconet, who reached beyond his previous, largely decorative work to achieve a new monumentalism that reflected the arrogance and elegance of his patroness, Catherine the Great. Unveiled amidst thundering canonfire and a massive military review, Catherine's monument to Peter subsequently provided the model for a vast body of civic statuary that encouraged the pretentions of one ruler in the guise of commemorating another.

At its best, the tradition of memorializing national heroes provided the obelisk in Petersburg's Palace Square, which commemorated the victory over Napoleon; the longest single piece of monolithic granite in the world, it was topped with an angel of victory whose face portrayed that of Alexander I. At its worst, the tradition was to provide, after World War II, the omnipresent oversized metal statues of Stalin. The suffering, silent people of Russia also acquired more moving and modest monuments through the quiet development (partly under Baltic influence) of graveyard statuary. "The marble weeps," a contemporary said of the first examples of sentimentalized mausoleum statuary in the late eighteenth century. The weeping became almost literal in the Petersburg fountain of perpetual mourning, erected to Russian sailors killed in the war with Japan in 1904–05. Some of the monuments to the dead of World War II that were placed on public view during the post-Stalin era attained a measure of dignity by introducing a new simplicity and even a cautious measure of abstraction into sculpture.

A recent Soviet critic has suggested that the heroic statuary and architectural ensembles of aristocratic Petersburg constituted a mass art without being a popular art. This criticism, which might be even more effectively made of the spirit-deadening work of official planners and architects of the Stalin era, also has some validity for the graceful and gifted art of the eighteenth century. For it too used massive construction to impress an ideology on the masses while allowing them broad streets and fields for demonstrations of loyalty and military drill. Unfortunately for the imperial city, increasing numbers of its intellectual *demi-monde* came to feel that it had been built for parades rather than people, and to wonder if it should have been built elsewhere—or perhaps nowhere. Indeed, toward the end of the imperial period the city was inspiring a rich literature of apocalyptical premonition. There is the image of a ticking time bomb in Andrei Bely's 1910 novel *St. Petersburg* and the observation of his prolific contemporary, the critic Dmitry Merezhkovsky, that "In Kitezh, that which is real is invisible. Here, on the contrary, that which is visible is not real." By the turn of the century aristocratic and commercial Petersburg had become surrounded by a new industrial city of uprooted peasants working in large factories and living in squalid barracks. The broad avenues designed to extend imperial power out into the country began to invite proletarian demonstrations back into the center of the city. Thus, the city of the most impressive mass art of the eighteenth century gave birth to the most important mass movement of the twentieth century and took its new name—Leningrad—from the leader of the Revolutionary forces that came to power there.

To understand the restless reformist passion that helped spawn that revolution, one must move behind the buildings to the books of Petersburg and consider the literary culture which arose there and dominated the Russian imagination in the nineteenth century. The religious culture that had prevailed in Kiev and Moscow had been based on the language of the liturgy, Church Slavonic. Its highest Christian ideal

24

Scenes from Russia's past became a popular subject for painters during the latter half of the 1800's. Vasily Surikov from Siberia, land of political exiles and independent thinkers, depicted a seventeenth-century religious martyr, Fedosia Morozova, who followed the Old Believers in her refusal to adapt to the new religious interpretations then being instituted. In Surikov's epic painting (1881–83) the defiant boyarynya, or noblewoman, is being carried off to a convent prison in a sledge, amid the crowd's jeering and weeping; she died in the convent soon after her imprisonment.

was redemption through voluntary suffering in imitation of Christ and in hopes of providing the purification needed to hasten the coming of His kingdom. For Kievan Rus, the classic testament was the tragic tale of Boris and Gleb, the young princes who accepted assassination as a means of unifying their warring people, and who thereby became the first native Russian saints. For Muscovite Russia a final statement and example was the famous autobiography of the Old Believer, Archpriest Avvakum. Written in a dungeon in the far north just before he was burned at the stake, it proclaimed his total fidelity to the old ways of worship in the face of massive cultural change.

In eighteenth-century Petersburg there was still no single language for the new secular culture despite Peter's simplifying linguistic reforms and an increasing use of the vernacular. German was widely used by the upper military and civil service classes; Polish (soon supplanted by French) in the schools and salons of the ruling aristocracy; Yiddish, Armenian, and other tongues in commercial centers. Creative philosophers of the eighteenth century like Grigory Skovoroda wrote in a language closer to modern Ukrainian than to modern Russian; while poets imitated unnatural classical forms and a syllabic verse more appropriate to Polish than to Russian.

A distinctive Russian literary culture began with the rise of national self-consciousness in the late eighteenth century and—above all—with the literary creations of Alexander Pushkin in the early nineteenth. By the force of his example, Pushkin liberated Russian from its age-old tendency to recede into Church Slavonic archaisms rather than to advance into more supple, European modes of expression. In his great poem "The Bronze Horseman," he opens up the theme of the haunted Petersburg, depicting the insanity and death of the minor clerk Eugene, who imagines during a flood of the Neva that he is being pursued by Falconet's mounted metal statue of Peter. Nikolai Gogol, who succeeded Pushkin as Russia's leading writer, suggested at the end of his story *The Overcoat* that the humiliated clerk who had been robbed of his last threadbare protection against the northern winter might return to revenge himself upon the city. Gogol helped Russian writing move from poetry to prose. His search for a new prose for modern Russia began a process that put poetry and art-for-art's-sake in permanent eclipse in Russia except for a brief if spectacular resurgence in the silver age of the early twentieth century.

Russia's supreme gift to world literature came through prose fiction in the 1860's and 1870's, when the realistic movement in European art suddenly reached unprecedented heights in Russia. Defeat in the Crimean War and emancipation of the serfs had damaged the self-esteem of imperial Russia and had shaken the complacency of its ruling aristocracy.

The young were driven by raw energy and by the belated discovery of philosophical speculation—an intellectual arena officially denied to Russians for years by the political fears of an insecure bureaucracy and the continued reliance of both Church and State on vindication through historical deed rather than rational persuasion. In a land with no legal political opposition, ideological passion had to be either illegal or extralegal, channeled either into subversive organizations or into literature. "Thick journals" and intense discussion "circles" became the points of contact for a new and polyglot elite that succeeded the monks of Muscovy and the salon aristocrats of Petersburg as heroes and creators of a new culture.

This extremely youthful, sometimes suicidally sincere, and generally iconoclastic elite was denounced by the older generation with the word that the liberal Turgenev had introduced in *Fathers and Sons: nihilist.* But it is more accurately characterized by another term that Russian literature also introduced into the world at this time: *intelligentsia.* They were united not only by a common dedication to ideas, but also by a growing sense of frustration in a society that seemed to offer no prospect for meaningful reform. The traditional dominance of the Church, the army, and the bureaucracy seemed to be seriously challenged only by rising commercial and industrial forces which were, if anything, even more *bezydeyny,* or "idea-less." Thus, the young created their own elite of alienated, revolutionary "new men."

Feeling a special urgency to find in reality something to replace the certainty that they had lost in religion, the Russians created prose masterpieces that made use of almost every stylistic form. Above all others rose Fedor Dostoevsky and Leo Tolstoy, each with his own intensified form of realism. Dostoevsky brought the power of the medieval mystery play into the modern novel. From *Crime and Punishment* through *The Brothers Karamazov* the Dostoevskian detective story presented—with uncanny psychological penetration into both man's basest motives and his highest aspirations—the drama of human beings interacting under stress. Tolstoy brought the sweep of the Homeric epic into the European novel. The panoramic Tolstoyan tableaux of armies and families in the early parts of *War and Peace* gradually focused on the enigma of what makes these enduring forms of society work: victorious armies in *War and Peace* and family happiness in *Anna Karenina*. But these two men were not—as André Gide once suggested—just lonely peaks on a barren steppe. Indeed, almost any other age would have hailed as a sufficient if not surpassing literary achievement in prose fiction the limpidly written novellas of Ivan Turgenev and the satire of Mikhail Saltykov.

The ideological passion of the age animated its prose and could not tolerate detached description by the unengaged. Thus, Turgenev's objectivity—evident in his classic portrayal of the raging conflict of generations in *Fathers and Sons* of 1862—rendered him equally offensive to young revolutionaries and to neoconservatives like Dostoevsky.

In these same, intensely ideological early 1860's were born both the school of propagandistic, Populist art (called "the Wanderers" after their itinerant exhibitions) and the distinctly Russian musical school of programmatic composers (the so-called "mighty handful"). The new painters were following in the footsteps of Alexander Ivanov, who left the Petersburg Academy of Fine Arts and spent most of his adult life trying to capture with both total realism and redemptive effect the moment of Christ's first appearance to the people (a study for which appears on page 177). The realistic portrayal of ordinary Russians was the goal of the Wanderers, but their idealized images of the common man in bare feet and peasant blouse were often little more than stylized ideographs calling directly for pity or anger. Lenin's personal secretary, Vladimir Bonch-Bruevich, recalled how earlier Russian revolutionaries had sworn vows before Ilya Repin's famed "Haulers on the Volga" in the way old Russian warriors had sworn before icons. Not surprisingly, this art became the model for the even more mediocre and exhortative poster art of "socialist realism" in the Stalin era.

But the original "realists" reached a measure of artistic distinction in the late years of the nineteenth century insofar as they responded to aesthetic impulse and chose their subject matter from history—precisely that area of reality that was inaccessible to direct observation. Thus, Vasily Surikov, inspired by the sight of a black crow on white snow, painted his massive canvas of the Old Believer heroine of the seventeenth century, the Lady Morozov, being hauled off to prison and martyrdom (shown on pages 24–25).

In music, too, Mussorgsky led the "mighty handful" (which included Mily Balakirev, Tsezar Kyui, Borodin, and Rimsky-Korsakov) back into Russian history in his two masterpieces, *Boris Godunov* and *Khovanshchina*. Like the famous canvases of this era—Surikov's "Execution of the Streltsy" and Repin's "Ivan the Terrible's Murder of his Son"—Mussorgsky was preoccupied with periods of suffering and division in the Russian past. However, the last and most long-labored canvas of the Populist era, Repin's "Zaporozh Cossacks Drafting a Reply to the Turkish Sultan" (shown on pages 178–79), presents a final idealized icon of popular spontaneity.

The renewed interest in Russian folklore that swept the Russian art world around the turn of the century is nowhere more apparent than in the set and costume designs of those artists associated with Sergei Diaghilev's World of Art society. The works of two such artists are shown here: opposite, Nikolai Rerikh's design for a gusli player's costume; below, Ivan Bilibin's pilgrim costumes for the opera Prince Igor.

COLLECTION OF S. BELIZ, PARIS

Both the painters and the musicians were dominated by the ideological passions of the great prose writers. Ivanov was deeply involved in the creative life of Gogol—as the painter Nikolai Ge was with Tolstoy—and can almost be described as an iconographer of the writer's anguish. Nikolai Dargomyzhsky was determined to fathom the musical depths of the Russian tongue by providing a totally authentic musical equivalent of a Pushkin text. Mussorgsky wanted to try the same impossible thing with Gogol's more unmusical and ideological prose. From Gogol, whom he felt was closest to Russian popular speech, Mussorgsky went on to try to extract music from the marketplace, to unlock the "treasure" which "awaits the composer in the speech of the people." Mussorgsky ended up helping create what he could not altogether find: a Russian national folk music. In the inspired and original Kromy Forest scene after the death of Boris Godunov (first heard at the opera's première early in 1874), the mob sings an anti-authoritarian chorus that was actually carried out into the countryside by singing students during the "mad summer" of that same year.

Music was the last of the major artistic media to come to full maturity in Russia. The emphasis in the Russian national school on music with a message was in some respects only a faithful continuation of the Russian tradition whereby music had always been subordinated to the meaning of the text it accompanied—whether of a popular epic related by a *bayan* or a prayer chanted by a priest. The prominence of the bass voice and the chorus in Russian operas reflects the continuing hold of the liturgical tradition in which the dominant sounds were those of the deep-voiced priest chanting the office and of the responding congregation.

As elsewhere in the nineteenth century, romantics in Russia believed that music had magical powers as yet untapped. It was the language of the will—capable of engaging as well as expressing the emotions, of unifying the conglomerate, post-aristocratic audience, and of expressing the peculiar genius of a nation. The characteristic passion of nineteenth-century Russian art for unvarnished truth made Mussorgsky's final operatic message one of despair—both in the lacerating lament of the Holy Fool that ends *Boris Godunov* and in the self-immolation of the Old Believers that ends *Khovanshchina*. Tchaikovsky also ended on a somewhat dark note in his last opera, *The Queen of Spades*. But Rimsky-Korsakov, the final survivor of the "mighty handful," pointed to new directions with his last two operas: the mystical and orchestrally rich *Invisible City of Kitezh*, and then the chromatic flight into folklore in his *Golden Cockerel*.

The full flight into musical modernism was launched by Rimsky's pupil, Igor Stravinsky, in his three successive compositions of 1910–12, *The Firebird, Petrushka,* and *The Rite of Spring*. At the very time that Kandinsky, inspired by old icons and wood prints, was freeing paintings from objective reality, Stravinsky was turning to pagan folklore and the

Alexander Tishler, born in a Jewish community in the Ukraine at the turn of the century, maintained his personal vision of art in private during the Stalinist years, after he was attacked in official circles for being too formalistic in his approach. But in 1966 he was given a retrospective exhibition in one of Moscow's major galleries. Above is his "Portrait of a Girl," which he painted in 1936.

Dionysian rites, freeing music from its servitude to traditional tonality and melodic cliché. Even more important, Stravinsky linked music with dance rather than speech, with movement in the body rather than meaning for the mind. Collaborating with Mikhail Fokin as choreographer, Léon Bakst and Nikolai Rerikh as set designers and virtuoso performers like Vaslav Nijinsky, Stravinsky became part of a fusion of the arts that engaged all the senses amidst the rich artistic flowering of the pre-World War I era. After the triumphal Paris season of the Ballet Russe staged by the impresario Sergei Diaghilev in May and June, 1909, all Europe fell under the spell of what was both the culmination of a long Russian tradition in the discipline of classical ballet and a long overdue outburst of romantic sensuality in defiance of Russia's ingrained puritanism.

A kind of erotic energy seemed to drive the Russian creative spirit on from one artistic medium to another—but always one that involved the human body in motion if not in flight. Diaghilev had organized an exhibition of Russian painting in Paris during one season, then moved on to a season of opera, and thence to the ballet; and his remarkable ensemble progressed from the classicism of 1909 to the expressionism and liberated modernity of subsequent seasons. By 1915 the old masters had been reincarnated. Peter Tchaikovsky's music was transformed into Fokin's weirdly symbolic ballet *Eros*; Rimsky's was wedded to the bold new sets of the Rayonnist painter Mikhail Larionov in the folkloristic ballet *Midnight Sun,* which also brought to view the first choreography of the young Leonid Massin, another figure who was to transfer the unleashed exuberance of the Russian dance to the West.

The striving for a new, more erotic musical language had reached a climax in Alexander Scriabin's 1906 *Poem of Ecstasy*, originally entitled *Orgiastic Poem.* "When you listen to 'Ecstasy,'" Scriabin advised a friend, "look straight into the eye of the Sun." Russian artists were in these years as visually blinding as Scriabin's brass section was deafening. The creative spirit was in many ways returning to the half-real, half-imagined paganism of ancient Russia, with its sun god and fertility cults. Artists were seeking native roots for a new sensuality. The repeal of the censorship and adoption of partially constitutional rule that followed in the wake of the revolution of 1905 permitted the emergence of a pornographic art to which writers like Fedor Sologub and painters like Larionov contributed. There was even a curious anticipation of Hippie culture in the so-called *ogarki* (or "burnt-out candles"), a small group that combined exotic dress with an interest in drugs and Oriental mysticism. Freedom from censorship lasted throughout the revolutionary era until 1922, but that brief respite helped encourage a profusion of artistic experiment that bespeaks not only the excitement of a revolutionary era but also the latent energies and native exuberance of the Russian people themselves.

A high point in the fusion of the arts was reached in *Mystery*, Scriabin's final work, which remained uncompleted and unperformed at his death in 1915. His fifth and last symphony, *Prometheus: the Poem of Fire*, was written to include a solemn, white-robed chorus and a "light-keyboard" which was to accompany the music with a play of colors on a screen. In *Mystery* he went even further, planning a ritual that was to involve perfumes as well as colored lights in the score, and dance and oratory for the cast of two thousand. White robes were to be worn by the audience, for all were to participate in what Scriabin called the "prefatory action" which was to begin symbolically in Tibet—the guardian of the ultimate mysteries of the East—and end, presumably, with the transformation of the human race. The final, though incomplete text of this "action" is a kind of ecstatic paean to the sun god and to damp mother earth. Waves, fields, and forests hail the sun, and the desert ends the text exalting "the moist elements."

For all his radicalism, Scriabin was in essence returning to the concept of total theater implicit in the celebration of the Christian liturgy which had dominated earlier Russian culture. Sight, sound, smell (incense), and gesture were all used to amplify the meaning of the Christian "mystery," which like Scriabin's tolerated no spectators (there are still no seats in Russian churches). All were participants in the liturgical drama, the climax of which was the "grand entrance" of the celebrating priest through the "royal doors" of the icon screen, symbolically re-enacting Christ's entry into Jerusalem and his subsequent death and resurrection. The purpose of the drama was to transform the believers and, through them, the world into the Kingdom of God.

Since all Orthodox Russia was thought to be the scene of this continuing drama, there had been a drift toward the theatrical in the celebration of the great Christian feasts. The Christmas season, for instance, though less important than Easter in Orthodox ritual, began during Advent with the "furnace show" (in which the three Israelites, Shadrach, Meshach, and Abednego, are rescued from Nebuchadnezzar's fire and sent out to proclaim the coming of Christ) and reached its climax on Epiphany with the combined feast of lights and blessing of waters (for which grandstands were traditionally erected on the banks of the Moskva River). Secular Petersburg, too, was a kind of open-air theater for the aristocracy long before it became the theater of revolution. The tsars filled it with public spectacles as well as public works, and developed a highly ceremonial and theatrical court. Since public life was so somber, stylized, and rehearsed, there was a compensatory desire to make the private stage sparkle with comedy. With the satirical successes of Denis Fonvizin in the eighteenth century, Russian comedy became superior to Russian tragedy; and Catherine the Great herself wrote for the satirical stage. But because Russian playwrights felt an obligation to be truthful and not merely diverting, the "laughter through tears" of Gogol and Chekhov became the most distinctive form of comedy in the nineteenth century.

Anton Chekhov captured the immobility and languor of Old Russia in the face of change; but the Chekhovian plays, intended originally as light comedies, were given their classic interpretation as semitragic mood pieces of *fin de siècle* melancholia by the new Moscow Art Theater. The theater's director, Konstantin Stanislavsky, insisted on a rapid pace and on the actor's total involvment in the feelings of the personality being depicted. His "method" acting represented an unleashing of motion and emotion similar to that which was simultaneously taking place in the ballet. Even more innovative (and more typical of the revolutionary age that followed Chekhov's death in 1904) were the theatrical productions of Stanislavsky's pupil and eventual rival, Vsevolod Meyerhold. Bringing gesture, dance, nonrepresentational staging, and dissonant sound onto the stage, he engaged the talents of poets, choreographers, and architects in his experimental theater of the early twenties. In this, the early

Soviet era, artists of all kinds were projecting for the stage their visions of a utopian future which the depleted economy did not permit them to construct in real life.

Among many experimental groups was the Constructivist school, which sought to create new forms in industrial and architectural design and in photo montage, posters, and typography—all intended to generate harmony between the working man and the geometric shapes and mechanical rhythms of the new industrial era. One of the more ambitious of many unrealized schemes was that of Vladimir Tatlin, an independent-minded friend of the Constructivists, who designed the plans (shown on page 310) for a monument in Moscow to the newly formed Communist International. It was to be twice the height of the Empire State Building, and the model, exhibited in 1920, was described by Tatlin as a dynamic "union of purely artistic forms [painting, sculpture, and architecture] for a utilitarian purpose." Intended as a functioning political center, it was also to be a kind of kinetic calendar for the direct transmission of proclamations to the masses. Inside a giant spiral of swirling iron were to be three glass shapes superimposed on one another: a cylinder, a cone, and a cube—each revolving on its axis once a year, month, and day, respectively, and housing legislative, executive, and propaganda functions for the new order. News and directives were to be radiated out by every known medium of communication—including the projection of a daily slogan on the clouds during overcast days.

The most famous Constructivist monument of this era was the Lenin mausoleum in Red Square, built after the leader's death in 1924 and subsequently translated from rough wood into smooth granite. Unfortunately, much of the genuinely innovative and revolutionary spirit also died out in the midtwenties. The posthumous cult of Lenin that began bringing interminable lines of pilgrims to the mausoleum heralded not so much the advent of a new Communist culture as the return to old Russian forms. The displaying of Lenin's embalmed body in the manner of the early Russian saints, Stalin's incantation of oaths at the funeral, and especially his policies when in full power—all heralded a kind of return to Orthodoxy without Christianity.

Stalinist culture in the thirties brought a return to suppression of emotion in art except enthusiasm for industrial production. Catechistic prose supplanted all other forms of verbal expression, photographic realism replaced multisensual expressionism in the arts. The old Russian intelligentsia (and indeed the original revolutionary movement itself) was all but annihilated during the purge period and replaced by what Stalin called "the new Soviet intelligentsia" —technologically trained and totally oriented toward material construction of "socialism in one country."

Artists were now, in Stalin's words, "engineers of the human soul"; and the true "artistic" monuments of the Stalin era were, appropriately, the great triumphs of engineering—the mammoth, pseudo-baroque Moscow subway, the totally new industrial cities like Magnitogorsk, which was artificially thrown up alongside a metal-rich mountain in the deep interior, the hydroelectric dams (beginning with Dnepropetrovsk), and the long canals (such as the Volga-Don). Russia became at last an urban empire, as the city population, which had more than doubled between 1917 and 1940, more than doubled again by 1968. Yet much of the new Soviet construction was haunted by the memory of the forced labor that had helped build it, and was dominated by architectural styles that were simply pretentious imitations of the pseudo-classical façades and spires of Petersburg and the heaviness of Muscovy.

There was no real drama on the stage of Stalin's Russia. Yet all Russia was the scene of innumerable acts of heroism and of tragedy—born of Stalin's purges and Hitler's invasion. At the center of power in Moscow a ritual theatrocracy provided a kind of drama with Kremlin entrances and exits, Red Square processions, and mysterious rearrangements of leading personalities on a reviewing stand or in a theater box.

Amidst this strange mixture of medieval ritualism and forced modernization, the continued flourishing of the classical, aristocratic ballet seems incongruous. Yet the Soviet rulers' reverence for an essentially unchanged imperial ballet expresses well their museum-keeper approach to culture which makes classics of the past available in unprecedented numbers, even as creative innovation in the present is being suppressed. At the same time, the ordinary citizen's love for Tchaikovsky's *Sleeping Beauty* and *Nutcracker* and for Sergei Prokofiev's *Cinderella* also provides many with a consoling flight of fantasy from the two-dimensional world of socialist realism. In some ways the intense popular love of the gossamer world of traditional ballet is similar to the earlier veneration for the ethereal figures and rich decor of Russian religious art. Both provided an image of a distant yet not completely unattainable ideal; a hint of grace amidst suffering, a moment of compensation for the drabness of real life.

The Stalin era came to regulate form as well as content; and Sergei Eisenstein complained in vain that the required style of exaggerated grimace and rolling eyeballs (a bastardization of the Moscow Art Theater tradition) was "a kindergarten for mental defectives." But, in his movies of the thirties and forties he, too, was forced to accept this style as well as the prescribed patriotic themes.

Despite the vulgarity and the degradation of the creative spirit, the attempt to bring culture to the masses did have some mollifying humanizing effects. If the best contemporary poets were frequently hounded into silence, diverted into translating the works of others, or—not infrequently—sent to prison or death, millions were exposed for the first time to the best of past poetry, and thousands attended the occasional readings by those poets who wore the crown of persecution for the pursuit of higher truth. And in such relatively new fields as puppet and children's theater, Soviet accomplishment was genuine and qualitative and not merely a statistical multiplication of past productions.

Thus, while live actors were transformed into puppets under Stalin, puppets in turn slowly began to come alive and quietly assumed a humanizing, satirical role. Similarly, though the prose of officially approved writers often treated the adult population of the U.S.S.R. as children, literature written for children often acquired powerful adult meaning. In the late Stalin era, for instance, the fairy tales of Hans Christian Anderson were skillfully rewritten for the children's puppet theater by Yevgeny Shvarts into anti-authoritarian dramas that subsequently received full stagings under Khrushchev. *The Naked King* and *The Shadow* transformed *The Emperor's New Clothes* and *The Man Who Lost His Shadow* into attacks on Stalin and his courtiers, but Shvarts' *Dragon* also packed a punch for Khrushchev in the guise of ridiculing the legendary Saint George. (The play showed that the rotund saint who slayed the dragon—Stalin—was in truth little better than his subhuman victim once in control.)

The adult theater and other long-persecuted arts enjoyed a quiet partial recovery of former vitality which lasted in most areas for a year or two after the fall of Khrushchev in October, 1964. Color, music, and the dance began to make intrusions onto the stage. The most popular playwright became the antiheroic Bertolt Brecht, and there were hints of fresh ferment for the freedom on which creativity depends. This ferment was less daring and flamboyant, but perhaps more solid and enduring than earlier spectacular open-air poetry readings. A characteristic and memorable moment came when the old historian in the play *Filming a Movie* tells how he prostrated himself to authority by changing his books with every shift in the political wind: "It is not frightening that there are bad people . . . what is frightening is when people are afraid of them."

No one can say whether the creative impulses of the young will be able to overcome inhibiting fears that have been internalized out of long habit—or whether the ruling bureaucracy in the U.S.S.R. will be able to overcome its fear of the entire creative process. But in a technological society in which mathematicians and physicists tend to be among the principal patrons of unofficial modern art, and their students the principal patrons of the new unofficial oral culture (the international guitar having replaced the Russian *gusli* and *balalaika*), there would seem to be some hope for a fuller culture to come. Surrounded by the beauties and resources of an only-partly-despoiled nature and by the memorabilia of an only-partly-destroyed historical past, the remarkable Russian people could yet find new ways to add to their inventory of accomplishment and aspiration. It will be uniquely theirs to create; but—to some degree in an increasingly interrelated world—for all men to share.

Among the most powerful and accomplished of Soviet monumental sculptures, "Machine Tractor Driver and Collective Farm Girl" (below) is a triumph of socialist realism, full of confidence in the heroic energies of the people. Created by Vera Mukhina (1889–1953), one of the foremost of Soviet sculptors, it symbolizes the union of agriculture and industry under socialism. The statue stands in Moscow, at the main entrance to the U.S.S.R. Economic Achievement Exhibition.

ERROL RAINNESS

Dominions of the Spirit

Churches and Monasteries

"The temples of the idols were destroyed, and the churches were built." So wrote Ilarion, the eleventh-century metropolitan of Kiev, exulting in the downfall of pagan gods. "The idols were broken and the icons of the saints appeared. . . . They adorned all the sanctuary and vested holy churches with beauty." Russia had thrown off paganism in 988, with the conversion to Christianity of Vladimir I, prince of Kiev —a conversion said to have been inspired by his emissaries' reports of the beauty and splendor of Constantinople's churches. "We knew not," they told their prince, "whether we were in heaven or on earth." Thus was established Russia's cultural dependence upon Byzantium, a tie further strengthened by Vladimir's timely marriage to the emperor's sister.

As the last peoples to enter the Orthodox world, the Russians passively accepted the established theological doctrines. Slavic energies and imaginations were not fired by abstract ideas, but rather by the aesthetics of Byzantine art and architecture. The glorification of God was expressed through tangibles—the building and decoration of cathedrals.

The first churches were of wood—the inevitable building material in a land rich in forests. Masonry was a foreign craft brought from Byzantium by Greek artisans who arrived in

The Church of the Intercession of the Virgin, near Vladimir, was built in 1165 by Prince Andrei Bogolyubsky. It stands beside the River Nerl, once a waterway for eastern merchants and diplomats.

the train of Greek priests and scholars. At Kiev, Russia's first important architectural center, the basic ground plan for the early churches was purely Byzantine—a Greek cross within a rectangle, the central dome set on the intersection of the arms of the cross, with subordinate domes at lower levels. Significantly, Russian taste and influence was immediately evinced in Kiev's first stone-built church, the Desyatinnaya. Consecrated in 996 and destroyed by the Mongols in 1240, it was exuberantly fashioned with twenty-five domes, an architectural plethora unknown in Byzantium. Kiev's Cathedral of St. Sophia, founded in 1036, was designed to equal the splendors of Constantinople's St. Sophia and was adorned, recorded the chronicles, "with gold and silver and churchly vessels." The original structure, however —a sophisticated expression of Byzantine design—has been so extensively remodeled and enlarged over the years that the exterior today is predominantly eighteenth-century baroque.

In 1169 Kiev was conquered and sacked by Andrei Bogolyubsky, the warrior prince of Vladimir and Suzdal. Kiev's prestige waned, and Vladimir-Suzdal entered a golden age of art and architecture. "God," wrote a chronicler, "brought artists . . . from all parts of the earth." Foreign and native craftsmen, working together, created a distinctive architectural style: richly sculptured exteriors, a soaring harmony of line, an exquisite amalgamation of Russian, Byzantine, and Caucasian designs, similar to European Romanesque.

The Byzantine Tradition

S. FREDERICK STARR

The city-state of Novgorod, northwest of Vladimir-Suzdal, was a bustling crossroads of world trade, linked to Constantinople and the Eastern markets by way of the Dnieper River and, as a member of the Hanseatic League, in direct contact with western Europe by way of the Baltic Sea. At Novgorod the architectural adaptions of Byzantine designs reflected the temper of the town—practical, straightforward, businesslike. Novgorod was essentially a republic, with the ruling princes playing a minor role. Hence, ecclesiastical architecture displayed none of the royal extravagances or aristocratic refinements of Kiev and Vladimir, and was almost spartan in its austerity and dignity. The city's smaller churches were sturdy and stocky, in imitation of native wooden construction. Larger buildings, such as the Cathedral of St. Sophia (opposite) and the Church of the Saviour (on the following page), were massive in their proportions and majestic in their simplicity, conveying a fortress-like impression by the absence of exterior decoration and the limited use of windows. Indeed, many of Novgorod's churches, built by guilds of local merchants and artisans, were also designed as strongholds for the storage of goods and business accounts, providing protection both from enemy attack and from the continuing threat of fire.

Novgorod's original St. Sophia, for example—a wooden church, described as having thirteen domes or "fancy roofs" —was destroyed by flames in 1044. The new stone cathedral, constructed between 1045 and 1052 within the city's kremlin on the River Volkhov, was built to endure—a symbol of the power and spiritual strength of Lord Novgorod the Great, as the citizens named their beloved city. St. Sophia (from the Greek, meaning "holy wisdom") also housed a library and school, as well as collections of art, metalwork, and jewelry, and vaults were provided for the city treasury. The interior, however, remained relatively plain compared to the lavishly wrought and richly finished interiors of the churches in Kiev, which were encrusted with glittering mosaics and brilliant frescoes. In keeping with the townspeople's practical nature, the principal interior decoration at Novgorod was confined to frescoes, painted without highlights, but achieving, nonetheless, a towering grandeur.

Novgorod has been credited with having had the first onion domes, the traditional and unmistakable trademark of Russian church design. According to recent research, the bulbous shape is thought to have evolved during the building of wooden cupolas, when it was found that the stress placed on the timbers was best absorbed by an onion-shaped construction. St. Sophia carries several early examples, probably added during the 1300's to replace the original hemispheric Byzantine domes damaged by a series of roof fires.

Novgorod's Cathedral of St. Sophia remains substantially as it was built, the city having escaped the ravages of Mongol invaders. On the west front are a set of twelfth-century doors, Saxon-work from Magdeburg, with twenty-six bronze, oak-mounted panels depicting scenes from the scriptures. The panel at left is "The Presentation in the Temple." The doors were a gift from medieval merchants.

In the 1500's Novgorod was repeatedly assaulted and ultimately conquered by Moscow,
an event foretold in a midnight vision, as shown in the contemporary icon opposite. A
humble verger, Trasy, was visited by Saint Varlaam as he prayed for the deliverance
of the city. Sent by Saint Varlaam to a church tower, the verger saw spread before him
a view of Novgorod's imminent downfall amid fire, plague, and flood, while saints and
guardian angels offered heavenly intercession. The city, divided by the Volkhov River, is
clearly mapped in the icon, with the red-walled kremlin and St. Sophia on the bank to
the right, and the verger Trasy in the looming tower on the bank to the left. The Church
of the Saviour, above, dating from the 1370's, is in the classical Novgorod style; falling across it is the shadow of a much later church, having fully evolved onion domes.

The Cathedral of St. Dmitry in Vladimir was built by Vsevolod III, between 1193 and 1197. Like the Church of the Intercession (page 32), built by Vsevolod's brother Prince Bogolyubsky, St. Dmitry's exemplifies the grace, delicacy, and elegance of line that characterizes Vladimir-Suzdal architecture. However, where earlier churches were but lightly touched with exterior ornamentation, St. Dmitry's flowers in a fantasia of sculptured decoration that combines Christian and pagan motifs. The dove of the holy spirit, David and his harp, saints and angels, were carved amid a mélange of mythical beasts—basilisks, griffins, harpies, and dragons. Contemporary chronicles omit mention of St. Dmitry's in a list of buildings erected by Vsevolod, and it has been conjectured that the church fathers were displeased by the prodigal display of "graven images" and pagan grotesques in Orthodox architecture.

St. Sophia in Kiev, "the great and holy temple of Divine Wisdom," as it was called by Ilarion, the metropolitan of medieval Kiev, is the oldest surviving church in Russia. It was built between 1037 and 1046, and though its exterior was drastically altered in the eighteenth century, its interior—adorned with brilliantly colored mosaics and frescoes—remains the dazzling re-creation of Byzantine splendor that its architects intended. The mosaics are the work of both Greek and Russian masters, and stylistic differences indicate that there were at least eight of them. The mosaics consist of cubes of glass (tesserae) set into a plaster bed and angled to catch the light, thus creating an effect of shimmering luminosity. Dominating the interior decoration is the image of Christ as Pantocrator (above), the All-Ruler of heaven and earth, who appears at the crest of the dome; in His left hand He holds the apocalyptic book that will be opened on the Day of Judgment. The frescoes of St. Sophia, most of which date from the eleventh and twelfth centuries, were badly preserved and, in the nineteenth century, badly restored by artists who imposed on them their own modern styles. Yet even in such heavily restored images as that of the archangel at left, the original Byzantine iconography is still apparent: the frontal pose, the shield and firmly grasped scepter, and the stylized drapery.

Of Stone and Timber Built

In northeastern Russia, the use of wood as the primary building material was dictated not merely by the country's extensive timberlands, but also by the scarcity of stone suitable for masonry. Native masters in the building trades, therefore, were skilled in carpentry, and under medieval Russian law were paid a daily wage in gold—plus their living expenses. In Novgorod, for example, where local carpenters were renowned as shipwrights and bridge builders, even the streets were paved with wood—wide planks laid across ties of logs —and the city's drainage system was made of large wooden pipes, caulked at the joints with birchbark wrappings. In 1016, according to the chronicles, on the eve of a battle between Kiev and Novgorod, the Kievan general "scoffed at the men of Novgorod, 'Why did you come hither . . . you carpenters? We shall put you to work on our houses.' "

Meanwhile, the techniques of architectural masonry were being learned under the guidance of Greek craftsmen. The principle sources of good stone were in the upper Volga valley and in such tributary valleys as those along the Kama and Oka rivers. From these quarries supplies of stone were laboriously hauled to distant building sites. It has been recorded that when work began on St. Sophia in Kiev in the twelfth century, Prince Yaroslav sent out an urgent call for carters, many of whom were presumably needed to aid in the transportation of stone, and a pay wagon was stationed at the city gate as a pledge of prompt wages. Prompt wages, in turn, assured a steady delivery of the necessary building materials. Six centuries later, when Peter the Great founded St. Petersburg, he assured himself of having the requisite amounts of precious stone by the direct expedient of forbidding its use in any masonry whatsoever, except that of his new capital, which was emerging from a northern marsh.

The Byzantine introduction of masonry, however, had not precluded the use of timber in conjunction with stonework. St. Sophia in Kiev, for instance, was built on oak foundations, and there was extensive use of wooden beams for the support of cupolas. Many early rooftops were probably covered with slate, as well as with wooden shingling. A tiny, octagonal stone chapel, built in the late 1600's at the Trinity-Sergius Monastery, was roofed in ornately shaped wooden tiles. St. Sophia in Novgorod, beset by a series of fires, was re-roofed in 1261 with sheets of lead soldered at the joints, a type of roofing generally supplanted in the seventeenth century by thin sheets of iron joined by rivets.

Bricks, of course, served as an alternative to stone, and local skills in the firing and the handling of brick construction developed quickly in eleventh-century Russia. One such brick kiln was unearthed, during archaeological excavations, near Kiev's St. Sophia, clearly indicating that the bricks used in the construction of the cathedral were fired on the spot. The combination of brick and stone in so much of Russia's early church masonry followed the techniques established in Byzantium. Rows of stone were alternated with courses of brickwork, thus creating a pattern of horizontal stripes, typically in tones of pink and white; these were left exposed—again in accordance with Byzantine architectural tradition. St. Sophia in Novgorod, however, was whitewashed in the twelfth century—perhaps initiating, as some scholars have suggested, the medieval fashion of covering striated masonry with plaster, whitewash, or stucco. The effect produced was imitative, after all, of the white stone so highly prized in the northern forest country. Russian folk epics speak repeatedly of stone palaces as the epitome of beauty and regal splendor.

The city of Vladimir became an important medieval center for stone- and brick-building industries, a tradition that lasted well into the nineteenth century when migrant peasant masons, traveling between jobs in St. Petersburg and Moscow, claimed the Vladimir area as their home. It was in Vladimir, around the twelfth century, that local masons devised what was apparently a unique method of construction —one that may well have contributed to the airy appearance of the Vladimir-Suzdal church architecture. Rather than building their walls of solid blocks of sandstone, Vladimir-Suzdal designers often used thinner cuts of stone set in parallel lines, and then poured a cement mixture into the hollow area between. Both in construction and design, Vladimir's churches came to be revered as the finest expression of early Russian architecture. It was to Vladimir that Ivan III dispatched one of his Italian architects, Ridolfo Fioravanti, instructing him to study local design and to emulate Vladimir's classic proportions in the rising city of Moscow. The result was the Cathedral of the Assumption (opposite), erected on the site of an earlier cathedral built by native workmen. So successful was Fioravanti's version of Vladimir design, that centuries later it was used as a model—by royal decree—for all new churches built in the reign of the Empress Elizabeth.

The Cathedral of the Assumption, or Uspensky Cathedral, built between 1474 and 1479, is shown in cross section. Its design was considered the quintessence of early Russian church architecture. Below (left) is the ground plan with five apses and six interior columns, four of which support the central cupola. The plan of the upper level, at right, shows partial details of overhead vaulting and disposition of the domes.

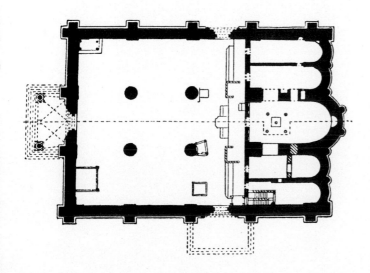

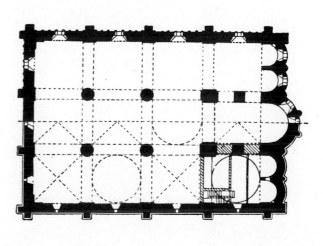

A Mighty Fortress

"If any part of the realm be better or sweeter than other," wrote the English ambassador to Moscow in 1588, "there standeth a friary or a monastery." The ideals of monastacism had been bequeathed to Russia by Byzantium, and under the aegis of the nobility, religious communes sprang up throughout the countryside. Though one eleventh-century monk decried those monasteries founded by princes and emperors as spiritually inferior to those "founded by tears, fasting, prayer and vigil," royal patronage proved judicious. Far-flung religious outposts were incorporated into a network of fortress-monasteries. As Moscow rose in power, the nearby Trinity-Sergius Monastery was transformed from a compound of wooden shelters into a walled city, and over the years, the buildings within became a rich architectural catalog ranging from Russian-Byzantine designs of the late 1400's to baroque confections of the 1700's.

The original monastery, founded by Sergius of Radonezh (1314?–92), most venerated of Russia's saints, had indeed been created through fasting and prayer (an account of Sergius' life in the wilderness appears on page 137). Despite Sergius' ideal of humility, the monastery grew in splendor. A later account by the seventeenth-century Byzantine priest Paul of Aleppo describes the monastery's magnificent buildings as being furnished with "objects surprising to the mind, and dazzling to the sight," vestments "loaded with gold, gems, and pearls," paneling studded with rubies and emeralds, and feasts of "princely meats . . . and infinite variety of royal liquors." Though he complained of the fleas that kept him from his sleep, and of a six-hour service that began at two in the morning, Paul of Aleppo could not but judge the monastery and its elegant appointments "perfect in all respects."

BOTH: S. FREDERICK STARR

Bell towers, bastions, and onion domes shape the skyline of the Trinity-Sergius Monastery (above). "When looking from afar in the clear sunlight at an old Russian monastery or town," wrote a recent Russian essayist, "it seems to be burning with a many-colored flame; and when these flames glimmer from afar, they attract us to them like a distant, ethereal vision of the City of God." The doorway with clustered pillars (at left) is from the monastery's fifteenth-century Cathedral of the Trinity.

Saint Sergius, who had asked that he be buried among the poor, found his final resting place in the gold-domed Cathedral of the Trinity (at right), built in 1422, and the first of the monastery's stone structures. There his coffin was enshrined "in a silver chest," wrote Paul of Aleppo, "covered with huge plates of pure silver, and veiled, with a portrait of the Saint in gold tissue, set with pearls and precious gems." The portrait below, embroidered about 1420 upon a ceremonial pall, shows bearded Saint Sergius as the ascetic, with lean figure, piercing eyes, and hollow cheeks.

Another link in Moscow's chain of outer defences was the Novodevichy Monastery, primarily a convent for women, but nevertheless a strategic stronghold built at a bend of the Moskva River, in order to control an important crossroads. Novodevichy was founded in 1525 by Vasily III, in fulfillment of a vow taken when he had set forth to free the town of Smolensk from Lithuanian rule. In 1591 artillery fired from the monastery battlements turned back an invasion led by the Crimean khan. In 1612 the monastery assisted in defending Moscow against a Polish assault. The fortifications, shown below in an eighteenth-century plan, were continually restored and strengthened. But by the end of the 1700's Moscow's borders had spread far beyond Novodevichy and the other fortress-monasteries, and builders and restorers began concentrating less on defense than on ornamentation. The ubiquitous Paul of Aleppo marveled at the five-domed Smolensk Cathedral (left), dating from the founding of Novodevichy and standing at the heart of the convent. "This church is of vast dimensions," he wrote, "and raised to great height, upon four pillars. . . . The cupola over the table is admirable, being all covered with gold, with arch over arch, supported by angels. . . . We found no likeness, not even among the Emperor's churches, to the beauties of this church. The Patriarch told our master from his own mouth: 'We possess no convent equal to this in riches; and this is, because all the Nuns who reside in it, and successively resort to it, are . . . widows, or maiden daughters of the grandees of the empire, who come with all their property and possessions, their plate, gold and jewels, which they settle upon the convent.' "

A sixteenth-century tower stands at each of the four corners of Novodevichy's walls. Sofia, Peter the Great's sister and arch rival, was imprisoned in one of these towers in 1689 for plotting against the Crown. The portrait, painted by Ilya Repin in 1879, shows the outraged Sofia in her convent quarters, before whose windows Peter had strung up the corpses of her fellow conspirators. There they hung for five months, a day-after-day reminder of her brother's vengeance and fury. Confined for life, Sofia devoted herself to construction projects at Novodevichy. Several chapels and a church were built, as well as a hospital, bell tower, refectory, and rooms for convent servants.

Moscow, The Third Rome

"Suddenly I saw spring up thousands of painted towers and sparkling domes," exclaimed the Marquis de Custine, French traveler and journalist, in recording his approach to Moscow on an August evening in 1839. "This first view of the capital of the Empire of the Slavs, which rises brilliantly in the cold solitudes of the Christian East, produces an impression one cannot forget. You have before you a sad landscape, but vast like the ocean, and to animate the emptiness, a poetic city whose architecture has no name."

Moscow, founded on a bluff overlooking the Moskva River, was little more than a frontier stockade when it was first mentioned in the chronicles in 1147. As Russia expanded, however, Moscow became a vital center, geographically and commercially. Its political and cultural power was consolidated in the early 1300's when the seat of the metropolitan of the Russian Church was moved to Moscow from Vladimir, and Moscow's ruler, Ivan I, was granted the title and privileges of grand prince by his Mongol overlords. Thus, in Ivan's reign began the aggrandizement of Moscow. At the heart of the city, where the first stockade had stood, successive rulers rebuilt the rude oak-fenced kremlin into a vast stone fortress, enclosing within its walls an ever-growing number of stone cathedrals and palaces, as well as an arsenal, an armory, a senate building. It was a city within a city, an exotic architectural wonderland, and—above all—the citadel of Church and State. Shown at right in a seventeenth-century engraving are the Kremlin fortifications and Spassky (Saviour) Gate, built by Italian architects in the late 1400's. The clock tower above the gate, constructed jointly by an English clockmaker and a Russian stonemason, was added about 1625. To the left is St. Basil's Cathedral, built by native-born architects during Ivan the Terrible's reign (1533–84). Moscow's spiritual and temporal power was eulogized by a sixteenth-century monk, writing to Vasily III: "The first Rome fell because of the Apollinarian heresy, the second Rome, Constantinople, was captured and pillaged by the infidel Turks, but a new third Rome has sprung up in thy sovereign kingdom. . . . the Third Rome, Moscow, will stand. . . ."

Christ's entry into Jerusalem was celebrated in medieval Moscow with a procession from the Kremlin to St. Basil's. At the head was a "palm tree" hung with raisins and apples (left), followed by icon and incense bearers, clergy, nobles, and boyars. The patriarch (right) rode an "ass," a linen-swathed horse led by the emperor. "Meanwhile," wrote a marveling visitor, "the bells rang violently, so that the earth trembled."

Kremlin.

Porte du Sauveur.

53

"A church marvellous in size and height, in brightness and resonance, and of wondrous spaciousness." So reads the Chronicle of Nikon in praise of the Cathedral of the Assumption of the Virgin (Uspensky Cathedral), the largest church in the Moscow Kremlin and the mother church of Russia. Here the patriarchs and metropolitans were buried, and here the tsars were crowned. A cross section of the cathedral is shown on page 43. An icon fragment (above), dating from the late 1500's, shows the laying of the foundation for the church first built on the site in 1326. This original structure collapsed in an earthquake, but Fioravanti, Ivan III's Italian architect, deepened the foundations and strengthened the new masonry by connecting walls and arches with tie rods. Illustrated at left is the slim-columned exterior of the new cathedral, completed in 1479. Its white limestone walls and arcading have clearly derived from the Vladimir-Suzdal style, which Fioravanti had studied closely —at Ivan's command. The paintings on the south portal (shown on the opposite page) were done in the seventeenth century and were recently refurbished.

OVERLEAF: *The holy hierarchy, saints, martyrs, and archangels sanctify and adorn the interior of the Cathedral of the Assumption. As legend records it, when the grand prince, bishops, and boyars first viewed these frescoes, they exclaimed, "We see heaven!" Centuries later, when Napoleon took Moscow, a cavalry unit was stabled in the cathedral.*

Glazed Fruits And Wedding Cakes

"A masterpiece of caprice," wrote the Marquis de Custine in 1839, viewing St. Basil's Cathedral in Moscow through French eyes. "Certainly the land where such a monument is called a place of prayer is not Europe; it is India, Persia, China, and the men who go to worship God in this box of glazed fruits are not Christians!" St. Basil's, among the most Russian of Russian churches, was built between 1555 and 1560, during the reign of Ivan the Terrible, and represents the culmination of a national style of architecture that reached its peak during the sixteenth century. In complete departure from traditional Byzantine design, inspiration was drawn from the bold patterns of native wooden churches—slender, tent-shaped roofs and tiers of massed gables, or *kokoshniki*. St. Basil's was the work of Russian-born architects, Barma and Posnik Yakovlev, the asymmetrical structure designed with no two onion domes alike. Built principally of brick and stone covered with stucco, the cathedral was originally white. Its dazzlingly variegated color scheme was a seventeenth-century addition. Basil (in Russian, Vasily) the Blessed, in whose name the cathedral was dedicated, was a mendicant miracle worker, a "holy fool" or "witless one," to whom Ivan credited Russia's victory over the Kazan Mongols in 1552. To be "idiotic for Christ's sake" was a common and deeply revered religious manifestation of the times.

As the story is told, Ivan the Terrible ordered his architects to be blinded after the completion of St. Basil's Cathedral, so that they would not be able to design another, more beautiful, church. Whether true or not, the story is significant; it epitomizes the legendary mad majesty of the tsar, here portrayed in a nineteenth-century painting by Viktor Vasnetsov. Despite Ivan's despotic temperament and the turmoil of his reign, it was an era of artistic advance. Such craftsmen as architects, masons, wood carvers, enamelers, and gold and silver smiths were brought to Moscow from all parts of Russia to combine their talents in the tsar's grandiose building program.

Yaroslavl, a northern principality ceded to Moscow in 1463, had been an established cultural center since the Middle Ages. In the 1600's Yaroslavl also became a rich commercial center, particularly known for its jewel trade. A number of new churches were built between 1660 and 1690, the city having been earlier swept by fire. And with the boundless funds contributed from the coffers of Yaroslavl's wealthy merchants, these churches were even larger and more luxurious than the ones in Moscow. Exteriors were embellished with elaborate brickwork patterns and with insets of colored tiles. Both were architectural motifs borrowed from the Near East and from India—the Asian world with which the city carried on an extensive trade. Shown here are details from the Church of the Epiphany, built between 1684 and 1693. The scaly roofing of the cupolas was typical of local design. The tiered gables are a further example of the kokoshniki used in the high Muscovite style.

The Church of the Intercession of the Holy Virgin, which has been described as "one of the brightest phenomena of Russian architecture," was built in 1693 at Fili, the suburban Moscow estate of the boyar Naryshkin, an uncle of Peter the Great. The basic form of the building is an elegant embodiment of Ukrainian pyramidal design—a series of diminishing octagonal drums. The ornamentation is a frosting of baroque details borrowed from Europe.

From the Forest

While masons and architects worked with stone in Russia's urban centers, carpenters and architects who worked with wood in the northern forest lands were perfecting their skills. The churches they created demonstrated a genius for design, proportion, and decoration. As one present-day Russian author has phrased it, "These forms became the inexhaustible source from which the arts of Russia, in their anemic period, drew new blood." The intricacies of wooden construction were accomplished without the use of metal nails and without the aid of a saw. In keeping with ancient Russian tradition, the workman's principal tool was the axe, whether for felling timber or shaping shingles. The tradition, in fact, was so strongly ingrained that the saw was looked upon as a "foreign" device until late in the seventeenth century; and Tolstoy later wrote that a Russian, equipped with nothing more than an axe, could "both build a house and shape a spoon." Possibly the masterpiece of all Russian wooden architecture is the Church of the Transfiguration, one of a group of ecclesiastical wooden structures on Kizhi Island at Lake Onega. The architect, Master Nester, designed the building in the pyramid form, the octagonal sections lavished with flights of domes. It has been said that when Nester completed the church he flung his axe into Lake Onega and said, "There has never been, is not, and never shall be such another."

Twenty-two domes, each bearing the Russian Orthodox cross of Saint Vladimir, crown the Church of the Transfiguration at Kizhi (left). The interior, a marvel of hand-hewn wood carvings, is shown above. A crucifix stands before the gilded iconostasis, or altar screen.

OVERLEAF: *The Church of the Transfiguration, built in 1714, and the smaller Church of Our Lady of the Veil, built in 1764, stand silhouetted against the northern sky of Russia.*

2

Images of Faith

Icons and Frescoes

Among all the Byzantine art forms introduced into tenth-century Russia along with Christianity, it was the icon that appealed most strongly to the Russians—both as an artistic and as a religious expression. The illumination of manuscripts never became widespread as it did in western Europe. Mosaic work was limited largely to the Kievan area and created solely by Byzantine-trained craftsmen. Fresco painting, while popular, was confined by the nature of the medium to stone buildings; and sculpture—the creation of "graven images"—was forbidden by the Church and therefore rarely practiced until the eighteenth century. Icons, however—with two-dimensional, ascetic figures that belonged unmistakably to the spiritual rather than the human world—were fully sanctioned by the Church, and were adopted so wholeheartedly into Russian life that they became the national art form. Icons, to the Russians, were not merely paintings. They were the visible evidence of divine powers that could transform the imperfect life on earth into a life of celestial perfection. As John of Damascus, an early Syrian theologian, wrote: "The icon is a song of triumph, and a revelation, and an enduring monument to the victory of the saints and the disgrace of the demons."

The Virgin of Vladimir was venerated as the guardian of Holy Russia for over eight hundred years. Though rare in Byzantine sacred art, motherly tenderness became a principal Russian theme.

The contemplative mood and dark colors of Byzantine iconography were modified by Russian artists into a more vigorous interpretation. Brighter, luminous colors were used, and outlines were simplified. Images that portrayed qualities of warmth and loving kindness became particularly favored in Russian iconography. The Virgin of Vladimir (opposite), painted by a Byzantine artist in the twelfth century, was immediately accorded affection by Russians. It was the image of divine compassion, as opposed to images of stern majesty.

This icon, a sacred treasure brought from Constantinople to newly Christianized Kiev, was later appropriated as a prize of war by Prince Andrei Bogolyubsky and taken to Vladimir. There, legends arose concerning the icon's wonder-working gifts, and thus the painting became known as the Miraculous Virgin of Vladimir. In the fourteenth century, when Tamerlane and his Mongol tribesmen advanced on Moscow, the precious icon was brought to the besieged city to offer divine intercession. It was said that on the day the icon arrived from Vladimir, Tamerlane saw a vision of a lady in purple robes who led a mighty army to defend the road to Moscow. The Mongols did indeed abruptly retreat into the Asian steppes from which they had come. Later, in 1612, the icon again saved Moscow when Russians, inspired by its presence, drove off invading Polish forces. "It is better," the Russians said, "for us to die than to deliver the image of the immaculate Mother of God of Vladimir to desecration."

Styles of Reverence

The Virgin of Kherson, a sixteenth-century icon of the Moscow school, copied the style formalized by the twelfth-century icon, the Virgin of Vladimir. Work derived from venerable models was often titled Kherson, after the port that had once been a gateway through which much of Byzantium's sacred art reached Russia.

In Russia, the cult of Mary stressed the concept of divine motherhood, rather than virginity, and the Mother of God became the mother image of all Russia. Icons of the Madonna were most widely represented by the type known as icons of tenderness, which were inspired by the cherished Virgin of Vladimir (which is shown on page 68). In icons of tenderness, the Mother presses her cheek to the Child's face in a gesture of all-embracing love, while her eyes are marked with sorrow and compassion, not only for her Son but for all mankind. Mary's veil was decorated with three stars, on the forehead and on each shoulder, as symbols of perpetual virginity. The Child was dressed not in swaddling clothes as an infant, but fully robed, symbolizing Christ Emmanuel clothed in wisdom. According to legend, several such icons, among them the Virgin of Vladimir, were painted during Mary's lifetime by Saint Luke, and she conferred her blessings upon her image. Thus, it was assumed that, by association, paintings copied after those attributed to Saint Luke were also recipients of Mary's words of blessing.

Though most painters rigorously adhered to the conventional styles and forms, some—while still careful to stay within the bounds of iconographic tradition—began developing distinctive styles and modes of expression. The Virgin of the Don, for instance (shown opposite, at top), was painted in a manner characterized by an inner luminosity and a distinct approach toward a naturalistic portrayal. Painted late in the fourteenth century, it has been attributed to Theophanes the Greek, a master painter who came to Russia from Byzantium and worked in Novgorod and Moscow. Not far from Novgorod, the painters of Pskov, the northern town once known as "the younger brother of Lord Novgorod the Great," were painting icons in which faces and figures were angular and almost coarse in quality. Furthermore, unlike the artists of other northern provincial towns, those of Pskov rejected the brilliant colors favored by Novgorod's painters, and worked in dark, earthy tones that became the hallmark of the Pskovian school.

The Virgin of the Don (right) was said to have been carried into the Battle of Kulikovo in 1380—a battle miraculously won when the winds shifted, blinding the Mongol enemy with clouds of sand. The Virgin of Tenderness in the icon below is surrounded by a panoply of saints. At top left is Nicholas, Russia's patron, and protector of children and travelers. "If God dies," goes an old Russian saying, "we still have Saint Nicholas." The others are (moving clockwise): George, patron of plowmen and shepherds; Demetrius, champion of Russian Orthodoxy; Paraskeva, patron of women's tasks; the apostles Paul and John; Cosmas, patron of blacksmiths and doctors; Laurus and Florus, protectors of horses; Anastasia, patron of trade and commerce; Blaise, patron of cattlemen; Elijah, the protector of the home; and the apostle Peter.

In a sixteenth-century icon of the Moscow school, Mary and the apostles gather on the Mount of Olives to witness Christ's ascension. Though limited to the Eastern Church's established iconographic composition for scenes of the Ascension, the artist was still able to achieve a skillful delineation of character and drapery, as is apparent in the detail shown opposite.

Visions of Heaven

SOVFOTO

Removed from Byzantine centers of Orthodoxy and influenced by the native arts, the great fresco painters of Russia tended to develop their own techniques. In Novgorod's Church of the Saviour-on-the-Nereditsa, the monumental frescoes done in 1199 departed from Byzantine stylization to offer such energetic and rugged figures as that of Saint Peter of Alexandria (above). One of the greatest masters of the fresco, Theophanes the Greek, migrated from Byzantium in the 1370's, possibly to escape the increasingly dogmatic restrictions on artistic interpretation. In Novgorod and later in Moscow, Theophanes created an art that was freely expressed, incisive yet ethereal, using bold brush strokes and heightening his palette with bright Russian colors. "When he sketched or painted," wrote one admirer in 1415, "no one ever saw him looking at model drawings." Theophanes drew inspiration from within, "pondering wise and lofty thoughts in his mind." A later master, Dionysius (c. 1440–c. 1509), employed mainly in the Kremlin under Ivan III, is noted for the elongated grace of his figures, rich colors, and the mood of triumph (right).

Dionysius and his sons painted the Intercession of the Virgin between 1500 and 1502, at the Ferapont Monastery in northern Russia. The fresco celebrates Mary's appearance in a Constantinople church in the tenth century, when she was seen holding her veil over the congregation—a symbol of her intercession in their behalf. Saint Andrew, "a Fool in Christ," who witnessed the vision, is in the right foreground, emaciated and half naked. In the pulpit Saint Romanos the Melodist holds a Christmas hymn honoring the Virgin.

EDITIONS CERCLE D'ART, PARIS

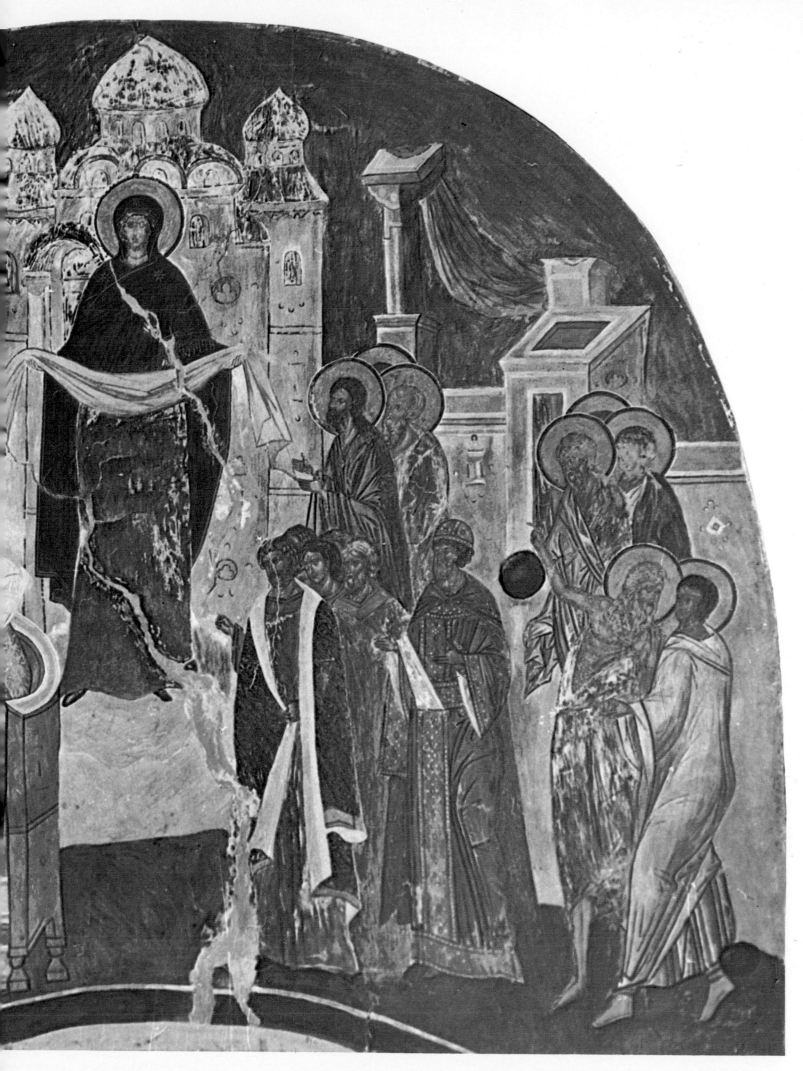

OVERLEAF: *Theophanes' fresco (1378), in Novgorod's Church of the Transfiguration, depicts the angelic Trinity that appeared to Abraham and Sarah.*

The Stroke of Genius

The greatest of all medieval Russian painters was the monk Andrei Rublyov (c. 1370–c. 1430), who lifted Russian art from the severity of its Byzantine legacy. By eliminating all unnecessary iconographic details, he created a purity of composition that emphasized the spiritual and aesthetic—an effect further heightened by the ethereal elongation of his figures. "His art is gentler, more poetic, and more luminous than that of his predecessors. The pigments of his palette are derived not from the traditional color canons, but from his native landscape." So wrote Viktor Lazarev, the Russian art historian. "His marvelous deep blue is suggested by the blue of the spring sky; his whites recall the birches so dear to a Russian; his green is close to the color of unripe rye; his golden ochre summons up memories of fallen autumn leaves; in his dark green colors there is something of the twilight shadows of the dense pine forest." This gift of color was delicately suffused with a misty atmosphere—a marked departure from the poster-like coloring typical of earlier painters. Rublyov's influence was immediate, and Russian art—in the fifteenth century—entered the golden age of the icon.

The precise details of Rublyov's life are uncertain, but it is known that he was a native of Moscow and entered the Trinity-Sergius Monastery as a young man, there to receive his initial training in art from the monk Prokhor. An early commission, in about 1404, took him to the monastery at Zvenigorod. Shortly thereafter, Rublyov and Prokhor worked as assistants to the aged Theophanes the Greek, who was then decorating the Cathedral of the Annunciation in the Moscow Kremlin. In 1408 Rublyov was commissioned to paint frescoes and icons in the Cathedral of the Assumption in Vladimir. Upon his return to his home monastery, Trinity-Sergius, he devoted many years to painting murals and icons (among them the Trinity that appears on page 83) in the cathedral built over the tomb of Saint Sergius. For a time he also lived and worked at the Andronikov Monastery in Moscow. After his death, Andrei Rublyov was beatified by the Russian Church, and his artistic innovations were wholly accepted into the iconographic tradition; in the mid-sixteenth century, the Council of One Hundred Chapters, a conclave of the clergy called together by Ivan IV to reinforce orthodoxy in art and ritual, officially sanctioned Rublyov's work as a model for other artists.

An icon of the Saviour, opposite, painted by Rublyov about 1410, exhibits the emotional intensity and fluidity of line so characteristic of his work. The painting, found by chance in a storehouse of the Zvenigorod Cathedral, was part of a Deesis—*the row of icons placed above the royal doors on an iconostasis. In the picture at left, Rublyov himself is portrayed on a scaffold as he gilds an icon of Christ on a wall of the Andronikov Monastery in Moscow. The illustration, from a manuscript on the life of Saint Sergius, dates from Rublyov's time.*

The Trinity (opposite), considered to be Rublyov's masterpiece, was painted in 1411 for the Trinity-Sergius Monastery, in Zagorsk. The Old Testament Trinity, as this type of icon is known, was an ancient Byzantine form rooted in Orthodox doctrine. In order to unify the Old Testament Church and the New Testament Church, the three heavenly beings who appeared to Abraham in the Book of Genesis were interpreted as a manifestation of the Holy Trinity, thus creating a theological continuity. As established in iconographic tradition, the angels were seated at a table, upon which lay the feast presented to them by Abraham and Sarah. (Theophanes' earlier fresco of this Old Testament scene appears on pages 78–79.) In his Trinity, Rublyov presented a flawlessly balanced composition, a mood of majestic calm, and a subtle harmony of coloring in the juxtaposition of blues and yellows. The angle given to the turn of the heads and the slight forward bend of the bodies created an unobtrusive impression of depth, without the use of perspective. These qualities were also achieved in the painting of Saint Peter (shown at left), which has been attributed to the school of Rublyov.

OVERLEAF: Rublyov's lucidity of line and color is illustrated in this detail of the first and second angels in the Trinity icon.

EDITIONS CERCLE D'ART, PARIS

Patrons and Protectors

Every aspect of Russian life, from birth to death, was attended by icons. Images of favorite saints were enshrined in every Orthodox household, whether princely or impoverished. Icons were hung on barns and stables to guard the livestock. They were set up at crossroads to guard the traveler. They were carried aloft in all religious and imperial processions, and led the armies of Russia into battle. They were the supreme authority before which oaths were given and vows taken. They were the ritual objects with which blessings were conferred—upon the newborn, upon a newly betrothed couple, or upon a son conscripted into the army. Icons known to possess the gift of healing were brought to the sick. And family icons followed in the funeral cortege that accompanied the dead to their graves.

The reverence paid to images of saints extended even to the purchase of icons. They were not "bought," because the customer would then be guilty of buying the saint himself; rather, the convention of barter was used, money being "given in exchange" for an icon. The chosen spot where family icons were displayed was the *krasny kut*, or "beautiful corner," before which each person who entered the house bowed in homage. In wealthy homes, an entire wall or even a room might be hung with icons, and family prayers held before these household shrines. The relationship with patron saints was intensely personal. If special prayers were answered, the icon might be thanked with the gift of a gold frame. If a prayer went unheeded, the icon might be turned to the wall as punishment.

In the procession above, led by the icon of the Virgin of Vladimir, the young tsar Mikhail Romanov kneels before his kneeling father, the patriarch Filaret, who returned from Polish captivity in 1619. A folk poem of the same year described the scene: "Our father has arrived, our lord Filaret Nikitich, from the land of the heretics. . . . Many princes, boyars, and many dignitaries have assembled to the mighty realm of Moscow. . . . Our lord, the orthodox tsar, has gone forth to meet his father, the Lord Filaret. . . ." The picture was painted for an account of Tsar Mikhail's reign written about 1672.

Saint Paraskeva (left) was martyred in the fourth century at the time of the persecution of Christians ordered by the Roman emperor Diocletian. In this painting, a detail from a Pskov icon dated c. 1400, Paraskeva wears a red cloak, the symbol of martyrdom. Besides being the patron of women's domestic tasks, Saint Paraskeva was also venerated as the patron of trade, because her Russian name, Pyatnitsa, meant "Friday," which was the traditional market day in Russia.

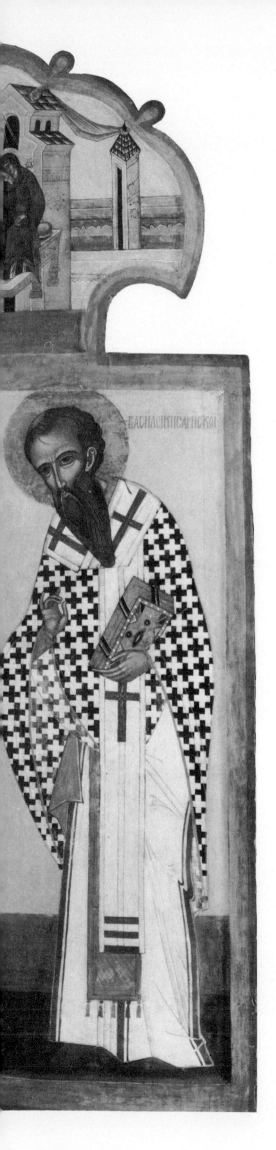

The iconostasis royal doors (left), said to date from 1700, were painted with the traditional images of two hierarchs of the Eastern Church: left, Saint John Chrysostom, or John the Golden Mouth, a bishop famed for his eloquence; facing him, Saint Basil the Great of Caesarea, also a bishop and early church father. Above them, again in iconographic tradition, is the Annunciation. The painting at right is of Saint John the Evangelist, in a detail from a Crucifixion scene.

Calendars of the liturgical year were painted on icons, with successive rows of figures and vignette illustrations giving the exact sequence of saints' feast days and of church festivals. Shown above are two panels, each close to six feet in height, that are part of a calendar icon painted in the sixteenth century by artists attached to the court of Ivan the Terrible. The complete set consists of twelve panels, one for each month.

OVERLEAF: *In a detail from a seventeenth-century icon at Yaroslavl's Cathedral of the Dormition, the prophet Elijah is carried to heaven in a fiery chariot, dropping his mantle to his disciple, Elisha. A popular icon theme, Elijah was believed to have power over fire and rainfall.*

The Arts of the Church

A Gallery of Treasures

For the Russian Church, art was a means of conveying the doctrines of Orthodoxy to the common people, of dramatizing dogma through organized symbols such as those found in icons and frescoes. But more importantly, art was also a means of creating an earthly image of God's heavenly realm, an awe-inspiring representation of the splendors of Paradise. Lamps of nielloed silver flickered amid the paintings glowing dimly from the walls of the cathedrals; finely wrought silver crosses stood on the altars, and were carried by priests and patriarchs; altar cloths and vestments were richly embroidered and appliquéd with pearls; censers of silver and gold perfumed the air; Bible covers were of gold or silver inlaid with enamel and precious stones; and the frames and royal doors of the iconostasis were carved and gilded.

In order to attain such opulent effects, the Church became a prime patron of the decorative arts. Monastic and lay artists, craftsmen, and jewelers were employed in large numbers by the wealthy patriarchs of Moscow, and in the 1650's the powerful Nikon even founded his own independent workshop near the patriarchal palace. Vast treasures also came to the Church as gifts from princes, boyars, and tsars, who hoped by their generosity to obtain their souls' repose. Occasionally the Church had to surrender parts of its treasure, as when private and church collections of silver were used to finance the war against Poland in the seventeenth century; fire, conquering armies, and revolution also took their toll. But enough of these precious objects were produced so that vast quantities still remain.

Despite the dictates of the hierarchy, the designs that were applied to church accouterments were not always confined to ecclesiastical traditions, nor could stylistic purity be maintained when craftsmen were being brought from such diverse areas as India, Islam, France, Germany, and Italy, as well as Byzantium. Thus, along with the Scythian and Teutonic animal motifs of pagan Russia, there also appear floral arabesques, intricate filigree patterns, bejeweled ornamentation, and calligraphic designs, creating a unique hybrid of styles.

Russian enamelwork derived originally from Greek and Scythian sources, and later from Byzantium. The cloisonné book cover opposite and the hand cross above both date from the seventeenth century.

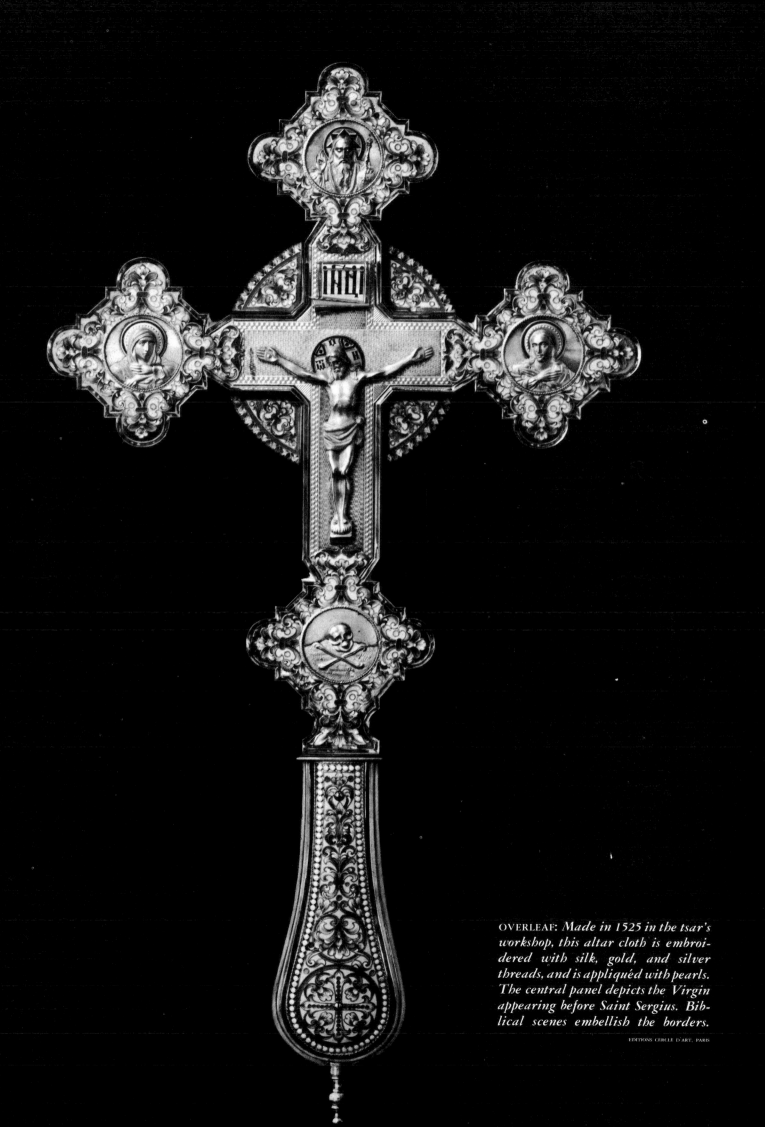

OVERLEAF: *Made in 1525 in the tsar's workshop, this altar cloth is embroidered with silk, gold, and silver threads, and is appliquéd with pearls. The central panel depicts the Virgin appearing before Saint Sergius. Biblical scenes embellish the borders.*

EDITIONS CERCLE D'ART, PARIS

"In the year 1666 on the 2nd of November the Holy Father Seth, Archbishop of Astrakhan, had the cup made for the Church of St. Nicholas." So reads the inscription on the gilded silver chalice at left, which is engraved with images of the Virgin, Christ, and John the Baptist. The silver candelabra at right, a gift from Boris Godunov to the Trinity-Sergius Monastery, was meant to illuminate the Trinity of Rublyov.

The bishop's miter above, a gift from Mikhail Romanov to his patriarch, is decorated with pearls and jewels.

ARMOURY OF THE KREMLIN, MOSCOW, NOVOSTI

Portable icons were frequently given as gifts in Russia. The one at right, a folding triptych, is reproduced here slightly larger than actual size. Created by the master jeweler Peter Carl Fabergé, it is of gilded silver and enamel set with rubies, emeralds, sapphires, and pearls, and is in the form of the royal doors of an iconostasis. The icon was presented by the nobility of St. Petersburg to Nicholas II and Alexandra Fedorovna on November 3, 1895, to celebrate the birth of their daughter, the Grand Duchess Olga. In the central panel are shown the patron saints of the tsar and tsaritsa; above them is Olga's patron. On the wings are angels and the evangelists.

The Peasants' Wealth

Folk Arts and Crafts

The folk arts were the only secular arts in early Russian history, the only record of the life experiences indigenous to the Russian people (the traditions of painting, architecture, and literature having been borrowed primarily from Byzantium and western Europe). Folk arts, like the ecclesiastical arts, were permeated with a utilitarian spirit that provided, in the words of the contemporary Russian-born sculptor Naum Gabo, "the link between the artist and the common man." The objects created by the peasant craftsmen—utensils, clothing, tools, and so forth—were intended exclusively for domestic use. Similarly, the symbols used in Russian folk art were expressive of the natural phenomena that shaped the course of the peasant's life: the seasons, plants and animals, wind, water, sun, and earth. Carved into stone and wood, stitched into linens and homespun, painted on ceramics and lacquerware, these motifs are centuries old, and many of them date back to pre-Christian times.

The forces of nature were, in large part, responsible for the extent to which the folk arts developed in Russia. The climate is harsh. (Moscow, in the center of Old Russia, is on the same latitude as the southern shore of Hudson Bay.) Agriculture, therefore, was possible only during about four

The relief, opposite, of a grinning lion is by a Russian craftsman of the seventeenth century, and was used to decorate the doorway of a building on the imperial estate at Kolomenskoe, near Moscow.

months of the year, and at that time every able-bodied peasant was at work in the fields. During the remaining months, the peasants turned to their crafts, both for pleasure and as a means of supplementing the meager income they earned from farming. Those engaged in some sort of craft were likely to live in better houses and to wear better clothes than peasants whose livelihood depended upon agriculture alone.

Most handicrafts—whether coarse wares bought by peasants, or luxury items such as silks and gold and silver objects intended for the wealthy—were produced by individual peasants and their families, working at home. But craftsmen also worked in village shops, and in communal groups, sharing materials and profits. Often the artisans of an entire town devoted themselves to a single craft, some towns becoming known for painting and wood carving, others for ceramics, embroidery, cotton printing, and so on.

The chief market places for the peasant's handicrafts were the towns and fairs. During the eighteenth and nineteenth centuries thousands of fairs were held each year in Russia. The greatest of them all—the one at Nizhny-Novgorod—was of international importance, situated as it was at the junction of the Volga and Oka rivers, the crossroads of Europe and Asia. Many a peasant craftsman, having carried his goods and perhaps those of his neighbors to markets such as this, found the peddler's wandering life exciting and profitable, and never again returned to his workbench.

The Carver's Art

The peasants who inhabited the rugged northern regions of Russia seem to have had an instinctive feeling for the artistic possibilities of the materials at hand. Using only a simple axe, a small chisel, and a knife (even carpenters frowned on using saws), they carved cottage beams and window frames, toys, furniture, utensils, looms, sleighs, wagons—any object that was part of their lives and could be hewn out of wood. A few carvers found stone to be a more congenial medium for their particular talents, and some of them were able to produce such sophisticated and elegant pieces as the fragment (shown on this page) from a fifteenth-century equestrian statue of Saint George. But more often the peasant chose to display his carving ingenuity in birch, oak, or limewood.

According to the early chronicles the pagan Slavs worshiped carved and elaborately decorated statues of the Slavic gods. When Christianity was introduced in 989 the Church attempted to destroy all pagan imagery and declared it heretical to carve wooden and stone figures. Once Orthodoxy was more securely established, native artisans were grudgingly allowed to carve church decorations, wooden icons, and other religious images. But the mass of the people, though Christian, retained vestiges of paganism, and the centuries-old pagan motifs continued to appear in secular woodwork. The ancient sun god, depicted as a circle or as a flaming horse—sometimes with three heads—was worked into mirror frames, and carved on the backs of benches and on distaffs. Later, peasant craftsmen also carved more mundane and light-hearted subjects, such as satirical dolls and toys portraying stock Russian characters. There was the fat clergyman, the snobbish military officer, the greedy merchant, and the peasant himself, working in the fields, eating, drinking, and being flogged.

The stone bust below is Christian Russia's earliest surviving example of figure sculpture in the round—carved in the late 1400's by a peasant builder and sculptor, Vasily Yermolin. He had been commissioned by Ivan III to create a pair of equestrian statues to decorate the Frolov Gate of the Kremlin. All that remains of his work is this bust, the head and shoulders of a young paladin who represents Saint George, his right arm raised for the spear thrust that will slay the dragon. The figure symbolized medieval Russia's invincibility and was included in Muscovy's coat of arms. Opposite is a detail from an eighteenth-century wooden sculpture of King David. Such carved images began appearing in Russian churches in the sixteenth century, and remained a major part of Orthodox iconography despite the hostility of the Church, which found them too reminiscent of pagan idols.

"Everything was of wood: the walls, the ceiling, the floor, the seats, the table. . . ." So the French traveler, the Marquis de Custine, described a Russian peasant's house in 1839, adding that "the rooftops are loaded with ornaments." In the north most peasant dwellings were likely to have a ridge beam carved on one end with the head of a horse, a goat, a deer, or a fantastic bird, while the tail of the beast appeared on the other end. Window and door frames were embellished with elaborately carved and painted figures like the mermaid below, who was considered protectress of the hearth. In more exalted households carvings of regal lions, like the one above dating from the eighteenth century, decorated the feet of chairs and thrones. The sailor too had his favorite carvings, among them the sun disc, a vestige of paganism; the one seen opposite was mounted atop the mast of a river boat.

OVERLEAF: *This carefully hand-carved flower and leaf pattern is a detail from a frieze that decorated a wooden house in northern Russia.*

Life in Rural Russia

The limewood statuette of a family of carvers, above, dates from the turn of the century. It is typical of the domestic scenes portrayed by artisans. The early nineteenth-century carvings shown opposite served as beehives; when bees flew through the eyes, the figures appeared to blink.

The Russian nobility often learned more about their peasants from books than by direct contact. One of the most influential studies was that of a foreign traveler, the German economist, the Baron August von Haxthausen, whose descriptions of nineteenth-century peasant life were first published in 1847. Excerpts are given below.

The peasants are usually dressed in sheepskins, with the hairy side inwards, but, particularly in summer, also in kaftans, which, among the poorer class, are of grey or brown homespun woollen cloth,—in the rich, of blue cloth; the latter are frequently girded with Turkish or Persian scarfs of a bright color. . . .

In warm weather the peasantry wear bast shoes, laced over the foot. The legs and feet are wrapped in rags, and the men have short loose trousers, over which the shirt is girded. The latter was formerly of coarse linen, but cotton is now becoming more common every day . . .; on the highroads bright-colored cotton shirts are almost universally seen, the principal color being necessarily red, as red and beautiful are identical terms with the genuine Russian, the language having only one word for both [*krasny*]. . . .

The peasant-women have generally a cloth wound round the head. Over their petticoats they wear a dress of woollen cloth,—among the poorer class of homespun, among the richer of blue cloth; it is low in the neck, has no sleeves, and is sometimes short, only reaching to the knee, but occasionally down to the feet; it is then called a *sarafan*. Over this, in winter, they wear a short fur pelisse, only reaching a little below the hips, which has the pretty name of "soulwarmer," and has been introduced into the rest of Europe, particularly as a dress for children.

. . . .

In the villages the men and boys are always seen in the roads, but a girl seldom, and women only when they have something to do. In the interior of the country, where the arrival of a carriage and strangers is a rare occurrence, the women and girls generally stand crowded together on some staircase; if any one approaches them, they immediately vanish into the house. This is perhaps a trace of Oriental manners. But when surprised in their dances in the streets, they are so grave and so absorbed in this important business as never to allow themselves to be disturbed by anything,—not even by the curious gaze of the stranger.

. . . .

The Russian has capacity and talent for everything. Of all peoples he has perhaps the greatest amount of practical ability in acquiring a position adapted to him. . . . [Yet] accident mostly decides which of the talents a boy possesses shall first be developed. The landed proprietor, without much examination, chooses among the boys of his serfs, who is to be a shoemaker, who a smith, who a cook, who a clerk, etc. Prudent landowners, in order to acquire better workmen, sometimes give the boys to master-artisans, under a contract for three to eight years to teach and exercise them in their work. The colonel of a regiment orders at once, and without much investigation, that so many men shall be saddlers, so many smiths or wheelwrights; these shall be musicians, those clerks. And they become all these, and almost invariably with ease and dexterity; and from them proceed in general the most solid and best artificers, workmen, and artists, because, being appointed and constrained by outward authority, they remain in the occupation they have adopted. In the case of the Crown peasants, on the other hand, the boy receives the first impulse from his parents or relatives, or chooses an occupation for himself. After adopting his calling, there is no question of any education such as the German artisan receives, nor of the settled apprenticeship with regular masters, nor advancement from the position of apprentice to that of journeyman, and ultimately on examination and trial to that of master, participating in important privileges. He learns as he can, from observation or accident, attempts and invents himself, and seeks employment wherever he can find it.

. . .

. . . the love of money and distinction are the rocks upon which in Russia every character is shipwrecked. The common man, the peasant, is estimable and good at heart; but as soon as he acquires money, and becomes a speculator or merchant, he is ruined and metamorphosed into an arrant rogue.

. . .

. . . it may be considered as a fixed rule in Russia, that he who has once had occasion, no matter from what reason, to abandon agricultural labor, never returns to it. This appears most clearly in the case of the soldiers after their period of service has expired. These have in general no property, and they be-

come anything else,—house-servants, watchmen, shopkeepers, etc., but never peasants as before.

. . .

[*Haxthausen here describes a house in a village some two hundred miles northeast of Moscow.*] There were several buildings adjoining each other, and a low shed . . . next to which stood the summer house; each building had a separate roof, but they were united internally in a convenient manner. The winter and summer houses contained only stalls and stables in the lower story; in the upper one was the dwelling. The winter house had the *izba* (black room) next the street; behind were the *tchulani* (chambers). The summer house contained the *sarai* (store for provisions), and in front the *gornitza*, or summer room, with large windows. Along the gables of the houses on both sides ran borders ornamented with a variety of carved work, which terminated in long planks, and beautiful filigree-work. In the inns the waiters and landlords carry a long narrow napkin, which they present when required to the guests in washing; at the end this cloth is about half a foot wide, worked like lace, and appears pinked with all sorts of arabesques. Now these planks with the filigree-work on the gables [look] like these napkins, one of which hangs upon the wall in every respectable peasant's house. . . .

. . .

. . . the Gulianie [at Nizhny-Novgorod] is a large open space south-west of the town upon the bank of the Oka, which is two hundred feet high,—a meadow without tree or bush. Here the people assemble in the afternoon once every week when the weather is fine, and amuse themselves until evening. . . . There were rows of tents and huts, made of the branches of trees, with food and drink. Over small fires, made in holes in the ground, the well-known Russian pies (*pirogi*) were everywhere cooking. These and the other eatables were carried about for sale by active young boys upon boards, which they balanced on their heads. Everywhere the people stood or lay in stationary groups, but the sexes were always separated; each group constituted a sort of separate Commune for the time being, in accordance with the fundamental principle of the Russian popular character,—an organic association, with its elected leader, Starosta, or master. Spectators only, belonging to the middle and higher classes, and not participators in the proceedings, promenaded about; the common Russian never promenades. In many of the groups of men we heard singing; among the women I never heard a song. The leader of the group commenced alone, in a monotonous plaintive note; the chorus answering, or repeating the concluding words. On one spot a circle of soldiers had assembled. The first singer stood in the middle with a tambourine; the songs were sung by several voices, and executed with great precision. In the comic songs . . . the leading singer addresses the circle, singing; the latter replies; the leader rejoins, jumps and gesticulates with the greatest vivacity. . . .

Feminine Artifice

In Russia, as in western Europe, weaving and embroidery were woman's work, so much so that the distaff became a symbol of womanhood. When a baby girl was born her umbilical cord was severed with a ritual distaff (a boy's was cleft with an axe). Russian girls grew up hearing the fairy tale about Maryushka, whose embroidery was the delight of her village, but who was turned into a firebird by an ogre when she refused to stitch for him alone.

As soon as the peasant girl could manage a needle she would spend long winter evenings learning from her mother the arts of spinning, weaving, and embroidery. And she would be warned to learn her arts well, for when the Russian girl became engaged she was expected to prepare embroidered gifts for her fiancé, as a measure of her ability and industry.

At an early age, Russian girls learned to decorate their linens and homespun—their pillowcases, sheets, towels, aprons, and dresses—with the traditional motifs. Mythological animals and birds (including the firebird), floral patterns, and geometrical designs were woven and stitched into even the most simple fabrics. Bed curtains, sometimes used to decorate the backs of sledges and wedding carriages, were embellished with swastikas, the Scythian symbol for good luck. Ceremonial towels, hung in peasant homes and brought to church as votive offerings, were often embroidered with a female figure surrounded by animals and trees—an evolution of the earth goddess motif found in the art of pre-Christian tribesmen. Thus, in their weaving and needlework, Russia's women preserved a valuable documentary record of pagan symbolism and primitive ornamental design.

The seventeenth-century wedding chest on the opposite page is filled with embroidered towels made in the Novgorod and Ryazan regions. (The lid of the chest is decorated with a painting of Sirin, the mythical bird said to live in Paradise, where it sings for the righteous.) The distaff at left held the tufts of raw wool that were spun into thread.

Designs in Clay

Long before the founding of Kievan Rus, Slavic craftsmen were making domestic pottery—crude earthenware bowls and jugs fashioned by hand, without the aid of a potter's wheel, and baked over an open fire. Gradually potters developed the art of glazing, by which a hard, glassy surface is baked onto the fired clay; and by the eleventh century, primitive kilns and pedal-driven wheels were operated in the pottery quarters of Russia's cities.

Earthenware was the basic material used by the Russians for domestic purposes: for pots, platters, kvass bottles, dishes, trays, toys, and dolls, all of which were embellished with colorful native designs. Even the aristocracy, who preferred gold and silver plate, had large quantities of pottery vessels. Tiles, made by peasant craftsmen and covered with complicated enamel designs, decorated the walls and floors of the palaces and churches. And when fine porcelain began to be produced in the eighteenth century, it was often created in imitation of the peasant's earthenware styles.

Ceramic jars like the one opposite, with a hole in the center for a chunk of ice, held kvass, a light beer. The primitive clay figures above are named for Vyatka (now Kirov), the town where they were made.

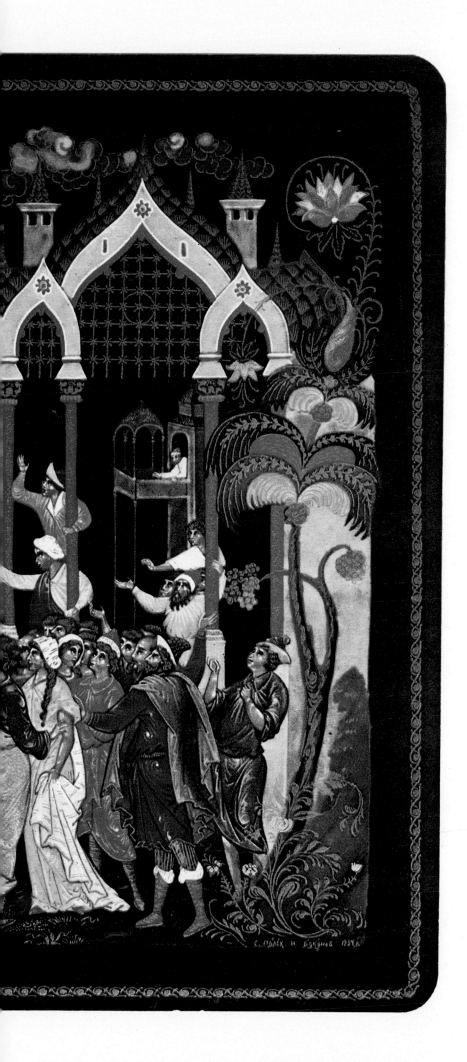

Lacquer Lore

The art of the palekh painters, said Maxim Gorky, is "one of those minor miracles that the revolution works . . . testimony to the awakening of creative energies among the masses of working folk." Prior to the 1917 revolution the working folk of Palekh, a town some two hundred miles northeast of Moscow, near Ivanovo, were using their presumably unawakened creative energies painting icons. Put out of business by the Revolution, some of them turned to making toys; some went off to seek a living in Moscow; but a few were determined not to forfeit their rich tradition.

Inspired by the painted lacquerware boxes of western Europe and the Russian imitations done in the early nineteenth century, the artists of Palekh began decorating plain lacquer boxes and caskets with the fantastic birds and beasts that they had once painted on icons. At first, the painters' secular figures tended to look like saints in street clothes, but gradually palekh painting reached maturity as an independent art form. Old religious themes were replaced by finely detailed and brilliantly colored paintings based on folk songs, fairy tales, Pushkin's poetry, and Gorky's stories. More recent compositions are contemporary, worldly, and often based upon the ideals of socialist realism.

The gaily decorated palekh box at left, dating from 1934, illustrates Pushkin's tale of the Golden Cockerel, in which a wizard sends a magic bird to defend a tsar's kingdom. Promised any reward he wishes, the wizard (in the scene shown here) demands the tsar's mistress.

In his story "The Singers," Ivan Turgenev describes how he heard, in the voice of a man singing at a country inn, "an uncounterfeited, profound passion, and youth, and strength, and sweetness, and some sort of enticingly heedless sorrowing. A Russian soul, true and ardent, sounded and breathed in it, and simply plucked at your heart, plucked right at its Russian chords." By the time the singer was finished, everyone in the room was in tears. A gayer scene is depicted in the ceramic tile above, showing a Ukrainian couple dancing to a fiddler's tune. The kobza (opposite) was a type of archlute; this one, from the Ukraine, is decorated with flowers and portraits of Lenin and Stalin. Other native instruments include the balalaika and the gusli, which is similar to a zither.

The Sound
Of Muzhiks

"The Russian song," one authority has written, "was born and sung in the open fields, and it has its roots in Mother Earth." At sowing and reaping, in cottages, around campfires, and during summer celebrations, the folk song was the voice of the peasant, the chronicle of his life, the relief of his burden. There were work songs, sung to the stroke of the hoe or scythe; songs and dances for courtships and weddings, for celebration and lament; historical songs praising the deeds of ancient heroes; songs, created by runaway serfs, glorifying the free life in the steppes; songs of satire and songs bemoaning the peasant's lot.

Folk music is *the* classic music of Russia, for until the nineteenth century there was no formal music that was not imported from Byzantium or western Europe. Church music had little to do with the peasant's daily life and was understood by only a few; and prior to the eighteenth century, when the importation of French and Italian music created a cleavage between popular music and court music, aristocrats as well as peasants entertained themselves with folk music.

The folk epics, or *byliny* (from *byl*, meaning "was," which emphasizes their real rather than imaginary origins), were half sung and half spoken. In rural areas folk songs were usually sung by two groups of people, one of which began the song while the other improvised a counterpoint. In the cities the performance was usually solo, supported by three-part voices.

Songs and dances created by the people were carried by the people themselves from one village to the next, or by *skomorokhi*, or buffoons—professional entertainers who traveled around the country visiting fairs, towns, and palaces. They were musicians, actors, magicians, acrobats, and animal trainers as well as singers, and those lucky enough to obtain the patronage of a prince occupied a high place in his court. It was often these *skomorokhi* who created the epics and tales of old Russia. They faded in the seventeenth century, when their ballads of peasant discontent began making the nobility nervous. Their songs, however, continued to be sung in rural Russia even into the twentieth century.

Peter the Great is the object of satire in the two luboks shown here. Conservatives opposed to his reforms characterized him (opposite) as "The Cat of Kazan," with trim whiskers. In "The Witch-Baby and the Bald Man" (below) Peter's wife compels him to dance and play pipes.

The hand-painted picture stories, or *luboks*, printed from wood blocks in the seventeenth and eighteenth centuries, are a vivid expression of the popular taste of the time. First introduced into Russia in the sixteenth century by German merchants, early luboks were modeled after Dutch and German biblical illustrations. Gradually the Russians evolved their own particular style, which is characterized by simple composition, deliberately crude line, and traditional folk art colors: reds, purples, yellows, and greens. By the middle of the seventeenth century they were being hawked in the market place along with the always popular icons. Originally religious in intent, the subject matter broadened with the luboks' popularity, and came to include themes that were social, political, satirical, ribald, didactic, and commemorative. Their importance as a folk art began to decline toward the end of the eighteenth century when copper engravings replaced them in public favor. But the luboks that survive provide an invaluable documentary on city life in Petrine Russia.

OVERLEAF: *The vanities and vagaries of fashion are mocked in this detail from "The Register of Beauty Spots and What They Mean," a lubok dating from the reign of Catherine the Great. A beauty spot on the left cheek implied happiness; one between the eyebrows, a lovers' meeting.*

D. A. ROVINSKY, *Russkie narodnie kartinki*, 1881

125

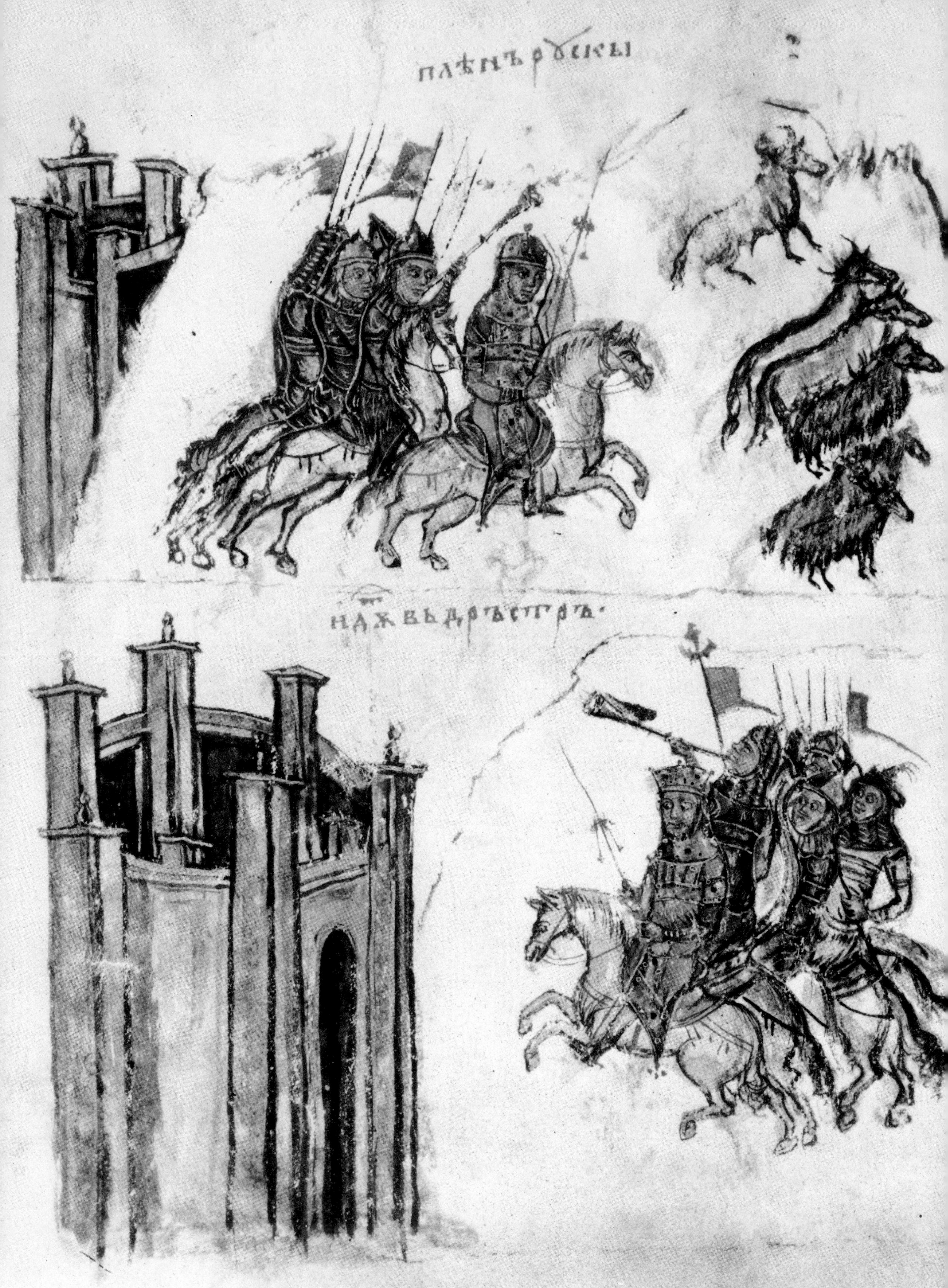
плѣнъ рѹскы
нажвъдръстръ.

4

Chronicles and Tales

Literature of Early Russia

"The enjoyment of words useful to the soul"—such was the spirit of early Russian literature, as expressed by a twelfth-century bishop, Cyril of Turov. It was a literature of the Church, written by clerics for the purpose of spreading the doctrine and ritual of Orthodoxy among the newly converted Russian peoples. It was a didactic literature, consisting of sermons, translations of the Bible and of the lives of the saints, and historical chronicles, all written in a solemn, elevated, and rather artificial language now called Church Slavonic. The script had been created in the ninth century—primarily by two Macedonian missionaries, the brothers Cyril and Methodius—in order to make the basic texts of Orthodoxy accessible to the Slavic peoples. The new Slavonic alphabet (now called Cyrillic) and the new written language were based on the style, syntax, and alphabet of Greek, and were applied to a primitive Bulgarian dialect.

In the late tenth and early eleventh centuries the heirs of Cyril and Methodius brought the new liturgical language to Kievan Russia. Since Russians already spoke a similar Slavic dialect and since many Byzantine liturgical and secular writings were already available in Slavonic translations, the literary culture of Byzantium spread rapidly. Within fifty years of Russia's conversion, during the 1030's, the first original Russian writings began to appear.

The exploits of Svyatoslav, father of Saint Vladimir, are portrayed in the fourteenth-century manuscript illustration on the opposite page. The prince is shown leading Russia's invasion of Bulgaria in 967.

Elements of colloquial Russian were frequently intermingled with Church Slavonic; similarly, the bards of the people, the minstrels and storytellers who brought the lore and history of Russia to court as well as to fairs, weddings, and village feasts, sometimes borrowed the lofty terms of Church Slavonic when describing such exalted subjects as Divine Justice or the virtues of a hero. But essentially the spoken and literary languages of Russia remained separate. Consequently the literature of the Church and court and the literature of the people had little influence on one another. Only the most elevated subjects—those that were instructive and inspiring—were considered worthy of Church Slavonic, which remained the official literary language of Russia until late in the seventeenth century. The oral tradition, however, long antedated the appearance of Christianity, and the elements of folk literature—songs, tales, and the epic and narrative poems called *byliny*—were therefore based less on the themes, legends, and language of Christianity than on those of pagan culture.

Folk literature flourished in the constant retelling. Regional lore, myth, songs and images, and contemporary political allusions were woven into the age-old fabric of the tales. In fact, the *byliny*, as well as the chronicles, were often devised specifically to identify a ruler with the popular heroes of the past, thereby creating a historical legitimacy for new or shaky regimes. Thus, in the course of the centuries, there evolved a literature without chronology, a literature in which legend became history, and history, legend.

Of Heroes and Princes

Among the favorite subjects of Russia's early writers were the exploits and adventures of heroes. Their deeds and virtues were celebrated in sermons as well as in chronicles and tales. The style and rhythms echoed those of the Bible and Byzantine liturgical writings—early authors' only written source of literary inspiration.

Nestor, the Chronicler

IGOR'S DEATH
AND OLGA'S REVENGE (c. 1118)

*Translated by Samuel Hazzard Cross
and Olgerd P. Sherbowitz-Wetzor*

The Primary Chronicle, *begun about 1060, was the earliest of the Russian annals. Nestor, who was among the last of its writers and editors, tells here of a couple who ruled Russia in the mid-tenth century. Their opponents, the Derevlians, were a Slavic tribe who lived to the west, between Kiev and the present Polish border.*

In [945], Igor's retinue said to him. "The servants of Sveinald are adorned with weapons and fine raiment but we are naked. Go forth with us, oh Prince, after tribute, that both you and we may profit thereby." Igor heeded their words, and he attacked Dereva in search of tribute. He sought to increase the previous tribute and collected it by violence from the people with the assistance of his followers. After thus gathering the tribute, he returned to his city. On his homeward way, he said to his followers, after some reflection, "Go forward with the tribute. I shall turn back, and rejoin you later." He dismissed his retainers on their journey homeward, but being desirous of still greater booty, he returned on his tracks with a few of his followers.

The Derevlians heard that he was again approaching, and consulted with Mal, their prince, saying: "If a wolf come among the sheep, he will take away the whole flock one by one, unless he be killed. If we do not thus kill him now, he will destroy us all." They then sent forward to Igor inquiring why he had returned, since he had collected all the tribute. But Igor did not heed them, and the Derevlians came forth from the city of Iskorosten and slew Igor and his company. . . . The Derevlians then said, "See, we have killed the Prince of Rus. Let us take his wife Olga for our Prince Mal, and then we shall obtain possession of Svyatoslav, and work our will upon him." So they sent their best men, twenty in number, to Olga by boat, and they arrived below Borichev in their boat. . . .

Olga was informed that the Derevlians had arrived, and summoned them to her presence with a gracious welcome. When the Derevlians had thus announced their arrival, Olga replied with an inquiry as to the reason of their coming. The Derevlians then announced that their tribe had sent them to report that they had slain her husband because he was like a wolf, crafty and ravening, but that their princes, who had thus preserved the land of Dereva, were good, and that Olga should come and marry their Prince Mal. . . .

Olga made this reply: "Your proposal is pleasing to me; indeed, my husband cannot rise again from the dead. But I desire to honor you tomorrow in the presence of my people. Return now to your boat, and remain there with an aspect of arrogance. I shall send for you on the morrow, and you shall say, 'We will not ride on horses nor go on foot; carry us in our boat.' And you shall be carried in your boat." Thus she dismissed them to their vessel.

Now Olga gave command that a large deep ditch should be dug in the castle with the hall, outside the city. Thus, on the morrow, Olga, as she sat in the hall, sent for the strangers, and her messengers approached them and said, "Olga summons you to great honor." But they replied, "We will not ride on horseback nor in wagons, nor go on foot; carry us in our boats." The people of Kiev then lamented: "Slavery is our lot. Our prince is killed, and our Princess intends to marry their prince." So they carried the Derevlians in their boat. The latter sat on the crossbenches in great robes, puffed up with pride. They thus were borne into the court before Olga, and when the men had brought the Derevlians in, they dropped them into the trench along with the boat. Olga bent over and inquired whether they found the honor to their taste. They answered that it was worse than the death of Igor. She then commanded that they should be buried alive, and they were thus buried.

Olga then sent messages to the Derevlians to the effect that, if they really required her presence, they should send after her their distinguished men, so that she might go to their Prince with due honor. . . . When the Derevlians arrived, Olga commanded that a bath should be made ready, and invited them to appear before her after they had bathed. The bathhouse was then heated, and the Derevlians entered in to bathe. Olga's men closed up the bathhouse behind them, and she gave orders to set it on fire from the doors, so that the Derevlians were all burned to death.

Olga then sent to the Derevlians the following message, "I am now coming to you, so prepare great quantities of mead in the city where you killed my husband, that I may weep over his grave and hold a funeral feast for him." When they heard these words, they gathered great quantities of honey and brewed mead. Taking a small escort, Olga made the journey with ease, and upon her arrival at Igor's tomb, she wept for her husband. She bade her followers pile up a great mound, and when they had piled it up, she also gave command that a funeral feast should be held. Thereupon the

Derevlians sat down to drink, and Olga bade her followers wait upon them. . . . When the Derevlians were drunk, she bade her followers fall upon them, and went about herself egging on her retinue to the Massacre of the Derevlians. . . .

Olga hastened with her son to the city of Iskorosten, for it was there that her husband had been slain, and they laid siege to the city. The Derevlians barricaded themselves within the city, and fought valiantly from it, for they realized that they had killed the prince, and to what fate they would in consequence surrender.

Olga remained there a year without being able to take the city, and then she thought out this plan. She sent into the town the following message: "Why do you persist in holding out? All your cities have surrendered to me and submitted to tribute. . . ."

The Derevlians then inquired what she desired of them, and expressed their readiness to pay honey and furs. Olga retorted . . . that she had one small request to make. "Give me three pigeons," she said, "and three sparrows from each house. I do not desire to impose a heavy tribute, like my husband, but I require only this small gift from you, for you are impoverished by the siege."

The Derevlians rejoiced, and collected from each house three pigeons and three sparrows, which they sent to Olga with their greetings. Olga then instructed them, in view of their submission, to return to their city, promising that on the morrow she would depart and return to her own capital. The Derevlians re-entered their city with gladness, and . . . the people of the town rejoiced.

Now Olga gave to each soldier in her army a pigeon or a sparrow, and ordered them to attach by a thread to each pigeon and sparrow a piece of sulphur bound with small pieces of cloth. When night fell, Olga bade her soldiers release the pigeons and the sparrows. So the birds flew to their nests, the pigeons to the cotes, and the sparrows under the eaves. Thus the dove-cotes, the coops, the porches, and the haymows were set on fire. There was not a house that was not consumed, and it was impossible to extinguish the flames. . . . The people fled from the city, and Olga ordered her soldiers to catch them. Thus she took the city and burned it, and captured the elders of the city. Some of the other captives she killed, while she gave others as slaves to her followers. The remnant she left to pay tribute. . . .

Metropolitan Ilarion

From EULOGY TO
OUR KAGAN VLADIMIR (c. 1050)

Translated by Serge Zenkovsky

The Sermon on Law and Grace, from which this eulogy is excerpted, is one of the earliest Russian literary works. Its author was the first Russian (rather than Greek) head of the Russian Church. Vladimir, who was considered a saint for having Christianized Russia, here is made the mentor of the destiny of the Russian people.

Arise from your grave, venerated prince,
Arise and shake off your sleep.
You are not dead,
but only sleep until the day of resurrection of all.
Arise! You are not dead,
for it is not right that you should die,
for you have believed in Christ,
the Sustainer of the whole world.
Shake off your deep sleep
and lift up your eyes
that you might see what honor the Lord has granted you,
and you still live upon this earth,
unforgotten through your sons.
Arise! Behold your child George,
Look upon your beloved one,
whom God has brought forth from your loins.
Behold him embellishing the throne of your land.
Rejoice and be of good cheer!
Behold the pious wife of your son, Irina.
Behold your grandchildren
and your great-grandchildren.
Behold how they live and how they are cared for by God.
Behold how they preserve devotion in your tradition,
how they partake of the Sacraments of the Holy Church,
how they glorify Christ,
how they venerate before his Holy Name.
Behold your city radiant with grandeur.
Behold your blossoming churches,
Behold Christianity flourishing.
Behold your city gleaming,
adorned with holy icons and
fragrant with thyme,
praising God and filling the air with sacred songs.
And beholding all this, rejoice and be of good cheer, and praise the Lord, the Creator of all which you have seen.

Vladimir Monomakh

From INSTRUCTIONS TO HIS CHILDREN (1096)

Translated by Nathan Haskell Dole

Vladimir Monomakh (r. 1113–25) was a great-grandson of the Vladimir eulogized by Ilarion. A learned man, he spoke five languages and is known to have practiced the virtues he taught his sons.

And now I shall tell you, my children, of my labors which I have performed either in my expeditions or on the chase these thirteen years. . . .

I have undergone many hardships in the chase. Near Chernigov I have with my own hand caught ten or twenty wild horses in the forests, and I have besides caught elsewhere many wild horses with my hands, as I used to travel through Russia. Two aurochses threw me and my horse with their horns; a stag butted me with his horns; an elk trampled me under his feet, and another butted me with his horns. A boar took away the sword at my side; a bear bit me into my knee covering; a grim animal [wolf] leaped at my loins and threw me with my horse: and yet God has preserved me. I have often fallen from my horse, I twice injured my head and frequently hurt my hands and feet in my youth, being reckless of my life and not sparing my head. Whatever there was to be done by my servants, I did myself, in war and in the chase, in daytime and at night, in the summer heat and in winter, without taking any rest. I depended neither on the posadniks [burgomasters] nor the heralds, but did all myself, and looked after my house. In the chase I looked myself after the hunting outfit, the horses, the falcons and the sparrowhawks. Also have I not permitted the mighty to offend the poor peasants and the destitute widows, and I have myself looked after the church property and the divine service.

Think not ill of me, my children, nor anyone else who may read this, for I do not boast of my daring, but praise God and proclaim His goodness for having preserved me, sinful and miserable man, for so many years from the hour of death, for having made me, miserable one, active in the performance of all humane acts. Having read this instruction, may you hasten to do all good acts and praise the Lord with His saints. Fear neither death, my children, nor war, nor beast, but do what behooves men to do, whatever God may send you. Just as I have come out hale from war, from encounters with animals, from the water, and from my falls, even so none of you can be injured or killed, if it be not so ordained by God. And if death come from the Lord, neither father, nor mother, nor brothers can save you. Though it is good to take care of oneself, yet God's protection is better than man's.

A Kievan Courtier

From THE LAY OF IGOR'S CAMPAIGN (c. 1185)

Translated by Bernard Guilbert Guerney

This epic by an unknown poet is the sole example of popular poetry in medieval Russia. Its subject—the defeat of a Christian hero and his army by a horde of pagan warriors—parallels that of the French medieval epic the Chanson de Roland. *Probably written within two years of Igor's defeat, it is a plea for unity among Russia's princes.*

II

Let us then begin, brethren mine,
This our song, our lay,
With Vladimir of the times of old,
And come down to Igor of this our own
                                        day,
Who his mind did gird with all fortitude,
And his heart within him whet
With all manliness,
And, with war fervor filled,
Did his brave troops lead
Against the Polovtsi,
And against their land,
That beyond the land
Of fair Russia lies.

And 'twas then Igor
Eyed the radiant sun—
And thereafter saw
That sun darkness spread
Over all his troops.

Thereupon Igor
To his nobles spake:

"Oh, my brethren all,
And my comrades brave!

Better slain to be
Than be taken slave.
Let us, brethren mine,
Mount our wind-swift steeds;
Let us feast our eyes
On blue-watered Don!"

And a longing seized
On the Prince's mind,
And the omen dread
Fled his yearning great
To behold and brave
the broad mighty Don.

Thereupon he spake:
"I would fain break lance
On the gory field 'gainst the Polovtsi;
Fain would I with ye,
Mighty Russian men,
Either lay my head
Down in eternal sleep,
Or from helmet deep
The Don's water quaff."

And Vsevolod, the Fierce Wild Ox,
Unto Igor spake:
"My only brother, thou, thou only one,
Thou most radiant Igor!

Yet both of us foster-sons of radiant
                                Svyatoslav!
Saddle, then, brother mine,
Thy wind-swift steeds,
For mine are already fully trained,
For mine already are saddled at Kursk!
As for my Kurians, they are tried in
                                war:
Swaddled to the blowing of war-horns,
Cradled within helmets,
Suckled upon the sharp tips of spears.
All the paths to them are familiar,
All the wellsprings in the ravines to
                        them are known.
Their bows are drawn taut,
Their quivers gape ready,
Their swords are whetted;
They skim over the plains
Like tawny wolves,
Seeking, for their Prince,
                        Glory,
And, for themselves,
                        Honor."

And Igor the Prince
Set his foot in his stirrup of gold
And rode off over
The vast open plain.

The eclipsed sun
On his path darkness spread;
The sudden night,
Moaning over the nearing storm,
Awakened every fowl;
Every tiny beast
Whimpered. . . .

III

Early Friday morn
They crushed underfoot
The Pagan troops
Of the Polovtsi;
And, scattering like arrows
Over the field,
They drove before them
The fair Polovets maids;
They bore off with these
    Gold,
    And gossamers,
    And precious samites.

With horsecloths,
And with purple palls,
And other fine weaves
So cunningly wrought by the Polovtsi,
They builded a way,
They carpeted a path,
Over swamps, over quagmires,
For the brave son
Of Svyatoslav!
    Scarlet his banner,
    White his oriflamme;
    Scarlet his pennon,
    Silver its staff. . . .

And next day, at morn,
At the morn's earliest hour,
A glow red as blood
Heralds the dawn. . . .

A great storm is brewing;
The rain will come slanting
Like arrows
From the mighty Don;
Many a spear
Is fated to be broken here;
Many a saber
To be blunted here
Against the helmets,
Against the helmets of the Polovtsi. . . .

And the winds,
Grandsons of Stribog, the god of all
                winds,
Dart in from the sea like arrows
Against the brave troops of Igor.

The earth rumbles,
The rivers flow turbidly,
Dust hovers over the plains and veils
                them,
The banners flutter in the wind:
'Tis the Polovtsi
Streaming from the Don,
Streaming from the sea;
And they the Russian troops
Encircle.

And the plains are barred:
The Seed of the Fiend barred them
With their rallying battle cry,
But the brave men of Russia
Barred them
With their scarlet shields. . . .

IV

Troy on a time knew wars.
The troublous years of Yaroslav are long
              since over.
Oleg, son of Svyatoslav, waged
    campaigns in his day also.
This Oleg
Wielded his sword as a hammer sedition
              to forge;
With his arrows he sowed the earth.

Thus in those olden times,
The times of Oleg the Woe-Bringing
              One,
Dissension was sown, e'en as grain,
And, e'en as grain, dissensions were
              garnered,
And therein was wasted the substance
              of the Russian,
That grandson of Dazhbog, the god of
              all fruitfulness:
Amid the dissensions of princes
The days of mankind
Were shortened.

And throughout the Russian land then
Rarely did the plowmen
Hail one another
Across the fields:
But, to make up for that,
How oft the corbies
Cawed,
The corpses among them sharing;
And the jackdaws also,
In their own tongue were choosing:
"Whither shall we fly now
To hold a fine feast?"
    Thus was it in those frays,
    And in those campaigns;

But such a carnage as this
Had never yet been heard of.

From early morn till even,
And from even to daybreak,
Fly arrows with barbs of chilled steel,
Swords thunder against helmets,
Spears of tempered steel crack
On an unfamiliar battlefield,
In the Polovetz land.

And the black ground
Under the horses' hooves
Was sown with bones
And watered with blood:
    And they came up
    As a crop of sorrow
    Throughout the Russian land.

    What is that din I hear,
    What rings in my ear—
    There, far away,
Early, before the break of day?
'Tis Igor, facing his troops about:
He feels for his brother,
For Vsevolod.

Thus they fought for a day;
They fought for another day;
But toward noon of the third day
The banners of Igor
Fell.

And it was then and there
That the brothers parted,
Near the swift-flowing Kayala,
On the bank of that River of Sorrow.

And the wine of blood
Thereupon ran short;
It was there the brave Russian men
Brought their feast to an end.
They gave their hosts their fill of
              drink,
But they themselves laid down their
              lives
For the Russian land.

The grasses wilt
From pity,
And each tree bends down to the earth
In sorrow.

Thus did it befall,
O brethren mine,
That a year of sadness came;
Thus the desert dust hid
The mighty war force. . . .

The Monks of Ryazan

PRINCE INGVAR
BURIES THE DEAD (c. fourteenth century)

Translated by Serge Zenkovsky

The Tale of the Destruction of Ryazan provides a vivid account of the Mongol invasions of the thirteenth century, during which two thirds of Russia's population was annihilated. Ryazan was the first city to fall. In this excerpt from the anonymous tale, the aftermath is described in tones echoing the Biblical Book of Lamentations.

Prince Ingvar Ingvarevich (the brother of Great Prince Yury Ingvarevich of Ryazan) returned from Chernigov, having been there with his relative, Prince Michael, at the time of the destruction of Ryazan. And so he was preserved by God from the enemy of all Christendom. Prince Ingvar Ingvarevich found his fatherland devastated, and learned that all his brothers had been killed by the impure, lawbreaking Batu. And he came to the city of Ryazan and found the city destroyed, and his mother and sisters-in-law, his relatives, and many other people lying dead. And he found the churches burned and all valuables taken from the common treasury of Chernigov and Ryazan. When Prince Ingvar saw this great and enduring destruction he shrieked aloud in his sorrow, sounding as a trumpet summoning the army. . . .

And Prince Ingvar searched through the bodies, and found the body of his mother, Princess Agrippina, and those of his brothers' wives. And he called a priest from villages that were preserved by God, and he buried his mother and the wives of his deceased brothers with great lamentations in place of the psalms and chants. And he cried and lamented terribly. And he buried the bodies of the other dead and he cleaned the city. And he had the city blessed by a priest and he gathered the few survivors and comforted them. And he lamented for a long time, thinking of his mother, his brothers, his relatives, and all the people of Ryazan. . . .

And all this happened because of our sins. There used to be the city of Ryazan in the land of Ryazan, but its wealth disappeared and its glory ceased, and there is nothing to be seen in the city excepting smoke, ashes, and barren earth. . . .

And Prince Ingvar went to the place where his brethren were killed by the impious emperor Batu. Great Prince Yury of Ryazan, Prince David of Murom, Prince Vsevolod of Pronsk, Prince Gleb of Kolomna, many other princes, boyars, voevodas [military commanders], and warriors—indeed, all the best souls of Ryazan—were lying on the barren earth and frozen grass. And they were covered with snow and ice, and no one cared for them. Beasts devoured their bodies and a multitude of birds tore them to pieces. And they were lying together, even as they had fallen together. They all drank the same bitter cup to the dregs.

And when Prince Ingvar Ingvarevich saw this great number of corpses lying on the earth, he shrieked bitterly, like a trumpet resounding. He fell to the ground, and tears flowed from his eyes in a stream. . . .

A Muscovite Poet

THE CAPTURE OF KAZAN (1552)

Translated by N. Kershaw Chadwick

This ancient tale, originally an oral epic, describes the capture of Kazan by Ivan the Terrible in 1552—an important victory in Russia's centuries-long struggle to free itself from Mongol rule.

Ye are to be told a wonderful thing, O guests,
A wonderful thing, and it is no trifle:
No less a thing than how the tsar captured Kazan.
He entrenched himself, and he lived on gruel . . .
He sank a mine under the River Kazanka,
He undermined the town of Kazan,
He rolled in barrels, barrels of oak,
Filled with violent, poisonous, black gunpowder,
And he lighted a fuse of pure wax.
The Tartars of Kazan were standing on the wall,
They were standing on the wall, and making insulting
        gestures:
"There's for you, sovereign tsar! and your taking of Kazan!"
The tsar's heart rose in anger,
He ordered his gunners to be executed, to be hanged.
Prudent men of the army came as deputies,
Prudent men, men of understanding:
"Hearken, our sovereign tsar, Ivan Vasilevich!
Do not order us to be executed, to be hanged,
Permit us, sovereign tsar, to speak a word:—
The fuse burns quickly in the open air,
But it burns slowly underground."
The tsar had not time to speak a word
Before the town of Kazan began to give way,
To give way, to be rent asunder, to be hurled in every
        direction,
And to fling all the Tartars of Kazan into the river.
The barrels of black gunpowder ignited,
A high mountain was raised up,
And the white stone palace was blown to pieces.
Then the mighty Prince of Moscow ran
On to this high mountain,
Where the royal palaces stood. . . .
And then the prince began to reign as a tsar. . . .

The Lives of the Saints

The most popular literature in medieval Russia was hagiography—lives of saints and holy but uncanonized monks. In sheer numbers these Russian vitae, *together with the stories of Byzantine saints, dominated the clerical and private libraries of the period. They served less as accurate biographies than as edifying examples of saintly living.*

Nestor, the Chronicler

THE MARTYRDOM OF BORIS AND GLEB (c. 1118)

Translated by Samuel Hazzard Cross and Olgerd P. Sherbowitz-Wetzor

The humble refusal of Boris and Gleb, sons of Saint Vladimir, to take up arms against their treacherous brother Svyatopolk, is represented by the chronicler as a martyrdom for peace in Russia. In death the sainted brothers became the exemplars of fraternal love.

When Boris returned with the army . . . he received the news that his father was dead. He mourned deeply for him, for he was beloved of his father before all the rest.

. . . His father's retainers then urged him to take his place in Kiev on his father's throne, since he had at his disposal the latter's retainers and troops. But Boris protested, "Be it not for me to raise my hand against my elder brother [Svyatopolk]. Now that my father has passed away, let him take the place of my father in my heart." When the soldiery heard these words, they departed from him. . . .

But Svyatopolk was filled with lawlessness. Adopting the device of Cain, he sent messages to Boris that he desired to live at peace with him, and would increase the territory he had received from his father. But he plotted against him now how he might kill him. So Svyatopolk came by night to Vyshgorod. After secretly summoning to his presence Put'sha and the boyars of the town, he inquired of them whether they were whole-heartedly devoted to him. Put'sha and the men of Vyshgorod replied, "We are ready to lay down our lives for you." He then commanded them to say nothing to any man, but to go and kill his brother Boris. . . .

These emissaries came to the Al'ta, and when they approached, they heard the sainted Boris singing matins. . . .

After offering [his prayers], he lay down upon his couch. Then they fell upon him like wild beasts about the tent, and pierced him with lances. They stabbed Boris and his servant, who cast himself upon his body. For he was beloved of Boris. He was a servant of Hungarian race, George by name, to whom Boris was greatly attached.

The desperadoes, after attacking Boris, wrapped him in a canvas, loaded him upon a wagon, and dragged him off, though he was still alive. When the impious Svyatopolk saw that he was still breathing, he sent two Varangians to finish him. When they came and saw that he was still alive, one of them drew his sword and plunged it into his heart. Thus died the blessed Boris. . . .

The impious Svyatopolk then reflected, "Behold, I have killed Boris; now how can I kill Gleb?" Adopting once more Cain's device, he craftily sent messages to Gleb to the effect that he should come quickly, because his father was very ill and desired his presence. Gleb quickly mounted his horse, and set out with a small company, for he was obedient to his father. When he came to the Volga, his horse stumbled in a ditch on the plain, and injured his leg slightly. He arrived at Smolensk, and setting out thence at daybreak, embarked in a boat on the Smyadyn. At this time, Yaroslav received from Predslava the tidings of their father's death, and he sent word to Gleb that he should not set out, because his father was dead and his brother had been murdered by Svyatopolk. Upon receiving these tidings, Gleb burst into tears, and mourned for his father, but still more deeply for his brother. He wept and prayed with the lament, "Woe is me, oh Lord! It were better for me to die with my brother than to live on in this world. Oh my brother, had I but seen thy angelic countenance, I should have died with thee. . . ."

While he was thus praying amid his tears, there suddenly arrived those sent by Svyatopolk for Gleb's destruction. These emissaries seized Gleb's boat, and drew their weapons. The servants of Gleb were terrified, and the impious messenger, Goryaser, gave orders that they should slay Gleb with despatch. Then Gleb's cook, Torchin by name, seized a knife, and stabbed Gleb. He was offered up as a sacrifice to God like an innocent lamb, a glorious offering amid the perfume of incense, and he received the crown of glory. Entering the heavenly mansions he beheld his long-desired brother, and rejoiced with him in the joy ineffable which they had attained through their brotherly love. . . .

From THE LIFE OF SAINT THEODOSIUS (c. 1118)

Translated by Helen Iswolsky

Theodosius, who died in 1074 and became the first monk canonized by the Russian Church, lived a humble, ascetic life of service in imitation of the life of Christ, at a time when Christ's awesomeness, rather than His humility, was being stressed throughout Christendom. Nestor's Life *provided a model for all Russian hagiography.*

When blessed Theodosius was about thirteen years old, his father died. From that time on, he applied himself even more zealously to his undertakings. That is, he now went into the fields with his serfs, where he did the humblest work. To prevent this, his mother used to keep him indoors. She also tried to prevail upon him to put on good clothes and go out to play with boys of his own age, for she said that if he were so poorly dressed, he would expose himself and his family to disgrace. But he would not obey her, and often she beat him in her vexation. She was robust of body, and if you could not see her, but could only hear her voice, you might well have mistaken her for a man.

The devout youth, meanwhile, was meditating and searching for the means of salvation. When he heard of the Holy Land where Our Lord had walked in the flesh, he longed to make a pilgrimage to this place. He prayed to God, saying, "My Lord Jesus, listen to my prayer, and grant that I may go to the Holy Land." After he had prayed in this manner for a long time some pilgrims came to the city. The holy youth rejoiced when he saw them. He went out to meet them and welcomed them affectionately, asking them whence they had come and whither they were going. And when they told him that they had come from the Holy Land and that, God permitting, they intended to return there, he begged to be taken with them. They promised to take him, and Theodosius returned home rejoicing. When the pilgrims had decided to set out on their journey they informed the boy of their intention, and rising in the night, he left his home secretly, taking nothing with him except the poor clothes he had on. It was in this manner that he set out to join the pilgrims. . . . After three days the mother learned that he had gone with the pilgrims, and taking her other son (who was younger than Theodosius) with her, she set out to overtake him. After a long pursuit, they caught up with him. Carried away by fury, she seized him by the hair, flung him to the ground, and trampled on him. Then, having rebuked the pilgrims, she returned home, leading the saint bound like a criminal. So greatly incensed was she, that when they had entered the house she beat her son until she was exhausted. Then she flung him into a room, shackled him, and locked the door. The holy youth suffered all this joyfully, giving thanks to God in prayer. . . . After two days his mother returned, unfastened him, and placed food before him. . . .

After some time Theodosius heard the words of the holy Gospel "He that loveth father or mother more than Me, is not worthy of Me." And again "Come to Me, all you that labor, and are burdened, and I will refresh you." And so, filled with devotion and with the love of Our Lord, the God-inspired youth cast about for the best way of escaping from his mother and finding a place where he might enter the religious life.

Now it was the will of God that his mother should go to the country at this time for a long visit. The saint rejoiced, prayed, and stole out of his home, taking with him nothing but the clothes he had on and enough food to sustain him. He went in the direction of Kiev, for he had heard that there were many monasteries in that city. . . .

Hearing that blessed Anthony was living in a cave outside Kiev, Theodosius went eagerly to the hermit's dwelling. When he saw Anthony, he wept and fell on his knees before him, begging for permission to remain in that place. The great Anthony replied, "My child, look about, and you shall see that this cave is dark and narrow. You are young and, I should think, unable to suffer such hardships." . . . The God-inspired Theodosius answered, with humble sincerity, "You know, most venerable father, that the all-seeing God has brought me to you because He desires my salvation. I will therefore obey you in all things." The blessed Anthony said to him, "My child, glory be to God, Who has given you strength for such a vocation. This is the place, remain here with me." . . .

I shall now tell of the primitive life of these monks. God alone can measure the suffering they endured because of the narrow space to which they were confined in the caves; human lips cannot describe it. They lived on rye bread and water. On Sundays and Saturdays they partook of a little boiled grain; sometimes, however, even such fare as this would be lacking, and they were satisfied with a small portion of cooked vegetables. They worked with their hands, weaving cowls and headgear for the brethren and plying other manual trades. . . .

Our father Theodosius surpassed all the other monks in wisdom and obedience, and he undertook greater labors than the others, for he was strong and healthy in body. He would assist his brethren in carrying water and fire-wood from the nearby forest. At night, while the other monks took their rest, he would remain wakeful, praising God. Moreover, the saint would grind all the grain which had been divided among the monks, and would leave the flour in its proper places. Sometimes at night, mosquitoes and gad-flies would swarm to the mouth of the cave; then Theodosius would go forth, and, stripping himself to the waist, sit in the open, spinning wool and singing the psalms of David. His body would be covered with blood drawn by the mosquitoes and flies which devoured it, but our father would sit there quietly until Matins. He entered the church before all the others, and never left his place, singing the divine praises with an untroubled mind. He was also the last to leave the church. Because of all these things, he was revered by the brethren, who loved him as a father, marvelling at his humility. . . .

Monk Polycarpe

MARKO THE GRAVEDIGGER WHO WAS OBEYED BY THE DEAD (c. 1225)

Translated by Serge Zenkovsky

Polycarpe was a monk at the Kievan Crypt Monastery, which had become the spiritual and cultural center of Russia after its founding by Theodosius and Anthony. This excerpt is one of Polycarpe's contributions to the Crypt's Paterikon, *the collection of historical (and sometimes fantastical) tales about the monastery's inhabitants.*

St. Marko used to live in the crypt, and during his life there the body of our father, Theodosius, was taken from the crypt into the great holy church. This Marko dug graves in the crypt with his own hands, and carried the earth away on his shoulders. He worked hard all day and all night. . . .

Once, according to his custom, he dug a grave and, laboring very much, became tired. However, the grave was not sufficiently wide. It so happened that this very day one of the brothers passed to God, and there was no grave available except this narrow one. The dead man was brought to the crypt, but because the grave was so very narrow he could not be placed in it. And the brethren began to grumble at Marko, for it was neither possible to adjust the dead man's robes nor to anoint him with holy oil. Marko, the monk of the cave, bowed to everyone with humility and said, "Forgive me, my fathers, but I could not finish the grave because of my poor health."

But the monks continued to reproach him still more. Then Marko addressed the dead man: "Brother, your grave is so narrow we cannot even anoint you with holy oil. Take the oil and anoint yourself."

The dead man raised up slightly, extended his hand, took the oil, and anointed his face and chest, making the sign of the cross. He then returned the vessel, adjusted his robes, lay down, and once more died. Awe and trembling seized everyone because of the miracle. . . .

Epiphanius the Wise

From THE LIFE, ACTS, AND MIRACLES OF
OUR REVERED AND HOLY FATHER
ABBOT SERGIUS (c. 1400)

Adapted by Nicholas Zernov with George P. Fedotov

Sergius, the first Russian mystic, was the patron of Muscovite Russia. His blessing of the troops before their first victory over the Mongols, in 1380, helped make him one of the country's most loved saints. His biographer, Epiphanius, was famed for his elegant style; abounding in panegyrics and epithets, his works became the models for much of the formal, ornamental writing of the next two centuries.

Blessed Bartholomew now came to [Stephen, later ordained Sergius], and begged him to accompany him in the search for some desert place. Stephen assented, and he and the saint together explored many parts of the forest, till finally they came to a waste space in the middle of the forest, near a stream. After inspecting the place they obeyed the voice of God and were satisfied. Having prayed, they set about chopping wood and carrying it. First they built a hut, and then constructed a small chapel. When the chapel was finished and the time had come to dedicate it, Blessed Bartholomew said to Stephen, "Now, my lord and eldest brother by birth and by blood, tell me, in honor·of whose feast shall this chapel be, and to which saint shall we dedicate it?"

Stephen answered: "Why do you ask me, and why put me to the test? You were chosen of God while you were yet in your mother's womb, and he gave a sign concerning you before ever you were born, that the child would be a disciple of the Blessed Trinity, and not he alone would have devout faith, for he would lead many others and teach them to believe in the Holy Trinity. It behooves you, therefore, to dedicate a chapel above all others to the Blessed Trinity."

The favored youth gave a deep sigh and said, "To tell the truth, my lord and brother, I asked you because I felt I must, although I wanted and thought likewise as you do, and desired with my whole soul to erect and dedicate this chapel to the Blessed Trinity, but out of humility I inquired of you. . . ."

Our saint, Sergius, had not taken monastic vows at this time for, as yet, he had not enough experience of monasteries, and of all that is required of a monk. After a while, however, he invited a spiritual elder, who held the dignity of priest and abbot, named Mitrofan, to come and visit him in his solitude. In great humility he entreated him, "Father, may the love of God be with us, and give me the tonsure of a monk. From childhood have I loved God and set my heart on him these many years, but my parents' needs withheld me. Now, my lord and father, I am free from all bonds, and I thirst, as the heart thirsteth for the springs of living water."

The abbot forthwith went into the chapel with him, and gave him the tonsure on the 7th day of October on the feast day of the blessed martyrs Sergius and Bacchus. And Sergius was the name he received as monk. . . .

At first Sergius did not wish to be raised to the priesthood and especially he did not want to become an abbot; this was by reason of his extreme humility. He constantly remarked that the beginning and root of all evil lay in pride of rank, and ambition to be an abbot. The monks were but few in number, about a dozen. They constructed themselves cells, not very large ones, within the enclosure, and put up gates at the entrance. Sergius built four cells with his own hands, and performed other monastic duties at the request of the brethren; he carried logs from the forest on his shoulders, chopped them up, and carried them into the cells. The monastery, indeed, came to be a wonderful place to look upon. The forest was not far distant from it as now it is; the shade and the murmur of trees hung above the cells; around the church was a space of trunks and stumps; here many kinds of vegetables were sown. . . .

After Vespers, and late at night, especially on long dark nights, the saint used to leave his cell and go the round of the monks' cells. If he heard anyone saying his prayers, or making genuflections, or busy with his own handiwork, he was gratified and gave thanks to God. If, on the other hand, he heard two or three monks chatting together, or laughing, he was displeased, rapped on the door or window, and passed on. In the morning he would send for them and, indirectly, quietly and gently, by means of some parable, reprove them. If he was a humble and submissive brother he would quickly admit his fault and, bowing low before St. Sergius, would beg his forgiveness. If, instead, he was not a humble brother, and stood erect thinking he was not the person referred to, then the saint, with patience, would make it clear to him, and order him to do a public penance. In this way they all learned to pray to God assiduously; not to chat with one another after Vespers, and to do their own handiwork with all their might; and to have the Psalms of David all day on their lips. . . .

The Life of the Church

The pastoral mission of Russia's clergymen made it only natural that they should often write homilies, lofty praises of the humble and saintly, and dire sermons on sin, repentance, and the awful wrath of God. But in their chronicles and clerical histories and, later, in their autobiographies, they also concerned themselves with such matter-of-fact subjects as episcopal politicking and the vehement and often bloody debates over the ritual and theology of Orthodoxy.

A Novgorod Chronicler

THE ELECTION OF ARCHBISHOP MANTURY (1193)

Translated by Serge Zenkovsky

The Novgorodian Chronicle was written by a succession of anonymous clerics whose interest in church affairs is apparent in this excerpt. Novgorod's archbishops were usually chosen by the prince and the citizens, but their election needed the approval of the metropolitan of Russia, who, in the twelfth century, resided at Kiev.

The archbishop of Novgorod, Gabriel, passed away on May 24th, the Day of Our Holy Father St. Simon. And he was solemnly buried in the porch of the Cathedral of St. Sophia next to his brother whose name was George after he took the holy vows. And then the people of Novgorod, the abbots, the Chapter of St. Sophia, and the clergy began their deliberations as to who should be the new archbishop. Some wanted to elect Mitrofan, while others wanted to elect Mantury, and still others wanted Grichina in this office. There was a great feud among them, and they decided to cast lots after High Mass in the Cathedral of St. Sophia. And they prepared the lots, and after the service they sent for a blind man and he was given to them by God. And with the help of divine Grace the blind man cast, and Mantury was chosen. And they sent for Mantury and they brought him to the Court of the Archbishop.

And they announced his election. . . .

Serapion of Vladimir

From SERMON ON OMENS (c. 1230)

Translated by Serge Zenkovsky

The author of this poetic sermon was abbot of the Kievan Crypt Monastery at the time of the first Mongol invasions, and became bishop of Vladimir after Kiev was overrun. The chronicles indicate that an earthquake occurred in 1230, just six years before the invasions.

The blessing of the Lord be with you!
Brethren, you have heard what the
Lord himself said in the Gospel:
"And there shall be signs in the sun,
and in the moon, and in the stars,
and there will be earthquakes in many places. . . ."

This prophecy of our Lord
has now been fulfilled in our days.
Many times have we seen the sun extinguished,
the moon darkened,
and the stars disquieted.
And recently with our own eyes
have we seen the quaking of the earth.
Now the earth, firm and immovable from time immemorial
by the will of God,
is today moved, quaking because of our sins,
unable to withstand our evil ways.

We have obeyed neither the Gospel
nor the Apostles,
nor the prophets. . . .

For this does God punish us,
bringing upon us calamities and earthquakes.
He no longer chastizes us with words,
but punishes us with afflictions.
God has castigated us in all ways,
yet he has not dispelled our evil ways.
Now he shakes the earth and makes it quake,
wishing to shake, like leaves from a tree,
our evil ways from the earth.
If any should declare that there have been earthquakes
before,
I should not deny it.
But what has happened to us after the earthquakes?
Were there not famines, plagues, and numerous wars?
But we did not repent.
Thus, by the will of God,
there fell upon us a merciless people
who devastated our land,
took entire cities off to captivity,
destroyed our holy churches,
put our fathers and brothers to death,
and defiled our mothers and sisters.
Now, brethren, that we have experienced such calamities,
let us pray to the Lord, and repent,
lest we incur the wrath of God even more,
and thus bring upon us an even greater castigation. . . .

Avvakum Petrovitch

From THE LIFE OF ARCHPRIEST
AVVAKUM, BY HIMSELF (c. 1675)

Translated by Jane Harrison and Hope Mireless

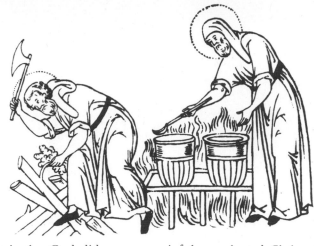

Avvakum was the leader of the Old Believers, a group of severely ascetic reformers who sought to raise the moral standards of the clergy and laity by insisting on strict observance of the ancient texts and rituals. In so doing they ran afoul of Patriarch Nikon, who was modernizing Orthodox liturgy and demanding submission to his authority. The Old Believers refused to submit and the result was schism and persecution. Avvakum himself remained a vigorous opponent of Nikon. In these excerpts from his autobiography, one of the masterpieces of vernacular Russian prose, he describes the events that led to his final exile in 1667. After living and writing in the far north for fifteen years, Avvakum was burned at the stake.

Thus having remained ten weeks in Pafnutiev in chains, they took me again to Moscow, and in the room of the Cross the bishops held disputation with me. They led me to the Cathedral church, and after the Elevation of the Host they sheared me and the deacon Theodore, and then they cursed us and I cursed them back. And I was heavy at heart for the Mass. And after I had stayed for a time at the patriarchal court, they took us by night to Ugresha, to the monastery of St. Nicholas—and the enemies of God shaved off my beard. What would you? It is like unto wolves not to pity the sheep; they tore at my hair like dogs and only left one forelock—such as the Poles wear on their foreheads. They did it carrying me not along the road to the monastery but by the marshes and the quagmires that people might not see me. They themselves saw that they were behaving as fools but they did not wish to cease from their folly; the devil had darkened their minds, why should one reproach them? . . . They kept me at Nikolas's in a cold room for seventeen weeks. . . . And the tsar came to the monastery and paid a visit to my prison cell and gave a groan and then left the monastery; it seems from that that he was sorry for me, the will of God lay in that. When they had shorn me there was a very great disturbance among them with the tsarina, God rest her soul! She, sweet lady, detected me at that time and asked to have me released from prison, as to which there is much to be said; God forgive them! As to my sufferings I do not hold them answerable, neither now nor hereafter; it sufficeth me to pray for them, be they alive or be they dead. The devil set discord between us but they were ever good toward me. . . . After this they took me again to the monastery of Pafnutiev, and there, having shut me up in the dark room, and put fetters on me, they kept me for well-nigh a year. . . . I will tell you yet more of my wanderings when they brought me out of the Pafnutiev Monastery in Moscow and placed me in the guesthouse, and after many wanderings they set me down in the Miracle Monastery, before the patriarchs of all Christendom, and the Russian Nikonites sat there like so many foxes. I spoke of many things in Holy Writ with the patriarchs. God did open my sinful mouth and Christ put them to shame. The last word they spoke to me was this: "Why," said they, "art thou stubborn? The folk of Palestine, Serbia, Albania, the Wallachians, they of Rome and Poland, all these do cross themselves with three fingers, only thou standest out in thine obstinacy and dost cross thyself with two fingers; it is not seemly." And I answered them for Christ thus: "O you teachers of Christendom, Rome fell away long ago and lies prostrate, and the Poles fell in the like ruin with her, being to the end the enemies of the Christian. And among you orthodoxy is of mongrel breed. . . . Nikon, the wolf, together with the devil, ordained that men should cross themselves with three fingers, but our first shepherds made the sign of the cross and blessed men as of old with two fingers, according to the tradition of our holy fathers. . . ." And the patriarchs fell to thinking, and our people began to howl like wolf cubs and to belch out words against their fathers saying, "Our Russian holy men were ignorant, and they understood nothing, they are unlearned folk," said they. "How can one trust them? They have no letters." O Holy God! How hast thou suffered so great reviling of thy holy ones? I, miserable one, was bitter in my heart, but I could do nothing. I abused them as hard as I could and I spake as follows: "I am pure, and the dust that cleaves to my feet do I shake off before you, as it is written— better one if he do the will of God than a thousand of the godless." Then louder than before they began to cry out against me: "Away with him, away with him; he hath outraged us all"; and they began to thrust at me and to beat me. . . . Then again they brought me to Moscow, to the guesthouse of the Nikolsky Monastery, and they demanded of us yet again a statement of the true faith. After that there were sent more than once to me gentlemen of the bedchamber, diverse persons, Artemon and Dementy. And they spake to me in the name of the tsar: "Archpriest!" they said, "I see thy life that it is pure and undefiled and pleasing unto God, I and the tsarina and our children, be entreated of us." The envoy wept as he spake, and for him I weep always. I was exceeding sorry for him. And again he spake: "I beg of thee, hearken to me. Be thou reconciled with the patriarchs." And I said, "Even if God will that I should die, I will not be joined together with apostates. Thou art my tsar, but they, what have they to do with thee? They have lost their tsar and they have come here to gobble you up. I—say I—will not cease to uplift my hands to heaven until God give thee over to me."

The last word I got from the tsar was, "Wherever," said he, "thou shalt be, do not forget us in thy prayers." And I, sinful one, now, as far as I may, pray to God for him.

The Lore of the Land

The popular literature of Russia was first recorded in the sixteenth century, by an Englishman, Richard James. Many of these songs, tales, and epic poems, or byliny, date from the oldest periods of Russian history. Often they concern heroes of Saint Vladimir's court. Recited at inns and around campfires, the songs and tales were still being sung, with variations, during the first decades of the twentieth century.

Folk Tales

From THE MERCHANT SADKO, THE RICH GUEST OF NOVGOROD (c. 1170)

Translated by Isabel Hapgood

The character of Sadko is apparently based on an actual merchant who, according to the chronicles, built a church in Novgorod in 1167. The "gusly" he plays is an ancient zither-like instrument.

In the glorious city of Novgorod dwelt Sadko the gusly-player. No golden treasures did he possess; he went about to the magnificent feasts of the merchants and nobles, and made all merry with his playing.

And it chanced on a certain day, that Sadko was bidden to no worshipful feast; neither on the second day nor the third was he bidden. Then he sorrowed greatly, and went to Lake Ilmen, and seated himself upon a blue stone. There he began to play upon his harp of maple-wood, and played all day, from early morn till far into the night.

The waves rose . . . , the water was clouded with sand. . . .

But Sadko summoned up his courage, and ceased not his playing. Then the Tzar Vodyanoi [the Water King] emerged from the lake, and spake these words:

"We thank thee, Sadko of Novgorod! Thou has diverted us of the lake. I held a banquet and a worshipful feast; and all my beloved guests hast thou rejoiced. And I know not, Sadko, how I may reward thee. Yet return now, Sadko, to thy Novgorod, and to-morrow they shall call thee to a rich feast. Many merchants of Novgorod shall be there, and they shall eat and drink, and wax boastful. One shall boast of his good horse, another of his deeds of youthful prowess; another shall take pride in his youth. But the wise man will boast of his aged father, his old mother, and the senseless fool of his young wife. And do thou, Sadko, boast also: 'I know what there is in Lake Ilmen—of a truth, fishes with golden fins.' Then shall they contend with thee, that there are no fish of that sort,—of gold. But do thou then lay a great wager with them; wager thy turbulent head, and demand from them their shops in the bazaar, with all their precious wares. Then weave thou a net of silk, and come cast it in Lake Ilmen. Three times must thou cast it in the lake, and at each cast I will give a fish, yea, a fish with fins of gold. So shalt thou receive those shops in the bazaar, with their precious wares. So shalt thou become Sadko the Merchant of Novgorod, the rich Guest." . . . [And so it happened as the Water King predicted, and Sadko became a very rich man.]

[Sadko] built thirty great ships, thirty dark-red ships and three. Their prows were in the likeness of wild beasts, their sides like dragons; their masts of red wood, the cordage of silk, the sails of linen, and the anchors of steel. Instead of eyes were precious jacinths; instead of brows, Siberian sables; and dark brown Siberian fox-skins in place of ears. His faithful guards, his clerks, loaded these red ships with the wares of Novgorod, and he sailed away down the Volkof to Lake Ladoga, and thence into the Neva, and through that river to the blue sea, directing his course towards the Golden Horde. There he sold his wares, receiving great gain. . . . They sailed away from the Golden Horde, Sadko leading the way in the Falcon ship, the finest of all the vessels. But on the blue sea the red ships halted; the waves dashed, the breeze whistled, the ships strained,—but could not move from that spot. . . .

And Sadko the merchant spake to his men: "Ho there, my brave body-guard! Long have we sailed the seas, yea, twelve full years, yet have we paid no tribute to the Tzar Morskoi [the Sea King], and now he commandeth us down into the blue sea. Therefore, cast ye into the waves a cask of red gold." And they did so; but the waves beat, the sails tore, the ships strained, yet moved not.

Again spake Sadko the rich guest: "Lo, this is but a small gift for the Tzar Morskoi, in his blue sea. Cast ye another cask, a cask of pure silver, to him." Yet the dark-red ships moved not, though they cast in also a cask of seed pearls.

Then spake Sadko once again: "My brave, beloved body-guard, 'tis plain the Tzar Morskoi calleth a living man from among us into his blue sea. Make ye therefore lots of alder-wood, and let each man write his name upon his own, and the lots of all just souls shall float. But that man of us whose lot sinketh, he also shall go from among us into the blue sea." So it was done as he commanded:—but Sadko's lot was a cluster of hopflowers. And all the lots swam like ducks save Sadko's, and that went to the bottom like a stone.

Again spake Sadko the rich merchant to his troop: "These lots are not fair. Make ye to yourselves others of willow-wood, and set your names thereon, every man." This they did; but Sadko made his lot of blue damascened steel from beyond the sea, in weight ten poods. And it sank while all the others swam lightly on the blue sea. . . .

Then said Sadko the rich guest: " 'Tis plain that Sadko can do nothing. The Tzar Morskoi demandeth Sadko. . . ."

Then took he in his right hand an image of St. Mikola, and in his left his little harp of maple-wood, with its fine strings of gold, and put on him a rich cloak of sables; and bitterly he wept as he bade farewell to his brave company, to the white world, and Novgorod the glorious. He descended upon [an] oaken plank, and was borne upon the blue sea, and his dark-red ships sped on. . . .

Then was Sadko the rich merchant of Novgorod greatly terrified, as he floated over the blue sea on his plank of oak; but he fell asleep, and lo! when he awoke it was at the very bottom of the ocean-sea. He beheld the red sun burning through the clear waves, and saw that he was standing beside a palace of white stone where sat the Tzar Morskoi. . . .

The Tzar Morskoi spake these words: "Thou art welcome, Sadko, thou rich merchant of Novgorod! Long hast thou sailed the seas, yet offered no tribute to the Lord of the sea. And now thou art come as a gift to me. . . .

"It is said that thou are a master-player on the harp," said the Tzar Morskoi then; "play for me upon thy harp of maple-wood."

Sadko saw that in the blue sea he could do naught but obey, and he began to pluck his harp. And as he played, the Tzar Morskoi began to jump about, beating time with the skirts of his garment, and waving his mantle; fair sea-maidens led choral dances, and the lesser sea-folk squatted and leaped.

Then the blue sea was churned with yellow sands, great billows surged over it, breaking many ships asunder, drowning many men, and ingulfing vast possessions. . . .

Then Sadko [realizing what havoc was being caused] brake his harp, and snapped its golden strings; and when the Tzar Morskoi commanded him to play yet two hours, he answered him boldly that the harp was broken. . . .

"Wilt thou not take a wife here?" the Tzar Morskoi said, "wilt thou not wed some fair maid in the blue sea?"

And Sadko answered: "In the blue sea, I obey thy will."

[And of the nine hundred maidens offered him by the Tzar] he chose the last of all, the maiden called Chernava.

Then the Tzar Morskoi made him a great feast; and afterwards Sadko lay down and fell into a heavy sleep. And when he awoke, he found himself on the steep banks of the Chernava river. . . .

And thenceforth he sailed no more upon the blue sea, but dwelt and took his ease in his own town.

From ILYA OF MUROM AND NIGHTINGALE THE ROBBER (c. 1200)

Translated by N. Kershaw Chadwick

Ilya, who used his supernatural strength to battle the enemies of Kievan Russia, was the favorite hero of the byliny *singers. He has been variously identified as Ilias, "a great chief and mighty warrior" of the twelfth century, and as a possible half brother of Vladimir Monomakh. Nightingale may have been a bandit chief of the period.*

Ilya of Murom urged on his heroic steed.
He rode off along the direct high-road,
He took his silken whip in his hand,
He struck his steed on his sleek flank,
He made his steed gallop with all his mighty strength.
His good heroic steed sped on,
Leaping from mountain to mountain,
Springing from hill to hill,
Passing over rivers and lakes at a stride.
He galloped up to that Black Morass,
To the glorious leaning birch tree,
To the cross of Levanidov,
To the glorious River Smorodina.
Whereupon Nightingale the Robber, the son of Odikhmantov,
                                    began to whistle;
He whistled like a nightingale,
That rascal robber roared out like a wild beast:
The dark forests bowed to the earth,
Every mortal creature lay lifeless.
The good steed of Ilya of Murom began to stumble;
He struck the steed on its sleek flank,
He struck the steed and addressed it:
"Ho, you food for wolves, you grass-bag;
Will you not go on, or can you not carry me?
Never can you have heard the whistle of a nightingale . . .
That you now stumble over roots, you dog!"
He brought his heroic steed to a stand,
He unhitched his taut, resilient bow,
From his right stirrup of steel;
He fixed a tempered arrow,
And drew his silken bow-string;
He shot at Nightingale the Robber,
Putting out his right eye from its socket.
Nightingale fell to the damp earth;
The old Cossack, Ilya of Murom,
He bound him to his right stirrup,
To his right stirrup of steel.
He rode over the free, open plain. . . .
He rode to the city of Kiev,
To gracious Prince Vladimir.
He entered the prince's spacious court-yard,
He stood his horse in the middle of the court-yard,
He went into the palace of white stone. . . .
He crossed himself in the prescribed manner,
He made his bow as it is enjoined,
On three, on four, on all sides he bowed,
To Prince Vladimir in particular,
And to all his royal retinue.
Prince Vladimir began to question him:
"Whence do you come, mighty, noble youth?
By what name do they call you?
How do they address you, bold youth, in your own home?"
Ilya answered him as follows:
"I come from the town of Murom,
From the glorious village of Karachoro;
They call me Ilya by name,
Ilya of Murom, the son of Ivanov. . . .
I attended Matins in Murom
And arrived in time for Mass at the royal city of Kiev.
My business on the road delayed me:
I came by the direct high-road,

The high-road past the glorious city of Chernigov,
Past the glorious River Smorodina."
Vladimir spoke as follows:
"You mock us to our faces, fellow!
You lie in our faces, fellow!
Under the city of Chernigov lies the infidel host,
By the River Smorodina sits Nightingale the Robber, the son
                                           of Odikhmantov—
Nightingale who whistles like a nightingale,
The rascal robber, who roars like a wild beast."
Ilya spoke as follows:
"Vladimir, prince of royal Kiev!
Nightingale the Robber is in your court-yard,
Chained to my right stirrup of steel."
Then Vladimir, prince of royal Kiev,
Instantly leapt to his nimble feet,
Flung his mantle of marten-skins over one shoulder,
His sable cap over one ear,
Very, very quickly he ran into the spacious court-yard,
And went up to Nightingale the Robber.
He addressed Nightingale as follows:
"Come, give us a whistle, Nightingale, like a nightingale;
Give a roar, now, rascal, like a wild beast!"
Nightingale answered Prince Vladimir:
"Vladimir, prince of royal Kiev!
I do not eat your food to-day,
And I will not obey you.
I eat with the old Cossack, Ilya of Murom;
And him I will obey."
Vladimir said to Ilya of Murom:
"Oh, old Cossack, Ilya of Murom,
Tell him to whistle like a nightingale,
Tell him to roar like a wild beast." . . .
Ilya of Murom said to him:
"Come, now, whistle up, Nightingale!—but only half the
                             whistle of a nightingale!
Give a roar now!—but only half the roar of a wild beast!"
Then Nightingale began to whistle like a nightingale;
He gave a roar, the wretch, like a wild beast.
At that nightingale whistle,
At that wild beast roar,
A tremendous pother arose.
The dark forests bowed to the earth,
And the pinnacles of the houses were bent awry,
The glass windows were shattered,
And every mortal creature lay lifeless;
But Vladimir, prince of royal Kiev,
Stood firm, for he covered himself up in his cloak of marten-
                                           skins.

This occurrence exasperated Ilya of Murom.
He mounted his good steed,
Rode out into the free, open plain,
He cut off Nightingale's turbulent head,
He cut off his head, and he cried:
"You have caused enough fathers and mothers to weep,
You have widowed enough young wives,
You have orphaned enough little children!"
Then they sang the dirge for Nightingale.

THE BOYAR'S EXECUTION (date unknown)

Translated by Talvi

*The historical background of this ballad is not known, though it
probably dates from the Muscovite period, which began in the fourteenth century during the reign of Ivan I. The Butcher's street and
Butcher's gate that are mentioned in the second verse were on
the route in Moscow along which criminals were led to execution.*

"Thou, my head, alas! my head,
Long hast served me, and well, my head;
Full three-and-thirty summers long;
Ever astride of my gallant steed,
Never my foot from its stirrup drawn.
But alas! thou has gained, my head,
Nothing of joy or other good;
Nothing of honors or even thanks."

Yonder along the Butcher's street,
Out to the fields through the Butcher's gate,
They are leading a prince and peer.

Priests and deacons are walking before,
In their hands a great book open;
Then there follows a soldier troop,
With their drawn sabres flashing bright.
At his right, the headsman goes,
Holds in his hand the keen-edged sword;
At his left goes his sister dear,
And she weeps as the torrent pours,
And she sobs as the fountains gush.

Comforting speaks her brother to her:
"Weep not, weep not, my sister dear!
Weep not away thy eyes so clear,
Dim not, O dim not thy face so fair,
Make not heavy thy joyous heart!
Say, for what is it thou weepest so?
Is 't for my goods, my inheritance?
Is 't for my lands, so rich and wide?
Is 't for my silver, or is 't for my gold?
Or dost thou weep for my life alone?"

"Ah, thou, my light, my brother dear,
Not for thy goods or inheritance,
Not for thy lands, so rich and wide,
Is 't that my eyes are weeping so;
Not for thy silver and not for thy gold,
'Tis for thy life, I am weeping so."

"Ah, thou, my light, my sister sweet!
Thou mayest weep, but it won't avail;
Thou mayest beg, but 'tis all in vain;
Pray to the Tzar, but he will not yield.
Merciful truly was God to me,
Truly gracious to me the Tzar,
So he commanded my traitor head
Off should be hewn from my shoulders strong."

Now the scaffold the prince ascends,
Calmly mounts to the place of death;
Prays to his Great Redeemer there,
Humbly salutes the crowd around;
"Farewell world, and thou people of God;
Pray for my sins that burden me sore!"

Scarce had the people ventured then
On him to look, when his traitor head
Off was hewn from his shoulders strong.

From FROL SKOBEEV, THE ROGUE (c. 1680)

Translated by Serge Zenkovsky

Seventeenth-century Russian literature had become thoroughly secularized. In this anonymous tale of a roguish provincial squire there is not a hint of the didactic moralizing that permeated the earlier ecclesiastical literature. A satire on the rise of the new bourgeois gentry, the tale ends with clever Frol not only winning the girl, but inheriting her father's wealth and property as well.

When the time of the Christmas holidays arrived, during which there is much merrymaking and the girls often have pretexts to pass the time gaily, the daughter of Stolnik Nadrin-Nashchekin, Annushka, told her nurse to go to all noblemen who had young daughters and whose estates were in the vicinity and ask them to come to Annushka's party and have some fun. The nurse went and asked all the daughters of noblemen, and they all promised to come to Annushka's party. Since the nurse knew that Frol Skobeev had a young sister who was unmarried, she went to Frol's house and asked his sister to come to . . . Annushka's party. . . .

The sister went to Frol and told him: "The nurse of Stolnik Nadrin-Nashchekin's daughter has arrived, and asks that I come to Annushka's party."

Frol Skobeev told his sister: "Go and tell this nurse that you will go, but with another girl, a nobleman's daughter."

The sister pondered on what her brother had told her to tell the nurse. However, she did not dare to disobey her brother, and told the nurse that she would go that very evening with the daughter of another nobleman. Then the nurse returned to her mistress, Annushka.

In the meantime Frol Skobeev began to speak with his sister, saying, "Well, sister, it is time for you to get dressed to go to the party." When his sister began to don feminine attire, Frol ordered her: "Sister, bring me also a girl's attire. I shall don it, and we shall go together to Annushka, the stolnik's daughter."

The sister was very much afraid that people might recognize him, and then certainly there would be much trouble for her brother, for the stolnik was much liked by the tsar. Still, she did not dare to disobey her brother, and she brought him the attire of a girl. Frol, having dressed himself as a girl, went with his sister to Annushka, the stolnik's daughter.

There had already gathered many daughters of noblemen, but no one was able to recognize Frol in his feminine attire.

Then the girls began to play parlor games, and enjoyed themselves. Frol also played the games, and was not recognized by anyone. Finally Frol left the room for his needs, and was accompanied through the corridor by the nurse, who carried a taper. On leaving, he told her, "Oh, my dear nurse, there are many girls here, and many of them ask services of you, but none of them would give you any gift for such services." Still the nurse did not recognize him. Then Frol gave her five rubles, which she accepted gratefully.

Seeing that the nurse still did not recognize him, Frol fell on his knees and explained to her that he was a nobleman, Frol Skobeev, and that he had come in feminine attire so that he might marry Annushka. When the nurse realized that he really was Frol Skobeev, she became frightened and did not know what to do. Still, remembering . . . his generous [gift], she said to him, "Well, my lord Skobeev, I am ready to do everything you may ask, in view of your gracious generosity."

Returning to the place where the girls were enjoying themselves, she spoke not a word about Frol Skobeev, but soon after she told her mistress. "Well, girls, you have had enough of these games. I suggest you play another game, one that was played when I was young." . . .

And the nurse told them of her game, saying: "Please, dear Annushka, play the role of the bride." Pointing to Frol Skobeev, she said: "And this girl will be the bridegroom." And then she led the two into a nice chamber, to the bed, as a bride and bridegroom are usually led after the wedding. The girls accompanied them to the bedroom and then, leaving the two alone, went to the rooms in which they had been playing their parlor games. . . .

Lying with Annushka on the bed, Frol told her that he was a nobleman, Frol Skobeev, from the district of Novgorod, and not a girl. Annushka was seized by great fright. But Frol, despite the fact that he was himself afraid, became daring and forced her to submit to his will. Thereafter, Annushka begged Frol not to bring shame upon her by telling of this to others. Later on, when the nurse and the girls returned to the chamber where Frol and Annushka were, they realized from Annushka's expression that something had happened. . . . However, the girls still did not recognize Frol Skobeev, for he was again in feminine attire. But Annushka took her nurse by the hand, led her away from the girls, and said to her: "What have you done to me! The one who was with me was not a girl. He is a man, Frol Skobeev."

However, the nurse answered: "I tell you the truth, my gracious lady, when I say that I was not able to recognize him. I thought that he was a girl like the others. If he has committed such a shameful deed, we can kill him and hide his body in some secret place, for we have plenty of servants."

But Annushka took pity on Frol Skobeev. And she told the nurse, "Well, nurse, let it be this way, for never again shall I regain my chastity."

Thereafter, all the girls, as well as Frol Skobeev, went to the reception room, and all enjoyed themselves until late into the night. Afterward, all the girls went to bed. And Annushka went to bed with Frol Skobeev. . . .

In the morning, when everyone had got up, the girls returned to their homes. Frol Skobeev also wanted to leave with his sister, but Annushka, who permitted all the others to go, kept Frol Skobeev in her house. Frol Skobeev remained at Annushka's house for three days, always in feminine attire, so that he might not be recognized by the house servants. And he and Annushka enjoyed themselves, and only after three days did Frol go home with his sister. . . .

Folk Songs

THE FAITHLESS LOVER

Translated by Talvi

Russian folk songs were intimately connected with the ancient life of the peasant. There were songs for the seasons and the weather; for feasts and funerals; for births and marriages; for happiness and sorrow. Here are two songs of love, requited and otherwise. Their dates and authors are unknown, but they are probably centuries old.

Nightingale, O nightingale,
Nightingale so full of song,
Tell me, tell me, where thou fliest,
Where to sing now in the night?
Will another maiden hear thee
Like to me, poor me, all night
Sleepless, restless, comfortless,
Ever full of tears her eyes?
Fly, O fly, dear nightingale,
Over hundred countries fly,
Over the blue sea so far;
Spy the distant countries through,
Town and village, hill and dell,
Whether thou find'st any one,
Who so sad is, as I am?

O, I bore a necklace once,
All of pearls like morning dew;
And I bore a finger-ring,
With a precious stone thereon;
And I bore deep in my heart
Love, a love so warm and true.
When the sad, sad autumn came,
Were the pearls no longer clear;
And in winter burst my ring,
On my finger, of itself!
Ah! and when the spring came on,
Had forgotten me my love.

MARRIAGE SONG

Translated by W. R. S. Ralston

Her mother has counselled Maryushka,
Has given counsel to her dear Efimovna.
"Go not, my child,
Go not, my darling,

Into thy father's garden for apples,
Nor catch the mottled butterflies,
Nor frighten the little birds,
Nor interrupt the clear-voiced nightingale.
For should'st thou pluck the apples
The tree will wither away;
Or seize the mottled butterfly,
The butterfly will die.
And should'st thou frighten a little bird,
That bird will fly away;
Or interrupt the clear-voiced nightingale,
The nightingale will be mute:
But catch, my child,
My dear one, catch
The falcon bright in the open field,
The green, the open field."
Maryushka dear has caught,
Caught has the dear Efimovna,
The falcon bright in the open field,
The green, the open field.
She has perched him on her hand,
She has brought him to her mother.
"Mother mine, Gosudaruinya,
I have caught the falcon bright."

Proverbs

THE SALT OF LIFE

Translated by Bernard Guilbert Guerney

The first collection of proverbs was made by order of Catherine the Great in the eighteenth century. In the nineteenth, a Russian lexicographer collected thirty-eight thousand of them. The few given here demonstrate both the humor of the peasant and his native distrust of clergymen, officials, judges, and men of wealth and power.

Pray once when going to the wars; pray twice when going to sea; but pray thrice when going to get married.

A wife is no balalaika; you can't
put her on the shelf after playing.

When money speaks, Truth keeps its mouth shut.

Don't trust a landlord till he's six feet under.

A man's a fool to make his doctor his heir.

If you're a rooster, crow; if you're a hen, lay eggs.

You can pull and pull, but you can't milk a bull.

Lie down with dogs and you'll get up with fleas.

A good friend is better than a hundred relatives.

The greatest Tsar must be put to bed with a shovel at last.

Pray to God, but keep rowing toward shore.

Born, baptized, married, or in the earth
laid—always the priest has to be paid.

Be righteous before God; be wealthy before a judge.

The Law is like an axle—you can turn it whichever way you please, if you give it plenty of grease.

The eighteenth-century engraving above is one panel from a series illustrating a fable, "The Tale of the Chicken and the Flattering Fox."

5

Splendors of the Court

Palaces, Riches, and Regalia

On Christmas Day, 1553, Ivan the Terrible gave a feast in the Throne Room of the Palace of Facets, in the heart of the Kremlin. "There dined that day in the Emperor's presence above 500 strangers and 200 Russians, and all they were served in vessels of gold." So marveled Richard Chancellor, the first Englishman to visit Russia, and one of Ivan's guests. Some years later, in 1588, the Greek Archbishop Arsenius visited the Kremlin's fabled royal residence, the Terem Palace, and described the "apartment of the Tsaritsa, which was spherical in shape, [and] shone with the purest gold. . . . The vault was covered with . . . wonderful paintings. The walls were adorned with the costliest mosaics . . . the floor was covered with cunningly wrought carpets, on which the sports of hawking and hunting were represented lifelike; . . . figures of birds and beasts, carved in precious metals, glittered on all sides. . . ."

In the three centuries during which the tsars ruled Russia from the Kremlin (early 1400's–1712), they constructed dazzling palaces and displayed exotic treasures to impress upon native princes and foreign envoys their supremacy as absolute rulers of a mighty land. Ivan III was the first tsar to make a practice of deliberate ostentation. He summoned

The Small Throne Room (opposite) of St. Petersburg's Winter Palace was created in 1833 in memory of Peter the Great, whose portrait hangs over a silver-gilt throne made by a London craftsman in 1731.

architects from Italy and bade them fill the Kremlin with magnificent churches and palaces of stone. His glittering reception hall, the Palace of Facets, built c. 1490, is Moscow's oldest surviving civil edifice in stone, and is named for its faceted exterior. The lower floor was used for administrative purposes; the more important upper floor—comprising a single chamber with a vaulted ceiling supported by a massive central pillar—was used as a throne room and audience hall by Ivan and his successors. Ivan also commissioned a masonry residence for himself, the Terem Palace, which remained the official residence of the tsars until the capital was transferred to St. Petersburg. Though badly burned and considerably rebuilt in the next two centuries, it still offers a vivid picture of the homes of the tsars: a color-drenched, labyrinthine structure, whose low corridors, arabesque arches, and vaulted chambers bespeak barbaric magnificence.

Peter the Great abandoned the Kremlin, shrouded as it was in mysticism and medieval splendor, and built St. Petersburg in the style of a Western, eighteenth-century city. He imbued it with the sedate austerity of Dutch architecture and the refined elegance of the French grand manner. Elizabeth I championed the ornate Russian baroque style, but her successor, Catherine the Great, popularized the formal neoclassical manner, which came to dominate Russian architecture for the better part of a century, and continues to influence it even to the present.

Versailles of the North

Peter the Great turned against the claustrophobic traditions of medieval Muscovy and gave Russia a "window on the West" in 1712 when he transferred the capital to St. Petersburg, a northern settlement he had built on a marshy site at the mouth of the Neva River. The move symbolized his drive to open Russia to the advanced culture and technology of Europe. Foreign architects began constructing the city in 1703, and later Peter ordered the court and nobility to take up residence there and to build houses and palaces of stone.

St. Petersburg vaunted Peter's tastes and predilections, many of which were formed during his year-long sojourn in western Europe. Favoring the practical sobriety of Dutch architecture, he sought to make his "paradise," as he called his city, a second Amsterdam. Unlike other Russian cities, which sprang up from villages and grew randomly into haphazard mazes of winding streets, Petersburg was as rationally conceived as a Renaissance painting, with wide avenues laid out in regular patterns, and buildings, squares, and parks designed to create a unified composition. Peter was also impressed with the magnificence of Versailles, and in 1715 he commissioned Louis XIV's architect, Jean Baptiste LeBlond, to design a palace at Peterhof, his estate near St. Petersburg on the shores of the Gulf of Finland. When completed, the Summer Palace and gardens (subsequently enlarged and altered by the master Italian architect Bartolomeo Rastrelli) were worthy rivals of the Sun King's residence.

Peterhof was the most spectacular of the imperial estates surrounding St. Petersburg. This Versailles of the North was the favorite resort of the tsars and the scene of lavish balls and firework displays. Crowning a majestic cliff, its Great Palace (above) commands a sweeping vista of cascades and fountains, culminating in a magnificent view of the Gulf of Finland and the Finnish coast in the distance. The Samson Fountain—so named after the central bronze figure (opposite) of Samson forcing open the lion's jaw—connects with a canal that leads into the gulf.

Tsarskoe Selo (now Pushkin), with its palaces, pleasure gardens, and pavilions, was one of the imperial family's favorite summer estates near St. Petersburg. Massive, brilliantly colored, and heavily windowed, the Catherine Palace exemplifies the Russian baroque style of the architect, Bartolomeo Rastrelli. Its façade (left), embellished with wrought-iron balconies, telamons, columns, and carved wood and stucco window ornaments, is one of his most unrestrained creations, and the wrought-iron palace gate below typifies his fanciful idiom. At Tsarskoe Selo he also built several pavilions and laid out formal gardens inspired by those at Versailles. Rastrelli's palace interiors were filled with intricate moldings, parquet floors, and grand staircases, but many were altered by subsequent rulers and severely damaged in World War II. Catherine the Great, who declared, "There is going to be a terrible turnout at Tsarskoe Selo," had the Scottish architect Charles Cameron redecorate many rooms and add a pavilion and a gallery, all in the less ornate neoclassical style.

Rastrelli the Magnificent

Peter the Great's daughter and fifth successor, the "gay tsaritsa" Elizabeth (r. 1741–62) devoted herself whole-heartedly to the pursuit of pleasure. She was capricious, extravagant, and self-indulgent even though the imperial treasury was usually as bare as a serf's cupboard. In keeping with her flamboyant personality, Elizabeth rejected the sober, labored decor and architecture popularized by her father and created an environment that satisfied her craving for lavish display and ornamentation. Her palaces were honeycombed with lofty, mirrored halls shimmering with brocades and crystal chandeliers.

The most important architect of Elizabeth's reign was Bartolomeo Rastrelli, whose exuberant Russianized rococo creations matched the empress' wildest flights of fancy. Born in 1700 and brought up in the Paris of Louis XIV, he was the son of the Italian sculptor Carlo Rastrelli, who arrived in Russia with the Sun King's architect, LeBlond, in 1715, and subsequently enjoyed great prominence. Rastrelli the Magnificent, as Elizabeth's architect was called, was a prolific worker. From the 1720's on, he constructed palaces, public buildings, and churches in Moscow, Kiev, the Baltic area, and St. Petersburg. For the nobility, who eagerly followed the fashion set by imperial tastes, Rastrelli created numerous small palaces. However, his fertile imagination manifested itself most fully in the residences he built for Elizabeth in

St. Petersburg and its environs. These palaces—with their immense frontages and elaborately colored and sculpted exteriors, as well as their theatrical, rococo interiors and staircases—epitomize the Russian baroque style. Rastrelli enlarged Peterhof (1747–52) to accommodate the throngs of pleasure seekers who clustered around Elizabeth, but was careful to retain LeBlond's original concept. In his two last and most important imperial palaces, Rastrelli's talents reached their most exalted forms. He rebuilt (1749–56) the Great Palace at Tsarskoe Selo, later known as the Catherine Palace after Catherine the Great, and built (1754–62) St. Petersburg's ornate Winter Palace, which now houses part of the Hermitage Museum.

The reign of Catherine the Great marked Rastrelli's fall from favor and the emergence of neoclassicism as the dominant style in Russia. In the 1760's and 1770's two Russians, Yury Velten and Vasily Bazhenov, and an Italian, Antonio Rinaldi, created buildings that represented the transitional phases between the baroque and the neoclassical. This more simplified style reached the height of refinement in the last decades of Catherine's reign, under the direction of another international trio—an Italian, Giacomo Quarenghi, a Scotsman, Charles Cameron, and a Russian, Ivan Starov. As if overcome by baroque opulence, the empress and the nobility had thus turned to the quiet elegance of neoclassicism.

In his palace designs, Bartolomeo Rastrelli, the master architect of Russian baroque whose portrait appears at right, above, combined elaborate sculptural ornamentation with a grand scale, monumental columns, and wide expanses of windows. The engraving above depicts his Great Palace at Tsarskoe Selo as it looked in 1761. Below is the Stroganov Palace in St. Petersburg, dating from the 1750's—one of the many lesser palaces that Rastrelli designed for the nobility.

MARY ANN JOULWAN

The ornate Gallery of the History of Ancient Painting (above) of the Winter
Palace, now housing a collection of neoclassical sculpture, is decorated with
murals depicting the influence of ancient culture on the development of art. The
Pavilion Hall (right) is in the Small Hermitage, which was constructed in
the 1760's for Catherine the Great and rebuilt in the mid-nineteenth century.

154

In this early 1800's print Alexander I's troops pass in review before Rastrelli's Winter Palace in Petersburg. (The spired Admiralty is in the

distance at left.) The main imperial residence from the 1760's until 1917, the palace was severely damaged by fire in 1837 and was remodeled.

All That Glitters

"Never in my life have I seen things more precious, or more beautiful," reported the ambassador of Maximilian II, the Holy Roman Emperor, of his visit to Ivan the Terrible's court in 1576. Ivan's regalia, he claimed, far outshone European crown jewels. The gem-studded and brilliantly enameled Russian accouterments of power—the thrones, crowns, scepters, and orbs that symbolized the tsar's divinely granted authority over his subjects —reflect the prodigal luxury of the tsarist court.

The rulers of Russia prized their regalia for the sense of legitimacy it imparted to their frequently tenuous claims to power. For instance, when Ivan III married Zoë (later, Sofia) Paleologus, the niece of the last Byzantine emperor, in 1472, he adopted as his crest the Byzantine double-headed eagle to symbolize that his succession was inherited from Byzantium. The Romanovs were still using it as their standard in 1917. According to one legend, the oldest Russian crown, the fur-rimmed Cap of Monomakh, once belonged to Augustus Caesar, but experts believe its earliest portion dates from the 1200's, and the first actual record of its use was in 1498. After that time, every tsar through Peter the Great was crowned with it, and it was subsequently carried in all coronation processions.

The orb, scepter, and fur-trimmed crown (or chapka) *above belonged to Tsar Mikhail I (r. 1613–45), the founder of the Romanov dynasty. The portrait opposite depicts his son, Alexei, in full robes and regalia.*

th
m
pl
or
ce
ce
Ba
th
at
as
ch

The seats of the tsars were as splendid as their jewels. Ivan the Terrible's Ivory Throne (left) is one of the Kremlin's great treasures. According to legend, Ivan III's wife, Sofia Paleologus, brought it to the Kremlin from Constantinople. Most likely, it was made in western Europe in the 1500's. Its wooden frame is entirely covered with ivory plates on which are carved scenes from mythology, heraldry, history, and everyday life. Beginning with Alexei in 1645, all the rulers of Russia used it at their coronations. Mikhail Romanov's saddle (right) is decorated in gold, enamel, and precious stones. Catherine the Great's English-made summer coach (below) was a gift from her lover, Count Orlov, in 1779. Its carved woodwork resembles cast metal, and its body is decorated with paintings in the manner of François Boucher.

co
do
m
m
va
wa
th
we
all
se
wi
wh
of

th
zli
ba
se
vc
so
by
th
se
be
th
so
fo
th
Ca
we
pre
of
wi
ing
do
th
En
Ch

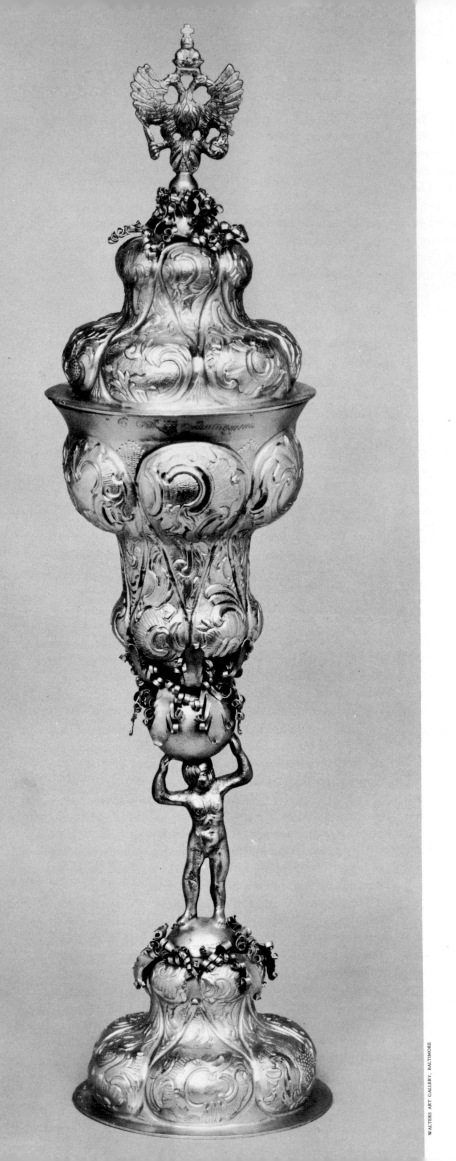

Stately Vessels

The two main influences in Russian art, the geometric patterns and arabesques of the Orient and the naturalism of the West, always appear under a veneer of Russianisms. The Oriental flavor dominated during the great flowering of the applied arts in Russia in the 1500's and 1600's. Foreign and native craftsmen in the Kremlin workshops produced vast quantities of gold and silver vessels—often encrusted with gems or richly decorated in polychrome enamels— to adorn the banquet tables of the tsars. The Eastern influence was particularly evident in the decoration of various types of drinking cups used on festive or ceremonial occasions and generally bearing inscriptions in stylized Slavonic lettering. One of the most typically Russian vessels is the low, boat-shaped *kovsh,* or dipper, that was originally used for ladling mead, beer, or kvass. The earliest ones were made of wood, and these continued to be used by the peasantry until recent times. For the nobility, *kovshi* of precious metals were being made as early as the 1300's. By the 1650's, however, many types of drinking vessels produced in Russia, notably flasks and goblets, began to take on a European appearance, and thereafter, the metal *kovshi* were used mainly as trophies, presented to faithful subjects by grateful tsars.

Echoes of the Oriental are apparent in the enameled silver-gilt bowl above, which dates from the late 1600's. As seen here, its exterior is embellished with tulips enameled in various shades, and edged with a filigree of twisted silver wire, a characteristically Russian technique. Also distinctly Russian is the golden kovsh (left), a dipper made in the late 1500's for Boris Godunov. The covered silver standing cup opposite, fashioned in Moscow in 1760, has a more Western appearance. Its structure and the assymetrical scrolls that embellish it are derived from German models.

OVERLEAF: The red- and gold-trimmed porcelain dinner service in the banquet room of Paul I's palace of Pavlovsk, near St. Petersburg, contains more than six hundred pieces, some of which depict Russian costumes.

Craftsmen working for Fabergé, who is shown in the medallion opposite, created the sprig of mistletoe above; the stem is of gold, the leaves of jade, the blossoms of moonstones. The imperial Easter egg at far right is known as the Chanticleer Egg, after the rooster that, at each hour, rises from within the shell, flaps its wings, crows, and then retires. The Coronation Box, right, was presented by Tsaritsa Alexandra to Nicholas II on Easter Sunday, 1897, the same day he gave her the similarly decorated Coronation Egg that is shown on pages 170–71.

Eggs à la Russe

Peter Carl Fabergé, the favorite goldsmith of Tsars Alexander III and Nicholas II and their courts, was born to a Russian family of Huguenot descent. In 1870 he took charge of his father's jewelry and goldsmith shop in his native St. Petersburg. Concentrating on articles of fantasy—flowers of precious stones, jeweled boxes, clocks, and Easter Eggs—he developed a thriving business, with branches in Moscow, Kiev, and Odessa. Fabergé did not himself make all the items that flowed from his workshops; he designed the most important pieces and co-ordinated the skills of his craftsmen. The bibelots produced by the House of Fabergé are often made with semiprecious stones or enamels, and while they have little intrinsic value, the imaginative craftsmanship with which they were fashioned renders them priceless to collectors. The imperial Easter eggs have come to symbolize Fabergé's unique creative flair. The first was commissioned by Alexander III for his wife, in 1883, and the tsar was so delighted with it that he asked Fabergé to make him one each year, stipulating only that it open to reveal a surprise.

OVERLEAF: *Nicholas II continued the Easter egg custom begun by his father. This Coronation Egg, which Nicholas gave to his wife, is made of red gold and is covered with translucent enamel. The miniature coach, the egg's "surprise," is a replica of the coach used by the imperial couple at their coronation in 1896. Fabergé made his last imperial Easter egg in 1917, but was not allowed to deliver it. The following year, the House of Fabergé was taken over by the Bolsheviks.*

A. KENNETH SNOWMAN, *The Art of Carl Fabergé*; IN THE COLLECTION OF WARTSKI JEWELERS, LONDON

À LA VIEILLE RUSSIE, NEW YORK

Russian sculptors did not begin to master European techniques until the late eighteenth century, and their work was very much in the French neoclassical manner. Mikhail Kozlovsky (1753–1802), one of the more competent sculptors, executed the statue of Samson appearing on page 149. Shown here are works by two later sculptors: above, "Lad Playing Nails," by Alexander Loganovsky (1815–55); and, opposite, "Satyr and Bacchante," by Boris Orlovsky (1796–1837).

Genre scenes became popular subjects for Russian painters during the nineteenth century, and they long retained vestiges of the exalted art of the Academy. Opposite is a study for "Christ Before the People," by Alexander Ivanov (1806–58), an artist who was deeply concerned with creating landscapes faithful to nature, but whose figures were based on classical ideals. "Bleaching the Linen," below, painted by Vasily Serebryakov in 1884, is a late example of the romanticized social realism represented in France by François Millet.

OVERLEAF: *"Zaporozh Cossacks Drafting a Reply to the Turkish Sultan" was painted c. 1890 by Ilya Repin, who was Academy-educated but supported the "Wanderer" rebels. His insightful, precise renderings of nature and his passionate portrayals of Russian life made Repin's work the epitome of Russian realism.*

6

Masters of the Pen

Nineteenth-Century Writers

During the 1600's Western ideas had been filtering into Russia at a slow but steady pace. Peter the Great removed all impediments and made Westernization a matter of public policy. While securing his empire by military victories and colonial expansion, Peter set about telescoping centuries of cultural development lost to Russia by initiating social, political, and educational reforms, and by repudiating old customs and values—such as long beards and native dress —in favor of Western fashions. His heirs continued his programs, and the intellectual life of the 1700's was dominated by a frantic assimilation and imitation of European culture. Royal whim dictated which influence was to be preferred, the empress Anna favoring Germans, while Elizabeth and Catherine looked to the French. Eager pupils, the Russians learned quickly; by the end of the century, they were not simply emulating their neighbors, but producing original, thought-provoking works.

A later intellectual stimulus came from the young officers and diplomats who accompanied Alexander I on his triumphal tour of Europe after Napoleon's defeat. Exposed to revolutionary ideas and a way of life forbidden by their autocratic ruler, they returned home with mixed feelings of

By 1800 the intelligentsia had turned from religion and politics to philosophy, history, and literature. Pushkin, the poetic genius of the era, is shown here (second from left) communing with friends.

pride in their victorious nation and dissatisfaction with its social and political conditions. Alexander's growing conservatism forced them underground into secret societies, where they continued to discuss plans for improving Russia. Their idealism culminated in an attempt to form a constitutional monarchy when Nicholas I was crowned in 1825. The immediate outcome was a series of executions and exiles, but the "Decembrists," named after the month of their abortive coup, left a heritage of liberalism.

Despite Nicholas I's heavy censorship, great advances were made in the humanities and sciences in the 1830's and 1840's. Literary journals burgeoned, the universities seethed with excitement, and artists intensified their criticism of life in Russia. The tradition of dissent was continued by the "intelligentsia," a new breed of intellectuals coming from all classes, not just from the nobility.

The ideas that later inspired Dostoevsky, Tolstoy, and Turgenev were shaped during the "Extraordinary Decade, 1838–1848," as it was called in a memoir of that era. The main division in thought was between the Slavophiles, who hoped to create reforms based on the customs of pre-Petrine Russia, and the Westernizers, who wanted to strip their country of characteristics separating it from the West. It was this dilemma—created by Peter when he attempted to turn Muscovy into a modern European state—that fired the imaginations of the great writers of the 1800's.

Founding Fathers

"One day," wrote Princess Dashkova, an intimate and powerful friend of Catherine the Great, "whilst I was walking with the Empress in the gardens of Tsarskoe Selo, our conversation turned on the beauty and richness of the Russian language. . . . I observed that nothing was wanting but rules, and a good dictionary, to render our language wholly independent of those foreign terms and phrases, so very inferior to our own in expression and energy." At Catherine's behest was founded the Academy for the Study of the Russian Language, which published the first Russian dictionary, established periodicals, and encouraged young writers. Standards of language were established where before there had been a chaotic jumble of Church Slavonic and native Russian. Though Russian writers still drew inspiration from the styles and modes of neoclassical France and Germany, they were nevertheless creating in their work a basis for a distinctly Russian literature.

GAVRIILA DERZHAVIN, *Sochinenia Derzhavina*

*Early in her reign Catherine the Great (above) encouraged the spread of European liter-
ature and ideas in Russia; she was herself a competent author of plays and tales, and she
corresponded voluminously with, among others, Voltaire and Diderot. The linguist, scientist, and poet Mikhail Lomonosov (top left) created the first fixed standards for the Russian
literary language, while Gavriila Derzhavin (bottom left) wrote poems that were the epitome of lofty classicism, praising God, waterfalls, and the greatness of empire. Under the
influence of Nikolai Karamzin (center), literary Russian took a turn to the French; the
language and subjects of his essays and tales marked the beginning of the sentimental age.*

The Prince
Of Poets

The outstanding poet of Russia's golden age, Alexander Pushkin was born in 1799 to a family whose origins went back to the Russian boyars and to an Abyssinian prince, a protégé of Peter the Great. Schooled at an exclusive lyceum founded by Alexander I on the imperial estate at Tsarskoe Selo, Pushkin was acclaimed for his writing talents while he was still a student. His life style was also established at an early age when, after graduating from Tsarskoe Selo, he plunged into the social whirl of Petersburg, dividing his time between serious intellectual pursuits and the pastimes of a wellborn rake—the theater, balls, amatory escapades, and dueling.

In 1820, as punishment for his poetic attacks on politicians (including the tsar), Pushkin was exiled to Russia's southern frontiers. There he experimented with narrative poems à la Byron ("The Captive of the Caucasus," "The Fountain of Bakhchisaray," and "The Gypsies"), set in the exotic regions he had visited during his travels.

An affair with the wife of the viceroy of Odessa resulted in Pushkin's banishment in 1824 to his parents' estate outside Moscow. This first of many stays there gave him the opportunity to become more familiar with the language and customs of the peasant, and it marked the beginning of his love for Russian history and folk tales.

Pushkin's enforced absence from Petersburg spared him the punishment meted out to his Decembrist friends after their uprising in 1825. He was permitted to return to the capital in 1826 under the supervision of the tsar. From 1825 to 1831, at the height of his creative powers, Pushkin finished *Eugene Onegin*, wrote his best lyric verse, the historical poem "Poltava," the plays *Boris Godunov* and *The Little Tragedies*, and turned to prose in his *Tales of Belkin*. However, his marriage to a young featherbrain in 1831 signaled a decline in literary productivity and brought about his death. In 1837 he was shot dueling with one of his wife's too-ardent admirers; he died two days later.

The statue of Pushkin opposite is located on the grounds of the former lyceum at Tsarskoe Selo, where the student Pushkin achieved his first success as a poet and spent his happiest years. He was, as one of his schoolfellows wrote, "always without a penny, always in debt, often without even a decent evening suit, with constant scandals, frequent duels, intimately acquainted with all the innkeepers, procuresses, and harlots of Petersburg." Much less enjoyable were the three years Pushkin spent in exile in Kishinyov, a dusty garrison town in southwestern Russia; the house he lived in is shown in the engraving above. Below is a sketch drawn by Pushkin to illustrate one of the stories in his Tales of Belkin, *and at far right, above, is a portrait of Pushkin's wife, Natalya, whose seductive beauty attracted the attention of even the tsar, sending Pushkin into jealous fits of rage.*

The profile study of Pushkin (above) is one of the dozens of doodles that swarm over the poet's manuscripts: portraits of himself, his current flames, and his friends and enemies. At left is a palekh box illustrating Pushkin's prologue to his narrative poem Ruslan and Ludmila, which is set in the time of Prince Vladimir. In the prologue, which has been a favorite of Russian school children for generations, Pushkin sought to make his tale acceptable as actual legend by identifying his heroes and villains with those of Russian folklore, who surround him here as he sits beneath an oak tree at the seashore. His companion is a learned cat who sings and tells tales. Lurking behind them is a furry wood spirit, and up in the tree is a rusalka, an ondine who lures men to their death in streams and ponds. The figures on the right, from top to bottom, are: Baba Yaga, a witch who flies on a mortar and pestle; a magician, gloating over an underground cache of gold; and a young prince capturing a fearsome tsar. To the left, from top to bottom, are: a princess languishing in a tower guarded by a wolf; a wizard carrying a warrior through the air and people waiting below with nets; Baba Yaga's hut, which has neither doors nor windows and rests on chicken legs; and a troupe of brave knights and their leader seen emerging from the sea.

Flights
Of Fantasy

In Nikolai Gogol's life as in his work, the dividing line between reality and fantasy was often blurred by his hyperactive imagination and his paranoid habit of concocting tales about himself to deceive his family and friends. Thus it was difficult for many of his biographers to distinguish between Gogol's fanciful mirages and his authentic but sometimes equally bizarre actions.

Gogol was born in the Ukraine in 1809, the son of a petty landowner. In 1828 he left the provinces for St. Petersburg, hoping to become an actor or writer. Rejected by stage managers and derided by critics for his first book, a long poetic idyll, Gogol was ready to abandon his ambitions when, in 1831, a collection of his stories about the Ukraine proved a success and convinced him that his talents lay in writing prose.

On the surface, Gogol's life was uneventful, and there was little to distinguish him from the homely, sickly

188

clerks who peopled his stories. His puny physique, secretive manner, and sensitive ego put off many of his contemporaries. But his mind was full of fantasy, and when he read his works aloud he could transfix an audience.

With the success of each new work—three volumes of stories were published between 1832 and 1835—Gogol's fantasies began encroaching on his reason, prompting him to believe that he was the divinely appointed teacher of the Russian people. At the same time, he became increasingly sensitive to criticism. In 1836, to escape the furor created by his play *The Inspector General*, he fled to Rome, where he spent the next few years writing *Dead Souls*, the *Inferno* section of what he intended to be a Russian *Divine Comedy*. As his religious fervor grew, his literary powers dwindled. In 1852, after ten years' work on his *Purgatorio*, he burned the manuscript in despair. He died shortly afterward.

NIKOLAI GOGOL, *Nevsky Prospekt*

The pencil sketch of Gogol opposite was done in 1840, when the author's whimsical stories, Gothic tales, and satirical plays had brought him to the pinnacle of success. One of his best pieces, Nevsky Prospect, *concerns two young men who try to seduce the girls they meet on the famous St. Petersburg avenue. In the water color above, from a series of illustrations painted by Valentin Serov, one of the heroes, Pirogov, is shown dancing with his prey. The drawing at left, attributed to Gogol, portrays the last scene of* The Inspector General, *when the corrupt officials of a provincial town learn to their horror that the inspector has arrived.*

189

Of Life and Art

One of the philosophical issues preoccupying the intelligentsia of Russia and western Europe at the beginning of the 1800's was whether life imitated art, or art, life. Mikhail Lermontov, whom contemporaries considered the literary heir to Pushkin, embodied the issue. His life provided the substance and feelings for his poetry and prose, but on occasion, events in his work also anticipated events in his life. Both were full of Byronic romance and adventure, as well as skepticism and melancholy. He was himself one of the superfluous men of whom he wrote, the bitter drones whose young lives, once full of promise and idealism, were stifled by the bland and complacent atmosphere of Russia under Nicholas I. And his death in a duel eerily recreated a scene from his novel *A Hero of Our Times*.

Lermontov was born in 1814, and grew up under the tutelage of a doting grandmother, who did nothing to discourage his flourishing vanity. He began reading and writing verse when he was thirteen and adopted Byron as his hero. After briefly preparing for a literary career at Moscow University, he decided the soldier's life was more to his taste. He went to St. Petersburg, enlisted as a hussar, and gave himself up to the life of the young roué. Outraged by the news of Pushkin's death, Lermontov wrote a poem condemning the killer and the courtiers who had encouraged him. The poem brought him instant recognition for his poetic gifts, and his attacks on the court brought him the same punishment as Pushkin—exile to the Caucasus. He spent the next four years in varying degrees of disfavor with the government, alternating between stays in St. Petersburg and enforced military service in the Caucasus. It was there that he was killed in 1841, in a duel that he had provoked by his sarcasms.

Lermontov tried to conceal his reserved and shy nature by posing as a dashing, cynical man of the world, and he chose an army career in hopes of strengthening the illusion. The portrait at top, opposite, however, shows him in a sensitive, melancholy mood. Unlike Pushkin, he was unable to create spontaneously and labored long hours over his works. (His desk at his country estate is shown at left.) A gifted draftsman as well as a poet, Lermontov drew the sketches shown here. Mountain landscapes like the one above were his milieu during his exile in the Caucasus, and the sketch below may also have been inspired by his days at southern military posts.

191

The semi-autobiographical hero of Lermontov's
The Demon *is a fallen angel whose love for a
mortal maid drives him to despair, and the girl
to her death. In his declaration of love, the passage excerpted below, the demon unburdens his
melancholy soul. His portrait shown at right
is one of a series of illustrations for the poem
created c. 1890 by the Russian art nouveau
painter Mikhail Vrubel. The poem was also the
inspiration for an opera by Anton Rubinstein.*

I am one by all the living hated,
By whom all hope is desolated.
I am the scourge of men's defeat,
The bane of nature, God's enemy!
I am the lord of liberty
And thought! Behold me at your feet!
I bring to you my heart's confession,
And all my tender love and fears;
I bring my suffering and passion,
My first humility of tears.
O hear me, hear me with compassion!
By just a word you could restore
My life to heaven and to good;
Clad in your godlike love, I would
In brightness new appear before
The empyrean brotherhood. . . .
If you could only comprehend
This nameless bitterness of living
Age after age, this unforgiving
In joy or sorrow without end,—
For evil deeds no praise receiving,
And no reward for good! For ages
To lust for self and live a life
Of emptiness, in fields of strife
That never peace nor fame assuages!
To live with hate against my will,
All knowing, nothing yet desiring,
And nothing in the world admiring,
But hating ever deeper still! . . .
When God proclaimed my great
                          disgrace
And curse upon me, from that day
All things celestial turned away
From me and spurned my warm
                          embrace.

A Continental Gentleman

Turgenev, the dapper young aristocrat, is shown in the portrait opposite as he appeared in 1844, shortly before giving up a civil service career to devote himself entirely to literature. Above is the author's bed at the family estate south of Moscow —to which Turgenev returned between sojourns in western Europe. The two manuscript illustrations at right were done by Turgenev in Paris, to accompany descriptions of character types. At top is "an old teacher of French grammar and syntax.... Awkward, small-minded, passionately fond of snuff, a bore, but not bad at heart, loves making jokes in a pedantic fashion. Tall, stooping, hollow-chested.... Never leaves the house without his umbrella and always wears large green gloves." At bottom is the "important employee or important industrialist—lacking in invention and originality—but possessing authority, integrity, clarity.... Though his family is afraid of him, he is by no means ill-natured."

The first Russian novelist to achieve eminence in western Europe, Ivan Turgenev was noted for his urbanity and charm, admired for his literary talent, and much sought after by Europe's intellectuals. Among his friends were Henry James, George Sand, Gustave Flaubert, and Emile Zola. His position as a Russian gentleman (he was born in 1818 to a family of wealthy landowners) and his cosmopolitan education made him equally at home in Russia and Europe. He tended, however, to be charming and graceful among the French, but arrogant in the presence of Russians.

Sent to study abroad in 1838, Turgenev returned to Russia three years later and became caught up in the ferment then arising between Slavophiles and Westernizers. He allied himself with the latter, many of whom were his friends from student days. Serfdom was one of the social ills causing anguish to Turgenev and his contemporaries. His *Sportsman's Sketches*, published in 1852 under the guise of innocent pastoral vignettes, drew attention to the indignity and misery of the peasants' lives. It slipped past the censors and created a furor; later it was said to have influenced Alexander II in his decision to abolish serfdom in 1861.

Turgenev spent the latter part of his life in Europe drifting around in the wake of his only love, the soprano Pauline Viardot. Like his admirer Henry James, he wrote about his own country and people, even though separated from them. His novels published between 1856 and 1862—*Rudin, A Nest of Gentlefolk, On the Eve,* and *Fathers and Sons*— reflect the changing political climate in Russia, as their heroes progress from the ineffectual idealists of the 1840's to the revolutionaries of the 1860's. His later works are less topical and more retrospective in nature. He died in 1883, at Bougival on the Viardot estate near Paris.

I cannot tell you to what extent your opinion of *Fathers and Sons* has made me happy. It isn't a question of satisfying one's pride but in the assurance that you haven't made a mistake and haven't missed the mark, and that labor hasn't been wasted. That was the more important for me since people whom I trust very much . . . seriously advised me to throw my work into the fire—and only recently (but this is confidential) Pisemsky [a novelist and playwright] wrote me that Bazarov [the main character in the book] is a complete failure. How can one then not doubt oneself and be led astray? It is hard for an author *immediately* to feel to what extent his idea has come to life, and whether it is true, and whether he has mastered it, etc. In his own work he is lost in the woods.

Letter from Turgenev to Dostoevsky, March 18, 1862

Notes From the Underground

Few novelists have equaled Fedor Dostoevsky in penetrating the human psyche or portraying the tragic, and if insight was a natural gift, tragedy too was drawn from his own troubled life. Dostoevsky lived for sixty years (1821–81), during which the pain and affliction of many lifetimes were condensed into one. His first encounter with misfortune was the murder of his father, a gloomy, despotic man who took to drink after his wife's death, began brutally mistreating his serfs, and was killed by them. It was the elder Dostoevsky who served as model for the father in *The Brothers Karamazov*.

After his father's death, Dostoevsky's incipient epilepsy surfaced to haunt him until his death. Both Prince Myshkin in *The Idiot* and Smerdyakov in *The Brothers Karamazov* are epileptics. Similarly, material for *The House of the Dead*, an account of life in a prison camp, for *The Possessed*, a story of young revolutionaries, and for *Crime and Punishment* was gleaned from Dostoevsky's ordeals as a political prisoner and exile in Siberia.

Two women loved by Dostoevsky were the prototypes for heroines of his works. One was Maria Isaeva, a high-strung consumptive whom he courted and married while in Siberia; *The Eternal Husband* dramatizes their tormented relations. The other was Polina Suslova, a bluestocking of the 1860's, the original for Dostoevsky's "infernal women." His love and hate for her is described in *The Gambler*. She is also Nastasya Filippovna in *The Idiot* and Grushenka in *The Brothers Karamazov*.

It was not until late in his life that Dostoevsky found calm and ease. He had a happy second marriage, and the publication of *The Possessed* in 1873 brought him material comfort. By the time he died he was so admired that thirty thousand people attended his funeral.

"About this place, with its tattered population, its dirty, evil-smelling courtyards and many alleys, Raskolnikov loved to roam in his aimless wanderings." Thus is described, in Crime and Punishment, *the Haymarket in Petersburg, shown in the lithograph (c. 1840) opposite. The student Dostoevsky lived the same penniless existence, in the same surroundings, as his mad hero. The bust above graces Dostoevsky's grave.*

As a professional journalist Dostoevsky was used to meeting deadlines and was fascinated with news reports. He wrote his novels feverishly, sending them off chapter by chapter to impatient publishers who had advanced him money toward the completed work. The manuscript page above is from The Possessed, *a novel inspired by an actual event—the liquidation of a terrorist by his fellow conspirators, who were attempting to overthrow Alexander II. Shown opposite is Dostoevsky's desk in his Moscow home.*

Tolstoy at War And Peace

Tolstoy, lion-maned and messianic in the 1906 photograph reproduced on the opposite page, was born and lived most of his life at Yasnaya Polyana (meaning Clear Glade or Ash Glade, after the ash trees that grew there in abundance), the family estate one hundred and thirty miles south of Moscow. Above is the main house; below, the spartan bedroom Tolstoy adopted during his later years.

"No man is more worthy than he of the name of genius; more complicated, contradictory, great in everything—yes, yes, in everything." Thus wrote Maxim Gorky, reminiscing about Leo Tolstoy, and if the comment seems extreme, such was the nature of Tolstoy's life. For him mediocrity did not exist. His appetites were insatiable, his strength was herculean, and his moral conscience stringent. To convey his vision he needed to create literary canvases of monumental proportions.

Tolstoy's sensuality, his spirituality, and his keen intellect were constantly at war, buffeting him from one extreme to another—from debauchery to asceticism, from haughty arrogance to unaffected simplicity. His quest for moral and rational perfection drove him all his life. From the self-absorbed, pleasure-seeking scion of the Russian nobility, Tolstoy evolved into the ascetic prophet of nonviolence, having renounced his birthright, his literary glory, and his worldly joys. When he died in 1910 he was fleeing from his family, who he felt were destroying his spiritual progress.

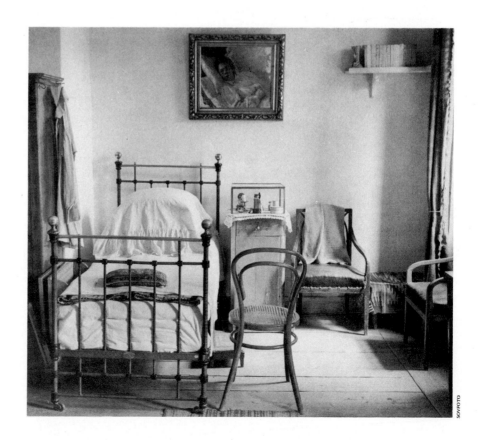

The habits, tastes, and values that Tolstoy acquired in his youth plagued him like demons for the rest of his life. Born in 1828 to an aristocratic family, Count Leo Nikolaevich Tolstoy reveled in the role of the young nobleman. He grew indolent, arrogant, and sensual, leaving the University of Kazan in 1847 because he was bored, being obsessed with behaving like the proper aristocrat, and going on frequent and riotous bouts of drinking and wenching, only to reprove himself remorsefully after each escapade. In 1851, repentant of his frivolous life and inspired by his older brother Nikolai, a dashing artillery officer, Tolstoy enlisted in the army and went off with him to fight rebellious tribesmen in the Caucasus. (The brothers are shown in the photograph at top, opposite, taken before their departure.) The fighting was sporadic, and during the frequent lulls Tolstoy wrote Childhood, *an autobiographical tale that was his first published work. A manuscript page is shown at right. He then transferred to Sevastopol, where he took part in some of the fiercest battles of the Crimean war. His impressions were recorded in the* Sevastopol Stories, *and provided him with material for the vivid battle scenes in* War and Peace, *such as that at Borodino, portrayed above. Opposite is a passage from the latter account.*

The battle began with a cannonade from several hundreds of guns on both sides. Then, when the whole plain was covered with smoke on the French side, the two divisions of Desaix and Compans advanced on the right upon the fleches, and on the left the viceroy's regiments advanced upon Borodino. . . . The soldiers of Desaix's division, advancing upon the fleches, were in sight until they disappeared from view in the hollow that lay between them and the fleches. As soon as they dropped down into the hollow, the smoke of the cannon and muskets on the fleches became so thick that it concealed the whole slope on that side of the hollow. Through the smoke could be caught glimpses of something black, probably men, and sometimes the gleam of bayonets. But whether they were stationary or moving, whether they were French or Russian, could not be seen. . . .

On the fleches themselves, occupied now together, now alternately by French and Russians, living, dead, and wounded, the frightened and frantic soldiers had no idea what they were doing. For several hours together, in the midst of incessant cannon and musket fire, the Russians and French, infantry and cavalry, had captured the place in turn; they rushed upon it, fell, fired, came into collision, did not know what to do with each other, screamed, and ran back again. . . .

In reality all these movements forward and back again hardly improved or affected the position of the troops. All their onslaughts on one another did little harm; the harm, the death and disablement was the work of the cannon balls and bullets, that were flying all about the open space, where those men ran to and fro. As soon as they got out of that exposed space, over which the balls and bullets were flying, their superior officer promptly formed them in good order, and restored discipline, and under the influence of that discipline led them back under fire again; and there again, under the influence of the terror of death, they lost all discipline, and dashed to and fro at the chance promptings of the crowd.

The battle of Borodino, as described in War and Peace

After his marriage in 1862, Tolstoy was at first content to spend his time managing his estates and writing, completing War and Peace *and* Anna Karenina *between 1865 and 1877. However, during the next three years his growing fear of death brought about a religious crisis. Thereafter he lived simply, doing manual labor, dressing in peasant clothes, and even making his own boots. The photographs below and at right show him attending a country fair and returning from a river swim. The sketches of Tolstoy mowing (left) were done in 1893 by the portraitist Leonid Pasternak, father of the writer Boris Pasternak and one of the many famous artists to visit Tolstoy's estate. Another visitor—and a frequent one—was Anton Chekhov, who is shown with Tolstoy in the photograph at far left, which dates from 1901.*

OVERLEAF: *The sage of Yasnaya Polyana entertains family and friends at a picnic, in this 1888 photograph. Tolstoy and his wife Sonya are seated at center, on either side of the samovar.*

7

The Golden Age

Writing from Pushkin to Tolstoy

When Peter the Great set about Westernizing Russian society in the early eighteenth century, he hoped for progress and cultural enlightenment. What he got was progress and cultural confusion. The new intelligentsia spawned by his social reforms indeed became familiar with Diderot and Leibnitz; but Russian translators who sought equivalents for foreign literary and technological terms often found themselves defeated by the limitations of their own written language—the ancient Church Slavonic. At least one of their number is known to have attempted suicide over the intricacies of French.

For the greater part of the century, Russian writers sought to create a language that would fix standards of usage for secular literature and accommodate nuances of style in odes, essays, and comedies that were being modeled after those of neoclassical writers such as Boileau and Racine. (Peter himself aided in this effort by devising a civil script to replace the traditional one used by the Church.) Finally, around 1790, there emerged a language that was more subtle, more flexible, and thus better suited to the needs of contemporary Russian writers.

In the meantime, another sort of written language had been developing among the less educated townspeople—a curious mixture of Church Slavonic and vernacular which

The giant of an age, Leo Tolstoy is portrayed (opposite) at work in the study of his home at Yasnaya Polyana. The painting, done in 1893, is one of many portraits of Tolstoy by his friend Ilya Repin.

had been improvised in the previous century to translate and imitate European tales of chivalry. After about 1750, when the volume of printed books increased considerably in Russia, these crudely written picaresques, or *povesti*, became more popular than ever. It was in these cavalier and ribald stories that techniques of narrative fiction were first used in Russian literature; and it was in this genre of plain speech that the vitality of Russian life was most clearly revealed.

A few aristocratic writers captured something of the same earthy spirit in satires and comic dramas. But it remained for a single brilliant writer of a later generation—a nobleman with a jester's sense of mischief—to combine elegance with common humor and produce a truly national literary style. That writer was Alexander Pushkin, whose "novels in verse" of the early 1820's inaugurated two classic decades of poetry and also laid the foundation for the realistic novel that was to dominate Russian literature for nearly the rest of the century. In Pushkin's poems, in Gogol's fantasies, in Turgenev's pastorales, in Dostoevsky's dark broodings, and in Tolstoy's monumental visions, the language found its golden age. And through all the literary battles that raged during this period of unusually intense social and political argument, the language itself remained a common source of pride.

Gogol put it this way, in a passage from his novel *Dead Souls*: "there is never a word which can be so sweeping, so boisterous, which would burst out so, from out the very heart, which would seethe so, and quiver and throb so much like a living thing, as an aptly uttered Russian word!"

Building a Language

Half a dozen Russian writers of the eighteenth and early nineteenth centuries stand out as forefathers of the golden age. Most were noblemen who cultivated European literary styles, though nearly all added touches of the vernacular. Still, linguistic traditions remained divided until the time of Pushkin.

Antiokh Kantemir

From SATIRE I: TO MY MIND (1750)

Translated by Harold B. Segel

Russia's first important modern writer typified the progressive nobleman, well educated and well traveled. In his chef-d'oeuvre, nine satires on various aspects of Russian culture, he often exchanged neoclassical rhetoric for spirited colloquialisms. Here he refers to the muses as "barefoot sisters" and invents names for types of cultural Philistines: Criton, a religious hypocrite; Silvan, a miserly landowner; Luka, a drunken sot; and Medor, a fop.

O unripe mind, brief learning's fruit, be still!
Do not compel my hand to take the quill.
One can, not writing all one's days, find fame
And not possess an author's wide acclaim.
In our time many easy paths lead there
On which bold steps can travel free of care.
Nine barefoot sisters traced the worst of all,
For many ere they reach it fail and fall. . . .
    "Schismatics, heretics are learning's sons;
The more one knows, the more the truth one shuns;
The bookworm into atheism tumbles,"
Thus, beads in hand, old Criton sighs and grumbles
And, pious soul, with bitter tears beseeks
To view what harm among us knowledge wreaks. . . .
    Now Silvan too finds fault with education
"Learning," he says, "just leads us to starvation.
We lived ere learning Latin well before,
Compared to now we had a great deal more.
In ignorance we reaped more grain; instead,
Now, learning foreign tongues, we've lost our bread. . . ."
    The red-faced Luka, belching thrice, declares:
"The brotherhood of man all learning tears.
God made us social creatures, and we own
The gift of reason not for us alone.
My hiding in a closet serves what ends
If for the dead I give up living friends? . . ."
    Medor complains that too much paper goes
On books and letters, and he thinks it shows
None will remain to twist up frizzled hair;
For Seneca no talcum would he spare. . . .
This is the talk that daily dins my ears—
Thus mind, I warn, be silent, heed my fears:
When work small profit holds, praise makes one care;
Without it—hearts are quick to know despair.

To suffer blame, not praise, how much the more!
Worse than a drunkard's having naught to pour,
Or priests not celebrating Holy Week,
Or merchants forced to guzzle beer too weak. . . .
    You'd be a bishop—then a cassock find;
Above, let striped chasuble bedeck
Your frame with pride; gold chain around your neck.
Head hide with cowl and belly with a beard,
And pompously have crutch before you steered;
Then stretched out in a handsome equipage
You bless to right and left, though heart a rage,
And in these signs all must the Shepherd know
And call you Father, with esteem bow low.
Of what use learning? Where the Church's gain?
While writing sermons, deeds aside are lain,
Which hurts the Church's income, and 'tis here
Its rights are based and its renown so dear.
    You'd be a judge? Then don a wig with bands,
Abuse the man who pleads with empty hands;
Let hardened heart see through the poor's despair;
Sleep, while the clerk reads briefs, upon your chair;
If one remind you of the civil laws,
Or people's rights, or natural law and cause,
Spit in his mug, tell him he's talking rot—
Impose on judges such a heavy lot! . . .
    The time's not come when wisdom shall preside
O'er all, and it alone awards decide,
And it alone to highest goals the way.
The golden age has not yet graced our day. . . .

Mikhail Lomonosov

From LETTER ON THE USE OF GLASS (1752)

Translated by Harold B. Segel

The son of a fisherman, Lomonosov became renowned both as a writer and as a scientist. He did more to modernize Russian poetry than any other writer of his time, and he set the first standards for a new literary language by compiling grammars that distinguished "Lofty," "Middle," and "Low" types of diction. It is thought that in this mock-epic letter written to his patron he was seeking permission to establish a factory for the manufacture of colored glassware.

They think unjustly about things, Shuvalov, who esteem
Glass less than Minerals which shine in the eyes with alluring

rays. There is no less use in it, no less beauty. I often leave the heights of Parnassus for it; but now I return to its summit and before you I sing praise, enraptured, not to precious stones, nor gold, but to Glass. And as I recall it in praise I do not present the frailty of false happiness—this should not serve as an example of perishability, for even a mighty fire, the common denominator of other earthly things, cannot devour it. Glass was born of it; fire is its parent.

. . . From pure Glass we drink wine and beer and see in it an example of guileless hearts: whom one can see through the Glass cannot really be a liar. In drinks Glass cannot conceal the mixture from us, and a clear conscience tears apart the rotten curtain of pretenses. . . .

Our short span of life on earth is filled with weaknesses. Man often falls into illness! He seeks help, and wishing to be saved from torment and to prolong his life he delivers himself into the hands of doctors. They can often give us comfort, knowing how to prescribe the proper medicines, medicines that they preserve and compound in Glass. . . .

When a violent storm raging in all its resilience hinders us with frost, man, not enduring great and severe change, hides himself behind thick walls. He would be forced to sit behind them without light or, trembling, suffer unbearable cold. But through Glass he lets in the rays of the sun and in this way repulses the cruelty of the cold. To be at one time open and closed, do we not call that creating miracles?

. . . Glass, in beads resembling pearls, is a favorite the whole world over. The people in the plains of the midnight sun adorn themselves with it. So does the Negro on southern shores. Simpletons, we hear, live in America who willingly give precious metal from a silver river to European merchants and take in exchange a countless quantity of beads. In this, I believe, they are wiser than we, for they drive from their eyes the cause of untold woes. They will never forget the times when their fathers fell slain for gold. Oh, what a terrible evil! For that did man go on perilous journeys across unknown seas; for that, having broken all the laws of nature, did he go about the whole world in frail ships; for that did he come to lovely shores to reveal himself a vicious enemy? . . .

After leaving innocence so trampled upon, the Castilians hurry home across the Ocean with their wealth, hoping at once to purchase all Europe with it. But it is impossible to calm the waves of the seas with gold. A storm akin to their own hearts in violence shook the depths and put an end to their lives and barbarism. . . . From evil, evil has been born! Was Glass the cause of such misfortunes! Not at all! Everywhere it delights the spirit, useful to the young and helpful to the old. . . .

Gavriila Derzhavin

INVITATION TO DINNER (1798)

Translated by Harold B. Segel

The favorite poet of Catherine the Great, Derzhavin flouted convention by writing neoclassical odes in a light, offhand style. He wrote this "invitation" to the same Count Shuvalov who had been Lomonosov's patron forty years earlier. ("Kaimak," in the first stanza, is a Turkish-derived name for a cream served with borsht.)

Gold sturgeon from the river Sheksna,
Kaimak and borsht already wait;
Shining with ice, reflecting crystal,
Wines in carafes and punch allure.
Perfuming pans diffuse aromas,
Fruits gaily laugh among the baskets.
The servants cannot catch their breath
Awaiting you about the table.
The hostess, dignified and youthful,
Is set to take you by the hand.

I beg you come, old benefactor,
Doer of good for twenty years!
Come grace my home now with a visit.
Although by no means elegant
And without sculpture, gold, or silver—
Its wealth is pleasantness and neatness
And my firm, honest character.
Come rest yourself from your affairs,
Eat, drink, enjoy yourself a little,
Fear nothing harmful to your health.

Not prominence, nor rank, nor favor
But kindliness alone I asked
To come to my plain Russian dinner,
And whosoever does me harm
Will be no witness to this party.
You guardian angel, benefactor,
Come on—enjoy the good things here,
And let the hostile spirits vanish;
No ill-intentioned step shall darken
The threshold of my humble home.

I dedicate this day to friendship,
To friendship and to beauty too.
I can esteem the worth of others,
And life I know is but a shade;
That we no sooner pass our youthhood
Than to old age we come already
And Death peers at us through a fence.
Alas!—How not to stop and ponder,
For once not covering all with flowers,
Forsaking not a somber look?

I have been privy to the secret
That even kings are sometimes sad;
That day and night they are tormented,
Though others have peace thanks to them.
Although he may have fame and glory,
But oh!—is the throne always pleasant
To one whose life is spent in care,
Whom treachery and downfall threaten?
How that poor sentinel is piteous
Who stands his hours eternally!

And so, as long as nasty weather
Does not cast gloom o'er cloudy days,
And Lady Fortune keeps caressing
And fondling us with tender hand;
As long as frosts are not yet with us
And roses have perfumed the gardens,
Let us not tarry to their scent.
Yes! Let us then delight in living
And take our comforts as we get them—
The cloth says how the coat is cut.

And should it be that you or others
Of the nice guests I've summoned here,
Prefer instead the golden chambers
Or honeyed victuals of kings,
Give up the thought of dining with me,
And pay heed to my explanation:
Bliss lies not in porphyry rays,
Nor in food's taste, or tender converse;
But in good health and peace of spirit—
The finest feast is temperance.

Denis Fonvizin

From THE MINOR (1782)

Translated by Leo Wiener

Nicknamed "the Vulture" for the caustic wit he displayed in the salons of St. Petersburg, Fonvizin unremittingly satirized the crudities of the rural gentry. The Minor, studded with lively dialogue, was his masterpiece and the first great realistic Russian comedy.

ACT I, SCENE 1. *Mrs. Uncouth, Mitrofan [her son], Eremyeevna [Mitrofan's nurse]*

MRS. UNCOUTH (*examining Mitrofan's caftan*). The caftan is all ruined. Eremyeevna, bring here that thief Trishka! (*Exit Eremyeevna.*) That rascal has made it too tight all around. Mitrofan, my sweet darling, you must feel dreadfully uncomfortable in your caftan! Go call father. (*Exit Mitrofan.*)

SCENE 2. *Mrs. Uncouth, Eremyeevna, Trishka [a tailor]*

MRS. UNCOUTH (*to Trishka*). You beast, come here. Didn't I tell you, you thief's snout, to make the caftan wide enough? In the first place, the child is growing; in the second place, the child is delicate enough, without wearing a tight caftan. Tell me, you clod, what is your excuse?

TRISHKA. You know, madam, I never learned tailoring. I begged you then to give it to a tailor.

MRS. UNCOUTH. So you have got to be a tailor to be able to make a decent caftan! What beastly reasoning!

TRISHKA. But a tailor has learned how to do it, madam, and I haven't.

MRS. UNCOUTH. How dare you contradict me! One tailor has learned it from another; that one from a third, and so on. But from whom did the first tailor learn? Talk, stupid!

TRISHKA. I guess the first tailor made a worse caftan than I.

MITROFAN (*running in*). I called dad. He sent word he'll be here in a minute.

MRS. UNCOUTH. Go fetch him by force, if you can't by kindness.

MITROFAN. Here is dad.

SCENE 3. *The same and [Mr.] Uncouth*

MRS. UNCOUTH. You have been hiding from me! Now see yourself, sir, what I have come to through your indulgence! What do you think of our son's new dress for his uncle's betrothal? What do you think of the caftan that Trishka has gotten up?

UNCOUTH (*timidly stammering*). A li-ittle baggy.

MRS. UNCOUTH. You are baggy yourself, you wiseacre!

UNCOUTH. I thought, wifey, that you thought that way.

MRS. UNCOUTH. Are you blind yourself?

UNCOUTH. My eyes see nothing by the side of yours.

MRS. UNCOUTH. A fine husband the Lord has blessed me with! He can't even make out what is loose and what tight.

UNCOUTH. I have always relied upon you in such matters, and rely even now.

MRS. UNCOUTH. You may rely also upon this, that I will not let the churls do as they please. Go right away, sir, and tell them to flog——

SCENE 4. *The same and Beastly [Mrs. Uncouth's brother]*

BEASTLY. Whom? For what? On the day of my betrothal! I beg you, sister, for the sake of the celebration, put off the flogging until to-morrow, and to-morrow, if you wish, I'll gladly take a hand in it myself. My name is not Taras Beastly, if I don't make every offence a serious matter. In such things my custom is the same as yours, sister. But what has made you so angry?

MRS. UNCOUTH. Here, brother, I'll leave it to you. Mitrofan, just come here! Is this caftan baggy?

BEASTLY. No.

UNCOUTH. I see now myself, wifey, that it is too tight.

BEASTLY. But I don't see that. My good fellow, the caftan is just right.

MRS. UNCOUTH (*to Trishka*). Get out, you beast! (*To Eremyeevna.*) Go, Eremyeevna, and give the child his breakfast. I am afraid the teachers will soon be here.

EREMYEEVNA. My lady, he has deigned to eat five rolls ere this.

MRS. UNCOUTH. So you are too stingy to give him the sixth, you beast? What zeal! I declare!

EREMYEEVNA. I meant it for his health, my lady. I am looking out for Mitrofan Terentevich: he has been ill all night.

MRS. UNCOUTH. Oh, Holy Virgin! What was the matter with you, darling Mitrofan?

MITROFAN. I don't know what, mamma. I was bent with pain ever since last night's supper.

BEASTLY. . . . I guess you have had too solid a supper.

MITROFAN. Why, uncle! I have eaten hardly anything.

UNCOUTH. If I remember rightly, my dear, you did have something.

MITROFAN. Not much of anything: some three slices of salt bacon, and five or six pies, I do not remember which.

EREMYEEVNA. He kept on begging for something to drink all night long. He deigned to empty a pitcher of kvas.

MITROFAN. And even now I am walking around distracted. All kinds of stuff passed before my eyes all night long.

MRS. UNCOUTH. What kind of stuff, darling Mitrofan?

MITROFAN. At times you, mamma, at others—dad.

MRS. UNCOUTH. How so?

MITROFAN. No sooner did I close my eyes, than I saw you, mamma, drubbing dad.

UNCOUTH (aside). It is my misfortune, the dream has come to pass!

MITROFAN (tenderly). And I felt so sorry.

MRS. UNCOUTH (angrily). For whom, Mitrofan?

MITROFAN. For you, mamma: you got so tired drubbing dad.

MRS. UNCOUTH. Embrace me, darling of my heart! Son, you are my comfort. . . .

Nikolai Karamzin

From LETTERS OF A
RUSSIAN TRAVELLER (1791–92)

Translated by Leo Wiener

By ignoring hundreds of Slavonic expressions and introducing current French ones, Karamzin gave the new literary language its final polishing of the century. The cosmopolitan charm and elegance of his travel notes—which he published in his own Moscow monthly review—made him the most fashionable Russian writer of the time.

London, September, 1790

There was a time, when I had hardly seen any Englishmen, when I went into ecstasy over them, and imagined England to be of all countries the most agreeable to my heart. . . . If I am not mistaken, novels were the chief foundation for this opinion. Now I see the English at close range, and I . . . praise them, but my praise is as cold as they themselves are.

Above all, I should not like to pass my life in England on account of its damp, gloomy, sombre climate. I know that one may be happy even in Siberia when the heart is satisfied and joyful, but a cheerful climate makes us more cheerful, and here one feels, in a fit of pining and melancholy, more than elsewhere like committing suicide. The groves, parks, fields, gardens—all that is beautiful in England; but it is all covered with fogs, darkness, and coal smoke. The sun rarely peeps through, and then only for a short time; but without it life upon earth is not a pleasure. . . . How, then, can an Englishman keep himself from looking like September?

In the second place, their cold natures do not please me in the least. "It is a snow-covered volcano," a French emigrant said of them smilingly to me. But I stand, watch, see no flame, and meanwhile freeze. My Russian heart loves to bubble in a sincere, lively conversation, loves the play of the eyes, the rapid changes of the face, the expressive motion of the hands. The Englishman is reticent, indifferent, and speaks as he reads, without ever expressing those sudden mental convulsions that electrify our whole physical system. They say he is profounder than others. Is it not rather that he *seems* profounder? Is it not because his thick blood moves more slowly in him, and gives him the aspect of being deep in thoughts, though he often has none? . . .

Ivan Krylov

THE QUARTET (c. 1815)

Translated by Bernard Pares

For years a struggling playwright and journalist, Krylov achieved fame as a writer of fables—which, by the beginning of the nineteenth century, had become a national craze. Whatever their allegories, his antic tales reflect a simple middle-class philosophy that expresses little regard for intellectualism or for inaptitude.

The tricksome little monkey.
The goat with tangled hair,
The donkey,
And the clumsy-fingered bear
A great quartet had planned to start;
They got the notes, viola, fiddles, bass,
And sat beneath a lime-tree, on the grass,
To charm creation with their art.
They struck the sounding strings; what discord, oh, my heart!
"Stop, boys," cries little Monkey, "wait a bit;
It can't go right like that; you don't know how to sit!
You face viola, Bear, with your bassoon;
First fiddle faces second; then, you'll see,
We'll play to quite another tune
And make the hills and forest dance for glee."
They change their places, start again;
Yet all attempts at tune are vain.
"Here, stop!" says Donkey, "I'll explain.
I'm sure we'll make it go
By sitting in a row."
The donkey's plan they tried,
Of sitting side by side;
But did it answer? No.
Why, only all the worse they got entangled,
And all the more they wrangled,
Of where to sit and why.
Attracted to the noise, a nightingale came by.
To him they all appeal to show them what's the way:
"Have patience with us, please," they say,
"We're trying a quartet, which will not go a bit;
We've notes, we've instruments; do tell us how to sit!"
The nightingale replies: "To sit is not enough.
Besides, my friends, your ears are much too rough.
Then change your seats, and fiddles too:
Yet chamber music's not for you!"

Pushkin and His Era

Having inherited a literary tradition divided between popular and elite tastes, Alexander Pushkin created a style of writing in the 1820's that gained wide appeal in Russia. A master of both neoclassical rhetoric and the Russian idiom, he developed a kind of poetry in which descriptive detail replaced lofty metaphor and in which sound and sense were skillfully united. Through his genius and the efforts of his successors, Mikhail Lermontov and Fedor Tyutchev, poetry dominated Russian literature for the better part of two decades.

Alexander Pushkin

From EUGENE ONEGIN (1825–33)

Translated by Walter Arndt

In his most famous work, Pushkin used the Byronic "tale in verse" to create his own hybrid of poem and novel: a story of a young aristocrat and his friends, told in a combination of character sketches, descriptions of Russian life, and philosophical ramblings— all woven on a rigid structure of four hundred sonnet-length stanzas and an intricate rhyme scheme. The first "chapter," which was written in 1823, delineates the fast, dandyish sort of life that Pushkin himself led during his early twenties in St. Petersburg.

Eugene's attainments were far vaster
Than I can take the time to show,
But where he really was a master,
Where he knew all there is to know,
What early meant in equal measure
His toil, his torment, and his pleasure,
What occupied at every phase
The leisured languor of his days,
Was the pursuit of that Fair Passion
Which Ovid sang, and for its sake
Was doomed to drain, in mutinous ache,
His glittering life's remaining ration
'Mid dear Moldavia's cloddish loam,
Far from his dear Italian home.

He learnt so early how to languish,
To reassure, compel belief,
Dissemble hope, feign jealous anguish,
Appear morose or sunk in grief,
To seem now proud and now obedient,
Cool or attentive, as expedient!
How dull he could be, with intent,
How passionately eloquent,
How casual-warm a letter-sender!
One goal in mind, one seeking most
How utterly he was engrossed!

How swift his glance was and how
                              tender,
Bold-shy, and when the time was here,
Aglitter with obedient tear!

Forever new and interesting,
He scared with ready-made despair,
Amazed the innocent with jesting,
With flattery amused the fair,
Seized the chance instant of compliance
To sway ingenuous youth's defiance
By ardor or astute finesse,
Lure the spontaneous caress,
Implore, nay, force a declaration,
Ambush the first-note of the heart,
Flush Love from cover, and then dart
To fix a secret assignation . . .
And after that, to educate
His prey in private tête-à-tête!

How soon he even set aflutter
Inveterate flirts' well-seasoned hearts!
What ruthless scandal could he utter,
Once he resolved with poisoned darts
To bring about a rival's ruin!
What snares he laid for his undoing!
Yet you, blithe husbands, by Fate's
                              whim
Remain on friendly terms with him:
Him of all men the shrewd spouse
                              fawns on,
Post-graduate of Faublas' old school,
And the most skeptical old fool
And the bombastic ass with horns on,
Contented ever with his life,
Himself, his dinner, and his wife.

The social notes are brought in gently,
While he is rising, or before.

What—invitations? Evidently,
Three for a single night, what's more,
A ball here, there a children's party;
Which will he skip to, our young hearty?
Which take up first now, let us see . . .
No matter—he can do all three.
Meanwhile there's boulevard parading;
Eugene, in faultless morning trim
And *Bolivar* with ample brim,
Drives out and joins the promenading,
Till the repeater's watchful peal
Recalls him to the midday meal.

Nightfall; the sleigh receives him.
                              Listen:
He's off with shouts of "way—away!"
His beaver collar starts to glisten
With hoarfrost dusting silver-gray.
On to Talon's, pace unabating,
Kaverin will no doubt be waiting.
He enters: corks begin to fly,
The Comet's vintage gushes high,
Here roast beef oozes bloody juices,
And near that flower of French cuisine,
The truffle, youth's delight, is seen
The deathless pie Strasbourg produces,
Mid Limburger's aroma bold
And the pineapple's luscious gold.

Their thirst for yet more goblets clamors
To douse the sizzling cutlet grease,
But the repeater's jingling hammers
Bid them to the new ballet piece.
The stage's arbiter exacting,
Who to the charming queens of acting
His fervent, fickle worship brings
Established freeman of the wings,
Eugene, of course, must not be missing
Where everyone without *faux pas*

Is free to cheer an *entrechat*,
Jeer Cleopatra, Phedre, with hissing,
Call out Moina (in a word,
Make sure that he is seen and heard).…

The house is full, the boxes gleaming,
Orchestra, pit, all is astir,
Impatient clapping from the teeming
Gallery—then the curtain's whir.
There stands ashimmer, half ethereal,
Obedient to the imperial
Musician's wand, amid her corps
Of nymphs, Istomina—to the floor
Touching one foot, the other shaping
A slow-drawn circle, then—surprise—
A sudden leap, and away she flies
Like down from Aeol's lip escaping,
Bends and unbends to rapid beat
And twirling trills her tiny feet.

Applause all round. Onegin enters,
Walks over toes along his row.
His double spyglass swoops and centers
On box-seat belles he does not know.
All tiers his scrutiny embraces,
He saw it all: the gowns and faces
Seemed clearly to offend his sight;
He traded bows on left and right
With gentlemen, at length conceded
An absent gaze at the ballet,
Then with a yawn he turned away.
And spoke: "In all things change is
                              needed;
On me ballets have lost their hold;
Didelot himself now leaves me cold."

While yet the cupids, devils, monkeys
Behind the footlights prance and swoop;
While yet the tired tribe of flunkies
Sleep on their furs around the stoop;
While yet they have not finished clapping,
Nose-blowing, coughing, hissing, tapping;
While yet the lanterns everywhere
Inside and outside shed their glare;
While yet chilled horses yank the tether
And harness-weary champ the bit,
And coachmen round the fires sit,
And, cursing, beat their palms together:
Onegin has already gone
To put his evening costume on.

Oh, will it be within my powers
To conjure up the private den
Where Fashion's acolyte spent hours
To dress, undress, and dress again?
What London makes for cultured whimsy
Of novelties polite and flimsy,
And ships upon the Baltic brine

To us for tallow and for pine,
All that Parisian modish passion
And earnest industry collect
To tempt the taste of the elect
With comfort and caress of fashion,
Adorned the boudoir of our green
Philosopher at age eighteen.

Bronze-work and china on the table
An ambered hookah from Stambul,
Spirits in crystal bottles, able
To soothe the brow with scented cool;
Steel files and little combs unending,
And scissors straight and scissors bending,
And brushes—recollection fails—
For hair and teeth and fingernails.
Rousseau—please pardon this digression—
Could not conceive how solemn Grimm
Dared clean his nails in front of *him*,
Great bard of silver-tongued obsession.
Our champion of Man's liberties
Here surely was too hard to please!

One can be capable and moral
With manicure upon one's mind:
Why vainly chide one's age and quarrel?
Custom is lord of all mankind.
Chadayev-like, Eugene was zealous,
Forestalling censure by the jealous,
To shun the least sartorial flaws—
A *swell*, as the expression was.
He used to squander many an hour
Before the mirrors in his room,
Until he issued forth abloom
Like playful Venus from her bower,
When in a man's disguise arrayed,
The goddess joins a masquerade.

AN ONEGIN GLOSSARY

Faublas   a roué, the hero of an eight-
eenth-century French novel
Bolivar   a black silk top hat
Talon   a well-known restaurateur
Kaverin   an officer of the Hussars and
a friend of Pushkin
Comet's vintage a champagne of 1811, a
year in which a comet appeared
Istomina a Russian ballerina
Didelot a celebrated French choreog-
rapher living in Russia
Grimm Frédéric-Melchior Grimm, a
Parisian journalist and confi-
dant of Catherine the Great
Chadayev a foppish friend of Pushkin
pantalons trousers
gilet waistcoat
frack dress coat

Now that this modish apparition
Has drawn your casual interest,
With the discerning world's permission,
I might describe how he was dressed;
I'd do it not without compunction;
Still, to describe is my true function—
But *pantalons, gilet* and *frack*—
With such words Russian has no truck,
For as it is, I keep inviting
Your censure for the way I use
Outlandish words of many hues
To deck my humble style of writing,
Although I used to draw upon
The Academic Lexicon.

But never mind this—we must hurry,
For while extraneous themes I broach,
Onegin in a headlong flurry
Drives to the ball by hired coach;
Along the housefronts past him speeding,
Down streets aslumber, fast receding,
The double carriage lanterns bright
Shed their exhilarating light
And brush the snow with rainbow flutters;
With sparkling lampions, row on row,
The splendid mansion stands aglow;
In shadow-play across the shutters
Flit profile heads of demoiselles
And fashionably well-groomed swells.

Now he has reached the frontal fareway,
Flashed past the stately doorman, and,
Pausing atop the marble stairway
To touch his hair up with his hand,
He enters. The great hall is swarming,

The band benumbed by its own storming,
In hum and hubbub, tightly pent,
The crowd's on the Mazurka bent;
Spurs ring, sparks glint from
          guardsmen's shoulders,
Belles' shapely feet and ankles sleek
Whirl by, and in their passing wreak
Much flaming havoc on beholders,
And fiddle music skirls and drowns
Sharp gibes of wives in modish gowns.

When ardent dreams and dissipations
Were with me still, I worshiped balls:
No safer place for declarations,
Or to deliver tender scrawls.
Beware, you estimable spouses,
Look to the honor of your houses!
I wish you well, and so here goes
An earnest word from one who knows . . .
And you, Mamas of daughters, leaven
Your wits and shelter well your pets,
Keep straight and polished your
          lorgnettes!
Or else . . . or else, oh, gracious Heaven!

Such sound advice comes to my tongue
Because I haven't sinned so long.

I burnt so much of life's brief candle
In levity I now regret!
Still, balls—but for the moral scandal
They breed, I should adore them yet.
I thrill to ardent youth's outpouring,
The crush and blaze, the spirit's soaring,
Those beauties artfully arrayed;
I love their feet—though I'm afraid
Throughout our land you won't discover
Three pairs of shapely female feet.
Ah—one I long could not delete
From memory . . . and still they hover,
Burnt-out and sad as I may be,
About my dreams and trouble me. . . .

But what about Onegin? Nodding,
He's driven homeward from the ball,
While drumbeats have long since been
          prodding
To life the strenuous capital.
The peddler struts, the merchant dresses,

The cabman to the market presses,
With jars the nimble milkmaids go,
Their footsteps crunching in the snow.
The cheerful morning sounds and hustles
Begin, shops open, stacks have puffed
Tall trunks of slate-blue smoke aloft;
The baker, punctual German, bustles
White-capped behind his service hatch
And more than once has worked the latch.

But, worn-out by the ballroom's clamor,
And making midnight out of dawn,
The child of luxury and glamor
Sleeps tight, in blissful shade withdrawn.
At noon or so he wakes—already
Booked up till next dawn, in a steady
Motley routine of ceaseless play:
Tomorrow will be like Today.
In youth's bloom, free of prohibition,
With brilliant conquests to his name,
Each day a feast, his life a game,
Was he content with his condition?
Or was he hearty and inane
Amid carousals—but in vain? . . .

From TSAR NIKITA AND HIS FORTY DAUGHTERS (written 1822)

Translated by Walter Arndt

*A relatively unknown facet of Pushkin's
art is his bawdy verse. "Tsar Nikita" is but
one of a score of poems in which vitality
spills over into eroticism and sensuality.*

Tsar Nikita once reigned widely,
Richly, merrily, and idly,
Did no good or evil thing:
So his realm was flourishing.
He kept clear of toil and bother,
Ate and drank and praised our Father.
With some ladies he had squired
Forty daughters had he sired,
Forty maids with charming faces,
Four times ten celestial graces,
Sweet of temper, full of love.

Ah, what ankles, Heaven above!
Chestnut curls, the heart rejoices,
Eyes—a marvel, wondrous voices,
Minds—enough to lose your mind:
All from head to toe designed
To beguile one's heart and spirit;
There was but a sole demerit.
Oh? What fault was there to find?
None to speak of, never mind.
Or at most the merest tittle.
Still, a flaw (though very little).
How explain it, how disguise
So as not to scandalize
That cantankerous old drip,
Sanctimonious Censorship?
Help me, Muse—your poet begs!

Well—between the lassies' legs . . .
Stop! Already too explicit,
Too immodest, quite illicit . . .
Indirection here is best:
Aphrodite's lovely breast,
Lips, and feet set hearts afire,
But the focus of desire,
Dreamed-of goal of sense and touch,
What is that? Oh, nothing much.
Well then, it was this in fact
That the royal lassies lacked. . . .
All the nation when it heard
Ah'ed and oh'ed at such an earful,
Gaped and gasped, amazed and fearful;
Some guffawed, but most were leerier:
(This could land you in Siberia!) . . .

ELEGY (written c. 1829)

Translated by Maurice Baring

*Pushkin's short lyric poems often best dis-
play the textural beauty of his verse style
and its flexibility in evoking different moods.*

As leaden as the aftermath of wine
Is the dead mirth of my delirious days;
And as wine waxes strong with age, so
          weighs

More heavily the past on my decline.
My path is dim. The future's troubled
          sea
Foretokens only toil and grief to me.
But oh! my friends, I do not ask to die!
I crave more life, more dreams, more
          agony!
Midmost the care, the panic, the distress,

I know that I shall taste of happiness.
Once more I shall be drunk on strains
          divine
Be moved to tears by musings that are
          mine;
And haply when the last sad hour draws
          nigh,
Love with a farewell smile may gild the sky.

Mikhail Lermontov

From THE DEMON (written 1829–39)

Translated by Nadine Jarintzov

Fifteen years younger than Pushkin, Lermontov modeled his early verse after Byron and his life after Don Juan. "The Demon" was one of the most popular poems in Russia.

And over the Caucasian ranges
Flew the exile from Paradise;
Beneath, Kazbek, like diamond's edges,
Flashed its eternal snow and ice;
Black as a creviced den confining
A serpent, deep below ran twining
The narrow chasm of Daryal;

And down its way, like lion roaring,
There leapt the stream of Terek, foaming,
With a frayed main along its back.
Both mountain beast and soaring eagle
Circling against the azure sky
Harked to the calling of the waters;
And golden clouds, due north, all day
Flew rapidly along its way
From far-off southern countries roaming.
And closely crowding gloomy rocks,
Mysteriously still and pensive,
Inclined their heads with snowy locks,

Watching the flickering waves, attentive.
And castle-towers on the cliffs
Scowled with dark menace through the
                hazes—
The giants, there to dominate
Where Caucasus its gateway raises!
Both wild and glorious was the world
Around him; but the haughty ghost
Contemptuously cast a glance
On the creations of his Lord,
And naught of what he saw or thought
Reflected in his countenance.

THE TESTAMENT (1840)

Translated by Maurice Baring

I want to be alone with you,
A moment quite alone.
The minutes left to me are few,
They say I'll soon be gone.
And you are going home on leave,
Then say . . . but why? I do believe
There's not a soul who'll greatly care
To hear about me over there.

And yet if someone questions you,
Whoever it may be,—
Tell them a bullet hit me through

The chest,—and did for me.
And say I died, and for the Tsar,
And say what fools the doctors are:—
And that I shook you by the hand,
And spoke about my native land.

My father and my mother, both,
By now are surely dead—
To tell the truth, I would be loth
To send them tears to shed.
If one of them is living, say

I'm bad at writing home, and they
Have told the regiment to pack,—
And that I shan't be coming back.

We had a neighbor, as you know,
And you remember I
And she. . . . How very long ago
It is we said good-bye!
She won't ask after me, nor care,
But tell her ev'rything, don't spare
Her empty heart; and let her cry;—
To her it doesn't signify.

Fedor Tyutchev

SILENTIUM (written 1833)

Translated by Babette Deutsch

Tyutchev's verse first appeared in quarterlies in the 1830's, but his literary importance was not recognized until two decades later.

Be silent, private, and conceal
What you may fancy or may feel.
Within your soul your dreams should rise
And set as the stars in the skies

How soundlessly follow their route.
Behold, admire them, and be mute.

How can a heart at will unfold
Its secret? Who will grasp, if told,
Whatever you are living by?
Spoken, a thought becomes a lie.
The springs men force they but pollute.

Drink of those waters, and be mute.

Within yourself learn how to live;
A world of thoughts not fugitive
Is there: mysterious, spellbound,
That worldly clamor will have drowned,
Dispersed by the day they dispute;
Heed that hushed music, and be mute.

A Tale of Superfluous Men

In 1829 a fad developed in Russia for the romantic novel, inspired principally by the Waverley Novels of Sir Walter Scott. Within a decade, the novel had become entrenched as the dominant form in the national literature, and its subject matter had changed from imaginary exploits in exotic lands to the very real social problems in Russia itself. A theme that recurred frequently in the new novel was the "superfluous" nobleman of Pushkin's generation—the kind of monarchist who had proved to be ineffectual in leading the country through social reform, and whose blasé spirit incurred the contempt of idealistic youth. Pushkin's own Eugene Onegin was such a man; and so was the corrupt Pechorin of A Hero of Our Times, *one of the earliest of the "psychological" Russian novels.*

Mikhail Lermontov

From A HERO OF OUR TIMES (1840)

Translated by Vladimir Nabokov

The tragic hero of Lermontov's novel is a young officer who has become bored with life and cynical toward everyone, yet who is still capable of passion and generosity. In this selection from his "journals"—which comprise three of the novel's five stories—Pechorin describes his malevolent seduction of Mary, a young princess, in a Caucasian spa; his indifference toward Vera, the woman who loves him; and his cold-hearted manipulation of his friend Grushnitski.

May 29th

During all these days, I never once departed from my system. The young princess begins to like my conversation. I told her some of the strange occurrences in my life, and she begins to see in me an extraordinary person. I laugh at everything in the world, especially at feelings: this is beginning to frighten her. In my presence she does not dare to launch upon sentimental debates with Grushnitski, and has several times already replied to his sallies with a mocking smile; but every time that Grushnitski comes up to her, I assume a humble air and leave them alone together. The first time she was glad of it or tried to make it seem so; the second time she became cross with me; the third time she became cross with Grushnitski.

"You have very little vanity!" she said to me yesterday. "Why do you think that I have more fun with Grushnitski?"

I answered that I was sacrificing to a pal's happiness, my own pleasure.

"And mine," she added.

I looked at her intently and assumed a serious air. After this, I did not say another word to her all day. In the evening, she was pensive, this morning, at the well, she was more pensive still. When I went up to her, she was absently listening to Grushnitski, who, it seems, was being rhapsodical about nature; but as soon as she saw me, she began to laugh (very much *mal à propos*), pretending not to notice me. I walked off some distance and stealthily watched her; she turned away from her interlocutor and yawned twice. Decidedly, Grushnitski has begun to bore her. I shall not speak to her for two more days.

June 3rd

I often wonder, why I do so stubbornly try to gain the love of a little maiden whom I do not wish to seduce, and whom I shall never marry? Why this feminine coquetry? Vera loves me more than Princess Mary will ever love anyone: if she had seemed to me to be an unconquerable belle, then perhaps I might have been fascinated by the difficulty of the enterprise.

But it is nothing of the sort! Consequently, this is not that restless need for love that torments us in the first years of youth, and drives us from one woman to another, until we find one who cannot abide us: and here begins our constancy—that true, infinite passion, which can be mathematically expressed by means of a line falling from a given point into space: the secret of that infinity lies solely in the impossibility of reaching a goal. . . .

Why then do I take all this trouble? Because I envy Grushnitski? Poor thing! He has not earned it at all. Or is it the outcome of that nasty but unconquerable feeling which urges us to destroy the sweet delusions of a fellow man, in order to have the petty satisfaction of saying to him, when he asks in despair, what is it he should believe:

"My friend, the same thing happened to me, and still, you see, I dine, I sup, I sleep in perfect peace, and hope to be able to die without cries and tears."

And then again . . . there is boundless delight in the possession of a young, barely unfolded soul! It is like a flower whose best fragrance emanates to meet the first ray of the sun. It should be plucked that very minute and after inhaling one's fill of it, one should throw it away on the road: perchance, someone will pick it up! I feel in myself this insatiable avidity, which engulfs everything met on the way. I look upon the sufferings and joys of others only in relation to myself as on the food sustaining the strength of my soul. I am no longer capable myself of frenzy under the influence of passion: ambition with me has been suppressed by circumstances, but it has manifested itself in another form, since ambition is nothing else than thirst for power, and my main pleasure—which is to subjugate to my will all that surrounds me, and to excite the emotions of love, devotion, and fear in relation to me—is it not the main sign and greatest triumph of power? To be to somebody the cause of sufferings and joys, without having any positive right to it—is this not the sweetest possible nourishment for our pride? And what is happiness? Sated pride. If I considered myself to be better and more powerful than anyone in the world, I would be happy; if everybody loved me, I would find in myself infinite sources of love. Evil begets evil: the first ache gives us an idea of the pleasure of tormenting another. The idea of evil cannot enter a person's head without his wanting to apply it to reality: ideas are organic creations. Someone has said that their very birth endows them with a form, and this form is action; he in whose head more ideas have been born is more active than others. This is why a genius chained to an office desk must die or go mad. . . .

The passions are nothing else but ideas in their first phase of development; they are an attribute of the youth of the heart; and he is a fool who thinks he will be agitated by them all his life. Many a calm river begins as a turbulent waterfall, yet none hurtles and foams all the way to the sea. But that calm is often the sign of great, though concealed, strength; the plenitude and depth of feelings and thoughts does not tolerate frantic surgings; the soul, while experiencing pain or pleasure, gives itself a strict account of everything and becomes convinced that so it must be; it knows that without storms, a constantly torrid sun will wither it. . . .

On re-reading this page, I notice that I have strayed far from my subject . . . But what does it matter? . . . I write this journal for myself and, consequently, anything that I may toss into it will become, in time, for me, a precious memory.

.   .   .

. . . In the evening, a numerous party set out on foot for The Hollow.

In the opinion of local scientists, that "hollow" is nothing else than an extinguished crater: it is situated on a slope of Mount Mashuk, less than a mile from town. To it leads a narrow trail, among bushes and cliffs. As we went up the mountain, I offered the young princess my arm, and she never abandoned it during the entire walk.

Our conversation began with gossip: I passed in review our acquaintances, both present and absent: first, I brought out their comic traits, and then their evil ones. My bile began to stir. I started in jest and finished in frank waspishness. At first it amused her, then frightened her.

"You are a dangerous man!" she said to me. "I would sooner find myself in a wood under a murderer's knife than be the victim of your sharp tongue . . . I ask you seriously, when it occurs to you to talk badly about me, better take a knife and cut my throat: I don't think you will find it very difficult."

"Do I look like a murderer?"

"You are worse. . . ."

I thought a moment, and then said, assuming a deeply touched air:

"Yes, such was my lot since my very childhood! Everybody read in my face the signs of bad inclinations which were not there, but they were supposed to be there—and so they came into existence. I was modest—they accused me of being crafty: I became secretive. I felt deeply good and evil—nobody caressed me, everybody offended me: I became rancorous. I was gloomy—other children were merry and talkative. I felt myself superior to them—but was considered inferior: I became envious. I was ready to love the whole world—none understood me: and I learned to hate. My colorless youth was spent in a struggle with myself and with the world. Fearing mockery, I buried my best feelings at the bottom of my heart: there they died. I spoke the truth—I was not believed: I began to deceive. When I got to know well the fashionable world and the mechanism of society, I became skilled in the science of life, and saw how others were happy without that skill, enjoying, at no cost to themselves, all those advantages which I so indefatigably pursued. And then in my breast despair was born—not that despair which is cured with the pistol's muzzle, but cold, helpless despair, concealed under amiability and a good-natured smile. I became a moral cripple. One half of my soul did not exist; it had withered away, it had evaporated, it had died. I cut it off and threw it away—while the other half stirred and lived, at the service of everybody. And this nobody noticed, because nobody knew that its dead half had ever existed; but now you have aroused its memory in me, and I have read to you its epitaph. To many people, all epitaphs, in general, seem ridiculous, but not so to me; especially when I recall what lies beneath them. However, I do not ask you to share my views; if my outburst seems to you ridiculous, please, laugh: I warn you, that it will not distress me in any way."

At that moment, I met her eyes: tears danced in them; her arm, leaning on mine, trembled, her cheeks glowed; she was sorry for me! Compassion—an emotion to which all women so easily submit—had sunk its claws into her inexperienced heart. During the whole walk she was absent-minded, did not coquet with anyone—and that is a great sign!

We reached The Hollow: the ladies left their escorts, but she did not abandon my arm. The witticisms of the local dandies did not amuse her; the steepness of the precipice near which she stood did not frighten her, while the other young ladies squealed and closed their eyes.

On the way back, I did not renew our melancholy conversation, but to my trivial questions and jokes she replied briefly and absently.

"Have you ever loved?" I asked her at last.

She glanced at me intently, shook her head and again became lost in thought: it was evident that she wanted to say something, but she did not know how to begin. Her breast heaved . . . What would you—a muslin sleeve is little protection, and an electric spark ran from my wrist to hers. Almost all passions start thus; and we often deceive ourselves greatly in thinking that a woman loves us for our physical or moral qualities. Of course, they prepare and incline their hearts for the reception of the sacred fire: nonetheless, it is the first contact that decides the matter.

"Don't you think I was very amiable today?" said the young princess to me, with a forced smile when we returned from the excursion.

We parted.

She is displeased with herself; she accuses herself of having treated me coldly . . . Oh, this is the first, the main triumph!

Tomorrow she will want to recompense me. I know it all by heart—that is what is so boring.

The Fantastical Gogol

The initiator of Russian realistic prose, Nikolai Gogol was a keen portrayer and satirist of Russian life—especially its vulgar aspects. But he was also a romantic in his flights of poetic fancy and his dramatic juxtapositions of humor and horror. Gogol's caricatures, moreover, were strangely introspective—as if they mirrored images more of himself than of his supposed subjects. In his artful maneuvering between reality and fantasy, Gogol anticipated surrealistic writing of the next century.

From THE DIARY OF A MADMAN (1835)

Translated by Andrew R. MacAndrew

Gogol's The Diary of a Madman *was published a few years after he had renounced a career in the Civil Service at St. Petersburg.*

December 3

. . . Why am I a clerk? Why should I be a clerk? Perhaps I'm really a general or a count and only seem to be a clerk? Maybe I don't really know who I am? There are plenty of instances in history when somebody quite ordinary, not necessarily an aristocrat, some middle-class person or even a peasant, suddenly turns out to be a public figure and perhaps even the ruler of a country. If a peasant can turn into someone so important, where are the limits to the possibilities for a man of breeding? Imagine, for instance, me, entering a room in a general's uniform. There's an epaulet on my right shoulder, an epaulet on my left, a blue ribbon across my chest. How would that be? What tune would my beauty sing then? . . . But I can't be promoted to general or governor or anything like that overnight. What I'd like to know is, why am I a clerk? Why precisely a clerk?

December 5

I read the newspapers all morning. Strange things are happening in Spain. I can't even make them out properly. They write that the throne has been vacated and that the ranking grandees are having difficulty in selecting an heir. It seems there's discontent. Sounds very strange to me. How can a throne be vacant? They say that some donna may accede. A donna cannot accede to a throne. It's absolutely impossible. A king should sit on a throne. But they say there is no king. It's impossible that there should be no king. There must be a king but he's hidden away somewhere in anonymity. It's even possible that he's around but is being forced to remain in hiding for family reasons or for fear of some neighboring country such as France. Or there may be other reasons.

December 8

I was on the point of going to the office but various considerations held me back. I couldn't get those Spanish affairs out of my head. . . . I confess I was so perturbed and hurt by these events that I could do nothing all day. Marva remarked that I was very absent-minded during dinner. . . . In fact, I believe I absent-mindedly threw a couple of plates on the floor, where they broke at once. After dinner, I walked the streets, uphill and downhill. Came across nothing of interest. Then, mostly lay on my bed and thought about the Spanish question.

Year 2000, April 43

This is a day of great jubilation. Spain has a king. They've found him. *I* am the King. I discovered it today. It all came to me in a flash. It's incredible to me now that I could have imagined that I was a civil-service clerk. How could such a crazy idea ever have entered my head? Thank God no one thought of slapping me into a lunatic asylum. Now I see everything clearly, as clearly as if it lay in the palm of my hand. But what was happening to me before? Then things loomed at me out of a fog. Now, I believe that all troubles stem from the misconception that human brains are located in the head. They are not: human brains are blown in by the winds from somewhere around the Caspian Sea.

Marva was the first to whom I revealed my identity. When she heard that she was facing the King of Spain, she flung up her hands in awe. She almost died of terror. The silly woman had never seen a King of Spain before. However, I tried to calm her and, speaking graciously, did my best to assure her of my royal favor. I was not going to hold against her all the times she had failed to shine my boots properly. The masses are so ignorant. One can't talk to them on lofty subjects. Probably she was so frightened because she thought that all kings of Spain are like Philip II. But I carefully pointed out that I wasn't like Philip II at all. I didn't go to the office. The hell with it. No, my friends, you won't entice me there now; never again shall I copy your dreadful documents.

From THE INSPECTOR GENERAL (1836)

Translated by F. D. Reeve

Generally considered the greatest of all Russian comic plays, Gogol's satire on bureaucratic corruption infuriated contemporary censors.

ACT I. *A room in the Mayor's house. The Mayor [Anton Antonovich], the Trustee of Social Welfare Institutions [Artemy Filipovich], the Superintendent of Schools [Luka Lukich], the Judge [Ammos Fyodorovich], the Chief of Police, the District Doctor [Khristian Ivanovich], two policemen.*

MAYOR. I asked you in, gentlemen, in order to inform you of some most unpleasant news. An inspector general is coming to our town.

AMMOS FYODOROVICH. What do you mean, an inspector general?

ARTEMY FILIPOVICH. What do you mean, an inspector general?

MAYOR. An inspector general from Petersburg, incognito. And with a secret directive.

AMMOS FYODOROVICH. Well, I'll be—!

ARTEMY FILIPOVICH. We had it easy so far, so now we're going to get it.

LUKA LUKICH. My Lord, and even with a secret directive.

MAYOR. I somehow saw it coming: all last night I dreamed of some kind of a couple of strange rats. Really, I never ever saw such rats before: black, unnaturally big! They came, they sniffed—and went away. Here, I'll read you the letter which I got from Andrei Ivanovich Chymkov, whom you, Artemy Filipovich, know. Here's what he writes: "Dearest friend, neighbor, and benefactor" (mutters, glancing over it quickly) "... and to inform you." Ah! here: "I hasten by the way to inform you that an official with a directive came to look over the whole province and especially our county (significantly raises his finger). I learned of this from the most reliable sources, although he poses as a non-official. Since I know that you, just like any man, have some little faults, because you are an intelligent man and don't like to let go of what finds its way into your hands ..." (pausing) well, here ..."so I advise you to take precautions, for he may arrive at any moment, if he has not already arrived and is not living somewhere incognito." ...

LUKA LUKICH. What for, Anton Antonovich, why is this? Why an inspector general to us?

MAYOR. Why? But, it's obvious, it's fate! (Sighing) Up to this moment, thanks be to God, they sneaked up on other towns. Now it's our turn.

AMMOS FYODOROVICH. I think, Anton Antonovich, that here there's a subtle and more political reason. Here's what I mean now: Russia ... um, yes ... wants to start war, and the ministry now, you see, has sent out a man to find out if there isn't treason somewhere.

MAYOR. Where'd you get that from! And an intelligent man, too. Treason in a district town! What's this, a border town? From here, even if you gallop for three years, you won't get to any other country at all.

AMMOS FYODOROVICH. No, let me tell you, you didn't get ... You didn't ... The authorities have sharp eyes: even if they're far away, nothing'll escape them.

MAYOR. Escape them or not, I have forewarned you, gentlemen—Watch out! in my own department I've given various instructions; I advise you to, too. Especially you, Artemy Filipovich. Without a doubt, an official passing through will want above all to look over the social welfare institutions within your jurisdiction—and therefore you arrange it so that everything is proper. The caps should be clean, and the sick shouldn't look like blacksmiths, the way they usually go around in their everyday clothes.

ARTEMY FILIPOVICH. Well, that's easy. They can even put on clean caps, most likely.

MAYOR. And then, too, you should put up at the head of each bed in Latin or some other such language—that's already in your department, Khristian Ivanovich—each illness, when the man got sick, what day of the week and date ... It's not good that in your place the sick smoke such strong tobacco that you always sneeze and sneeze when you go in. And then it would be better if there were fewer of them: right away it will be attributed to bad supervision or to the doctor's lack of skill.

ARTEMY FILIPOVICH. Oh, about the doctoring, Khristian Ivanovich and I have taken measures: the closer to nature, the better; we don't use expensive medicines. Man is easy: if he's going to die, he'll die anyway; if he's going to get well, he'll get well anyway. Besides, it would be sort of difficult for Khristian Ivanovich to have to express himself to them—he doesn't know a word of Russian. (Khristian Ivanovich lets out a sound partly similar to the letter i and partly to e.)

MAYOR. I would also advise you, Ammos Fyodorovich, to direct your attention to your offices. In your vestibule there, where the petitioners usually present themselves, the doormen have acquired some domestic geese and little goslings, which keep poking about underfoot. It is, of course, laudable for every man to settle down to domestic life, and so why should not a doorman, also, settle down? just, you know, in such a place it isn't decent ... I meant to mention this to you before, but somehow I kept forgetting.

AMMOS FYODOROVICH. I'll tell them right away today to pick them up and take them all out to the kitchen. If you want, come over for dinner.

MAYOR. In addition to which it's no good that all kinds of junk is hanging up to dry in your own office. . . . Also, your assessor . . . he is, of course, a very able man, but he smells so, as if he's just come out of a distillery—that's not good either. . . . There are remedies for this if it actually is, as he says, an odor he was born with. You can suggest he eat onions or garlic or something else. In that case Khristian Ivanovich can assist with various medications. (Khristian Ivanovich lets out the same sound.)

AMMOS FYODOROVICH. No, that's impossible to get rid of: he says his nurse bruised him when he was a child and ever since he's smelled a bit of vodka.

MAYOR. Yes, yes, I only wanted to mention it to you. Now about the internal dispositions and what Andrei Ivanovich in his letter terms little faults, I have nothing to say. Indeed, it would be unusual to say anything. There's not a man who doesn't have some kind of besetting sin. That's the way it was arranged by God Himself, and the Voltarians argue against it in vain.

AMMOS FYODOROVICH. What do you mean, Anton Antonovich, by little faults? There are all kinds of little faults. I tell everybody openly that I take bribes, but what kind of bribes? Borzoi puppies. That's a completely different thing.

MAYOR. Well, puppies or something else, bribes are bribes. . . .[The Mayor proceeds to caution the Superintendent of Schools about "the odd ways" of his teachers, whereupon the Postmaster, Ivan Kuzmich, enters.]

POSTMASTER. Explain it to me, gentlemen, what kind of official's coming?

MAYOR. You really haven't heard?

POSTMASTER. I heard from Pyotr Ivanovich Bobchinsky. He was just over at my office in the post office.

MAYOR. Well? What do you think of it? . . .

POSTMASTER. What do I think? What do you think, Anton [Antonovich]?

MAYOR. What do I think? There's no danger, but, well, just a little . . . The merchants and the citizenry disturb me. They say I've given them a hard time, but if, now, good Lord, I've taken anything from anyone why, really, it was without malice.—I even think (*takes him by the arm and leads him to one side*), I even think, maybe there was some kind of denunciation of me. What, in fact, is an inspector general coming here for? listen, Ivan Kuzmich, couldn't we, for our general good, you know, take each letter, which gets to your office in the post office, incoming or outgoing, open it just a little bit and read it: doesn't it contain, maybe, some kind of report or simply correspondence? If not, why, we could seal it up again; besides, we could even return the letter just like that, opened.

POSTMASTER. I know, I know . . . You can't teach this to me, I do it myself, not as a precaution but mostly out of curiosity—I've got a passion for finding out what's new in the world. I can tell you it's the most interesting reading. . . .

AMMOS FYODOROVICH. Be careful you don't get scolded for that some time.

POSTMASTER. Oh, goodness!

MAYOR. Nothing to it, nothing to it. It'd be completely different if you made something public of it, but you know it's all a family affair.

AMMOS FYODOROVICH. Indeed, we're in for a great deal of trouble! And, I must admit, Anton Antonovich, I was about to come over to your place to treat you to a puppy. The litter sister to that dog, you know. You surely heard that Sheptovich has concocted a lawsuit with Varkhovinsky, and I'm living in clover: I go hare-hunting on [their] property. . . .

MAYOR. Gentlemen, your hare aren't very close to my heart right now. A damned incognito is sitting in my head. Here we sit and wait, and suddenly the door'll open and—bang. . . .

From THE OVERCOAT (1842)

Translated by Bernard Guilbert Guerney

Dostoevsky later acknowledged the importance of this satirical masterpiece by saying, "we have all emerged from 'The Overcoat.' "

It is doubtful if you could find anywhere a man whose life lay so much in his work. It would hardly do to say that he worked with zeal; no, it was a labor of love. Thus, in this transcription of his, he visioned some sort of diversified and pleasant world all its own. His face expressed delight; certain letters were favorites of his and, whenever he came across them he would be beside himself with rapture: he'd chuckle, and wink, and help things along by working his lips, so that it seemed as if one could read on his face every letter his quill was outlining. If rewards had been meted out to him commensurately with his zeal, he might have, to his astonish-

ment, actually found himself among the State Councilors; but, as none other than those wits, his own co-workers, expressed it, all he'd worked himself up to was a button in a buttonhole too wide, and piles in his backside. . . .

He gave no thought whatsoever to his dress; the uniform frock coat on him wasn't the prescribed green at all, but rather of some rusty-flour hue. His collar was very tight and very low, so that his neck, even though it wasn't a long one, seemed extraordinarily long emerging therefrom, like those gypsum kittens with nodding heads which certain outlanders balance by the dozen atop their heads and peddle throughout Russia. And, always, something was bound to stick to his coat: a wisp of hay or some bit of thread; in addition to that, he had a peculiar knack whenever he walked through the streets of getting under some window at the precise moment when garbage of every sort was being thrown out of it, and for that reason always bore off on his hat watermelon and cantaloupe rinds and other such trifles. Not once in all his life had he ever turned his attention to the everyday things and doings out in the street. . . . But even if Akakii Akakiievich did look at anything, he saw thereon nothing but his own neatly, evenly penned lines of script, and only when some horse's nose, bobbing up from no one knew where, would be placed on his shoulder and let a whole gust of wind in his face through its nostrils, would he notice that he was not in the middle of a line of script but, rather, in the middle of the roadway.

On coming home he would immediately sit down at the table, gulp down his cabbage soup and bolt a piece of veal with onions, without noticing in the least the taste of either, eating everything together with the flies and whatever else God may have sent at that particular time of the year. On perceiving that his belly was beginning to bulge, he'd get up from the table, take out a small bottle of ink, and transcribe the papers he had brought home. If there were no homework, he would deliberately, for his own edification, make a copy of some paper for himself, especially if the document were remarkable not for its beauty of style but merely addressed to some new or important person.

. . . Having had his sweet fill of quill-driving, he would lie down to sleep, smiling at the thought of the next day: just what would God send him on the morrow? . . .

From DEAD SOULS (1842)

Translated by Andrew R. MacAndrew

Gogol's famous novel concerns a rogue named Chichikov who tries to persuade landowners to sell him their serfs who have died since the last census but who are still being taxed. His aim is to procure a bill of sale and mortgage the serfs as if they were still alive. Gogol worked on a sequel, but eventually he burned most of the manuscript—claiming he had been tricked into doing so by the devil.

"Nastasia Petrovna? A very nice name indeed. I have an aunt, my mother's own sister, who's also a Nastasia Petrovna."

"And what's your name? I suppose you're a tax assessor."

"Oh no, my good lady, I'm no tax assessor, I'm just traveling on personal business."

"Then you must have come to buy farm produce. What a shame—I sold my honey very cheaply to some merchants, and I'm sure you'd have bought it from me, my good sir."

"Now honey is something I wouldn't have bought from you."

"What did you want then? Hemp, perhaps? But I have only about twenty pounds left."

"No, no, ma'am, I need goods of a different sort: tell me, have any of your peasants died?"

"Oh, my good friend, eighteen of them!" the old woman said with a sigh. "And they were all such nice people, such good workers. True, since then some new ones have been born, but what's the good of that; they're all so young and yet the tax assessor came and demanded that I pay so much per soul. So the people are dead and I have to pay for them as though they were alive. Last week my blacksmith was burned to death. He was such a good blacksmith and a quite skilled locksmith as well." . . .

"God's will is in all things," Chichikov said and sighed. ". . . Well then, Nastasia Petrovna, will you sell them to me?"

"Sell what to you?"

"Why, all those serfs who died."

"How can I sell them to you?"

"Just like that. Sell them to me, and I'll pay you money for them."

"But how? I really can't make head or tail of it. Do you intend to dig them up or what?"

Chichikov realized that the old woman had not understood him and that he would have to explain what he was after. In a few words he conveyed to her that the sale, or transfer, would only be on paper and that the souls would figure in the transaction as though they were still alive.

"But what do you want them for?" the old woman asked, her eyes popping.

"Now that's my business."

"But since they're dead!"

"And who's trying to maintain they're alive? That's why you lose money on them, because they're dead: you have to pay for them and now I'll save you the payments and the worry. Do you understand? And I'll not only save you that, but also pay you fifteen rubles. . . . I'll even draw up a purchase deed at my own expense, you understand?". . .

"Really, I'm rather hesitant. I could lose money entering into such a transaction for the first time. . . . Maybe you're fooling me, my good sir, and they're really worth more." . . .

Chichikov was beginning to lose patience. . . .

"Believe me," she said, "this business is too much for me, inexperienced widow that I am. I think I'd better take some time to think it over—some merchants may drive in and then I could get some idea of the current prices."

"Shame on you, shame on you, my good lady, shame indeed! What are you saying? Just think for yourself—who do you imagine will buy them? What would a buyer do with them? What use can they be put to?"

"Well, maybe they would come in handy in a household . . ." the old woman replied, and without finishing, she stared at him open-mouthed, almost fearfully, curious to see what he would answer to that.

"Dead people in a household! What will you think of next! Unless you mean to scare off the sparrows at night in the vegetable gardens?"

"God bless their souls—what horrible things you say!" she said and crossed herself.

"Well then, what do you intend to use them for? Anyhow, you can hold on to the bones and the graves—all I want is a transfer on paper. Well then? You might at least give me an answer."

The old woman grew thoughtful once more. . . .

"My goodness, the merchandise you're after is rather strange and unusual!"

At this point Chichikov lost patience altogether, grabbed a chair, banged it against the floor, and expressed the wish that the devil might take her.

The lady landowner turned out to be very much afraid of the devil.

"Oh, for God's sake, don't mention him, leave him in peace," she cried, turning very pale. "The night before last I kept dreaming of the cursed one. I got a notion to lay out the cards and find my fortune after my evening prayers, and so God must have sent him as a punishment . . . he was so horrible, with horns longer than a bull's. . . ."

"I really wonder that you don't dream of devils by the dozen," Chichikov said. "I wanted to help you out of pure Christian charity: I saw a poor widow suffering a hardship. . . . I was going to buy all sorts of farm produce from you, because I also happen to supply the government. . . ."

Here he was lying, and although he did so in passing and without lengthy consideration, it turned out to be unexpectedly successful. This business of government supply had a considerable effect on Nastasia Petrovna, and she said in a conciliatory tone: "What are you getting so excited about? If I'd known you'd get so angry, I'd never have argued with you at all——"

"There's nothing to be angry about. The whole deal isn't worth an egg laid by a hen, and I'm supposed to get excited about it?"

"Well, all right, have it your own way. You can have them for fifteen rubles in banknotes. But just remember, my friend, the purchases for the government—if you ever need any rye or buckwheat or any other grain, or any slaughtered cattle, you won't let me down, will you?"

"No, my good lady, I'll never let you down," Chichikov said, using his hand to wipe away the sweat that was running down his face in three streams.

The Pastoral Turgenev

If Gogol was the most imaginative of the early realists of Russian prose, Ivan Turgenev was the most graceful. A meticulous observer of nature and rural life, he developed a style of narrative that was limber enough to accommodate long, detailed descriptions and dialogues. Praised and imitated by Henry James and by numerous Europeans, Turgenev was the first Russian novelist to appeal widely to Westerners.

From FOREST AND STEPPE (1852)

Translated by Bernard Guilbert Guerney

Turgenev's first successful publication, The Hunting Sketches, *was a collection of vignettes of country life at Spaskoe, his estate south of Moscow, where he frequently went hunting with his dog. This selection, a sustained description of nature, was the epilogue.*

It may well be that the reader has by now become somewhat wearied of my sketches; I hasten to reassure him by promising to limit myself to those fragments already in print; yet, in parting from him, I cannot refrain from saying a few words about hunting.

Hunting with gun and dog is splendid in itself, *für sich*, as they used to say in the old days; however, even if we suppose that you are not a hunter born, you, nonetheless, love nature; you cannot, therefore, help envying us of the hunting fraternity. . . . Hearken, then.

Do you know, for instance what a delight it is to venture forth in the spring, before the dawn glow? You come out on the front porch. Stars are blinking here and there in the dark-gray sky; a humid breeze comes surging in a light wave from time to time; you can catch the restrained, indistinct whispering of night; the trees, drenched in shadow, are faintly murmurous. There, a carpet is spread on the cart, the chest with the samovar is put at your feet. The off horses are shrinking from the chill, snorting, and shifting their legs daintily; a brace of white geese, who have awakened just now, makes its way silently and leisurely across the road. Beyond the wattle fence, in the garden, the watchman is peacefully snoring; every sound seems to remain fixed in the still air, seems to remain fixed and does not pass on.

There, you are seated; the horses spring forward as one, the cart has started with a great clatter. You are off, off past the church, going downhill to the right, crossing the dam. The vapor is barely beginning to swirl up like smoke from the pond. Feeling a trifle chill, you muffle your face in the collar of your overcoat; you feel like dozing. The horses splash their hoofs noisily through puddles, the driver is whistling softly and intermittently.

But now you have covered about three miles . . . the rim of the sky is glowing crimsonly; the jackdaws in the birches are awakening, flitting ungainly from branch to branch; the cock sparrows are chirking near the weather-beaten hayricks. The air grows light, the road is plainer, the sky becomes clear, the small clouds show white, the fields green. Rush-

lights burn red within huts; voices, still sleep-laden, are heard outside the gates. And in the meanwhile the dawn glow is bursting into flame: there, bands of gold have already stretched themselves across the sky, steaming mist is swirling in the ravines, skylarks are sonorously singing, the predawn wind has started to blow, and gently the purple sun floats to the surface. Light will burst forth in a very torrent; your heart will flutter into alertness, like a bird. What freshness, lightness, loveliness! You can see far all around you. There, beyond that copse, lies the village; there, somewhat farther off, is another, with a white church; over there is a small grove of birches on a hill; beyond it lies the swamp for which you are heading. Go faster, you horses, faster! Onward, at a full trot!

Only a couple of miles left, no more. The sun is rising fast; the sky is clear. The weather will be glorious. A herd of cows has started from the village, ambling toward you. By now you have gotten up on the hill. What a view! The river winds along for six miles or so, gleaming dully blue through the mist; beyond it lie meadows of a watery green, beyond the meadows are gently sloping knolls; lapwings, calling, are soaring over the swamp; through the moist glitter suffusing the air the far-off vista is clearly emerging—not at all the way it does in summer. How freely the breast breathes, how quickly the limbs move, how much stronger man grows when enveloped by the fresh breath of spring!

And what about a summer morning in July? Who, save a hunter, has experienced what a joy it is to roam at dawn through the bushes? The tracks of your feet fall in a green line on the dewy, whitened grass. You part a dripping bush —and the accumulated warm night smell breathes full upon you; the air is all saturated with the fresh bitterness of wormwood, the honey of buckwheat and clover; in the distance, like a wall, stands an oak forest, and it glistens and glows crimson in the sun; the air is still fresh, yet one already feels that sultriness is not far off. Your head spins languidly from the excess of sweet smells. There is no end to the brushwood —save that, here and there, the ripening rye shows yellow and the buckwheat reddens in short narrow streaks.

And now you catch the creaking of a cart; the muzhik drives at a walk and makes sure to put his horse in the shade beforehand. You exchange greetings with him and go on— the clanking of a scythe rings behind you. The sun is climbing higher, ever higher. The grass has dried quickly. There, the day has already become sultry. An hour passes, then another. The sky darkens at the edges; the motionless air breathes forth prickly sultriness.

"Where could a body get a drink of water here?" you ask a reaper.

"Why, you'll find a wellspring down there, in the ravine."

You make your way down, through thick hazelnut bushes entangled with clinging grass, to the bottom of the ravine. Sure enough, right by the steep side, a spring lurks; a scrub oak has greedily thrown its pawlike branches over the water; from the bottom, covered with fine, velvety moss, great silvery bubbles rise, swaying. You throw yourself on the ground; you drink your fill at last, yet you feel too lazy to stir. You are in the shade, breathing in the fragrant dampness, you feel fine, but across from you the bushes are becoming incandescent and seem to be turning yellow.

But what was that, just now? The wind has made a sudden swoop and sped by; the air has shuddered all about you: is it going to thunder, by any chance? You come out of the ravine: what's that leaden streak on the horizon? Is it the sultriness intensifying? Or a cloud drawing nearer? But there —a lightning flash shows faintly. Eh, but that's a thunderstorm coming up! The sun is still shining brightly all around: it's still possible to hunt. The cloud grows, however, its foremost edge balloons like a sleeve, bends over in an arc. The grass, the bushes, everything has suddenly darkened. Hurry! There, that looks like a hay barn—hurry! You've managed to reach it by running, have gone in. What a rain, eh? And those lightnings? Here and there, through the straw thatch, water drips on the fragrant hay.

However, the sun has begun to shine again blithely. The storm has passed; you step outside. My God, how gaily everything sparkles all around, how fresh the air is and how rarefied, what a smell there is of strawberries and mushrooms!

But now evening comes on. The evening glow has flamed into a conflagration and encompassed half the sky. The sun is setting. The air is, at close range, somehow especially transparent, just as though of glass; in the distance a soft glow, warming the eye, is nestling down; a crimson sheen is falling with the dew upon the meadows that so recently were drenched by torrents of liquid gold; from the trees, from the bushes, from the tall hayricks, long shadows have begun to scamper.

The sun has set; a star has kindled, and is quivering in the fiery sea of the sunset. There, it pales; the sky turns indigo; individual shadows disappear; the air becomes swollen with murk. Time to be heading home, to the village, to the hut where you are to pass the night. Throwing the gun over your shoulder you walk rapidly, disregarding your fatigue. And in the meanwhile night is coming on; by now you can't see a thing twenty paces off; the dogs are barely perceptible white blotches in the gloaming ahead. Over there, above the black bushes, the rim of the sky grows vaguely brighter. What can it be? A house burning? No; it is the moon rising. And over there, below, to the right, the little lights in the village are already aglimmer. And here, at last, is your hut. Through the small window you see the table, covered with a white cloth, a candle burning, the supper waiting. . . .

Or else you order the racing droshky to be harnessed and set out for the forest, after woodcock. It is a blithe thing to be making your way over a narrow path, between two walls of tall rye. The ears of grain flick your face gently; the cornflowers catch at the horse's legs, the quail are calling all around you; your horse is going at a lazy trot. And here is the forest. Shade and silence. The graceful aspens babble high above you; the long, drooping branches of the birches barely stir; a mighty oak stands, like some warrior, close to a beautiful linden. You are driving over a green path mottled with shadows; great yellow flies hang motionless in the aureate air and then suddenly fly off; the midges whirl in a pillar, growing lighter in the shade, darkening in the sunlight; the birds are singing peacefully. The golden little voice of the hedgesparrows sounds with innocent, garrulous joy: that voice is in keeping with the fragrance of the lilies of the valley. On, on, deeper into the forest. It becomes thicker. An inexplicable quietude falls upon your soul—and all around you, too, everything is so slumbrous and still. But now a wind has sprung up, and the treetops have turned noisy, and their noise is as of waves subsiding. Tall grasses grow here and there through last year's dark-brown leaves; there are mushrooms, standing aloof under their small caps. A white hare may leap out unexpectedly—your dog, barking resoundingly, will dash off after it. . . .

And how fine this very same forest is late in autumn, when the snipe come winging! They do not keep to the very heart of the forest; they must be sought along its edges. There is no wind, nor is there any sun, or light, or shade, or movement; an autumnal bouquet, like the bouquet of wine, is diffused through the air; a fine haze hangs in the distance over the yellow fields. Through the denuded, dark-brown boughs the still sky is serenely bleak; the last golden leaves dangle here and there upon the lindens. The dank earth is springy underfoot; the high dry stalks of grass never stir; long threads of caught gossamer shimmer on the blanched grass. The breast breathes tranquilly, yet a strange disquiet comes over your soul. You are walking along the skirt of the forest, keeping an eye on your dog, yet at the same time beloved images, beloved faces, those of the dead and the living, come to memory; long-slumbering impressions unexpectedly awaken; the imagination soars and sweeps along like some bird, and everything moves and stands so clearly before your eyes. The heart either suddenly quivers and pounds, passionately plunging ahead, or becomes irretrievably sunk in recollections. All your life unrolls before you lightly and quickly, like a scroll; a man is master of all his past, of all his senses, of all his forces, of all his soul. And nothing around him hinders him—there is no sun, nor wind, nor noise. . . .

And what of the autumnal day, clear, a trifle chill (actually frosty in the morning), when some birch, as though it were a tree out of a fairy tale, all of gold, stands out like a beautiful painting against the pale-blue sky; when the low sun no longer warms yet shines brighter than the sun of summer, while the small grove of aspens is shot through and through with glitter, as though it were a lissome and light thing for it to be standing there denuded; when the hoarfrost is still showing white at the bottom of the dales, while the fresh breeze stirs, ever so quietly, the fallen, mummified leaves and drives them along; when blue waves race joyously along the river, making the geese and ducks scattered over it bob rhythmically, and a mill, half-screened by osiers, is clattering away in the distance, with pigeons rapidly circling over it, turning the radiant air to motley. . . .

Fine, also, are the misty days of summer, even though hunters have no great love for them. On such days you can't shoot: a bird, fluttering out from under your very feet, vanishes instantly in the whitish murk of the unmoving fog. But how still, how inexpressibly still, everything around you is! Everything has awakened, and everything is keeping silent. You walk past a tree—it will not stir: it is blissfully slothful. Through the fine haze evenly diffused in the air a long furrow shows black before you. You take it for a forest close by; you approach: the forest transforms itself into a high hedge of wormwood growing on the boundary of a field. Above you, around you—everywhere—is the fog. But now the breeze stirs slightly: a tatter of pale-blue sky emerges dimly through the thinning haze. . . .

But now you've gotten ready to ride off into the far-off plain, into the steppe. For some seven miles you have been making your way over crossroads—and here is the highway, at last. You ride a long, long while past never-ending cart trains, past little wayside inns, each with a samovar hissing under an overhang, each with wide-open gates and its well, through fields the eye cannot take in, along green hemp fields. The crows flit from willow to willow; country wives, with long rakes in their hands, are wandering off into the fields; a wayfarer, in a worn caftan of nankeen, with a beggar's wallet over his shoulder, plods along with a weary step; a landowner's ponderous carriage, harnessed with six big and broken-down horses, is floating toward you. A corner of a pillow sticks out of the carriage window, while on the backboard, sitting sideways on a mat sack and holding onto a bit of rope, is an overcoated footman, spattered with mud. . . .

Now the steppe regions have begun. When you look down from a hill, what a view! Round, low knolls, plowed and sown to their very tops, surge out in broad waves; ravines grown over with bushes wind among them; small groves are scattered about like elongated islands; narrow paths run from village to village, and churches gleam whitely; between the willow bushes one glimpses the sparkle of a small river, girded in four places by dams; far off on the plain there is a single file of bustards that seem to be sticking out of the ground; a little old manor house, with its outbuildings, its orchard and threshing floor, has nestled up cozily to a small pond.

But you ride on and on. The knolls become smaller and smaller; there is almost no timber to be seen. Here it is at last—the steppe, illimitable, unencompassable to the eye!

And what about a day in winter, when you go after rabbits, wading through snowdrifts, breathing the frosty, nipping air, puckering your eyes involuntarily from the blinding, fine sparkle of the soft snow, admiring the green color of the sky over a reddish forest! . . . And what of the first days in spring, when everything around and about gleams and comes crashing down, when through the heavy vapor steaming up from thawed snow you can already scent the warmed earth; when above the thawed patches of earth,

under the oblique rays of the sun, the skylarks are trustfully singing and, with blithe bluster and roar, torrents go swirling from one ravine into another. . . .

However, it is time to be done. Quite apropos, I have mentioned the spring: in the spring parting comes easy; in the spring even those who are happy are drawn to far-off vistas. . . . Farewell, reader; I wish that all things may go steadfastly well with you.

From FATHERS AND SONS (1862)

Translated by Ralph E. Matlaw

In Bazarov, the chief character in this novel, Turgenev introduced a new social prototype to Russian literature—the young, antisentimental Nihilist. Denounced by both radicals and conservatives for failing to indicate praise or contempt for such a character, Turgenev left Russia and spent most of his remaining years in western Europe—which had already become his second home. In this passage, Bazarov is drawn into a long argument with Pavel and Nikolai Petrovich, the father and uncle of his friend Arkady. The scene is the Petrovich estate, where Arkady had brought Bazarov.

A tussle came off . . . at evening tea. Pavel Petrovich came into the drawing-room, all ready for the fray, irritable and determined. He was only waiting for an excuse to fall upon the enemy; but for a long while an excuse did not present itself. As a rule, Bazarov said little in the presence of the "old Kirsanovs" (that was how he spoke of the brothers), and that evening he felt out of humor, and drank off cup after cup of tea without a word. Pavel Petrovich was all aflame with impatience; his wishes were fulfilled at last.

The conversation turned on one of the neighboring landowners. "Trash, a rotten little aristocrat," observed Bazarov indifferently. He had met him in Petersburg.

"Allow me to ask you," began Pavel Petrovich, and his lips were trembling, "according to your ideas, have the words 'trash' and 'aristocrat' the same meaning?"

"I said 'rotten little aristocrat,'" replied Bazarov, lazily swallowing a sip of tea.

"Precisely so, sir; but I imagine you have the same opinion of aristocrats as of rotten little aristocrats. I consider it my duty to inform you that I do not share that opinion. I venture to say that every one knows me for a man of liberal ideas and devoted to progress; but, exactly for that reason, I respect aristocrats—real aristocrats. Kindly remember, sir" (at these words Bazarov lifted his eyes and looked at Pavel Petrovich), "kindly remember, sir," he repeated, with acrimony—"the English aristocracy. They do not abate one iota of their rights, and for that reason they respect the rights of others; they demand the fulfillment of obligations in dealing with them, and for that reason they fulfill their own obligations. The aristocracy has given freedom to England, and supports it for her."

"We've heard that song a good many times," replied Bazarov; but what are you trying to prove by that?"

"I am tryin' to prove by that, sir" (when Pavel Petrovich was angry he intentionally clipped his words in this way, though, of course, he knew very well that such forms are not strictly grammatical. In this whim could be discerned a survival of the habits of the times of Alexander I. The exquisites of those days, on the rare occasions when they spoke their own language, made use of such slipshod forms; as much as to say, "We, of course are genuine Russians, at the same time we are grandees, who are at liberty to neglect the rules of scholars"); I am tryin' to prove by that, sir, that without the sense of personal dignity, without self-respect—and these two sentiments are well developed in the aristocrat—there is no secure foundation for the social . . . *bien public* . . . the social fabric. Character, sir—that is the chief thing; a man's character must be firm as a rock, since everything is built on it. I am very well aware, for instance, that you are pleased to consider my habits, my dress, my neatness, in short, ridiculous; but all that proceeds from a sense of self-respect, from a sense of duty—yes sir, yes sir, of duty. I live in the country, in the wilds, but I will not lower myself. I respect the dignity of man in myself."

"Let me ask you, Pavel Petrovich," said Bazarov; "you respect yourself, and sit with your arms folded; what sort of benefit does that do to the *bien public?* If you didn't respect yourself, you'd do just the same."

Pavel Petrovich turned white. "That's a different question. It's absolutely unnecessary for me to explain to you now why I sit with my arms folded, as you are pleased to express yourself. I wish only to tell you that aristocracy is a *principe*, and in our days none but immoral or silly people can live without *principes*. I said that to Arkady the day after he came home, and I repeat it now. Isn't it so, Nikolai?"

Nikolai Petrovich nodded his head.

"Aristocracy, Liberalism, progress, principles," Bazarov was saying meanwhile; "if you think of it, what a lot of foreign . . . and useless words! No Russian needs them, even as a gift."

"What is good for something according to you? According to you we are outside humanity, outside its laws. Come—the logic of history demands . . ."

"But what's that logic to us? We can get on without it too."

"How do you mean?"

"Why, this. You don't need logic, I hope, to put a piece of bread in your mouth when you're hungry. What are these abstractions to us?"

Pavel Petrovich flung up his hands.

"I don't understand you, after that. You insult the Russian people. I don't understand how it's possible not to acknowledge *principes*, rules! By virtue of what do you act then?"

"I've told you already, uncle, that we don't recognize any authorities," put in Arkady.

"We act by virtue of what we recognize as useful," observed Bazarov. "At the present time, negation is the most useful of all—and we deny—"

"Everything?"

"Everything!"

"What, not only art and poetry . . . but even. . . ."

"Everything," repeated Bazarov, with indescribable composure.

Pavel Petrovich stared at him. He had not expected this; while Arkady fairly blushed with delight.

"Allow me, though," began Nikolai Petrovich. "You deny everything; or, speaking more precisely, you destroy everything . . . But one must construct too, you know."

"That's not our business now. . . . The ground has to be cleared first."

"The present condition of the people requires it," added Arkady, with dignity; "we are bound to carry out these requirements, we have no right to yield to the satisfaction of our personal egoism."

This last phrase apparently displeased Bazarov; there was a flavor of philosophy, that is to say, romanticism about it, for Bazarov called philosophy, too, romanticism, but he did not think it necessary to correct his young disciple.

"No, no!" cried Pavel Petrovich, with sudden energy. "I'm not willing to believe that you, gentlemen, know the Russian people really, that you are the representatives of their requirements, their aspirations! No; the Russian people is not what you imagine it. It holds tradition sacred; it is a patriarchal people; it cannot live without faith . . ."

"I'm not going to dispute that," Bazarov interrupted. "I'm even ready to agree that in *that* you're right."

"But if I am right. . . ."

"It still proves nothing."

THE RUSSIAN TONGUE (written 1882)

Translated by Constance Garnett

In his last few years, grown old and melancholy, Turgenev wrote a number of short, poignant prose poems, which he published in a volume called Senilia *during his final brief return to his native land.*

In days of doubt, in days of dreary musings on my country's fate, thou alone art my stay and support, mighty, true, free Russian speech! But for thee, how not fall into despair, seeing all that is done at home? But who can think that such a tongue is not the gift of a great people!

ON THE RACK (written 1882)

Translated by Constance Garnett

"Why all this groaning?"

"I am in pain, in great pain."

"Have you listened to the babbling of a brook as it runs over stones?"

"Yes—but what is the point of the question?"

"The point of the question is that the babbling of the brook and your groans are both just sounds and nothing more. There is only this difference, perhaps: the babbling of the brook may gladden someone's ear, whereas your groans leave the listener quite unmoved. Don't try to contain them, however—just remember that they are merely sounds, sounds like the crash of a falling tree . . . sounds . . . and nothing more."

The Dark Dostoevsky

*Pessimistic about life but compassionate toward his fellow man, Fedor Dostoevsky
once wrote that he sought in his work to portray "the depths of the human soul."
Though often called a psychologist, he preferred to be thought of as a realist who
examined universal human qualities—not only passion and pathology, but also
man's religious instincts and his feeling for his native land. Dostoevsky's milieu
was the Russian city—in particular, the streets and gloomy rooms of St. Petersburg.*

From POOR PEOPLE (1846)

Translated by David Magarshack

*Dostoevsky's first novel became the most celebrated work of early
Russian realistic prose. Constructed in the form of correspondence
between a clerk and an indigent young girl next door, it traces the
clerk's efforts to help her by sacrificing his own meager financial
security. He loves her but is too shy to tell her so. This excerpt is
from the girl's diary, which she sends with one of her letters.
Pokrovsky is her lover, an impoverished student; Sasha is her
cousin, in whose house the girl and her mother had once been living.*

A little, grey-haired old man used to visit our house sometimes. He was dirty, badly dressed, awkward, ungainly—in
short, as strange-looking as could be. At first glance one got
the impression that he was ashamed of himself for some
reason. That was why he was so ill-at-ease, why he had such
awkward gestures. Indeed, he had such strange mannerisms
that one could not help concluding that he was not in his
right mind. He used to arrive at our house and remain standing in the hall by the glass doors, not daring to enter. If anyone—Sasha, a maid or myself—happened to pass whom he
knew to be well-disposed towards him, he would begin to
wave and beckon and make all sorts of signs, and it was only
when that person nodded or called him in—the agreed sign
that there was no visitor in the house and that he could come
in when he liked—it was only then that the old man opened
the door quietly, smiled happily, rubbed his hands with satisfaction, and tiptoed into Pokrovsky's room. The old man
was Pokrovsky's father.

Later I came to know the story of that poor old man. He
had a job in some government office but, possessing no abil-
ities of any kind, had occupied a very low, insignificant post
in the civil service. After his first wife (Pokrovsky's mother)
had died, he took it into his head to marry again, this time a
shopkeeper's daughter. His second wife turned the whole
house upside down, made life a hell for everybody, and took
everybody in hand. . . .

Old man Pokrovsky, driven to desperation by his wife's
cruelties, gave himself up to a life of dissipation and was
hardly ever sober. His wife beat him and made him live in the
kitchen. She brought him to such a state that in the end he
got used to blows and ill treatment and no longer complained. He was not yet really old, but his bad habits had almost driven him out of his mind. The only sign of decent
human feelings was his great love for his son, who was said
to bear a striking resemblance to his mother. Was it the
memory of his first kind wife that was responsible for his
great love for his son? The old man would not speak of anything else [and when his son became Sasha's tutor] he visited
the boy twice a week without fail. He dared not come more
often because young Pokrovsky hated his father's visits. The
chief and most important of his faults was his lack of respect
for his father. No doubt his father sometimes was the most
obnoxious man in the world. To begin with, he was terribly
inquisitive and, besides, by his conversation and his most in-
sipid and inane questions, he constantly interfered with his
son's studies, not to mention the fact that he sometimes arrived drunk. Gradually, however, the son weaned his father
from his evil ways, from inquisitiveness and everlasting chat-
ter, and in the end got the old man to listen to him as though
he were an oracle, and the father dared not open his mouth
without his son's permission. The poor old fellow could not
help admiring and doting on Petenka (as he called his son,
Peter). Yet, when he came to see him, the old man almost
always looked tired and worried, probably because he was
uncertain about the reception he might expect from his son.
As a rule, he could not bring himself to enter the room for a
long time, and when I happened to be there, he would question me for about twenty minutes as to whether his Petenka
was well, what sort of mood he was in, whether he was engaged on some important work, what exactly he was doing,
whether he was writing something, or whether he was lost in
meditation. When I had sufficiently encouraged and reas-
sured the old man, he would at last make up his mind to go
in. He would open the door very quietly and very cautiously,
first poke his head through the door, and if he saw that his
son was not cross and nodded to him to come in, he would
enter the room, take off his ragged overcoat and his hat,
which was crumpled and in holes and with a torn brim, hang
them up on a hook—quietly and without a sound. Next he
would carefully sit down somewhere on a chair and, without
taking his eyes off his son, follow his every movement in an
effort to discover his Petenka's mood. If his son did not appear to be in a very good mood, the old fellow would notice
it, would get up from his seat at once, and after remarking,
"I've only looked in for a moment, Petenka," go on to explain that he had been out "for a long walk" and happened

"to pass by" and dropped in "for a rest." He then would silently and humbly put on his coat and hat and, opening the door quietly again, go out, forcing himself to smile so as to conceal his aching heart from his son.

But when the son was glad to see his father, the old man would be struck dumb with joy. His face beamed with pleasure, and this could be detected in his gestures and movements. If his son spoke to him, the old man would invariably rise a little in his chair and reply quietly, humbly, almost reverentially, always trying to choose the choicest, that is to say, the most ridiculous, expressions. But the gift of words did not come easy to him: he would always grow confused, he would lose courage, so that he would not know what to do with his hands or with himself, and a long time afterwards he would whisper his answer, as though wishing to correct himself. If, however, he succeeded in giving a good answer, he would sit up happily, straighten his waistcoat, cravat and frockcoat, and assume an air of self-conscious dignity. Occasionally, indeed, he would feel so emboldened, he would let his courage go so far as to get up quietly from his chair, walk up to the bookshelves, take out a book and even proceed to read something, whatever the book happened to be. All this he would do with an air of feigned indifference and self-composure, as though he could always do as he liked with his son's books, as though his son's kindness was nothing unusual as far as he was concerned. Yet one day I chanced to see the poor old man frightened when his son told him not to touch his books. He grew confused, hastened to put the book back, but did so upside down, then, wishing to put it right, turned it with its back to the wall, smiled, blushed, and was at a loss as to how to make amends for his misdemeanor. Pokrovsky, by his hints, gradually weaned his father from his bad habits, and whenever his father was sober three times running, he gave him a quarter or half a rouble or even more on parting. Sometimes he would buy his father a pair of boots or a tie or a waistcoat. The old fellow would be as proud of his new acquisition as a peacock. . . .

From CROCODILE (c. 1865)

Translated by Rosalind A. Zoglin

Dostoevsky is thought to have written this casual satire to rebuke a Russian political economist whose materialistic attitudes he deplored. In the story a Russian gentleman is swallowed by a crocodile at an entertainment gallery owned by a German. Here the victim's friends discuss his predicament, and their best course of action.

"And so, Timofey Semyonich? Give advice, guidance as befits an experienced man, like a relative. What should we do? . . . Suppose he suffocates?". . .

"Hmm," he said, twirling the snuff in his hands. . . . "Naturally, he musn't be allowed to suffocate and that is why it is necessary to take certain basic precautions for the preservation of his health—well, to avoid taking cold, etc. . . . As for the German, it is my personal opinion that he is completely within his rights, and even more, because it is *his* crocodile that was invaded without permission and it was not *he* who

entered into Ivan Matveyich's crocodile without a by-your-leave who, as I recall, never even had a crocodile. Thus, since a crocodile constitutes property, it is impossible to have him cut open without recompense."

"Not even to save a human being . . . ?"

"It's his own fault. Who stuck him in there? Perhaps it will be necessary to hire a nurse for him there at the state's expense, but that isn't in the regulations. But the main thing is that the crocodile is property and thus the so-called economic principle is in action here, and the economic principle has priority. The other day at Luka Andreyich's meeting, Ignaty Prokofich spoke. Do you know him? He is a great capitalist. 'We need industry,' he said, 'we have very little foreign trade. It is essential to create it. We have to create capital, therefore, we must also create a middle class, the so-called bourgeoisie. And since we don't have capital, we must attract it from abroad. First of all, we must do what is done abroad. . . . We must encourage foreign companies . . . to buy up the whole of our land in large parcels and then split it up and . . . sell it as private property or rather not sell, but rent it. Then,' he said, 'all the land will be in the hands of foreign companies, they can fix any rent they like. And so the peasant will work three times as hard to earn his daily bread and he can be turned out at will and so he will feel that and become industrious and submissive and will work much harder for the same wages. But as it is now in the commune—what does he care? He knows he won't die of hunger, and he can continue to be lazy and drunk. And meanwhile money will be attracted to Russia and capital will be created. . . .'"

"But how about Ivan Matveyich?". . .

"Yes, well, how about Ivan Matveyich? I am coming to that. Here we are anxious to attract foreign capital, and now consider this. As soon as the capital of a foreigner who came to Petersburg has been doubled through Ivan Matveyich, we, instead of protecting the foreign capitalist, want to rip open the belly of his original capital, namely, the crocodile. In my opinion, Ivan Matveyich, as a true, devoted son of his fatherland, should rejoice and take pride in the fact that due to him the value of this foreign capital, namely the crocodile, has been doubled, possibly trebled. That's just what's needed to attract foreign capital. If one man succeeds with a crocodile then another will come with two or even three, and capital will grow around them, and then you'll have a bourgeoisie—It must be encouraged."

From THE IDIOT (1868)

Translated by Henry and Olga Carlisle

The "idiot" in this later novel is a Russian prince, Myshkin, whose simple, childlike nature is often mistaken for witlessness. In this chapter Myshkin ends a visit to his friend and rival, Rogozhin, following a quarrel over the girl to whom they have both been attracted.

They went through the same rooms the prince had passed through before; Rogozhin walked a little ahead, the prince followed him. They entered the large drawing room. On the walls there were some pictures, all of them portraits of bish-

ops or dark landscapes in which nothing could be seen. Over the doorway into the next room there hung an oddly shaped picture, about five feet wide and less than a foot high. It was of the Savior, who had just been taken down from the cross. The prince glanced narrowly at it as if he was trying to remember something, but he was about to pass through the door without stopping. He felt very depressed and wanted to get out of this house. But Rogozhin suddenly stopped in front of the painting.

"All these pictures were picked up at auctions for a rouble or two by my late father," he said. "He liked them. A man who knows paintings looked at all the paintings here. He said they were trash, all except this one, the one over the doorway. . . ."

Rogozhin suddenly stopped looking at the painting and walked ahead. No doubt his distraction and the strangely irritable mood that had come over him so suddenly might explain this abruptness; nevertheless the prince found it odd that he would break off a conversation which he had started himself. . . .

"Tell me, Lev Nikolayevitch," said Rogozhin suddenly, having walked on a few steps. "I've been meaning to ask you a long time, do you believe in God or not?"

"How strangely you ask that and—how strangely you look at me," observed the prince involuntarily.

"I like looking at that painting," Rogozhin murmured after a short silence, as if he had forgotten his question again.

"At that painting!" exclaimed the prince, struck by a sudden thought. "At that painting! Why, that's a painting that might make some people lose their faith!"

"Yes, faith may be lost too," assented Rogozhin unexpectedly. By now they had reached the front door.

"What do you mean?" said the prince, suddenly stopping.

"What is the matter? I said it almost as a joke, but you're so serious! And why do you ask whether I believe in God?"

"Oh, like that, for no reason. I've meant to ask you before. Lots of people don't believe these days. . . ."

Rogozhin smiled bitterly. After he had asked his question he suddenly opened the door and waited with his hand on the lock for the prince to go out. . . .

The prince went down one step and turned around.

"As for faith," he said, smiling—plainly not wishing to leave Rogozhin this way—and inspired by a sudden recollection. "As for faith, I had four different encounters in two days last week. One morning I was traveling on the new railway line and I talked for four hours with a certain S.; we had just become acquainted. I'd already heard a lot about

him, among other things that he was an atheist. He is really a very learned man, and I was glad to have the chance to talk to such a person. Besides that, he is an unusually well-bred man, and he talked with me as if I was his equal in knowledge and understanding. He doesn't believe in God. Except one thing struck me: he didn't seem to be talking about that at all, the whole time, and this struck me precisely because whenever I've met disbelievers before, and no matter how many of their books I read, it has always struck me that they seem to be speaking and writing about something else, though on the surface it seems to be that. I told him this at the time, but I probably didn't say it clearly, or did not know how to express it, because he didn't understand a thing. That evening I stopped for the night at a provincial hotel where a murder had happened the night before, and everyone was talking about it when I arrived. Two peasants, older men who had known each other a long time and were friends, neither of them drunk, were having tea and were meaning to go sleep in the little room they had taken together. But for the past two days one of them had been noticing that the other wore a silver watch on a beaded ribbon, which apparently he had not known that he had before. The first was not a thief, he was in fact an honest man and for a peasant not at all poor. But he was so taken by this watch, so tempted by it that he finally could not restrain himself, he took a knife and when his friend's back was turned came up cautiously behind him, took aim, raised his eyes to heaven, crossed himself, and bitterly and silently prayed, 'Lord, forgive me for Christ's sake!' and he cut his friend's throat with one stroke like a sheep, and took his watch."

Rogozhin rocked back and forth with laughter. He laughed as if he was having a fit of some kind. It was indeed strange to see him laughing like this so soon after his somber mood.

"Oh, I like that! No, that really beats everything!" he cried, gasping for breath. "One fellow doesn't believe in God at all, while the other believes in Him so much he murders people with a prayer on his lips. No, my dear Prince, you could never have just invented that. Ha, ha, ha! No, that beats everything!"

"Next morning I went out to walk around the town," continued the prince when Rogozhin had stopped laughing, though spasmodic laughter still burst from his lips, "and I saw a drunken soldier swaying along the wooden sidewalk in a terrible state. He came up to me and said, 'Buy this silver cross, sir. You can have it for twenty kopecks. It's silver!' I saw the cross in his hand—he must have just taken it off— on a dirty blue ribbon; but you could tell at first glance it was only made of tin, a big, eight-branched one, of a regular Byzantine design. I took out twenty kopecks and gave them to him, and at once put the cross around my neck and I could see in his face how pleased he was to have cheated a stupid gentleman. He went off immediately to drink up the proceeds of the cross; there wasn't the least doubt of that. As for me, my dear friend, I was at the time tremendously impressed by everything that came pouring upon me in Russia; I had understood nothing about the country before, as if I had grown up unable to express myself; and my memories of it during my five years abroad were somehow fantastic. So I went away and I thought, 'No, it's too soon for me to condemn this peddler of Christ. God alone knows what is hidden in those weak and drunken hearts.' An hour later as I was going back to the hotel I came upon a peasant woman with a tiny baby. The woman was still quite young, the child about six weeks old. The child smiled at her for the first time in its life. I watched and suddenly she crossed herself with great devotion. 'What are you doing, my dear?' (I was always asking questions in those days.) 'There is joy for a mother in her child's first smile, just as God rejoices when from heaven he sees a sinner praying to Him with his whole heart.' This is what that peasant woman said to me, almost in those very words, such a profound, subtle, and truly religious thought, in which the whole essence of Christianity is expressed—I mean the whole conception of God as our own Father and of God's joy in man, like a father's in his own child—Christ's fundamental thought! A simple peasant woman! It's true she was a mother—and, who knows, perhaps she was the wife of that soldier. Listen, Parfyon, you asked me a question before, and here's my answer: the essence of religious feeling doesn't depend on reasoning, and it has nothing to do with wrongdoing or crime or with atheism. There is something else there and there always will be, and atheists will always pass over it and will never be talking about *that*. But the important thing is that you will recognize it most quickly and clearly in the Russian heart—that's my conclusion! It's one of the main convictions I have received from our Russia. There is much to be done, Parfyon! There is much to be done in our Russian world, believe me! Remember how in Moscow we used to meet and talk then, you and I—no, I didn't want to come back here at all! And I never, never thought I'd be meeting you like this! Well, it's done! Good-bye for now. May God be with you!" He turned and went down the stairs.

"Lev Nikolayevitch!" Parfyon shouted from above, when the prince reached the first landing. "That cross you bought from the soldier—do you have it with you?"

"Yes, I'm wearing it." And once again he stopped.

"Show me."

Again something strange! He thought a moment, then went up and showed him the cross without taking it off his neck.

"Give it to me," said Rogozhin.

"Why? Do you—" The prince did not want to part with the cross.

"I'll wear it, and I'll give you mine, for you to wear."

"You want to exchange crosses? By all means, Parfyon, if you want to I'm delighted. We will be brothers."

The prince took off his tin cross, Parfyon his gold one, and they exchanged. Parfyon was silent. With pained surprise the prince observed the same mistrust, the same bitter and almost sarcastic smile on the face of his adoptive brother; at least at times it could be plainly seen. Finally, in silence, Rogozhin took the prince's hand and stood for some time, as though he could not make up his mind about something. At last he suddenly drew him after him and, in a barely audible voice, said, "Come on." They crossed the first floor landing and rang at the door facing the one they had come out. It was soon opened to them. An old woman, all bent and dressed in black, wearing a kerchief over her head, silently bowed low to Rogozhin. He asked her something rapidly and without waiting for an answer led the prince inside. Again they went through dark rooms, of a somehow extraordinarily cold cleanliness, coldly and somberly furnished with ancient furniture under clean white covers. Without announcing himself, Rogozhin led the prince straight into a fairly small room like a drawing room, divided by a polished mahogany partition with doors at each end, behind which there was probably a bedroom. In the corner of the drawing room by the stove sat a little old woman in an armchair. . . .

"Mother," said Rogozhin, kissing her hand, "this is my great friend, Prince Lev Nikolayevitch Myshkin. We have exchanged crosses. He was like a real brother to me in Moscow at one time, he did a lot for me. Bless him, Mother, as you would bless your own son. Wait, old lady, like this; let me fix your fingers right."

But before Parfyon had time to do this, the old woman raised her right hand, with three fingers held up, and three times devotedly made the sign of the cross over the prince. Then, once again she nodded her head tenderly and affectionately to him.

"Well, let's be going, Lev Nikolayevitch," said Parfyon. "That's all I brought you here for."

When they came out on the landing again, he added, "She doesn't understand a thing, she didn't understand a word I said, and yet she blessed you. That means she wanted to do it herself. Well, good-bye, it's time for me to go, and you too."

And he opened his own door.

"But let me at least embrace you before we part, you strange fellow!" cried the prince, looking at him with tender reproach, and was about to embrace him. But Parfyon had barely raised his arms when he let them fall again. He could not bring himself to do it, he tried to avoid looking at the prince. He did not want to embrace him.

"Have no fear! Though I took your cross, I'm not going to knife you for your watch!" he muttered to himself indistinctly, and suddenly laughed in a strange way. But then his whole face changed: he turned terribly pale, his lips trembled, his eyes blazed. He raised his arms, embraced the prince warmly, and said in a breathless voice: "Well, take her, then, since it's fated to be! She's yours! I'm letting you have her. Remember Rogozhin!"

And turning away from the prince without looking at him, he went quickly inside and slammed the door behind him.

Satirists and Populists

From 1840 to 1870 the Russian reading public had trebled in size. The printed word had become a powerful medium, and after the abolition of serfdom in 1861, novelists and journalists used it more than ever before to promote social and political ideas. Some writers, fascinated with Darwin's new theories, shared the Nihilism of the notorious Bazarov in Turgenev's Fathers and Sons. *Others, called Populists, romanticized the provincial peasant and villager and censured the rural aristocracy. Two Populists in particular—Leskov and Saltykov—and a realist—Goncharov—captured the flavor of the period in broad satires.*

Ivan Goncharov

From OBLOMOV (1859)

Translated by Natalie Duddington

In Ilya Ilyitch Oblomov, the protagonist of this novel, Goncharov created a classic caricature of the serf owner of the 1850's. "Oblomovism," symbolizing aristocratic indolence, soon became a household word. This excerpt is taken from the beginning of the story.

Ilya Ilyitch Oblomov was lying in bed one morning in his flat in Gorohovy Street, in one of the big houses that had almost as many inhabitants as a whole country town. He was a man of thirty-two or three, of medium height and pleasant appearance, with dark-grey eyes that strayed idly from the walls to the ceiling with a vague dreaminess which showed that nothing troubled or occupied him. His attitude and the very folds of his dressing-gown expressed the same untroubled ease as his face. At times his eyes were dimmed by something like weariness or boredom; but neither weariness nor boredom could banish for a moment the softness which was the dominant and permanent expression not merely of his face but of his whole being. A serene, open, candid mind was reflected in his eyes, his smile, in every movement of his head and his hands. A cold and superficial observer would glance at Oblomov and say: "A good-hearted, simple fellow, I should think." A kinder and more thoughtful man would gaze into his face for some time and walk off smiling in pleasant uncertainty.

Ilya Ilyitch's complexion was neither rosy nor dark nor pale, but indefinite, or perhaps it seemed so because there was a certain slackness about the muscles of his face, unusual at his age; this may have been due to lack of fresh air or exercise, or to some other reason. The smooth and excessively white skin of his neck, his small soft hands and plump shoulders, suggested a certain physical effeminacy. His movements were restrained and gentle; there was a certain lazy gracefulness about them even if he were alarmed. If his mind was troubled, his eyes were clouded, his forehead wrinkled, and an interplay of hesitation, sadness, and fear was reflected in his face; but the disturbance seldom took the form of a definite idea and still more seldom reached the point of a decision. . . .

How well Oblomov's dress suited his calm features and soft body! He wore a dressing-gown of Persian material, a regular Eastern dressing-gown without anything European about it—no tassels, no velvet, no waist, and so roomy that he could wrap it round him twice. The sleeves, in true Asiatic fashion, gradually widened from the wrists to the shoulders. Although the dressing-gown had lost its original freshness and was shiny in places with an acquired and not a natural lustre, it still preserved its brilliant Eastern coloring, and the stuff was as strong as ever.

The dressing-gown had a number of invaluable qualities in Oblomov's eyes: it was soft and pliable; it did not get in his way; it obeyed the least movement of his body. . . .

Oblomov never wore a tie or a waistcoat at home because he liked comfort and freedom. He wore long, soft, wide slippers; when he got up from bed he put his feet straight into them without looking.

Lying down was not for Ilya Ilyitch either a necessity as it is for a sick or a sleepy man, or an occasional need as it is for a person who is tired, or a pleasure as it is for a sluggard: it was his normal state. When he was at home—and he was almost always at home—he was lying down, and invariably in the same room, the one in which we have found him and which served him as bedroom, study, and reception-room. He had three more rooms, but he seldom looked into them, only, perhaps, in the morning when his servant swept his study—which did not happen every day. In those other rooms the furniture was covered and the curtains were drawn.

The room in which Ilya Ilyitch was lying at the first glance seemed splendid. It had a mahogany bureau, two silk-upholstered sofas, a handsome screen embroidered with fruit and flowers never to be seen in nature. It had silk curtains, carpets, several pictures, bronze, and china, and a number of pretty knick-knacks. But the experienced eye of a person of good taste would detect at once that all these things were put there merely to comply with unavoidable conventions. This was all Oblomov had in mind when he furnished his study. . . .

The owner himself, however, looked at the furniture of his study coldly and unconcernedly, as though wondering who could have brought all this stuff there. It was because of Oblomov's indifference towards his property, and perhaps because of the still greater indifference of his servant, Zahar, that the study struck one, at a more careful inspection, by its neglected and untidy condition. Dusty cobwebs hung in festoons round the pictures on the walls; mirrors, instead of reflecting objects, might have served as tablets for writing memoranda in the dust; there were stains on the carpets; a towel had been left on the sofa. Almost every morning a dirty plate, with a salt-cellar and a bone from the previous night's supper, was to be seen on the crumb-covered table.

If it had not been for this plate and for a freshly smoked pipe by the bed, and for the owner himself lying in it, one might have thought that the room was uninhabited. . . .

Ilya Ilyitch had, contrary to his habits, woken up very early—about eight o'clock. He was much perturbed. His expression kept changing from one of alarm to that of distress and vexation. He was obviously suffering from an inward conflict and his intellect had not yet come to his aid.

The fact was that the evening before Oblomov had received a disagreeable letter from the bailiff of his estate. Everyone knows what kind of disagreeable news a bailiff can write: bad harvest, debts, smaller income, etc. Although the bailiff had written exactly the same letter the year before and the year before that, his last letter had the effect of an unpleasant surprise.

It was no joke! One had to think of taking some measures. In justice to Ilya Ilyitch it must be said that, after receiving the bailiff's first unpleasant letter several years before, he had begun to think of various changes and improvements in the management of his estate. He proposed introducing fresh economic, administrative, and other measures. But the plan was not yet thoroughly thought out, and the bailiff's unpleasant letters came every year inciting him to action and disturbing his peace of mind. Oblomov knew it was necessary to do something decisive.

As soon as he woke he made up his mind to get up and wash, and, after drinking tea, to think matters over, taking various things into consideration and writing them down, and altogether to go into the subject thoroughly. He lay for half an hour tormented by his decision; but afterwards he reflected that he would have time to think after breakfast, which he could have in bed as usual, especially since one can think just as well lying down.

This was what he did. After his morning tea he sat up and very nearly got out of bed; looking at his slippers, he began lowering one foot down towards them, but at once drew it back again.

It struck half-past nine. Ilya Ilyitch roused himself. "What am I thinking of?" he said aloud with vexation. "It's disgraceful: I must set to work! If I let myself go, I'll never . . .

"Zahar!" he shouted.

Something like a dog's growl followed by the sound of jumping feet came from the room divided by a narrow passage from Ilya Ilyitch's study. It was Zahar jumping off the stove, where he generally sat dozing.

An elderly man, wearing a grey waistcoat with brass buttons and a grey coat torn under the arm and showing his shirt, came into the room; his skull was perfectly bare, but each of his big side-whiskers, light brown streaked with grey, was thick enough to make three beards.

Zahar made no attempt to change either the appearance, which Providence had bestowed upon him, or the costume he had worn in the country. His clothes were made after the pattern he had brought from Oblomov's estate. He liked the grey coat and waistcoat because they vaguely reminded him of the livery he had worn in the old days when he accompanied his late master and mistress to church or on a visit to friends; and the livery was the only thing in his memories that expressed the dignity of the Oblomov family. There was nothing else to remind the old man of the peace and plenty of his master's house in the depths of the country. The old master and mistress were dead; the family portraits had been left behind and were probably lying somewhere in the attic; tales of the old way of living and the family grandeur were being forgotten and only lived in the memory of a few old people who had remained on the estate. . . .

It was some minutes before Ilya Ilyitch, absorbed with his thoughts, noticed Zahar. Zahar stood before him in silence. At last he coughed.

"What is it?" asked Ilya Ilyitch.

"You called me, didn't you?"

"Called, did I? What could I have called you for—I don't remember!" he answered, stretching himself. "Go now and I will try and remember."

Zahar left the room and Ilya Ilyitch went on lying and thinking of the accursed letter.

Nikolai Leskov

From LADY MACBETH OF MTSENSK (1865)

Translated by Ethel O. Bronstein

A Populist with a keen ear for provincial slang, Leskov has been called the most Russian of Russian writers. The melodramatic short story excerpted here in two of its chapters was later adapted as the libretto to an opera of the same name by Dmitry Shostakovich.

Zinovii had been away from home for a week, and that whole week his wife had whiled each night away, till the white dawn broke, with Serghei.

Much wine from the father-in-law's cellar was drunk during those same nights in the bedroom of Zinovii Borisich, and many sweet sweets eaten, and many a kiss sipped from the young mistress' honeyed lips, and much toying with black curls was there on the soft pillows. But no road runs smooth all the way; there's also rough going here and there.

Sleep would not come to Boris Timotheich; the old man wandered about the quiet house in his nightshirt of lurid calico; he came to one window, came to another, looked out, and there below him, slipping quiet as quiet down a post under his daughter-in-law's window, was the red shirt of that fine lad Serghei. Boris Timotheich dashed out and grabbed the Lothario by his legs. The latter swung back, as if to plant a haymaker on his master's ear, he was so vexed, but held back, after deciding there would be a row.

"Tell me," said Boris Timotheich, "where was you at, you thief?"

"Where was I, says he! Wherever it was, I'm not there now, Boris Timotheich, my dear Sir," answered Serghei.

"You spent the night in my daughter-in-law's room?"

"As to that, master, once again—I know where I spent the night; but here's what, Boris Timotheich, you take my word for it; you can't bring back what's past; don't you go bringing shame down on your decent merchant household, at least. Just you tell me what you want of me now? What satisfaction would you like?"

"I'd like, you varmint, for to give you five hundred lashes," answered Boris Timotheich.

"Mine was the guilt—your will be done," the gallant agreed. "Tell me where I'm to follow you; have yourself a good time—lap up my blood."

So old Boris led Serghei to a small stone storeroom he had, and he lashed away at him with a quirt till there was no more strength left in him. Not a groan did Serghei let out of him, but he did chew up half the shirt-sleeve he'd sunk his teeth into.

And after that old Boris left Serghei lying in that storeroom, until his back, beaten so livid that it looked like cast iron, might heal, shoved in a clay pitcher of water, snapped shut the big lock, and sent for his son.

But, even in our time, six miles over the byroads of Russia are not to be traversed rapidly, whereas Katerina could no longer bear to pass an extra hour without Serghei. She had developed suddenly in all the fullness of her awakened nature and had become so resolute that there was no restraining her. She ferreted out Serghei's whereabouts, talked things over with him through the iron door, and dashed off in search of the keys.

"Let Serghei go, Father dear," she appealed to her father-in-law.

The old man simply turned green. Never had he expected such brazen daring from his sinful but always, up to now, submissive daughter-in-law.

"What are you up to, you so-and-so?" he began shaming Katerina.

"Let him go," she said. "I swear to you on my conscience that there's been nothing wrong between us yet."

"'No wrong!' says she!"—and he just plain ground his teeth. "And what was you two passing your time at up there of nights? Fluffing up your husband's pillows?"

But she wouldn't let him be, harping on her one note: Let him go, and let him go.

"If that's the way you'd have it," said old Boris, "then get this: when your husband gets back, we'll flog you with our own hands out in the stable, honest wife that you are; and as for him, I'll send that low-down villain to prison tomorrow."

That's what Boris Timotheich decided; the only thing was that his decision was never carried out.

.   .   .

That night old Boris ate some mushrooms with buckwheat porridge, and after that heartburn set in; he was seized with sudden pain in the pit of his stomach: he was racked by dreadful vomiting spells, and toward morning he died, and, as it happened, in the very same way that the rats died in his warehouses, for whose benefit Katerina would always prepare a special mess with her own hands, using a dangerous white powder that was entrusted into her keeping.

Katerina freed her Serghei from the old man's stone storeroom and, without the least shame, before the eyes of all the people, made him comfortable in her husband's bed to recover from her father-in-law's beatings, whilst the father-in-law himself was, without any delay, interred with all Christian rites. Remarkably enough, no doubts occurred to anyone: if Boris Timotheich died, why, then, die he did, after eating mushrooms, just as did so many others after eating them. Old Boris was buried in all haste without even waiting for his son, for the weather at that time of year was sultry, and the messenger had not found Zinovii Borisich at the mill. He had chanced to get some forest land cheap, more than sixty miles still further, had gone to look at it, and hadn't told anyone clearly just where he was going.

Having disposed of this matter, Katerina became completely unbridled. She had never been one of your timid women, but now one could not at all divine what she had in mind; she went about bold as you please, managed everything about the house, and simply wouldn't let Serghei go a step from her side. Everyone on the place began wondering at all this, but Katerina managed to get on the right side of each in her openhanded way, and all wondering ceased at once. . . .

And in the meantime Serghei had gotten his health back, and his suppleness, and again, like the bravest of brave fellows, had begun circling like a very falcon over Katerina, and again began their ever so pleasant life. But time was rolling on not for them alone: Zinovii Borisich, the much-wronged husband, was hastening home after his prolonged absence.

Mikhail Saltykov

From THE GOLOVLOVS (1876)

Translated by Andrew R. MacAndrew

Known in his own time chiefly by the pseudonym N. Shchedrin, Saltykov was the leading Populist writer of the seventies. In this novel he invents a chronicle of a gentry family dominated by one of the younger sons, nicknamed Judas, whom Saltykov describes as "pettifogging, deceitful, loquacious, boundlessly ignorant, and afraid of the devil." Here, Judas sadistically mocks his dying brother, Pavel, who is the appointed heir to the coveted family estate.

"Why? Where from? Who let him in?" Pavel cried, instinctively letting his head fall back limply on the pillow.

Judas stood by the bed looking at the sick man, sorrowfully shaking his head.

"Does it hurt?" he asked, in his sweetest possible voice.

Pavel fixed his mad eyes on him as if trying desperately to understand something. Suddenly Judas turned, went over to the icon, knelt by it, bowed three times to the ground, got up and returned to the bed.

"All right, Brother, you can get up. God has been merciful!" he said cheerfully, installing himself in the armchair with such an air of satisfaction that one might really have thought he had an assurance of God's "mercy" in his pocket.

Finally Pavel understood that this was not a phantom but his brother Judas in the flesh. He started shivering, feeling suddenly shrunken. Judas's eyes were looking at him with a warm, brotherly expression, but the sick man saw the noose that was hidden in them, a noose that at any moment would come flying through the air and tighten around his neck.

"Ah, Brother, Brother, what a sight you've become!" Judas went on, switching to a friendly, teasing tone. "Why, cheer up, get up on your feet and run down to see Mamma, show her what a fine fellow you've become! Come on, up you go!"

"Get out of here, Bloodsucker!" the sick man shouted in exasperation.

"Oh, my dear, dear brother! I come in all friendship to comfort you and you . . . what a terrible word to use! It's a terrible sin, you know, to say such things! How could you call your own brother that? You should be ashamed of yourself, my boy! Wait, let me plump up your pillow!"

Judas rose from the armchair and poked the pillow with his finger.

"That's better now! Now you'll be nice and comfortable! Have a good rest, you'll be comfortable now till tomorrow."

"You get out!"

"My, I must say sickness has spoiled you quite a bit. It has even changed your character—you've become so querulous! You keep sending me away, but think for yourself. How can I go away and leave you? Suppose you want a drink? I'll go and get you some water. . . ."

"Go away, Bloodsucker!"

"You see, you insult me while I'm praying to God for you. I know very well that it's your sickness that makes you say these things. But I'm accustomed to forgiving people and I forgive you everything. Today, for instance, driving here to see you, we came across a peasant on the road who said something. . . . Well, what of it? I only hope God will forgive him! He defiled his own tongue. But I didn't lose my temper at all. On the contrary, I made the sign of the cross over him—that's the truth!"

"I suppose you robbed him too . . . that peasant."

"Who, me? No, Brother, you're wrong. Highwaymen rob people, not me. I act strictly according to the law. I caught his horse in my meadow. All right, friend, go and complain to the judge! Now, if the judge says it's all right to graze your animals in other people's meadows, then God bless him, he can have his horse back. But if the judge says it isn't all right, well then, let him pay for it. I obey the law, my dear brother. I always obey the law!"

"You're Judas-the-Betrayer, you've robbed your mother of everything!"

"Again, think what you like, but I must repeat that what you say doesn't make much sense. And, if I weren't a good Christian, I might strongly resent that statement."

"Yes, yes, yes, you robbed her, made a beggar out of her."

"Wait a minute, wait a minute, calm yourself! I'll say a prayer—perhaps that'll make you feel a bit better. . . ."

Judas's control over himself was very strong, but the dying man's insults stung him so sharply that his lips twisted and paled. However, his hypocrisy was so deeply ingrained that he couldn't break off the comedy he was playing. He actually got down on his knees and remained there for a quarter of an hour, whispering and raising his arms to heaven. When he had gone through this and returned to the dying man's bed, his face was again relaxed, almost serene.

"As a matter of fact, Brother dear, I came here to talk business with you," he said.

He sat down in the armchair again. "While you go on insulting me," he continued, "I keep thinking of the salvation of your soul. Now tell me, how long is it since you last confessed?"

"What is this? Hey, Ulita! Agashka! Someone! Take him away from here!" Pavel groaned.

"Come, come, don't get so excited, my boy. I know you don't like to talk about these things. You've always been a very poor Christian and I suppose you always will be. Still, it might be a good thing if, in a moment like this, you gave some thought to your soul. You see, the soul is a delicate thing and must be handled carefully. Now, what does the Church teach us? Bring me, it tells us, thanksgiving and supplication. . . . And then too, we pray for a dignified, painless, Christian end to our existence. . . ."

Pavel's face was purple and he was almost choking. If he could have smashed his own head, he would certainly have done so.

"Then I wanted to talk to you about the estate; have you made any arrangements yet?" Judas added. "It's a nice little estate you've got here, no doubt about that! The soil is even richer than in Golovlovo; there's more loam in it. And then there's the capital, of course. As you can imagine, I know nothing about your affairs, except that the government must have paid you for the land you made over to the peasants. I've never poked my nose into your affairs, but today, while driving over here, it occurred to me: 'Why, my brother Pavel must have some capital, and if he does, he must have made some arrangements already.'"

Pavel turned away, breathing deeply.

"You haven't made any arrangements? Oh, so much the better, my dear friend! It's much fairer if it passes to the rightful successor. That way the property won't go to a stranger, it'll remain in the family. Now take me, for instance. My health is very poor—you might even say I have one foot in the grave. Nevertheless, I don't bother with making a will. Why should I when I know that the law will take care of it for me? And think of the advantages of doing things that way—no quarrels, no envy, no intrigues. Just leave the law to do the job!"

This was sinister. Pavel had the nightmarish sensation that he had been placed in his coffin while he was still alive, that he was lying fettered by lethargy, that he couldn't make the smallest movement, and that Judas the bloodsucker was jeering at his motionless body. . . .

The Prodigious Tolstoy

A writer of such skill that he could present more than five hundred characters in his novel War and Peace *without resorting to stereotypes—and maintain a smooth narrative at the same time—Leo Tolstoy brought to maturity the realistic tradition that began with Gogol. His work won him international fame; yet he remained a humble man, whose greatest admiration was for the peasants, the "poor, simple, unlettered folk."*

From CHILDHOOD (1852)

Translated by Rosemary Edmonds

Childhood *was Tolstoy's first published work, a fictionalized autobiography that he later followed with two other volumes—*Boyhood *and* Youth. *This selection from the first chapter of the book describes Karl Ivanych, who tutored young Tolstoy and his brothers.*

On the 12th of August 18—, exactly three days after my tenth birthday, for which I had received such wonderful presents, Karl Ivanych woke me at seven in the morning by hitting at a fly just over my head with a flap made of sugar-bag paper fastened to a stick. His action was so clumsy that he caught the little ikon of my patron-saint, which hung on the headboard of my oak bedstead, and the dead fly fell right on my head. I put my nose out from under the bedclothes, steadied with my hand the ikon which was still wobbling, flicked the dead fly on to the floor, and looked at Karl Ivanych with wrathful if sleepy eyes. He, however, in his bright-colored quilted dressing-gown, with a belt of the same material round the waist, a red knitted skull-cap with a tassel on his head and soft goat-skin boots on his feet, continued to walk round the room, taking aim and smacking at the flies on the walls.

"Of course I am only a small boy," I thought, "but still he ought not to disturb me. Why doesn't he go killing flies round Volodya's bed? There are heaps of them there. But no, Volodya is older than me: I am the youngest of all—that is why I am tormented. All he thinks of every day of his life is how to be nasty to me," I muttered. "He is perfectly well aware that he woke me up and startled me, but he pretends not to notice it . . . disgusting man! And his dressing-gown and the skull-cap and the tassel too—they're all disgusting!"

While I was thus mentally expressing my vexation with Karl Ivanych he went up to his own bed, looked at his watch which was suspended above it in a little shoe embroidered with glass beads, hung the fly-swat on a nail and turned to us, obviously in the best of moods.

"*Auf, Kinder, auf! . . . 's ist Zeit. Die Mutter ist schon im Saal!*" [Get up, children, get up! . . . It's time. Your Mother is already in the dining-room!] he cried in his kindly German voice. Then he came over to me, sat down at the foot of my bed and took his snuff-box from his pocket. I pretended to be asleep. Karl Ivanych first took a pinch of snuff, wiped his nose, snapped his fingers, and only then began on me. With a chuckle he started tickling my heels. "*Nun, nun, Faulenzer!*" [Now then, lazy-bones!]

Much as I dreaded being tickled, I did not jump out of bed or answer him but merely hid my head deeper under the pillow and kicked out with all my might, doing my utmost to keep from laughing.

"How nice he is, and how fond of us!" I said to myself. "How could I have had such horrid thoughts about him just now?"

I was annoyed with myself and with Karl Ivanych; I wanted to laugh and cry at the same time. I was all upset. "*Ach, lassen Sie* [Oh, leave me alone], Karl Ivanych!" I cried with tears in my eyes, thrusting my head from under the pillows.

Karl Ivanych was taken aback. He stopped tickling my feet and began to ask anxiously what was the matter with me? Had I had a bad dream? His kind German face and the solicitude with which he tried to discover the cause of my tears made them flow all the faster. I felt ashamed and could not understand how only a moment before I had hated Karl Ivanych and thought his dressing-gown, skull-cap and the tassel repulsive. Now, on the contrary, I liked them all very much indeed and even the tassel seemed to be a clear testimony to his goodness. I told him I was crying because of a bad dream: I had dreamt that mamma was dead and they were taking her away to bury her. I invented all this, for I really could not remember what I had been dreaming that night; but when Karl Ivanych, affected by my story, tried to comfort and soothe me it seemed to me that I actually had dreamt that awful dream and I now shed tears for a different reason.

. . . In the schoolroom Karl Ivanych was an entirely different person: there he was the tutor. I dressed myself quickly, washed and with the brush still in my hand smoothing down my wet hair appeared at his call.

Karl Ivanych, spectacles on nose and book in hand, was sitting in his usual place between the door and the window. To the left of the door were two shelves: one of them belonged to us children—the other was Karl Ivanych's *own* shelf. On ours were all sorts of books—lesson-books and story-books, some standing, others lying flat. Only two big volumes of *Histoire des Voyages* in red bindings rested decorously against the wall, and then came tall books and thick books, big books and little, bindings without books and books without bindings, since everything got pushed and crammed in anyhow when playtime arrived and we were told to tidy up the "library," as Karl Ivanych pompously labelled this shelf. . . .

Among the things that lay on Karl Ivanych's shelf was one which recalls him to me more than all the rest. It was a round piece of cardboard attached to a wooden stand which could be moved up and down by means of small pegs. A caricature of a lady and a wig-maker was pasted on to the cardboard. Karl Ivanych, who was very clever at that sort of thing, had thought of and made this contrivance himself to protect his weak eyes from any very strong light.

I can see before me now his tall figure in the quilted dressing-gown and his thin grey hair visible beneath the red skull-cap. I see him sitting beside a little table on which stands the cardboard circle with the picture of the wig-maker; it cast its shadow on his face; he holds his book in one hand, the other rests on the arm of his chair; near him lie his watch with the figure of a huntsman painted on the dial, a checkered pocket-handkerchief, a round black snuff-box, his green spectacle-case and a pair of snuffers on their tray. Everything is arranged so precisely and carefully in its proper place that this orderliness alone is enough to suggest that Karl Ivanych's conscience is clear and his soul at peace.

If we got tired of running about the *salon* downstairs and crept upstairs on tiptoe to the schoolroom—there was Karl Ivanych sitting by himself in his arm-chair and reading one or other of his beloved books, with a calm, stately expression on his face. Sometimes I caught him when he was not reading: his spectacles had dropped down on his big aquiline nose, his half-closed blue eyes had a peculiar look in them and a sad smile played on his lips. All would be quiet in the room; his even breathing and the ticking of the watch with the huntsman on the dial were the only sounds.

Sometimes he did not notice me and I used to stand at the door and think; "Poor, poor old man! There are a lot of us, we can play and enjoy ourselves; but he is all alone with no one to make a fuss of him. It is true what he says when he talks about being an orphan. And the story of his life is such a dreadful one! I remember him telling Nikolai about it— how awful to be in his position!" And I would feel so sorry for him that sometimes I would go up and take his hand and say, "*Lieber* Karl Ivanych!" He liked to have me say that, and would always pet me and show that he was touched.

From SEVASTOPOL IN DECEMBER, 1854 (1855)

Translated by Louise and Aylmer Maude

This is the first of three Crimean War accounts Tolstoy wrote for a St. Petersburg magazine. Unflinching descriptions of the horrors of battle, they anticipated War and Peace *and influenced such later war correspondents as Stephen Crane and Ernest Hemingway.*

Crowds of gray-clad soldiers, sailors in black, and gayly-dressed women, throng noisily about the quay. Here are women selling buns, Russian peasants with samovars are shouting, "Hot sbiten!" [treacle and lemon] and here too on the very steps lie rusty cannon-balls, bombs, grapeshot, and cannon of various sizes. A little farther on is a large open space where some enormous beams are lying, together with gun carriages and sleeping soldiers. Horses, carts, cannon, green ammunition wagons, and stacked muskets, are standing there. Soldiers, sailors, officers, women, children, and tradespeople, are moving about, carts loaded with hay, sacks, and casks, are passing, and now and then a Cossack, a mounted officer, or a general in a vehicle. To the right is a street closed by a barricade on which some small guns are mounted in embrasures and beside which sits a sailor smoking a pipe. To the left is a handsome building with Roman figures engraved on its frontage and before which soldiers are standing with bloodstained stretchers. Everywhere you will see the unpleasant indications of a war camp. Your first impressions will certainly be most disagreeable: the strange mixture of camp-life and town-life—of a fine town and a dirty bivouac. . . . You will look in vain in any of these faces for signs of disquiet, perplexity, or even of enthusiasm, determination, or readiness for death—there is nothing of the kind. What you see are ordinary people quietly occupied with ordinary activities, so that perhaps you may reproach yourself for having felt undue enthusiasm and may doubt the justice of the ideas you had formed of the heroism of the defenders of Sevastopol, based on the tales and descriptions and sights and sounds seen and heard from the North Side. But before yielding to such doubts go to the bastions and see the defenders of Sevastopol at the very place of the defense. . . .

. . . You meet and overtake detachments of soldiers, Cossacks, officers, and occasionally a woman or a child; only it will not be a woman wearing a bonnet, but a sailor's wife wearing an old cloak and soldiers' boots. After you have descended a little slope farther down the . . . street you will no longer see any houses, but only ruined walls amid strange heaps of bricks, boards, clay, and beams, and before you, up a steep hill, you see a black untidy space cut up by ditches. This space you are approaching is the Fourth Bastion. . . . Here you will meet still fewer people and no women at all, the soldiers walk briskly by, there are traces of blood on the road, and you are sure to meet four soldiers carrying a stretcher and on the stretcher probably a pale yellow face and a bloodstained overcoat. . . . After walking a couple of hundred yards you come to a muddy place much cut up, surrounded by gabions, cellars, platforms, and dugouts, and on which large cast-iron cannon are mounted and cannon-balls lie piled in orderly heaps. It all seems placed without any plan, aim, connection, or order. Here a group of sailors are sitting in the battery; here in the middle of the open space, half sunk in mud, lies a shattered cannon; and there a foot-soldier is crossing the battery, drawing his feet with difficulty out of the sticky mud. . . .

"So this is the Fourth Bastion! This is that terrible, truly dreadful spot!" So you think, experiencing a slight feeling of pride and a strong feeling of suppressed fear. But you are mistaken, this is not the Fourth Bastion yet. This is only Yazonovsky Redoubt—comparatively a very safe and not at all dreadful place. To get to the Fourth Bastion you must turn to the right along that narrow trench where a foot-soldier has just passed, stooping down. In this trench you may again meet men with stretchers and perhaps a sailor or a soldier with a spade. You will see the mouths of mines, dugouts into which only two men can crawl, and there you will see the Cossacks of the Black Sea battalions changing their boots, eating, smoking their pipes, and, in short, living. And again you will see the same stinking mud, the traces of camp life and cast-iron refuse of every shape and form. When you have gone some three hundred steps more you will come out at another battery—a flat space with many holes, surrounded with gabions filled with earth, and cannons on platforms, and the whole walled in with earthworks. Here you will perhaps see four or five soldiers playing cards under shelter of the breastworks, and a naval officer, noticing that you are a stranger and inquisitive, will be pleased to show you his "household" and everything that can interest you. This officer sits on a cannon rolling a yellow cigarette so composedly, walks from one embrasure to another so quietly, talks to you so calmly and with such an absence of affectation, that in spite of the bullets whizzing around you oftener than before you yourself grow cooler, question him carefully and listen to his stories.

. . . It is even very likely that the naval officer from vanity, or merely for a little recreation, will wish to show you some firing. . . .

Suddenly the most fearful roar strikes not only your ears but your whole being and makes you shudder all over. It is followed by the whistle of the departing ball, and a thick cloud of powder-smoke envelops you, the platform, and the black moving figures of the sailors. . . . Soon after, you will see before you a flash and some smoke; the sentinel standing on the breastwork will call out "Can-n-non!" and then a ball will whiz past you and bury itself in the earth. . . . Or he will call out "Mortar!" and you will hear the regular and rather pleasant whistle—which it is difficult to connect with the thought of anything dreadful—of a bomb; you will hear this whistle coming nearer and faster towards you, then you will see a black ball, feel the shock as it strikes the ground, and will hear the ringing explosion. The bomb will fly apart into whizzing and shrieking fragments, stones will rattle in the air, and you will be bespattered with mud.

At these sounds you will experience a strange feeling of mingled pleasure and fear. At the moment you know the shot is flying towards you, you are sure to imagine that it will kill you, but a feeling of pride will support you and no one will know of the knife that cuts at your heart. But when the shot has flown past without hitting you, you revive and are seized, though only for a moment, by an inexpressibly joyful emotion, so that you feel a peculiar delight in the danger—in this game of life and death—and wish the bombs and balls to fall nearer and nearer to you.

But again the sentinel in his loud gruff voice shouts "Mortar!" Again a whistle, a fall, an explosion; and mingled with this last you are startled by a man's groans. You approach the wounded sailor just as the stretchers are brought. Covered with blood and dirt he presents a strange, scarcely human, appearance. Part of his breast has been torn away. For the first few moments only terror and the kind of feigned, premature, look of suffering, common to men in this state, appear on his mud-besprinkled face, but when the stretcher is brought and he himself lies down on it on his healthy side you notice that his expression changes. His eyes shine more brightly, his teeth are clenched, he raises his head higher with difficulty, and when the stretcher is lifted he stops the bearers for a moment and turning to his comrades says with an effort, in a trembling voice, "Forgive me, brothers [in Russian, an expression almost interchangeable with "Farewell . . ."]!" He wishes to say more, something pathetic, but only repeats, "Forgive me, brothers!" At this moment a sailor approaches him, places the cap on the head the wounded man holds up towards him, and then placidly swinging his arms returns quietly to his cannon.

"That's the way with seven or eight every day," the naval officer remarks to you, answering the look of horror on your face, and he yawns as he rolls another yellow cigarette.

So now you have seen the defenders of Sevastopol where they are defending it, and somehow you return with a tranquil heightened spirit, paying no heed to the balls and bombs whose whistle accompanies you all the way to the ruined theater. The principal thought you have brought away with you is a joyous conviction of the strength of the Russian people; and this conviction you have gained not by looking at all those traverses, breastworks, cunningly interlaced trenches, mines, cannon, one after another, of which you could make nothing; but from the eyes, words, and actions —in short from seeing what is called the "spirit"—of the defenders of Sevastopol. What they do is all done so simply, with so little effort, that you feel convinced that they could do a hundred times as much. . . .

From ANNA KARENINA (1877)

Translated by Constance Garnett

Tolstoy's Populist attitudes are clearly revealed in this episode from Anna Karenina, *in which the landowner Konstantin Levin— modeled after Tolstoy himself—spends a day working in his fields alongside the peasants. The excerpt begins the previous evening with a brief discussion between Levin and his brother Sergey Ivanovitch.*

At tea . . . Levin said to his brother:
"I fancy the fine weather will last," said he. "To-morrow I shall start mowing."
"I'm so fond of that form of field labor," said Sergey Ivanovitch.
"I'm awfully fond of it. I sometimes mow myself with the peasants, and to-morrow I want to try mowing the whole day."
Sergey Ivanovitch lifted his head, and looked with interest at his brother.
"How do you mean? Just like one of the peasants, all day long?"
"Yes, it's very pleasant," said Levin.
"It's splendid as exercise, only you'll hardly be able to stand it," said Sergey Ivanovitch, without a shade of irony.
"I've tried it. It's hard work at first, but you get into it. I dare say I shall manage to keep it up. . . ."
"Really! what an idea! But tell me, how do the peasants look at it? I suppose they laugh in their sleeves at their

master's being such a queer fish?"

"No, I don't think so; but it's so delightful, and at the same time such hard work, that one has no time to think about it."

"But how will you do about dining with them? To send you a bottle of Lafitte and roast turkey out there would be a little awkward."

"No, I'll simply come home at the time of their noonday rest."

Next morning Konstantin Levin got up earlier than usual, but he was detained giving directions on the farm, and when he reached the mowing-grass the mowers were already at their second row.

From the uplands he could get a view of the shaded cut part of the meadow below, with its grayish ridges of cut grass, and the black heaps of coats, taken off by the mowers at the place from which they had started cutting.

Gradually, as he rode towards the meadow, the peasants came into sight, some in coats, some in their shirts, mowing, one behind another in a long string, swinging their scythes differently. He counted forty-two of them.

They were mowing slowly over the uneven, low-lying parts of the meadow, where there had been an old dam. Levin recognized some of his own men. Here was old Yermil in a very long white smock, bending forward to swing a scythe; there was a young fellow, Vaska, who had been a coachman of Levin's, taking every row with a wide sweep. Here, too, was Tit, Levin's preceptor in the art of mowing, a thin little peasant. He was in front of all, and cut his wide row without bending, as though playing with the scythe.

Levin got off his mare, and fastening her up by the roadside went to meet Tit, who took a second scythe out of a bush and gave it to him.

"It's ready, sir; it's like a razor, cuts of itself," said Tit, taking off his cap with a smile and giving him the scythe.

Levin took the scythe, and began trying it. As they finished their rows, the mowers, hot and good-humored, came out into the road one after another, and, laughing a little, greeted the master. They all stared at him, but no one made any remark, till a tall old man, with a wrinkled, beardless face, wearing a short sheepskin jacket, came out into the road and accosted him.

"Look'ee now, master, once take hold of the rope there's no letting it go!" he said, and Levin heard smothered laughter among the mowers.

"I'll try not to let it go," he said, taking his stand behind Tit, and waiting for the time to begin.

"Mind'ee," repeated the old man.

Tit made room, and Levin started behind him. The grass was short close to the road, and Levin, who had not done any mowing for a long while, and was disconcerted by the eyes fastened upon him, cut badly for the first moments, though he swung his scythe vigorously. Behind him he heard voices:

"It's not set right; handle's too high; see how he has to stoop to it," said one.

"Press more on the heel," said another.

"Never mind, he'll get on all right," the old man resumed.

"He's made a start. . . . You swing it too wide, you'll tire yourself out. . . . The master, sure, does his best for himself! But see the grass missed out! For such work us fellows would catch it!"

The grass became softer, and Levin, listening without answering, followed Tit, trying to do the best he could. They moved a hundred paces. Tit kept moving on, without stopping, not showing the slightest weariness, but Levin was already beginning to be afraid he would not be able to keep it up: he was so tired.

He felt as he swung his scythe that he was at the very end of his strength, and was making up his mind to ask Tit to stop. But at that very moment Tit stopped of his own accord, and stooping down picked up some grass, rubbed his scythe, and began whetting it. Levin straightened himself, and drawing a deep breath looked round. Behind him came a peasant, and he too was evidently tired, for he stopped at once without waiting to mow up to Levin, and began whetting his scythe. Tit sharpened his scythe and Levin's, and they went on. The next time it was just the same. Tit moved on with sweep after sweep of his scythe, not stopping or showing signs of weariness. Levin followed him, trying not to get left behind, and he found it harder and harder: the moment came when he felt he had no strength left, but at that very moment Tit stopped and whetted the scythes.

So they mowed the first row. And this long row seemed particularly hard work to Levin; but when the end was reached and Tit, shouldering his scythe, began with deliberate stride returning on the tracks left by his heels in the cut grass, and Levin walked back in the same way over the space he had cut, in spite of the sweat that ran in streams over his face and fell in drops down his nose, and drenched his back as though he had been soaked in water, he felt very happy. What delighted him particularly was that now he knew he would be able to hold out. . . .

Another row, and yet another row, followed—long rows and short rows, with good grass and with poor grass. Levin lost all sense of time, and could not have told whether it was late or early now. A change began to come over his work, which gave him immense satisfaction. In the midst of his toil there were moments during which he forgot what he was doing, and it came all easy to him, and at those same moments his row was almost as smooth and well cut as Tit's. But so soon as he recollected what he was doing, and began trying to do better, he was at once conscious of all the difficulty of his task, and the row was badly mown.

On finishing yet another row he would have gone back to the top of the meadow again to begin the next, but Tit stopped, and going up to the old man said something in a low voice to him. They both looked at the sun. "What are they talking about, and why doesn't he go back?" thought Levin, not guessing that the peasants had been mowing no less than four hours without stopping, and it was time for their lunch.

"Lunch, sir," said the old man.

"Is it really time? That's right; lunch, then."

[After lunching at home, Levin rejoined his companions and mowed for several hours more—again oblivious to the time. Eventually, the peasants' children appeared with their fathers' dinners.]

"Come, master, dinner-time!". . . And on reaching the stream the mowers moved off across the lines of cut grass towards their pile of coats, where the children . . . were sitting waiting for them. The peasants gathered into groups—those further away under a cart, those nearer under a willow bush.

Levin sat down by them; he felt disinclined to go away.

All constraint with the master had disappeared long ago. The peasants got ready for dinner. Some washed, the young lads bathed in the stream, others made a place comfortable for a rest, untied their sacks of bread, and uncovered the pitchers of rye-beer. The old man crumbled up some bread in a cup, stirred it with the handle of a spoon, poured water on it from the dipper, broke up some more bread, and having seasoned it with salt, he turned to the east to say his prayer.

"Come, master, taste my sop," said he, kneeling down before the cup.

The sop was so good that Levin gave up the idea of going home. He dined with the old man, and talked to him about his family affairs, taking the keenest interest in them, and told him about his own affairs and all the circumstances that could be of interest to the old man. He felt much nearer to him than to his brother, and could not help smiling at the affection he felt for this man. When the old man got up again, said his prayer, and lay down under a bush, putting some grass under his head for a pillow, Levin did the same, and in spite of the clinging flies that were so persistent in the sunshine, and the midges that tickled his hot face and body, he fell asleep at once and only waked when the sun had passed to the other side of the bush and reached him. The old man had been awake a long while, and was sitting up whetting the scythes of the younger lads.

Levin looked about him and hardly recognized the place, everything was so changed. The immense stretch of meadow had been mown and was sparkling with a peculiar fresh brilliance, with its lines of already sweet-smelling grass in the slanting rays of the evening sun. And the bushes about the river had been cut down, and the river itself, not visible before, now gleaming like steel in its bends, and the moving, ascending peasants, and the sharp wall of grass of the unmown part of the meadow, and the hawks hovering over the stripped meadow—all was perfectly new. Raising himself, Levin began considering how much had been cut and how much more could still be done that day.

The work done was exceptionally much for forty-two men. They had cut the whole of the big meadow, which had, in the years of serf labor, taken thirty scythes two days to mow. . . . But Levin felt a longing to get as much mowing done that day as possible, and was vexed with the sun sinking so quickly in the sky. He felt no weariness; all he wanted was to get his work done more and more quickly and as much done as possible.

"Could you cut Mashkin Upland too?—what do you think?" he said to the old man.

"As God wills, the sun's not high. A little vodka for the lads?"

At the afternoon rest, when they were sitting down again, and those who smoked had lighted their pipes, the old man told the men that "Mashkin Upland's to be cut—there'll be some vodka."

"Why not cut it? Come on, Tit! We'll look sharp! We can eat at night. Come on!" cried voices, and eating up their bread, the mowers went back to work. . . .

The sun was already sinking into the trees when they went with their jingling dippers into the wooded ravine of Mashkin Upland. The grass was up to their waists in the middle of the hollow, soft, tender, and feathery, spotted here and there among the trees with wild heart's-ease.

After a brief consultation—whether to take the rows lengthwise or diagonally—Prohor Yermilin, also a renowned mower, a huge, black-haired peasant, went on ahead. He went up to the top, turned back again and started mowing, and they all proceeded to form in line behind him, going downhill through the hollow and uphill right up to the edge of the forest. The sun sank behind the forest. The dew was falling by now; the mowers were in the sun only on the hillside, but below, where a mist was rising, and on the opposite side, they mowed into the fresh, dewy shade. The work went rapidly. The grass cut with a juicy sound, and was at once laid in high, fragrant rows. The mowers from all sides, brought closer together in the short row, kept urging one another on to the sound of jingling dippers and clanging scythes, and the hiss of the whetstones sharpening them, and good-humored shouts.

Levin still kept between the young peasant and the old man. The old man, who had put on his short sheepskin jacket, was just as good-humored, jocose, and free in his movements. Among the trees they were continually cutting with their scythes the so-called "birch mushrooms," swollen fat in the succulent grass. But the old man bent down every time he came across a mushroom, picked it up and put it in his bosom. "Another present for my old woman," he said as he did so.

Easy as it was to mow the wet, soft grass, it was hard work going up and down the steep sides of the ravine. But this did not trouble the old man. Swinging his scythe just as ever, and moving his feet in their big, plaited shoes with firm, little steps, he climbed slowly up the steep place, and though his breeches hanging out below his smock, and his whole frame trembled with effort, he did not miss one blade of grass or one mushroom on his way, and kept making jokes with the peasants and Levin. Levin walked after him and often thought he must fall, as he climbed with a scythe up a steep cliff where it would have been hard work to clamber without anything. But he climbed up and did what he had to do. He felt as though some external force were moving him.

• • • •

Mashkin Upland was mown, the last row finished, the peasants had put on their coats and were gaily trudging home. Levin got on his horse, and parting regretfully from the peasants, rode homewards. On the hillside he looked back; he could not see them in the mist that had risen from the valley; he could only hear rough, good-humored voices, laughter, and the sound of clanking scythes.

The kind of scene that was popular with writers and artists of the late nineteenth century is shown in this detail from "The Reapers," a typical painting from the palette of the realist Grigory Myasoedov (1835–1911).

8

The World of the Stage

Theater, Music, and Dance

In the late 1600's, after hearing about the special entertainments provided other European monarchs, Tsar Alexei I lifted the Russian cultural curtain on Western music, theater, and ballet. The first attempts to master the European modes left something to be desired. Muscovites who were sent to the court of Louis XIV to learn dancing were reportedly inattentive, and new sounds of music at the Kremlin were compared to "screech owls, a nest of Jackdaws, a pack of hungry Wolves, seven Hogs on a windy day, and as many Cats." By 1673, however, a court dramatic theater was amusing Alexei for ten hours at a stretch.

Peter the Great was as avid a theater buff as his father. He installed a theater room at the Kremlin and compensated for the dearth of native actors by hiring a German troupe, who performed fifteen tragedies and comedies between 1702 and 1703. Dancing also made great strides during Peter's reign. By replacing cumbersome Russian robes and boots with European frock coats, petticoats, and shoes, Peter unfettered the human form. At his "assemblies," women, formerly kept in Oriental seclusion, took men as partners and tried the latest styles of ballroom dancing—the first steps in the development of the classical Russian ballet. Empress Anna

On the opposite page appears a scene from the ballet Le Diable à Quatre *(which was also known as* The Wilful Wife*). It exemplifies the romantic style of choreography so popular in the mid-1800's.*

deemed dancing a social grace worthy of the *Corps des Cadets.* More than a hundred of these young noblemen, taught by Jean Baptiste Landé, performed in the first professional court ballet, in 1736. Two years later, Landé established the Imperial Ballet School for children of palace servants. (This academy still exists under Soviet auspices and with a Soviet name.) Similarly, in the 1770's, ballet classes were instituted for Moscow's orphans, who were the ancestors of the famed Bolshoi Ballet company.

The performing arts also received encouragement from the empresses Elizabeth and Catherine. A St. Petersburg dramatic theater was sponsored by Elizabeth in 1756 and later incorporated into a state system of Imperial Theaters that survived until the 1917 revolution. Catherine, nearly tone-deaf, nevertheless cultivated opera and lighter forms of music, and during her reign more plays and ballets were performed than ever before. The plays were generally frivolous copies of French or Italian originals, but drama also had political overtones. When Catherine's son Paul wanted to see *Hamlet,* the censors cancelled the performance because the characters too closely resembled Russians living and dead. (Paul's father had been murdered with his mother's approval, and Catherine usurped the throne.) By the early 1800's, then, despite awkward beginnings and occasional lapses into uncertainty, the stage was set for the century in which the Russian performing arts would find their fullest expression.

N. A. YELIZAROVA, *Ostankino*

On the Boards

Serfs were given fleeting moments of theatrical glory in eighteenth-century Russia. By releasing the nobility from certain state obligations and tightening the bonds of serfdom, Catherine the Great unwittingly provided the gentry with an unprecedented amount of leisure, as well as a permanent source of entertainment. Rich landowners hired foreign instructors to mold retinues of servants into highly skilled troupes, whose repertoires were said to rival the imperial and public theaters of St. Petersburg and Moscow. In the late 1700's, twenty private serf theaters existed near Moscow alone. The finest belonged to one Count Sheremetev at his country estate of Kuskovo. After witnessing a performance there, one enthralled guest noted: "The poet and the musician who wrote the opera . . . the actors and actresses who played in the piece, the members of the ballet and the musicians . . . were all serfs."

The count also maintained a ballet company at his

Tatyana Granatova, above (her surname means "gar- net"), was a serf ballerina of the late 1700's, who danced in the theater on her master's estate at Ostan- kino. The theater, shown in the drawing at left, was converted into a museum after the 1917 revolution. In an earlier epoch, Fedor Volkov, below, also of humble origin, organized a group of amateur players in Ya- roslavl. Empress Elizabeth learned of the presentations and summoned the actor to Petersburg, where he helped found the first permanent Russian theater in 1756.

pleasure palace outside Moscow. Here, serf boys and girls were taught estate-composed ballets, containing folk dances as well as classical numbers. All of the ballerinas were named after precious stones, and one gem, the serf actress Praskovia Zhemchuzova (whose surname means "pearl"), married her owner, but died shortly afterward. Less enlightened masters inflicted cruel punishments on their chattel and sold them at whim. Advertisements such as this were typical: "For sale: Two domestic servants, one a leather-stitcher. . . . The other is a musician and a singer . . . plays the bassoon, with a bass voice." When the serf theater declined in popularity around 1800, noblemen who could not find a market for their peasant performers peddled them as common laborers. Luckier serfs were sold to the theaters of the big cities, and often obtained their freedom. In 1806 the last large company of serfs was bought by the Imperial Theaters in Moscow.

Themes and Variations

Spiritually attuned to the literary movements of his time, Mikhail Glinka, shown in the photograph above, derived inspiration for his opera Ruslan and Ludmila *from Alexander Pushkin's romantic poem of the same name. Based on a folk epic in which justice triumphs over evil, this musical fairy tale combines fantasy with aspects of Russian reality and has a happy ending, as seen in the engraving at right.* Ruslan and Ludmila *was Glinka's second and last opera. Five years in the making, the work was panned after its St. Petersburg première on December 9, 1842. Glinka's stylistic innovations along with an inadequately prepared cast caused the tsar's family to walk out on the performance before the final act. As a result, the opera was removed from the Russian repertory and it was not revived until many years after Glinka's death.*

Russian classical music was not notably Russian until the nineteenth century. Previously, Italian musicians monopolized the court, and conservatories were nonexistent. Political and social events in the early 1800's, however, fostered a new nationalism which was echoed in the arts. Russian composers discovered in folk songs, church chants, popular speech, and peasant life the sources of a unique national idiom. Mikhail Glinka fathered a national school of music by synthesizing Western forms with familiar Russian themes. His 1836 opera, *A Life for the Tsar,* was initially labeled "coachmen's music" by the aristocracy, but in a few years the patriotic work was considered *the* national opera.

After Glinka, the development of Russian music split into pro-Western and pan-Slavic schools. The Russian Music Society, founded in 1859, became the bastion of European classical tradition, as well as the official sponsor of conservatories at St. Petersburg and Moscow. The New Russian Music School, also known as "the Powerful *Kuchka* (Group)," or "the Five," provided effective counterpoint to the cosmopolitan policies of the Society. Its members, including Borodin, Rimsky-Korsakov, and Mussorgsky, sought to make Russian music "self-sufficient," claimed to reject the heritage of Bach, Haydn, and Mozart, and for good measure, denied the usefulness of institutionalized music education.

The era's greatest composer, Tchaikovsky, absorbed the technical training of the St. Petersburg Conservatory without its academic limitations, and like Glinka, created music that was Slavic in feeling, yet classical in form. The dissonance between the *Kuchka* and the Society gradually lessened, and after the 1860's the schools merged. Only Mussorgsky refused to modify his belief in musical nationalism, or accept the legacy of the West, maintaining that art must "plow up the . . . virgin soil . . . that no man has touched," rather than "reclaim tracts already fertilized."

The lyrical and psychological elements of Tchaikovsky's operatic style find their most poignant expression in Eugene Onegin, *completed in 1878 and successfully presented in St. Petersburg in 1884. Based on Pushkin's novel in verse, the opera contains little dramatic action, but instead concentrates on conveying the moods of its characters through music. The background of* Eugene Onegin *consists of a series of vignettes of Russian town and provincial life in the nineteenth century. The above scene takes place at a country ball, where the cynical Eugene tries to steal a lady from his friend and protégé, a young, idealistic poet, and suddenly finds himself challenged to a duel.*

PETER TCHAIKOVSKY *(1840–1893), Russia's internationally renowned composer, wrote ballets, operas, and symphonies. Continuing in the classic tradition of Beethoven, Tchaikovsky made his final work, the lyrical and tragic* Sixth Symphony *of 1893, the summation of his emotional and dramatic development, embodying his definition of a symphony as a "musical confession of the soul."*

MODEST MUSSORGSKY *(1839–1881), a former guards officer, championed a folkish realism in Russian music, seeking "dramatic truth" in the formless passions of the human soul, as well as in pleasant folk tunes. His 1869 opera,* Boris Godunov, *was initially rejected by the Imperial Theaters because it reflected Populist political ideas; but it was finally staged at St. Petersburg in 1874.*

NIKOLAI RIMSKY-KORSAKOV *(1844–1908), a naval officer turned musician, composed the first Russian symphony in 1864. Though he said he had "never written one counterpoint nor heard of the existence of a chord" before 1871, he was made a professor that year at the St. Petersburg Conservatory. His* Scheherazade *(1888) reveals a Slavic fantasy world through orchestral tone-painting.*

ALEXANDER BORODIN *(1834–1887), a founder of the Russian symphonic school, was a chemist and part-time composer. His greatest work, the opera* Prince Igor, *was based on the twelfth-century epic poem, and records the heroism of the Russian people against the Polovtsy, a nomadic tatar tribe. The "Polovetsian Dances" contain elements of Oriental folklore and some of Borodin's finest melodies.*

LUCIEN MAZENOD. *La Galerie des Hommes Célèbres.* ALL OTHERS: SOVFOTO

A Night at The Opera

In August, 1874, Vladimir, son of Tsar Alexander II, married a German grand duchess. The nuptial festivities included a gala by Glinka at the St. Petersburg Opera House, to which an American visitor, Thomas W. Knox, wangled a hard-to-get invitation. His report for Harper's New Monthly Magazine *follows below.*

Early on Sunday evening we put on our best clothes to attend the gala spectacle at the opera-house. . . . There were few people present when we arrived, but the house filled rapidly, and by eight o'clock . . . there was not a vacant place except in the imperial box, where a single servant was arranging the seats and burning a small brazier of incense, as if to fill the locality with sweet odors. The house was built a long time ago, and is not equal to the Grand Theatre at Moscow, La Scala at Milan, San Carlo at Naples, or the Academy of Music in New York. Its interior has been changed several times. . . . There are five ranges, including the bel étage and the gallery, and it is said that the house can contain three thousand persons—a statement which I am inclined to doubt. The stage is large, and is said to be one of the best equipped in Europe. The government gives a large subvention for the support of opera, and the money which *prime donne* have taken from the capital would amount to an almost fabulous sum. . . . What matter a few thousand pounds when the government foots the bills? . . . There was a general buzz of conversation all over the house, the predominance of voices being masculine. . . . The [lower floor] is entirely filled with the sterner sex; almost all are officers. . . . All are in full uniform, and sport their decorations, which are so profuse in quantity and rich in quality as to make each row of seats resemble the show-case of a jewelry store. . . . In the boxes nearly all the front seats are occupied by ladies in full evening dress; behind them are their cavaliers or others sit-

ting or standing, some in uniform and the rest in full evening costume. I don't think a man would be admitted here in a black frockcoat, even though he had a dozen tickets. . . . The imperial box faces the stage. . . . About twenty minutes past eight there is a commotion and buzz of whispers; all eyes are turned to the imperial box, and at the same time every body who has been sitting rises respectfully and faces the spot where the emperor is expected to appear. Preceded by . . . [the] Minister of the Imperial Household . . . the emperor . . . comes to the front of the box, followed by Vladimir and his bride. A hearty and prolonged but at the same time decorous and well-ordered cheer greets the party, and simultaneously the orchestra strikes up the imperial hymn, whose stately measures resound through the building and fill every nook and corner. The party bows its acknowledgment of the reception, and is seated. . . . The emperor is in the centre; on his right is the young bride, looking rather flushed and not altogether at ease; and then comes Vladimir, looking just a shade uneasier than the lady he has sworn to protect . . . all were richly dressed, and had more diamonds and decorations about them than any of us ever hope to have. . . . As soon as the imperial party were seated every body else sat down: it would have been great rudeness for any body to sit while they were standing; and if the emperor had risen at any time during the performance, it would have been the etiquette for every other person in the house to follow his example. . . . In a few minutes the curtain rises, and as we glance around the house we see that every body is on his good behavior. Two or three have leveled their glasses at the imperial box—evidently they are strangers and unaware of the custom, and before many minutes they have taken the hint and desisted. Every body sits erect, and the rows of seats look like those of a well-drilled school when heads are up for recitation pur-

The engraving at left depicts St. Petersburg's Bolshoi, or Grand, Theater as it appeared in about 1810. Designed in the neoclassical style, this historical home of Russian opera and ballet was erected in 1783, and seated two thousand people. Enlarged on an even grander scale in 1802, the building suffered the fate of so many candle-lit theaters—on New Year's, 1811, it burned to the ground. Twice rebuilt, the Bolshoi housed machinery providing for such elaborate effects as mountains toppling and ships sinking. The theater was declared unsafe in 1889, performances were discontinued, and the grand Bolshoi Theater became the St. Petersburg Conservatory.

poses. You can hardly find a better-looking, better-dressed, and better-behaving audience, go where you will. One of my friends suggests that we can make a sensation of hanging our boots over the edge of the gallery, *à la Bowery;* I quite agree with him, and offer him a new hat to do it, but he declines. On the whole, I am glad that he did, as there would have been more attention paid to our box than would have been agreeable. What the result would have been I am unable to say, as nobody ever performed the boot trick in the St. Petersburg opera-house on a gala night. The opera invariably selected . . . is *Djisn na Tsaria,* or "A Life for the Czar." It is a work by Glinka, Russia's most celebrated composer, and is famous for the beauty and sweetness of its melodies, which are all national. The plot of the opera runs upon the devotion of a peasant who saves the life of the Czar Michel by losing his own. . . . of course he dies happy, and is speedily revived with brandy and soda in his dressing-room or at a neighboring restaurant. Only the first act was given tonight. The scenery was well set and handled, and the movement of the piece was as easy as that of a comedy after it has had a steady run of a fortnight or more. . . . All the time from the rise to the fall of the curtain the audience sat almost without movement, and gazing at the stage as though at the theatre for the first time in their lives. There was not the faintest sound of applause, not a hand was clapped against another, not a stick or umbrella pounded the floor in delight, not a boot fell heavily on the planks, and not a voice indulged in a "Hi-hi." It was decorum theatrified. As soon as the curtain fell every body rose and faced the imperial box; the party there rose and retired, and we were at liberty to stand at ease. The door of every box opened, and at each was a servant with a tray of ices, which were served to all. . . . It was hinted that we had better descend to the buffet. . . . We did so, and found what

one of our party irreverently denominated a "free lunch." There were ices, cakes, fruit, and various odds and ends of solids; and there were tea, coffee, Cognac, soda, Seltzer water, sherry, and Champagne for the lubrication of the solids. . . . There was an abundance of every thing . . . so that every body could be properly refreshed. It was the emperor's treat, and I am bound to say that it was well managed. I wouldn't object to his standing treat every time I go to the opera. . . . The diplomatic corps were there in full force . . . and a fine appearance they presented in their brilliant dress. . . . The land of the free and the home of the brave was represented by a *chargé d'affaires,* who looked very insignificant in his plain black suit without a single decoration of any sort. For all that his dress showed . . . he might have been a waiter in a restaurant, or an undertaker's lieutenant. . . . We had half an hour for refreshment, and then a bell sounded the retreat. We returned to our places, so that all could be standing when the imperial party re-entered. They were seated . . . the audience again sat down, the music began, and the curtain rose . . . upon a ballet, of which I could see . . . only by craning my head forward over those in front of me. The little that I saw was superb in every way: *mise en scène,* faces, forms, figures, dress, and dance, all were perfection. The ballet was short. As the curtain fell every body rose and faced the imperial box . . . , its occupants bowed an adieu, the cheer that was given at their entrance was repeated, the orchestra played the imperial hymn once more, and when the last of the party had disappeared the audience was at liberty to disperse. We found our overcoats and returned to the hotel on foot as stiffly as we had come. We were rather "set up" at having been the guests of the emperor, and discussed the propriety of exacting in future not less than two shillings (in coin) from every man that ventured to shake hands with us.

Musical Footnotes

At the beginning of the nineteenth century, Russian ballet as a theatrical art was growing by leaps and bounds. State-sponsored Theater Schools at St. Petersburg and Moscow provided budding ballerinas and *danseurs* with sound professional training. Except for Napoleon's invasion of 1812, when patriotic sentiment made the enemy unwelcome, a steady influx of French choreographers arrived. Under the direction of Charles Didelot, Russian ballet became the finest in Europe. Between 1802 and 1829, Didelot mounted fifty works, containing such elements of romanticism as folk dancing, local color, free body movements, and the full *pointe* technique—a tiptoe stance expressing flight or weightlessness. Many of Didelot's dances were inspired by the poetry of Alexander Pushkin; the impressario and his great ballerina Avdotia Istomina were in turn "winged by fame" in

Pushkin's *Eugene Onegin:* she "stands ashimmer, half ethereal, Obedient to the imperial musician's wand."

The cult of the prima ballerina flourished in the 1830's and 1840's. Stars like Marie Taglioni, Yelena Andreyanova, and Fanny Elssler were idolized by adoring audiences, while *danseurs* generally performed "lifts." Around mid-century, the dance suffered a temporary decline. Mediocre choreographers catered primarily to court boxes and the so-called diamond row, reserved for rich balletomanes, whom a poet described as "starched dandies, youthful old men." Marius Petipa's thirty-five-year reign at St. Petersburg's Mariinsky Theater revived ballet in the 1870's and brought classical choreography to its climax. His vast repertoire included three masterpieces realizing the symphonic potential of ballet: *Sleeping Beauty, The Nutcracker,* and *Swan Lake.*

Marius Petipa, who is shown c. 1870 at top, opposite, was known as the master of Russian ballet. Indeed, both his own dancing and his choreography dominated the art during the latter half of the nineteenth century. His ability to create ballets charged with emotional life revolutionized the dance, though as head of the Petersburg ballet his eagerness to please the eye and the court often lead to theatrical excesses, as when a ballerina watered a "bed of dahlias"—the corps de ballet—*from a real watering can. "Snowflakes" from Tchaikovsky's Nutcracker, a production supervised by Petipa, appear in the 1892 photograph at left. The dancers created an illusion of falling snow by gliding across the stage in ever-shifting patterns. The bustled blithe spirit shown at far left is Petipa's daughter, Maria, in her role as the Lilac Fairy in the première (1890) of* The Sleeping Beauty.

OVERLEAF: *This scene from* La Esmeralda, *a ballet based on Victor Hugo's* Notre Dame de Paris, *shows its star, Fanny Elssler, in a swoon. The ballerina performed the role in Petersburg in 1848.*

Александръ Бенуа

9

Russian Renaissance

Art in the New Century

During the late 1800's and early 1900's there was a rebirth of imagination in Russian painting, architecture, music, literature, and the theater, revolving chiefly around the World of Art, a society, magazine, exhibiting organization, and state of mind. Its founders, a group of sophisticated young dilettantes, including Alexander Benois, Léon Bakst, and Sergei Diaghilev, denounced the utilitarian view of art upheld by the Academy and the Wanderers. The reform movement was based on their belief that art is a universe unto itself, outside the sphere of religion, politics, or social service. Together, these men sought to make Russia the cradle of a new cosmopolitan culture by initiating contact with the Western European *avant-garde* and renewing interest in Russia's artistic heritage.

Under Diaghilev's guidance, the World of Art circle began a series of creative enterprises. The impresario planned a periodical to "unite the whole of our artistic life. . . . As illustrations I shall use real paintings, the articles will be outspoken. . . . I propose to organize a series of annual exhibitions, and finally, to attract to the magazine the new industrial art which is developing in Moscow and Finland." The first issue of *Mir Iskusstva (The World of Art)* appeared

Alexander Benois, a leader of the World of Art society, used the spouting and sprouting forms of art nouveau *in a frontispiece (opposite) for a 1901 issue of the society's journal,* Mir Iskusstva.

in October, 1898. Ecstatic over the immediate success, Bakst, one of the editors, wrote: "'The World of Art' is above all earthly things, above the stars, there it reigns proud, secret and lonely as on a snowy peak." Lavishly designed, the review contained an article by Benois on the Impressionists, poems by French and Russian Symbolists, and a discussion of Alexander Scriabin's musical ideas.

In its early numbers, the magazine featured the *art nouveau* movement of western Europe, though neglecting the obvious parallel between the French discovery of primitive and folk art and the then-current revival of peasant crafts in Moscow. And in 1904 the journal introduced the paintings of Van Gogh, Gauguin, Cézanne, Matisse, and Picasso to the Russian public. After thus propagating Post-Impressionism, the World of Art leaders terminated the publication, but continued their exhibitions for a number of years. Their pioneer work was carried on by a younger generation of *avant-garde* artists, who soon voiced their own protests against the "old guard" attitudes of the parent organization.

The World of Art group now devoted themselves to purely artistic endeavor, making their most colorful contributions in theater. The ballet, in particular, provided the former collaborators, as well as a galaxy of talented newcomers, with an ideal medium in which to realize their goal of life-made-art, where choreography, music, costumes, and scenery would be harmoniously integrated.

In the late 1800's a new generation of artists turned against the prevailing mode of pictorial realism and ushered in the era of modern Russian painting. While Konstantin Korovin and other exponents of the "art for art's sake" aesthetic began brushing up on the French Impressionist technique, other innovators like Vrubel were drawing inspiration from the European *art nouveau* movement of William Morris and Gustave Klimt, and integrating it with their own cultural heritage. At the turn of the century, Russian art began an accelerated development and within a decade experimented with the most revolutionary phases of European painting—Post-Impressionism, Fauvism, Cubism, Futurism. Russian artists were exposed to foreign trends by a new picture-buying bourgeoisie who collected some of the world's finest modern works, and by exhibitions sponsored by such societies as the World of Art. Between 1910 and World War I, Russian artists ceased being eclectic imitators and became the *avant-garde* of modern art. The inventors of the Primitivist style, Larionov and Goncharova, synthesized the simple imagery of peasant art with the brilliant colors and bold distortions of the French *Fauves* (the wild beasts), and thus founded a new and uniquely Russian school. Their experiments with Rayonnism led Larionov to write, "From here begins the true freeing of art; a life which proceeds only according to the laws of painting." Indeed, before the decade was past, Russian artists had taken the leap into abstraction.

The Leap
To Modernism

The oil painting at left, "Lady in a Dining Room Drinking Tea," is typical of Konstantin Korovin's Impressionistic style. After visiting France in 1885, the artist adapted the Parisian palette to suit his Russian temperament and produced "fountains of color" and "feasts for the eye." When his sweeping brush strokes began to require more space than the canvas allowed, Korovin took to painting theatrical scenery. Mikhail Vrubel, whose "Fortune Teller" is shown above, was at the very heart of the Russian art nouveau, and like Paul Cézanne he was a transitional figure on the road from traditional to modern art. His belief in form rather than ideas in painting was to have great impact on those who followed his example.

Borrowing Impressionist, Cubist, and Expressionist techniques, Marc Chagall added his own stroke of genius and created enchanted, topsy turvy worlds in paint. Thoroughly immersed in the Jewish culture of his native city of Vitebsk (he is one of the few major artists of the time who was not working in Petersburg or Moscow), he also brought to his work the refinements of European culture. Chagall crowded his canvases with a kaleidoscopic array of Jewish symbols, cows and chickens, fiddlers on roofs, and lovers in transports of ecstasy. Chagall's rapture reached new heights in a series of paintings commemorating his early years of wedded bliss. In the "Double Portrait with Wineglass" of 1917, at left, the artist is swept off his feet by love, defying both gravity and his wife's weight-lifting capacity. After dabbling in a multitude of European styles, Mikhail Larionov denounced the "decadent" art of the West and sought a new and peculiarly Russian pictorial idiom to depict essences rather than appearances. From 1911 to 1914, he evolved a concept in painting called Rayonnism, whereby rays emanating from various objects were projected into space, with the points of intersection bathed in color. Larionov began his Rayonnist experiments in 1911 when he tried to trace the rays linking a mackerel to a sausage. In the same year, he exhibited his first Rayonnist painting, entitled "Glasses," shown below, at the Society of Free Esthetics in Moscow. Natalya Goncharova, a descendant of Alexander Pushkin and a lifelong companion of Larionov, adapted Russo-Byzantine and current European styles in her highly eclectic works. Her main contribution to the modern art movement consists of her use of forceful linear rhythms, rich ornament, and sensuous, brilliant colors. Goncharova's oil painting of a provincial fishing party, opposite, was executed in 1910 and reveals the influence of the French Fauvist school, as well as the simplified, roughhewn forms of the national Primitivist style.

Maxim Gorky's The Lower Depths, *first presented by the Moscow Art Theater in 1902, concerns a group of social dregs in a slum*

The main characters, a prostitute, a destitute baron, and a gambler, are portrayed here by Knipper-Chekhova, Kachalov, and Stanislavsky.

Flight of the Firebird

Throughout the winter, I worked strenuously at my ballet, and that brought me into constant touch with Diaghilev and his collaborators. Fokin created the choreography of *The Firebird*, section by section, as the music was handed to him. I attended every rehearsal with the company, and after rehearsals Diaghilev, Nijinsky, and myself . . . ended the day with a fine dinner washed down with good claret.

Stravinsky on composing The Firebird *ballet in 1910*

Pavlova was never really interested in art as such. The only thing that mattered to her was virtuosity, and she is a virtuoso without equal. When first I wanted her to do Stravinsky's *The Firebird*, especially designed for her, she declared that she wouldn't dance to such horrible music.

Diaghilev, after Pavlova refused to perform The Firebird

The Firebird. . . . is very dear to me . . . chiefly because it was a materialization of my artistic ideas of the unity of creative choreography and creative music. . . . [Stravinsky's] music. . . . expressed every moment of the tale and had an unheard-of, fantastic quality. . . . The costume of the Firebird . . . created by Bakst. . . . did not resemble the traditional figure of a ballerina. Everything was different: transparent

Karsavina appears in full plumage in the painting opposite. Above, Picasso, who designed for the Ballet Russe, caricatures (from right) Diaghilev, Bakst, and a young choreographer, Leonid Massin.

Oriental pantaloons . . . feathers, fantastic headgear, and long golden braids. . . . The performers gave an excellent account of themselves, with Tamara Karsavina dancing the title role. . . . The *corps de ballet* was wonderful. . . . Never again did I see . . . such an assorted collection of Russian folklore monsters. . . . The dance of the Firebird I staged on toe and with jumps. . . . The arms would now open like wings, now hug the torso. . . . Having recorded my happy recollections . . . I now proceed to . . . the other side of the ledger. . . . The flight of the Firebird proved to be a failure. . . . Karsavina was rolled in on some sort of saddle attached to a . . . plank in the floor . . . accompanied by loud, squeaky noises. Then, immediately, she "flew" backwards into the wings. The effect was exceedingly repulsive.

Fokin's recollections of The Firebird *from his memoirs*

I loved the Russian Ballet. I gave my heart and soul to it. I worked like an ox and I lived like a martyr. . . . I hated Diaghilev from the first days of our acquaintance, because I knew his power. . . . I knew well that if I left Diaghilev I would die of hunger because I was not ready for life. I was afraid of life. . . . I loved Karsavina. She excited me a little, because she was beautifully made, but one could not flirt with her and therefore I felt exasperated. I courted her . . . but [she] did not respond because she was married. . . . I realized that Diaghilev influenced her against me.

Excerpts from Nijinsky's diary, written in 1918–19

Diaghilev, Benois, and their World of Art group turned to the ballet partly for its own sake, and partly to provide avant-garde painting with a stage where it could be seen by a wide audience. Ballet and theater productions became visual extravaganzas in which artists brought mythic realms of folklore to life in modernistic sets and costumes. Goncharova's towered cityscape (opposite), for a revival of The Firebird, and Pavel Tchelishchev's costume for a 1921 ballet (left) draw their inspiration from the Oriental dreamworld of Russia's past. A futuristic vision is instilled in Larionov's peacock (opposite, top) for a 1916 ballet; in Alexandra Exter's mechanized designs (top left) of 1924; and in Sergei Soudeykin's rhythmic marching forms (above) of 1929.

276

Bakst's Dionysian designs, orgies of undulating line and color, included figures like the scantily clad nymph above, for the 1911 ballet Narcisse. Carrying his pagan vision further, in 1912, Bakst barely clothed Nijinsky, the star of L'Après-midi d'un Faune, in a pair of mottled tights (opposite). The costume, along with Nijinsky's voluptuous use of a veil as his symbolic partner in love, provoked a scandal that threatened Franco-Russian relations.

"L'APRÈS MIDI D'UN FAUNE"
(NIJINSKY)

BAKST

Bakst evoked the splendor of the Orient in his theatrical art and influenced contemporary fashion. His scenery and costumes for Les Orientales, *a suite of five ballets performed in 1910, created the illusion of a Persian miniature come to life. In the water color below, Nijinsky, who has been decked out by Bakst in the garb of an Eastern potentate, lurks seductively, as if awaiting his harem.*

281

In the teens and early twenties the cinema was attracting a large following among members of the art world, and the primary experimental movements of the period found their way into film. For the 1924 picture Aelita—a science fiction fantasy—the artist Alexandra Exter designed the mechanistic costumes for the scene opposite. One of the early Soviet sound films was Chapaev (1934), the story of a Red Army hero (seen manning a machine gun above). A vivid human portrait, the production was enormously successful with everyone: the public and the film makers, as well as the army and the government.

OVERLEAF: Themes and images from traditional Russian art recurred frequently in the cinema. This scene from Arsenal (1929), by the Ukrainian director Alexander Dovzhenko, echoes such nineteenth-century Populist art as Repin's "Zaporozh Cossacks" (pages 178–79).

10

The Silver Age

Writing from Chekhov to Babel

In the early 1880's Russian literature reached a turning point. With the deaths of Dostoevsky in 1881 and Turgenev in 1883, and Tolstoy's virtual abandonment of fiction in favor of moralistic writing, there were suddenly no living masters to inspire a younger generation of novelists. Furthermore, greater restrictions than before were placed on Russian writers in dealing with current social and political trends. Populism had been suppressed after the assassination of Alexander II, and censorship was imposed on all publications.

It was a bleak period, but by the end of the century new writers with new ideas had begun restoring life to their country's literature. Bleakness itself became a principal theme for the great storyteller and playwright Anton Chekhov, whose writings first appeared in the eighties. The hardships of the proletariat—the urban working classes that emerged as a result of industrial expansion—provided another young writer, Maxim Gorky, with a subject soon to become a rallying cry for political revolution. By the early 1900's Gorky had become a popular favorite of the Russian reading public.

Meantime, other young writers from educated families were rejecting the "drab materialism" of their confreres and seeking escape in mystical symbolism and individualism. Meeting in salons in Moscow and St. Petersburg, they found inspiration in Goethe and the German Romantics, and in the

Looking like one of the wistful, fin de siècle *heroines of a drama by Chekhov, the quietly reflective young lady gazing out the window (opposite) was painted by Konstanin Korovin in the early 1900's.*

forerunners of Western Symbolism, Baudelaire and Edgar Allan Poe. However, though they shared a preference for poetry over prose and chose themes centered on private emotions and perceptions, they diverged at times into two separate factions. Some were interested in poetry for its own sake, while others used a cultist language of symbols and considered themselves to be high priests, whose mission it was to interpret the world of ultimate reality for an uninitiated public.

During the early years of the century, culminating in the revolution of 1917, poetry dominated the national literature. While the Symbolists were at their zenith in 1912, two new groups of poets began to challenge their supremacy. One group who called themselves Acmeists produced a poetry of deliberate clarity, detached from religious mysticism. Another, the Futurists, declared literary war not only against Symbolism, but against all traditional art forms and revered authors, in an effort to free literature from the structures and mannerisms of the past.

A few of these poets became champions of the 1917 revolution, but with Lenin's death and the rise to power of Stalin's totalitarian regime, experimentalism in the arts was frowned upon and party-line orthodoxy encouraged. Some writers, unable to adapt to the new way of life, chose emigration or suicide. Literary activity was left to the proletarian writers who propagandized about building socialism, and to the "Fellow-travelers"—non-party members who described the Revolution as a brutal but necessary purging force.

The Chekhovian Mood

Born the son of a serf in 1860 and trained as a doctor, Anton Chekhov began his writing career by tossing off frothy burlesques, lampoons, and sketches for Moscow's comic papers. When, during his mid-twenties, his short stories started attracting critical attention, Chekhov began to devote himself seriously to literature, developing a strong, understated style and a type of fiction in which realistic effects are achieved through the suggestive power of a few vivid details. Though he was best known in Russia for his stories, Chekhov became internationally famous for his moody, evocative plays.

From ON OFFICIAL BUSINESS (1889)

Translated by Avrahm Yarmolinsky

Few storytellers engage their readers' attention as effectively as Chekhov. In the first sentences of a work, he not only sets the time and place and introduces the protagonists, he also establishes an emotional atmosphere which envelops the tale with an immediate sense of reality and sets the plot in motion. Following are the opening paragraphs from three of his more than seven hundred short stories.

The deputy examining magistrate and the county physician were on their way to an autopsy in the village of Syrnya. En route they were caught in a blizzard; they wasted a great deal of time traveling in circles and arrived at their destination not at midday, as they had intended, but in the evening when it was already dark. They put up for the night at the village headquarters. It was here that the dead body happened to be lying, the corpse of the Zemstvo insurance agent Lesnitzky, who had come to Syrnya three days previously and, after settling in the village headquarters and ordering the samovar, had shot himself, to the complete surprise of everyone; and the fact that he had ended his life under such strange circumstances, with the samovar before him and the food he had brought along laid out on the table, led many to suspect murder; an inquest was in order.

From ANNA ON THE NECK (1895)

Translated by Avrahm Yarmolinsky

After the ceremony not even light refreshments were served; the bride and groom each drank a glass of wine, changed their clothes, and drove to the station. Instead of having a gay ball and supper, instead of music and dancing, they traveled a hundred and fifty miles to perform their devotions at a shrine. Many people commended this, saying that Modest Alexeich had already reached a high rank in the service and was no longer young, and that a noisy wedding might not have seemed quite proper; and besides, music is likely to sound dreary when a fifty-two-year-old official marries a girl who has just turned eighteen. It was also said that Modest Alexeich, being a man of principle, had really arranged this visit to the monastery in order to make it clear to his young bride that in marriage, too, he gave the first place to religion and morality.

From IN THE RAVINE (1900)

Translated by Constance Garnett

The village of Ukleyevo lay in a ravine, so that only the belfry and the chimneys of the cotton mills could be seen from the highroad and the railway station. When visitors asked what village this was, they were told:

"That's the village where the sexton ate all the caviar at the funeral."

VANKA (1886)

Translated by Avrahm Yarmolinsky

This melancholy story, from Chekhov's early years as a professional writer in Moscow, was one of his first departures from pure comedy.

Vanka Zhukov, a nine-year-old boy, who had been apprenticed to Alyahin the shoemaker these three months, did not go to bed on Christmas Eve. After his master and mistress and the journeymen had gone to midnight Mass, he got an inkpot and a pen-holder with a rusty nib out of the master's cupboard and having spread out a crumpled sheet of paper, began writing. Before he formed the first letter he looked fearfully at the doors and windows several times, shot a glance at the dark icon, at either side of which stretched shelves filled with lasts, and heaved a broken sigh. He was kneeling before a bench on which his paper lay.

"Dear Granddaddy, Konstantin Makarych," he wrote. "And I am writing you a letter. I wish you a merry Christmas and everything good from the Lord God. I have neither father nor mother, you alone are left me."

Vanka shifted his glance to the dark window on which flickered the reflection of his candle and vividly pictured his grandfather to himself. Employed as a watchman by the Zhivaryovs, he was a short, thin, but extraordinarily lively and nimble old man of about sixty-five whose face was always crinkled with laughter and who had a toper's eyes. By day he slept in the servants' kitchen or cracked jokes with the cook; at night, wrapped in an ample sheepskin coat, he made the rounds of the estate, shaking his clapper. The old bitch, Brownie, and the dog called Wriggles, who had a black coat and a long body like a weasel's, followed him with hanging heads. This Wriggles was extraordinarily deferential and demonstrative, looked with equally friendly eyes both at his masters and at strangers, but did not enjoy a good reputation. His deference and meekness concealed the most Jesuitical spite. No one knew better than he how to creep up behind you and suddenly snap at your leg, how to slip into the icehouse, or how to steal a hen from a peasant. More than once his hind legs had been all but broken, twice he had been hanged, every week he was whipped till he was half dead, but he always managed to revive.

At the moment Grandfather was sure to be standing at the gates, screwing up his eyes at the bright-red windows of the church, stamping his felt boots, and cracking jokes with the servants. His clapper was tied to his belt. He was clapping his hands, shrugging with the cold, and, with a senile titter, pinching now the housemaid, now the cook.

"Shall we have a pinch of snuff?" he was saying, offering the women his snuffbox.

They each took a pinch and sneezed. Grandfather, indescribably delighted, went off into merry peals of laughter and shouted:

"Peel it off, it has frozen on!"

The dogs too are given a pinch of snuff. Brownie sneezes, wags her head, and walks away offended. Wriggles is too polite to sneeze and only wags his tail. And the weather is glorious. The air is still, clear, and fresh. The night is dark, but one can see the whole village with its white roofs and smoke streaming out of the chimneys, the trees silvery with hoarfrost, the snowdrifts. The entire sky is studded with gaily twinkling stars and the Milky Way is as distinctly visible as though it had been washed and rubbed with snow for the holiday. . . .

Vanka sighed, dipped his pen into the ink and went on writing:

"And yesterday I got it hot. The master pulled me out into the courtyard by the hair and gave me a hiding with a knee-strap because I was rocking the baby in its cradle and happened to fall asleep. And last week the mistress ordered me to clean a herring and I began with the tail, and she took the herring and jabbed me in the mug with it. The helpers make fun of me, send me to the pothouse for vodka and tell me to steal pickles for them from the master, and the master hits me with anything that comes handy. And there is nothing to eat. In the morning they give me bread, for dinner porridge, and in the evening bread again. As for tea or cabbage soup, the master and mistress bolt it all themselves. And they tell me to sleep in the entry, and when the baby cries I don't sleep at all, but rock the cradle. Dear Granddaddy, for God's sake have pity on me, take me away from here, take me home to the village, it's more than I can bear. I bow down at your feet and I will pray to God for you forever, take me away from here or I'll die."

Vanka puckered his mouth, rubbed his eyes with his black fist, and gave a sob.

"I will grind your snuff for you," he continued, "I will pray to God for you, and if anything happens, you may thrash me all you like. And if you think there's no situation for me, I will beg the manager for Christ's sake to let me clean boots, or I will take Fedka's place as a shepherd boy. Dear Granddaddy, it's more than I can bear, it will simply be

the death of me. I thought of running away to the village but I have no boots and I am afraid of the frost. And in return for this when I grow big, I will feed you and won't let anybody do you any harm, and when you die I will pray for the repose of your soul, just as for my Mom's.

"Moscow is a big city. The houses are all the kind the gentry live in, and there are lots of horses, but no sheep, and the dogs are not fierce. The boys here don't go caroling, carrying the star at Christmas, and they don't let anyone sing in the choir, and once in a shop window I saw fishing-hooks for sale all fitted up with a line, for every kind of fish, very fine ones, there was even one hook that will hold a forty-pound sheatfish. And I saw shops where there are all sorts of guns, like the master's at home, so maybe each one of them is a hundred rubles. And in butchers' shops there are woodcocks and partridge and hares, but where they shoot them the clerks won't tell.

"Dear Granddaddy, when they have a Christmas tree with presents at the master's, do get a gilt walnut and put it away in the little green chest. Ask the young lady, Olga Ignatyevna, for it, say it's for Vanka."

Vanka heaved a broken sigh and again stared at the window. He recalled that it was his grandfather who always went to the forest to get the Christmas tree for the master's family and that he would take his grandson with him. It was a jolly time! Grandfather grunted, the frost crackled, and, not to be outdone, Vanka too made a cheerful noise in his throat. Before chopping down the Christmas tree, Grandfather would smoke a pipe, slowly take a pinch of snuff, and poke fun at Vanka who looked chilled to the bone. The young firs draped in hoarfrost stood still, waiting to see which of them was to die. Suddenly, coming out of nowhere, a hare would dart across the snowdrifts like an arrow. Grandfather could not keep from shouting: "Hold him, hold him, hold him! Ah, the bob-tailed devil!"

When he had cut down the fir tree, Grandfather would drag it to the master's house, and there they would set to work decorating it. The young lady, Olga Ignatyevna, Vanka's favorite, was the busiest of all. When Vanka's mother, Pelageya, was alive and a chambermaid in the master's house, the young lady used to give him goodies, and, having nothing with which to occupy herself, taught him to read and write, to count up to a hundred, and even to dance the quadrille. When Pelageya died, Vanka had been relegated to the servants' kitchen to stay with his grandfather, and from the kitchen to the shoemaker's.

"Do come, dear Granddaddy," Vanka went on. "For Christ's sake, I beg you, take me away from here. Have pity on me, an unhappy orphan, here everyone beats me, and I am terribly hungry, and I am so blue, I can't tell you how, I keep crying. And the other day the master hit me on the head with a last, so that I fell down and it was a long time before I came to. My life is miserable, worse than a dog's—I also send greetings to Alyona, one-eyed Yegorka and the coachman, and don't give my harmonica to anyone. I remain, . . . Ivan Zhukov, dear Granddaddy, do come."

Vanka twice folded the sheet covered with writing and put it into an envelope he had bought for a kopeck the previous day. He reflected a while, then dipped the pen into the ink and wrote the address: *To Grandfather in the village.* Then he scratched himself, thought a little, and added: *Konstantin Makarych.* Glad that no one had interrupted him at his writing, he put on his cap and, without slipping on his coat, ran out into the street with nothing over his shirt.

The clerks at the butchers' whom he had questioned the day before had told him that letters were dropped into letter boxes and from the boxes they were carried all over the world in troikas with ringing bells and drunken drivers. Vanka ran to the nearest letter box and thrust the precious letter into the slit.

An hour later, lulled by sweet hopes, he was fast asleep. In his dream he saw the stove. On the stove sat grandfather, his bare legs hanging down, and read the letter to the cooks. Near the stove was Wriggles, wagging his tail.

From THE CHERRY ORCHARD (1904)

Translated by Avrahm Yarmolinsky

The Cherry Orchard *was at first considered static and "undramatic" by contemporary audiences and only later was acclaimed as an innovative lyric drama. Though Chekhov conceived it as a comedy poking fun at the impoverished rural gentry, the initial interpretation by Stanislavsky at the Moscow Art Theater established it as a somber lament. In this excerpt from Act III, Lopahin, a merchant, announces to Madame Ranevskaya, a landowner, that he has bought her beloved cherry orchard. Gayev is her brother; Anya and Varya are her daughters; Firs is an octogenarian servant; Yasha is a young valet; and Pishchik is another landowner.*

MME. RANEVSKAYA. Is that you, Yermolay Alexeyevich? What kept you so long? Where's Leonid?

LOPAHIN. Leonid Andreyevich arrived with me. He's coming.

MME. RANEVSKAYA. Well, what happened? Did the sale take place? Speak!

LOPAHIN (*embarrassed, fearful of revealing his joy*). The sale was over at four o'clock. We missed the train—had to wait till half past nine. (*Sighing heavily.*) Ugh. I'm a little dizzy. (*Enter Gayev. In his right hand he holds parcels, with his left he is wiping away his tears.*)

MME. RANEVSKAYA. Well, Leonid? What news? (*Impatiently, through tears.*) Be quick, for God's sake!

GAYEV (*not answering, simply waves his hand. Weeping, to Firs*). Here, take these; anchovies, Kerch herrings . . . I haven't eaten all day. What I've been through! (*The click of billiard balls comes through the open door of the billiard room and Yasha's voice is heard.*) "Seven and eighteen!"

GAYEV (*expression changes, he no longer weeps*). I'm terribly tired. Firs, help me change. (*Exits, followed by Firs.*)

PISHCHIK. How about the sale? Tell us what happened.

MME. RANEVSKAYA. Is the cherry orchard sold?

LOPAHIN. Sold

MME. RANEVSKAYA. Who bought it?

LOPAHIN. I bought it. (*Pause. Mme. Ranevskaya is overcome.*

She would fall to the floor, were it not for the chair and table near which she stands. Varya takes the keys from her belt, flings them on the floor in the middle of the drawingroom and goes out.)

LOPAHIN. I bought it. Wait a bit, ladies and gentlemen, please, my head is swimming. I can't talk. (*Laughs.*) We got to the auction and Deriganov was there already. Leonid Andreyevich had only 15,000 and straight off Deriganov bid 30,000 over and above the mortgage. I saw how the land lay, got into the fight, bid 40,000. He bid 45,000. I bid fifty-five. He kept adding five thousands, I ten. Well . . . it came to an end. I bid ninety above the mortgage and the estate was knocked down to me. Now the cherry orchard's mine! Mine! (*Laughs uproariously.*) Lord! God in Heaven! The cherry orchard's mine! Tell me that I'm drunk—out of my mind—that it's all a dream. (*Stamps his feet.*) Don't laugh at me! If my father and my grandfather could rise from their graves and see all that has happened—how their Yermolay, who used to be flogged, their half-literate Yermolay, who used to run about barefoot in winter, how that very Yermolay has bought the most magnificent estate in the world. I bought the estate where my father and grandfather were slaves, where they weren't even allowed to enter the kitchen. I'm asleep—it's only a dream—I only imagine it. . . . It's the fruit of your imagination, wrapped in the darkness of the unknown! (*Picks up the keys, smiling genially.*) She threw down the keys, wants to show she's no longer mistress here. (*Jingles keys.*) Well, no matter. (*The band is heard tuning up.*) Hey, musicians! Strike up! I want to hear you! Come, everybody, and see how Yermolay Lopahin will lay the ax to the cherry orchard and how the trees will fall to the ground. We will build summer cottages there, and our grandsons and great-grandsons will see a new life here. Music! Strike up! (*The band starts to play. Mme. Ranevskaya has sunk into a chair and is weeping bitterly.*)

LOPAHIN (*reproachfully*). Why, why didn't you listen to me? My dear friend, my poor friend, you can't bring it back now. (*Tearfully.*) Oh, if only this were over quickly! Oh, if only our wretched, disordered life were changed!

PISHCHIK (*takes him by the arm; sotto voce*). She's crying. Let's go into the ballroom. Let her be alone. Come. (*Takes his arm and leads him into the ballroom.*)

LOPAHIN. What's the matter? Musicians, play so I can hear you! Let me have things the way I want them. (*Ironically.*) Here comes the new master, the owner of the cherry orchard. (*Accidentally he trips over a little table, almost upsetting the candelabra.*) I can pay for everything. (*Exits with Pishchik. Mme. Ranevskaya, alone, sits huddled up, weeping bitterly. Music plays softly. Enter Anya. . . . Anya goes to her mother and falls on her knees before her.*)

ANYA. Mamma, mamma, you're crying! Dear, kind, good mamma, my precious, I love you, I bless you! The cherry orchard is sold, it's gone, that's true, quite true. But don't cry, mamma, life is still before you, you still have your kind, pure heart. Let us go, let us go away from here, darling. We will plant a new orchard, even more luxuriant than this one. You will see it, you will understand, and like the sun at evening, joy—deep, tranquil joy—will sink into your soul, and you will smile, mamma. Come, darling, let us go.

The Proletarian Gorky

The son of an upholsterer from a Volga riverport, Alexei Peshkov educated himself, and in his early twenties took up writing as a profession, adopting the pseudonym Maxim Gorky ("Maxim the Bitter"). Within a decade he became the best selling Russian author of his time—the first to create fictional heroes from the working classes of the industrial cities. His realistic style and Marxist political sympathies won him the admiration of young writers, and later, recognition as "the Father of Soviet Literature."

From THE LOWER DEPTHS (1902)

Translated by F. D. Reeve

First performed at the Moscow Art Theater, this strident play about the misfortunes of vagabonds and criminals, was barely passed by government censors. It became vastly successful, both in Russia and in western Europe. In the scene given here, a gambler, Satin, scolds his companions for having ridiculed a kindly old pilgrim, Luka, who had wandered into their cellar lodgings and tried to reform them. Nastya is a prostitute; the Baron is a nobleman gone to seed.

SATIN (*striking the table with his fist*). Shut up! You're—all of you—pigs! You woodenheads! . . . Shut up about the old man! (*More calmly.*) You, Baron, you're the worst of the lot! . . . You understand nothing . . . and keep talking nonsense! The old man was no fake. What's truth? Man. That's truth! He understood that . . . you don't! You've all got bricks in your heads . . . I understand the old man . . . yes! He was lying . . . but out of pity for you, God damn you! There're lots of people who live out of pity for their neighbors . . . I know! I've read about it! Lie handsomely, inspiredly, excitingly! . . . There's such a thing as a comforting lie, a reconciling lie . . . A lie explains away the weight that has crushed a workingman's hand . . . and indicts people dying of hunger . . . I know what a lie is! Whoever's weak inside . . . and whoever sucks his life from others—they need lies . . . A lie holds some of them up, others screen themselves behind it . . . But whoever's his own master . . . whoever's independent and doesn't live off somebody else, what's he want a lie for? Lying is the religion of slaves and masters . . . Truth's the god of the free man!

BARON. Bravo! Beautifully said! I agree! You talk . . . like an honest man! . . .

SATIN (*smiling*). The old man lives in himself . . . he sees everything his own way. Once I asked him: "Grampa, what're people living for?" (*Trying to talk with Luka's voice and imitating his manner.*) "Why, people, now, are living for something better, my boy! Like, say, there are carpenter-joiners and everything—trash—the people . . . And now, out of them gets born this joiner—a joiner such as the world's never seen before; he does better than everybody else and there's not a joiner equal to him. Puts his stamp on the whole trade of joinery . . . and right away moves the whole thing twenty years ahead . . . And so all the rest, too . . . the locksmiths, now . . . shoemakers and other working people . . . and all the peasants . . . and even the gentry—every-body's living for something better! Each thinks he's living for himself, but turns out it's for something better! . . .

BARON (*thoughtfully*). Hmm—yes . . . for something better? That . . . reminds me of our family . . . An ancient name . . . from the time of Catherine . . . nobility . . . soldier-heroes! . . . Frenchmen by birth . . . Joined the service, worked up higher and higher . . . Under Nicholas I, my grandfather, Gustave deBille . . . had a high position . . . wealth . . . hundreds of serfs . . . horses . . . cooks . . .

NASTYA. Bull! No such thing!

BARON (*jumping up*). Wha-at? We-ell . . . what else!

NASTYA. No such thing!

BARON (*shouts*). A house in Moscow! A house in Petersburg! Carriages . . . carriages with coats of arms on them! . . .

NASTYA. There weren't!

BARON. Shut up! I'm telling you . . . there were dozens of footmen! . . .

NASTYA (*with relish*). The-ere weren't!

BARON. I'll kill you!

NASTYA (*getting ready to run*). There were no carriages!

SATIN. Drop it, Nastenka! Don't get him irritated . . .

BARON. Just you wait . . . you piece of trash! My grandfather . . .

NASTYA. You had no grandfather! There was nothing! (*Satin bursts out laughing.*)

BARON (*tired from anger, sits down on the bench*). Satin, tell her . . . the slut . . . You—you're laughing, too? You . . . too —don't believe me? (*Shouts in despair, pounding the table with his fists.*) It all was real, God damn you all!!

NASTYA (*triumphant*). So-o, now you've set up a howl? Y'understand now what it's like for a person when nobody'll believe him? . . .

BARON. I . . . can't allow people to make fun of me! I have proofs . . . my papers, damn you!

SATIN. Forget them! And forget about your grandpa's carriages. You're not going to go anywhere in a carriage of the past . . .

BARON. But how can she dare! . . .

NASTYA. You tell me! How I do!

SATIN. See? she does! How's she any worse than you? Though for sure her past has not only no carriages and no grandpa in it, but not even a mother and father . . .

BARON (*calming down*). God damn you . . . You . . . know how to talk about things without getting worked up . . . But it seems . . . I've got no will of my own.

SATIN. Get yourself some. It's a useful thing . . .

Mystics and Decadents

The young poets who burst onto the literary stage of the 1890's were responsible for a renascence in Russian poetry that lasted two decades. Writing in a style that was derived from Western Symbolists, the Decadents reveled in experiments with sound and sense; the Mystics saw symbols as a means of understanding the world's confusion.

Vladimir Solovyov

IN THE MORNING MIST (1884)

Prose translation by Dimitry Obolensky

Solovyov, one of Russia's great philosophers, was more influential for his ideas than for his verse, which illustrated his cosmology: a belief in the dawning of an era when man would reach perfection.

In the morning mist I walked with wavering steps towards a mysterious and wonderful shore. Dawn was contending against the last stars, dreams were still hovering, and my soul, in the grip of dreams, prayed to unknown gods.

In the cold white day I tread, as before, a lonely road in an unknown land. The mist has lifted, and the eye sees clearly how difficult is the mountain track, and how far, far away is still all that I saw in my dreams.

And until midnight I shall still be walking with fearless steps towards the shore of my desires, to where, on a mountain beneath new stars, my promised temple, all ablaze with triumphal lights, awaits me.

Konstantin Balmont

I'M THE EXQUISITE VOICE (written 1902)

Translated by Vladimir Markov and Merrill Sparks

A vociferous early Decadent, Balmont was regarded by critics as a raving lunatic. In a style that echoes Whitman, he creates unusual metrical forms—and praises himself for doing so at the same time.

I'm the exquisite voice of the broad Russian tongue:
Other poets before were precursors who'd sung.
I was first to discover the speech-cadence bounds,
In which vary the angry, melodious sounds.

    I am that—sudden break.
    I am that—thunder shake.
    I am that—limpid lake.
    I am for all and no one.

Many-foamed, splash on splash, and discordantly fused . . .
Precious gems that the primeval world has oozed . . .
And the echoes through woods in the green, green of May . . .
I shall know. And from others I'll take all away.

Like a dream (always young),
I'm in love (so I'm strong)
With myself, with the throng—
I'm the exquisite poem.

Zinaida Gippius

SHE (written 1905)

Prose translation by Dimitry Obolensky

Gippius, an ardent revolutionary in 1905, became an equally ardent anti-Bolshevik in 1917. She wrote metaphysical verse styled after the Symbolists but conceived from an intellectual viewpoint.

In her shameless and despicable vileness she is grey as dust, as earthly ashes. And I am perishing from her nearness, from the indissoluble bond between her and me.

She is scabrous, prickly, cold—she is a serpent. Her repulsive, searing, and jagged scales have covered me with wounds.

If only I could feel a sharp sting! She is flaccid, dull, and still, so lumpish and sluggish; there is no access to her—she is deaf.

Coiling round me, she stubbornly and insinuatingly caresses and strangles me. And this dead, black, and fearsome thing is my soul!

Valery Bryusov

TORTURE CHAMBER (written 1904)

Translated by Vladimir Markov and Merrill Sparks

The first of the new poets to achieve notoriety in the early nineties, Valery Bryusov dominated modern literature in Russia for almost fifteen years. Both in his personal eccentricities and in his fondness for erotic themes, he established himself as a true Decadent.

Who could merge us for one purpose,
We two, enemies at heart?
Who, conjuring words of magic,
Called us from roads far apart?

Who let us look eye to eye, while

On this perilous abyss?
Who tied us with passion's torment,
Threw us breast to breast like this?

We did not know . . . nor expect that
Mutual doom was the intent . . .
For our distances were alien
And our dreams were different.

Frightened, trembling for a long time,
Eyes averted, would not budge . . .
Each of us denied the other
Before the face of the Judge.

He, the Wise One, He, the Strict One,
Gave us punishment. (What? Why?)
We pained with a muted anguish
When the hangman laughed nearby.

In the whirlwind . . . (Who, What are we?)
Leaves borne upward from the earth!
Dreams of ecstasy and languor,
Like coals, burnt through us from birth.

Here, fallen in helpless shudders,
Thunderstorms and lightnings' whack.
Where are we: On a bed of passion
Or upon a torture-rack?

Now co-crucified for suffering,
Old enemy and sister mine!
Give me your hand! Give me your hand!
Hurry! The sword's raised! It's time!

Fedor Sologub

THE DEVIL'S SWING (written 1907)

Translated by Babette Deutsch

Fedor Teternikov took the name of a nineteenth-century aristocrat to disguise his humble origins. His prose and poetry reflect his Manichaean belief that in the struggle between good and evil, evil triumphs; beauty is destroyed; ugliness, death, and Satan prevail.

Beneath a shaggy pine,
Where the loud waters sing,
The hairy-handed fiend
Pushes his fiendish swing.

He shoves and gives a crow:
  To and fro,
  To and fro.
The board creaks as it sags,
The rope is taut and drags
Against the heavy bough.

The weak, unsteady board
Creaks warningly and slides;
The devil can afford
To roar; he holds his sides.

In agony I swing:
  To and fro,
  To and fro.
I swing and cling and try
To look away, but no,
He holds me with his eye.

Above the darkening pine
The blue fiend's tauntings ring:
"The swing has trapped you—fine!
Then, devil take you, swing!"

Beneath the shaggy pine
The demon voices sing:
"The swing has trapped you—fine!
Then, devil take you, swing!"

The fiend will not let go,
The dizzy board not stay
Until that dread hand strikes
And I am swept away.

Until the hemp, rubbed thin
And frayed, breaks suddenly,
Until the broad black ground
Comes rushing up to me.

Above the pipe I'll fling
And plop! into the mire.
Then swing, devil, swing—
Higher, higher, higher!

Innokenty Annensky

POPPIES (1910)

Translated by Babette Deutsch

Annensky, a teacher by profession, did not achieve much recognition as a poet until a few years before his death (at 53) in 1909. His sharp imagery influenced many poets of the pre-revolutionary years who were then rebelling against the theories of Symbolism.

The joyful day is blazing. . . . The limp grass
Here throngs with poppies, poppies like the cries
Of avid impotence, like lips that tempt
And poison, like strange scarlet butterflies.

The joyful day is blazing. . . . But the weeds
Usurp a garden done with pleasuring.
And poppies, withered like old women's heads,
Are sheltered beneath heaven's shining wing.

The Master Symbolists

The experimentalism of the Mystics and Decadents, and their fine craftsmanship, paved the way for the great representative poets of the Symbolist movement: Bely, Blok, and Ivanov, all of whom made their literary debuts between 1900 and 1905. These three used Symbolism to express utopian and, later, apocalyptic philosophies.

Andrei Bely

From ST. PETERSBURG (1911–13)

Translated by John Cournos

Bely, whose strikingly innovative prose has often been compared to that of James Joyce, was born Boris Bugaev, but changed his name in order to dissociate himself from his father, a famous and eccentric mathematician. Bely's obsession with fathers and sons pervades the novel excerpted here, in which Nikolai Apollonovich trys to kill his father Apollon, using a time bomb hidden in a sardine can.

Apollon Apollonovich had his own secret: a world of contours, tremors and perception—a universe of singular phenomena. All this he saw before dropping off to sleep. On his way to sleep he recalled all the former inarticulations, rustlings, crystallographic figures, stars flitting. . . .

Before the final moment of diurnal consciousness, Apollon Apollonovich had noticed, as he dropped off to sleep, that a gurgling whirlpool was suddenly assuming the shape of a corridor that vanished in infinity; but what astonished him most was that the corridor began with his head and was the endless continuation of his head, whose crown suddenly opened into infinity. . . .

Wrapped in the blanket, head and all, he was already suspended above the bed; the lacquered floor had already fallen away from the legs of the bed into the unknown—and, at the same moment, he heard a distant clicking noise, like the clatter of hoofs.

This clicking noise came nearer. . . .

In his nightshirt, a lighted candle in his hand, he traveled through the rooms. The bulldog with a clipped tail followed his disturbed master, clinking his collar and slobbering. . . .

Apollon Apollonovich gathered courage and rushed into the salon; the clicking noise came from there.

"Tra-ta. . . . Tra-ta-ta . . ."

"On the basis of what statute in the *Code of Laws?*"

As he asked this, he observed the good-natured bulldog panting amiably at his side; but someone in the hall impudently replied:

"On the basis of the extraordinary law!"

Angered by this answer, he rushed into the hall.

The flaming brand melted in his hand: it filtered through his fingers like air. A tiny ray, it came to rest at his feet. The clicking noise was made by the tongue of some villainous Mongol; he had seen the face before when staying in Tokyo; yet it turned out to be Nikolai Apollonovich. . . .

"On the basis of what law?" the Senator asked again.

"And what paragraph in the Code?" he added.

"There are no paragraphs, and no laws!" The answer came from space.

Weightless, bereft of sensation, suddenly deprived of gravity, of every physical sense, he fixed the space of his eyes (he could not say positively that his eyes fixed it, because all bodily sensation had left him); he realized too that he no longer had any parietal bones, that in their place there was a gap; Apollon Apollonovich saw in himself this round gap which formed a blue circle. At the fatal moment when according to his calculation the Mongol, who was imprinted in his consciousness but was now no longer visible, was about to reach him, something resembling a roaring wind in a chimney rapidly began to pull his consciousness through the blue parietal breach—into infinity. . . .

There was primordial darkness; and the consciousness struggled within it—no universal consciousness, but a quite simple one. . . .

Then the consciousness saw its habitation: a little yellow old man, whose bare heels were pressing against a rug.

The consciousness, it seemed, was the little old man himself; as he sat on his bed, the little old man listened to the distant clatter.

And then Apollon Apollonovich suddenly understood: his journey through the corridor, through the salon, through his head—had been only a dream.

And no sooner did this thought occur to him than he awoke; it had been a double dream.

He was not sitting, but lying down with his head wrapped in a blanket: the clatter was that of a slamming door.

Nikolai Apollonovich had returned home. . . .

Alexander Blok

From THE SCYTHIANS (written 1918)

Adapted by Rose Styron with Olga Carlisle

The handsome idol of Russia's literary salons, Blok epitomized the romantic concept of The Poet, and his poems and plays confirmed the Symbolists' belief that life and literature were inseparable. His works parallel the changing mood of Russia in the first decades of the century, progressing from the shining imagery of idealistic youth to the staccato rhythms and harsh colors of the Revolutionary era.

You are but millions—we are an infinite number.
Measure yourselves against us, try.

We are the Scythians, we are the Asians
With slanted and greedy eye.

Centuries of your days are but an hour to us,
Yet like obedient slaves,
We've held a shield between two hostile races—
Europe, and the Mongol hordes. . . .

But time has come to term and the evil hour
Flaps its wings. Each day multiplies
Offenses: soon of your very Paestum
There will be no trace. . . .

From war and horror come to our open arms,
The embrace of kin,
Put the old sword away while there's time,
Hail us as brothers. . . .

Ah, Old World, before you have perished, join
Our fraternal banquet. Hear,
Perhaps for the last time summoning you,
The barbaric lyre.

From THE TWELVE (written 1918)

Translated by Olga Carlisle

Our sons have gone
to serve the Reds
to serve the Reds
to risk their heads!

O bitter, bitter pain,
Sweet living!
A torn overcoat
an Austrian gun!

—To get the bourgeois
We'll start a fire
a worldwide fire, and drench
           it in blood—
The good Lord bless us!

—O you bitter bitterness,
boring boredom,
deadly boredom.

This is how I will
spend my time.

This is how I will
scratch my head,

munch on seeds,
some sunflower seeds,

play with my knife
play with my knife.

You bourgeois, fly as a sparrow!
I'll drink your blood,

your warm blood, for love,
for dark-eyed love.

God, let this soul, your servant, rest in peace.

Such boredom!

Vyacheslav Ivanov

LOVE (1903)

Prose translation by Dimitry Obolensky

*Known as Vyacheslav the Magnificent, Ivanov was a classicist
turned poet, whose erudition, wit, and hospitality drew Russia's best
minds to his weekly soirees. His verse—a reflection of his flamboyant
personality—combines mystical philosophy with religious symbolism,
and archaic Russian with neologisms, all set to classical meter.*

We are two tree-trunks kindled by a thunderstorm, two
flames in a midnight forest; we are two meteors, flying
through the night, a two-pointed arrow of one destiny.

We are two horses, whose reins are. held by one hand,
and which are pricked by the same spur; we are two eyes
of a single vision, two quivering wings of one dream.

We are a sorrowful pair of shades above the marble of
a sacred tomb, where ancient Beauty sleeps.

A two-voiced mouthpiece of the same mysteries, we are
one and the same Sphinx for each other. We are the two
arms of a single cross.

TO THE TRANSLATOR (1904)

*Translated by Vladimir Markov
and Merrill Sparks*

Whether you hunt Virgil, the meadowlark,—
Or Baudelaire, the albatross,—or Verlaine,
The nightingale—you cannot lure free birds
To strange captivity without hard strain.

My dear bird-catcher, I'm sure you won't spare
Violence or treason, poet—or desist
Though you're shepherd of idylls or a friend
Of all nine muses or evil's botanist.

Since someone else's verse is Proteus,
A slippery god, you can't catch him with grasp
Or courage. You hold the fishtail and it

Pours through the flimsy nets. Be Proteus
With Proteus. Meet each mask with a mask!
Or else amuse them with your own tale's wit.

Poets at the Crossroads

The Symbolists, who had earlier been considered radicals, were thought to be passé by the poets whose works appear below. Those who belonged to the Acmeist school, represented here by Akhmatova and Mandelshtam, strove to restore clarity and freshness to a poetry obscured by the Symbolists' abstract musings. The Futurists, led by Mayakovsky, rejected all previous art forms and created new ones for the machine age. Meanwhile, Yesenin and the Imagists stressed striking imagery as the primary element in verse.

Anna Akhmatova

BROAD GOLD (written 1915)

Translated by Babette Deutsch

The young Akhmatova (pen name of Anna Gorenko) cut a dashing figure as the emancipated woman who wrote eloquently of feminine emotions. By the time she died, in 1966, she was considered one of Russia's greatest modern poets, admired for her verse and her courage in the face of government harassment and literary black-listing.

Broad gold, the evening heavens glow,
The April air is cool and tender.
You should have come ten years ago,
And yet in welcome I surrender.

Come here, sit closer to me, look
With eyes that twinkle, mouth that purses,
Into the little blue-bound book
That holds my awkward childish verses.

Forgive me that I long forsook
Joy's sunny paths, nor glanced toward any;
Forgive me those whom I mistook
For you—alas, they were too many.

ALL IS SOLD (written 1921)

Translated by Babette Deutsch

All is sold, all is lost, all is plundered,
Death's wing has flashed black on our sight,
All's gnawed bare with sore want and sick
                              longing—
Then how are we graced with this light?

By day there's a breath of wild cherry
In the city, from woods none descries;
At night new and strange constellations
Shine forth in the pale summer skies.

And these houses, this dirt, these mean ruins,
Are touched by the miracle, too;
It is close, the desired, the despaired of,
That all longed for, but none ever knew.

AN UNPARALLELED AUTUMN (written 1922)

Translated by Babette Deutsch

An unparalleled autumn erected a glorious dome;
All the clouds were commanded to leave it undarkened and
                              pure.
And men marveled: September is gone, and yet where are
                              the days
Shot with dampness and chill? How long can this wonder
                              endure?
In the turbid canals the mild waters shone emerald-clear,
And the nettles had fragrance more rich than the roses to
                              give;
And the sunsets that laid on the air their unbearable weight
Of demoniac crimson, we shall not forget while we live.
Like a rebel who enters the capital, thus the proud sun,
Which this autumn, so springlike, was hungry to smile at
                              and woo,
Till it seemed any moment a snowdrop, transparent, would
                              gleam—
Then I saw, on the path to my door, stepping quietly, you.

Osip Mandelshtam

ORIOLES LIVE IN THE ELMS (1914)

Adapted by Stanley Kunitz with Olga Carlisle

Mandelshtam, a scholarly essayist and poet from St. Petersburg, attempted to remain indifferent to Revolutionary politics. Like other writers, he was expected to turn out paeans for the government, but found himself unable to bend his subtle and refined poetry to the banalities of propaganda. Later he was sent into exile for criticizing Stalin. He died in 1938, en route to a Siberian prison camp.

Orioles live in the elms, and in classical verse
The length of the vowels alone determines the measure.
Once and once only a year nature knows quantity
Stretched to the limit as in Homer's meter.

O this is a day that yawns like a caesura:
Serene from the start, almost painfully slowed.
Oxen browse in the field, and a golden languor
Keeps me from drawing a rich, whole note from my reed.

MOSCOW (1916)

Adapted by Robert Lowell with Olga Carlisle

Somehow we got through the miles of Moscow,
left the Sparrow Hills, and found the small, familiar church.
Our open sled was filled with straw, and roughly hooded
with coarse, frozen cloth that hurt us.

Then in Uglitch the children played knucklebones.
When we drove through it, I reached for my lost hat,
the air smelled like bread left in the oven,
three candles were melting in the chapel.

They were not three candles but three meetings—
one of them had been blessed by the Lord Himself.
There couldn't be a fourth—Rome was so far away,
and the Lord had never really been Himself there.

Our sled stuck in a black rut,
and people shuffled by us to stare.
The men were all bones, the women were crows.
They gossiped and wasted time by the door.

Birds blackened the bare distance with spots—
his tied hands were icy. The Tsarevitch's
body was like a frozen sack when they drove him in,
and set fire to the reddish straw.

TRISTIA (1922)

Adapted by Stanley Kunitz with Olga Carlisle

I made myself an expert in farewells
By studying laments, the night-fall of a woman's hair.
Oxen chew their cud; anticipation lags;
It is the town's last restless hour;
And I praise that ritual night when the cocks crowed
And eyelids, heavy with the griefs that pass,
Opened to the light, while her weeping flowed
Into the sound of the Muses singing.

Who knows, when the time comes to say goodbye,
What separation we are meant to bear
And what for us cockcrow shall signify
When the acropolis burns like a flare,
And why, at the new daybreak of a life,
When the ox is ruminating in his stall,
The herald cock, prophetic of rebirth,
Should flap his wings on the town wall?

I bless the craft of spinning: the to-and-fro
Action of the shuttle, the way the spindle hums.
Look! barefooted Delia, light as a feather,
Hurries to meet you, flying as she comes.
Oh, how scrawny is the language of joy,
That weak foundation of our mortal lot!
Everything happened before; it will happen again.
Only the flash of recognition brings delight.

Be it so: a small transparent puppet lies,
Like a dried squirrel skin
Extended on a plate,
While a girl crouches, staring, over the image.
Wax is for women what bronze is for men.
We, who cannot prophesy of Erebus,
Only in battle dare confront our fate—
But their gift is to die while telling fortunes.

Vladimir Mayakovsky

From THE CLOUD IN TROUSERS (1915)

Translated by George Reavey

Mayakovsky, the leader of the Futurists, was at first an ardent supporter of the Revolution, preaching the overthrow of traditional forms in art and politics. But the Soviet regime proved hostile to his literary experimentalism and began censoring and ridiculing his works. In 1930, disillusioned and frustrated, he shot himself.

Glorify me!
For me the great are no match.
Upon every achievement
I stamp *nihil*.

I never want
to read anything.
Books?
What are books!

Formerly I believed
books were made like this:
a poet came,
lightly opened his lips,
and the inspired fool burst into song—
if you please!
But it seems,
before they can launch a song,
poets must tramp for days with callused feet,
and the sluggish fish of the imagination
flounders softly in the slush of the heart.
And while, with twittering rhymes, they boil a broth
of loves and nightingales,
the tongueless street merely writhes
for lack of something to shout or say.

In our pride, we raise up again
the cities' towers of Babel,
but god,
confusing tongues,
grinds
cities to pasture.

In silence the street pushed torment.
A shout stood erect in the gullet.
Wedged in the throat,

bulging taxis and bony cabs bristled.
Pedestrians have trodden my chest
flatter than consumption.

The city has locked the road in gloom.

But when—
nevertheless!—
the street coughed up the crush on the square,
pushing away the portico that was treading on its throat,
it looked as if:
in choirs of an archangel's chorale,
god, who had been plundered, was advancing in wrath!

But the street, squatting down, bawled:
"Let's go and guzzle!"

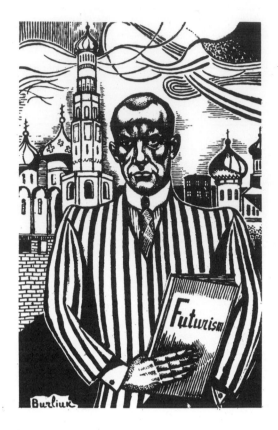

From TRASH (1921)

Translated by Bernard Guilbert Guerney

Glory, Glory, Glory to the heroes!!!
But, no doubt,
They
Have had their bellyful of glory-hash:
Today
Let us mere zeros
Talk about
Trash.

The storms of revolt are all dead as the Czar.
The Soviet whirlpools are covered with scum.
And there has peeped out
From behind the back of the USSR
The burgher's damned snout—
His day has come.

From BROOKLYN BRIDGE (written 1925)

Translated by George Reavey

Give, Coolidge,
a shout of joy!
I too will spare no words
                about good things.
Blush
      at my praise,
                go red as our flag,
however
        united-states
                     -of
-america you may be.
As a crazed believer
                enters
                    a church,
retreats
        into a monastery cell,
                                austere and plain;

so I,
      in graying evening
                        haze,
humbly set foot
                on Brooklyn Bridge. . . .
I am proud
          of just this
                      mile of steel;
upon it,
        my visions come to life, erect—
here's a fight
              for construction
                                instead of style,
an austere disposition
                      of bolts
                            and steel.
If
   the end of the world
                        befall—
and chaos
         smash our planet
                        to bits,
and what remains
                will be
                      this
bridge, rearing above the dust of destruction;
then,
     as huge ancient lizards
                            are rebuilt
from bones
          finer than needles,
                              to tower in museums,
so,
   from this bridge,

                    a geologist of the centuries
will succeed
        in recreating
                        our contemporary world.
By the cables
        of electric strands,
I recognize
        the era succeeding
                    the steam age—
here
    men
            had ranted
                    on radio.
Here
    men
        had ascended
                in planes.
For some,
        life
            here
                had no worries;
for others,
        it was a prolonged

                        and hungry howl.
From this spot,
                jobless men
leapt
        headlong
                into the Hudson.
Now
        my canvas
                    is unobstructed
as it stretches on cables of string
                                to the feet of the stars.
I see:
        here
                stood Mayakovsky,
stood,
            composing verse, syllable by syllable.
I stare
        as an Eskimo gapes at a train,
I seize on it
                as a tick fastens to an ear.
Brooklyn Bridge—
yes . . .
            That's quite a thing!

Sergei Yesenin

Yesenin was a naive farm boy who came to Petersburg from Ryazan to show his poetry to Blok and other writers. They recognized his talent immediately, and he was soon being lionized in the capital as "the peasant poet." But he was unable to adjust to the dissolute city life; his later poems express his nostalgia for the country.

I AM THE LAST POET (1921)

*Adapted by W. S. Merwin
with Vladimir Weidle*

I am the last poet of the villages
the plank bridge lifts a plain song
I stand at a farewell service
birches swinging leaves like censors

The golden flame will burn down
in the candle of waxen flesh
and the moon a wooden clock
will caw caw my midnight

On the track in the blue field
soon the iron guest will appear
his black hand will seize
oats that the dawn sowed

In a lifeless and alien grip
my poems will die too
only nodding oats

will mourn for their old master

The wind will take up their neighing
they will all dance in the morning
soon the moon a wooden clock
will caw caw my midnight

A MOONY THIN DESOLATION (1925)

Translated by Babette Deutsch

A moony thin desolation,
Vast plains in anguish immersed—
My carefree youth once knew this,
I loved it, like others, and cursed.

The roads with their dusty willows,
And the tune that the cartwheels play. . . .
Not for aught that I might be offered
Would I listen to it today.

I am weary of huts and hearthstones,
Spring storming the apple trees

I can love no longer for thinking
Of the fields in their poverty.

Now my heart is given elsewhere—
In the moon's consumptive light
I see stone and steel as the secret
Of my country's coming might.

Oh, Russia, give over dragging
Your wooden plow through the fields!
The birches ache, and the poplars,
When they see what the harvest yields.

Perhaps the new life will reject me,
My future is blank, but I feel
A longing to see beggared Russia
Become a Russia of steel.

And hearing the bark of the motors
Through the blizzards, shrill and strong,
I have no wish at all to listen
To the cartwheels' creaking song.

Laments and Prophecies

In the 1920's Russian writers were again turning to prose—mainly short stories and novellas—as the most effective medium for conveying glimpses of the social chaos that followed the Revolution. The masters among these writers, Zamyatin, Pilnyak, and Babel, were at first in sympathy with the Revolution (they were later disillusioned), believing it would abolish tyranny. Their works, seemingly fantastic, are accurate reflections of the times.

Yevgeny Zamyatin

From WE (written 1920)

Translated by Bernard Guilbert Guerney

Paraphrasing a remark by Chekhov, Zamyatin once said he was a bigamist—his two wives being shipbuilding and literature. A naval engineer by profession, he ended up devoting most of his time to writing. Zamyatin endorsed the Revolution, but not the Marxist dogmatism evolved by the Soviets, whose utopianism he satirized in We.

FIRST ENTRY: *An Announcement. The Wisest of Lines. A Poem.*
I am simply transcribing, word for word, what appeared in today's *State Gazette:*

"In 120 days the construction of the *Integral* will be completed. The great, the historic hour is near when the first *Integral* shall soar into universal space. A thousand years ago your heroic ancestors subdued the entire terrestrial globe to the domination of The One State. Now a still more glorious deed lies before you: that of integrating, by means of the glazed, electrified, fire-breathing *Integral*, the endless equalization of all Creation. There lies before you the subjugation of unknown creatures to the beneficent yoke of reason—creatures inhabiting other planets, perhaps still in the savage state of freedom. Should they fail to understand that we are bringing them a mathematically infallible happiness, it will be our duty to compel them to be happy. But, before resorting to weapons, we shall try words.

"In the name of The Benefactor it is hereby proclaimed to all the numbers of The One State:

"Everyone who feels able to do so is obligated to compose treatises, poems, odes and/or other pieces on the beauty and grandeur of The One State.

"This will be the first cargo to be borne by the *Integral*.

"All hail to The One State; all hail to the numbers; all hail to The Benefactor!"

I am writing this—and I feel my cheeks are flaming. Yes—we must carry through the integration of the grandiose, endless equalization of all Creation. Yes—we must unbend the wild curve, we must straighten it out at a tangent—at an asymptote—to a straight line! Inasmuch as the line of The One State is a straight line. The great, divine, exact, wise straight line—the wisest of lines!

I, D-503, the builder of the *Integral*—I am but one of the mathematicians of The One State. My pen, accustomed to figures, has not the power to create the music of assonances and rhymes. I shall merely attempt to record what I see, what I think—to be more exact, what *we* think (*we*, precisely, and let this *WE* serve as the title of the entries I am making). However, these things will be a derivative of our life, of the mathematically perfect life of The One State, and if that be so, will not all this be a poem *per se*, whether I will it or not? It will be a poem—I believe it and know it. . . .

SECOND ENTRY: *Ballet. Harmony of the Square. X.*
Spring. From beyond the Green Wall, from the wild plains that lie out of sight, the wind brings the honeyed yellow pollen of certain flowers. . . . On days such as this, one sees the blue depth of things, one sees certain of their equations, amazing and unknown until that moment—one sees them in something that may be ever so ordinary, ever so prosaic.

Why, consider ever this, for example: this morning I was at the launching site where the *Integral* is under construction—and I suddenly caught sight of the work benches. Sightlessly, in self-oblivion, the globes of the regulators rotated; the cranks, glittering, bent to right and left; a balanced beam swayed its shoulders proudly; the blade of a gouging lathe was doing a squatting dance in time to unheard music. I suddenly perceived all the beauty of this grandiose mechanical ballet, flood-lighted by the ethereal, azure-surrounded sun.

Then, continuing my train of thought, I asked myself: Why is all this beautiful? Why is this dance beautiful? The answer was: Because this was *nonfree* motion, because all of the profound meaning of the dance lay precisely in absolute, aesthetic submissiveness, in ideal *nonfreedom*. . . .

I will have to finish this thought later: the intercommunication board clicked at this point. I looked up—0–90, of course. In half a minute she herself will be here; she is coming to fetch me for a walk. . . .

We went down. The avenue was full of people—in such weather we usually spend the after-lunch Personal Hour in a supplementary walk. As always, the Musical Factory was chanting with all its pipes The March of The One State. The numbers—hundreds, thousands of numbers—all in light-blue unifs, all with gold badges on their chests, each badge bearing the State number of the particular he or she—the numbers were pacing along in even ranks of four each, exaltedly pounding their feet in time to the music. . . .

The sky of beatific blue, the suns, tiny as children's toys, reflected in all the badges, faces unclouded by the insanity of thoughts—rays, these, you understand: all this was formed of some unique, radiant, riant matter. As for the brazen beats—*tra-ta-ta-tam, tra-ta-ta-tam*—these were steps of brass that sparkled in the sun, and with every step you rose higher and higher into the vertiginous azure. . . . And then, just as it had happened this morning at the launching site, I again saw all things as if I were seeing them for the very first time in my life—I saw the irrevocably straight streets, the ray-spurting glass of the roadways, the divine parallelepipedons of the transparent dwellings, the square harmony of our gray-blue ranks. And so it struck me that it had not been the generations upon generations before me but I—precisely I—who had conquered the old God and the old life; that it was precisely I who had created all this. . . .

Boris Pilnyak

From THE NAKED YEAR (1922)

Translated by Alec Brown

Pilnyak's real name was Boris Vogau. A veterinarian's son, he spent his youth in provincial Russia and became fascinated by the earthy and the primitive. In his novella The Naked Year, *written in a chaotic "blizzard of words," Pilnyak ascribed the Revolution's success to a welling up of erotic, blind forces in the Russian people.*

In 1914 the war blazed up; and, after it, in 1917, the Revolution. In the ancient town people were summoned together and taught the craft of murder and were sent—to the swamps of Belovezh, to Galicia, to the Carpathians—to kill and to die. . . . In Ordynin, when soldiers went off, the town saw them off as far as the Yamskaya suburb.

The first of the town's casualties was *Classic-Spark*, honorable tavern-rat, dipsomaniac student—died—hung himself—leaving a note:

"I die because it is impossible to live without vodka. Citizens and comrades of the new dawning! When a class has come to the end of its meaning—it is time it died, and it had better put an end to itself.

"I die at the dawn of new life!" . . .

In 1916 the railway past Ordynin to the ironworks was laid and for the last time the merchants of the town—"fathers of the town"—used their cunning: the engineers suggested the town should fork up a bribe, and the fathers of the town agreed. But they suggested so ridiculously small a sum that the engineers felt obliged to put the station ten versts out, at the ironworks. The trains rushed past the town like crazy things—but in spite of that the residents made the coming of the first train a festival—all flocked down to the Vologa, and, to see better, the urchins climbed onto housetops and willows. . . .

About the ancient town, about the dead kremlin, they paraded with banners and sang red songs—sang songs and moved in crowds at an hour when the ancient canonic merchant town, with its monastery and its nunnery and its churches and its towers and its cobbled streets, would have been in the depth of sleep, with the only moving life, the life behind those walls where there were wolf-dogs on the gateposts. Around Ordynin lay woodlands, and out in the woods flared the red flames of burning manors, and from the woods came strings of peasants with sacks and corn. . . .

The salt market was broken up. From under the plank flooring the rats fled in their thousands—in the cellars putrid pork had been kept. At the foundations they found human skulls and skeletons. The salt market was destroyed . . . and in its place a *House of the People* began to spring up. . . .

Hunger in the town, misery and delight in the town, tears and laughter in the town; over the town pass springs, autumns, winters; and over the new road creep starving townsmen coming in with sacks from foraging in the villages; creep smallpox and typhus.

There is no longer that inscription on the gates of the Ordynin Kremlin:

> "Preserve, O Lord,
> This Town and Thy People,
> And Thy Benediction
> Be upon these gates"

For that matter, the town did not contain only merchants: there were nobles too, artisans and other commoners; the town, it must not be forgotten, lies a thousand versts from anywhere, in the lands the other side of the River Kama, among forest lands; and the Whites came to the town.

The chronicler says in his chronicles of the Ordynin lands:

"The town of Ordynin riseth out of rock. The lands are rich in the fiery stone and the lodestone to which adhereth iron."

And so, outside Ordynin, an ironworks sprang up. The Ordynin lands consist of: dry water-courses, streams, lakes, woodlands, copses, swamps, arable land, a tranquil sky, and are intersected by country roads, tracks of peasant carts. . . . The country roads creep along, and wind like twisted thread, with neither beginning nor end. And some folk, as they go along these winding roads, sing quiet songs that many would find as wearisome as the road itself. Ordynin was born amid them, with them, of them.

In his chronicles, in his *History of Great Russia, Religion, and Revolution,* the chronicler—the Archbishop of Ordynin, Silvester, says of the people of Ordynin:

"They lived in the woods like wild beasts, they ate all manner of unclean things, and foul words were upon their lips before their fathers and before womenfolk; there were no marriages among them, but revels between village and village, they coming together for revels and dancing and all manner of satanic antics, and here they took for themselves brides with whom they had made their pacts, and they had each man two or three wives, and if one of them died they did pagan funerals over him, and then made ready a great fire, a pyre, and put on it the dead man and burned him, and took the bones and put them in a small vessel and put this on a pillar by the roadside, which they do to this day."

And the song of these days is the song of the blizzard:

—Storm. And pines. And plains. And terror.

Ooooooaaah, oooooaaahhh, oooooooaaaaaahhhh. . . .

Eeeeiou, aaaaaaou, eeeiou, eeeeeeion, aaaou! and

Crr-a-a-sh!

Crr-a-a-sh!!

Ooooooah, eeeeiou, aaaaou. . . .

Crrr-a-a-sh!!!

Isaac Babel

GEDALI (1926)

Translated by Andrew R. MacAndrew

Babel was born and grew up in the Jewish sector of Odessa, the colorful seaport where many of his stories are set. Having witnessed the pogroms, Babel at first welcomed the Revolution, believing that it would bring an end to anti-Semitism. But the Soviet government dashed his hopes; Babel himself died a victim of Stalin's purges.

The opaque sadness of memories pervades me on Sabbath eves. Once, on those evenings, my grandfather's yellowed beard swept the volumes of Ibn Ezra while my old, lace-capped grandmother moaned sweetly as she told the future over the Sabbath candles with her knotty fingers. On those evenings, my heart, the heart of a child, rocked like a toy ship on the waves of an enchanted sea. Oh, the moldering Talmuds of my childhood! Oh, the opaque sadness of memories!

I roam around Zhitomir seeking a timid star. By the yellow and indifferent walls of the ancient synagogue, old Jews with the beards of prophets, pathetic tatters covering their sunken chests, sell chalk, wicks, and bluing.

Here before me is the market and the death of the market. The fat soul of plenty has been killed. Dumb padlocks hang on the shops and the granite pavement is as clear as the bald patch on a dead man's head. The timid star twinkles and goes out.

Success came to me later. It came just before sunset. Gedali's shop was lost among the rows of other, tightly padlocked shops. Where was your ghost that evening, Dickens? In that curiosity shop you would have seen gilt slippers, ship's cables, an ancient compass, a stuffed eagle, a Winchester rifle with the date 1810 engraved on it, and a broken saucepan.

Old Gedali walked among his treasures in the pink vacuum of the sunset—a small man in smoked glasses and a green smock that hung almost to the ground. He rubbed his small white hands together, tugged at his thin grayish beard, and with lowered head, listened to the voices of invisible people that floated down to him.

The little shop is like the treasure box of a self-important and inquisitive schoolboy who one day will become a teacher of botany. The shop has buttons to sell and also a dead butterfly. Its little owner's name is Gedali. Everyone has left the market place except Gedali, who stays on. . . .

We sit on empty beer barrels. Gedali winds and unwinds his narrow beard. His high silk hat sways above us. . . .

"We say *yes* to the Revolution," Gedali began, enmeshing me in the silky cords of his smoky eyes, "but why must we say *no* to the Sabbath? *Yes!* I shout to the Revolution, *yes, yes!* But what does it do? It hides from Gedali and sends out only rifle bullets."

"The sun can't get into closed eyes," I reply to the old man, "but we'll tear open the eyes that are shut."

"The Pole has closed my eyes for me," the old man whispers, hardly audibly, "the Pole—the vicious dog. He takes a Jew and tears out his beard. Ah, the dog! And now, they're giving that vicious beast a good beating. The Revolution, it's wonderful! And then, the Revolution which gave that beating to the Pole comes to me and says: 'Let me have your phonograph, Gedali, I must turn it over to the state.' 'But I love music, Mrs. Revolution,' I say to her. 'You don't know what's good for you, Gedali,' she says, 'but when I start firing at you, you'll find out, because I can't help firing, being the Revolution. . . .' "

"But the Pole fired at me, kind madam, because he was the Counterrevolution. And now you're firing because you're the Revolution. But surely, Revolution means joy, and having orphans in the house doesn't contribute to joy. A good person does good deeds and the Revolution is a good deed of good people. But good people don't kill. Then Revolution is made by wicked people. But the Poles are wicked people too. Who, then, will explain to Gedali where Revolution is and where Counterrevolution is? Once upon a time, I studied the Talmud. I like Rashi's commentaries and Maimonides' books. And besides me, there are other people who think in Zhitomir. And now, all of us learned people, we fall upon our faces and shout in one voice: 'Woe to us, where is she, the sweet Revolution?' "

The old man fell silent, and we saw the first star coming up along the Milky Way.

"The Sabbath is on its way," Gedali announced solemnly. "Jews must go to synagogue, Mr. Comrade," he added, getting up and picking up the top hat so that now the little black tower swayed on his head, "please send some nice people over to Zhitomir. Oi, there's a shortage of them in this town, a bad shortage! Get some kind people in here and we'll hand all the phonographs they want over to them. We are no ignoramuses. We know what the International is. I want an International of good men and I want every soul registered and receiving a first-category ration card. Here, soul—eat, help yourself, get a kick out of life. It's you, Mr. Comrade, who doesn't know what people eat the International with."

"They eat it with gunpowder," I said to the old man, "and they season it with the best blood."

And then the young Sabbath came out of the blue darkness and mounted its throne.

"Gedali," I said, "it's Friday tonight and its already dark. Where does one find a piece of Jewish pastry here, a Jewish glass of tea, with a whiff of that retired God in it?"

"Nowhere," Gedali said, putting the padlock on his little box. "You won't find it anywhere. There was a small restaurant next door and nice people used to run it, but no one eats there now—they just cry there."

He buttoned the three bone buttons of his green smock, dusted himself with the rooster-feather duster, sprinkled some water on his soft palms, and left—tiny, lonely, and dreamy in his black top hat, with a big prayer book under his arm.

The Sabbath was here. Gedali, the founder of the unrealizable International, left for the synagogue to pray.

The industrial society envisioned by Mstislav Doboujinsky in this undated ink drawing was a utopia for some writers of the twenties, a horror for others. Doboujinsky, a book illustrator and stage designer, was an early member of Diaghilev's World of Art society, and later emigrated to Europe and the United States.

11

Utopian Dreams

Artists in Revolt

The prevailing mood in Russia and Europe before World War I was summed up by the poet Alexander Blok. "I think," he wrote, "that a persistent feeling of catastrophe took root in the hearts of people of the latest generations. . . . a feeling of sickness, alarm, and alienation was lodged in all of us." In Russia the restlessness of the workers and peasants erupted in strikes, rural uprisings and political assassinations, including the 1905 revolution and the assassination of Premier Peter Stolypin in 1911. The government vacillated between appeasement and oppression, and intellectuals and aristocrats succumbed to despair, some of them turning for solace to wild living and others to religious mysticism.

In this tense atmosphere the generation of artists and writers that dominated Russian cultural life from 1917 to the late 1920's came to maturity. They felt the approaching crisis as keenly as their elders, but many placed their hopes on the success of revolution and the social reforms it would bring. Having first trained themselves in the modes of their predecessors—Symbolism and Realism in writing, Impressionism, Expressionism, and Fauvism in painting—the younger generation dismissed those schools as irrelevant and obsolete.

The poster opposite, "The Red Scepter of Communism Advances through Europe," was made just after the 1917 revolution; modernist works were later condemned as incomprehensible to the public.

Their first alternative was an exuberant anarchy, a total rejection of all traditional values in art and literature. Thenceforth, their new rule was that they would have no rules.

The most vocal among them were the Futurists, an alliance of poets and artists who issued their manifesto in 1912. Entitled "A Slap in the Face of Public Taste," it advocated new idioms for an age of machines and socialism. The Futurists delighted in jolting the complacent public by wearing freakish costumes and body paint, and by upsetting public functions with their raucous behavior. In a more productive vein, they arranged touring exhibitions to present their ideas to the Russian people and opened the way for the nonobjective art of the Suprematists and the engineering art of the Constructivists.

The majority of these groups joyfully accepted the March and the November revolutions of 1917, and their art became increasingly political. They worked hard to define and promote the new regime, writing slogans, painting posters, staging propaganda rallies, making films, creating art workshops, and designing everything from buildings to teapots. But often, the revolution in art was too far ahead of the political and educational revolutions to be fully appreciated, and by the 1920's the burst of experimentalism that had begun at the turn of the century had ceded to the demand for a popular socialist art that could be understood by the people, an art that would educate the masses and raise them to glory.

A Slap in the Face

In their heyday, from 1912 to the mid-1920's, the Futurists counted among their members and allies the artists Vasily Kandinsky, Kazimir Malevich, and Lazar Lissitsky; the poet-painters Vladimir Mayakovsky and David and Vladimir Burliuk; and the writers Velemir Khlebnikov and the young Boris Pasternak. Of all the groups of artists and writers kaleidoscopically forming, intermingling, and splintering, it was the Futurists whose art and ideas most reflected the chaotic atmosphere accompanying the change-over from an agrarian to an industrial society in the years succeeding the 1917 revolution. "The city," one of them proclaimed, "is replacing nature and her elements. . . . Telephones, airplanes, expresses, elevators . . . sidewalks, factory chimneys, massive stone buildings, soot, and smoke—these are the components of beauty in new urban nature." Futurists throughout Europe held in common a fascination with modern urban society and a concern for social problems, to which the Russians lent their own native color and daring. Their outrageous gestures—Mayakovsky's loud shirts and the wooden spoon he wore on his lapel, Burliuk's "I am Burliuk" painted on his forehead—dramatized their disdain for current values.

A man of many arts, Vladimir Mayakovsky wrote and acted in Futurist films (above) and drew dozens of anticapitalist posters and cartoons (left). He is shown opposite reciting his verse at an open-air gathering.

A Conflict of Visions

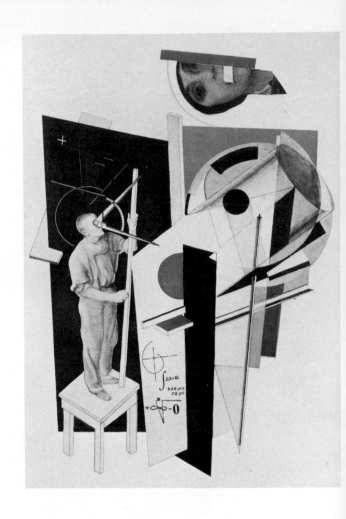

The excitement in the pre-war Russian art world was not always directed into the most creative channels. Just before the 1915 opening in Petersburg of "0.10 The Last Futurist Painting Exhibition," the main exhibitors came to blows. Kazimir Malevich, whose new Suprematist school of painting was to have its debut at the show, and Vladimir Tatlin, founder of Constructivism, were in violent disagreement over the validity of abstract art.

Malevich and his followers conceived of art as a spiritual activity whose purpose was to give man a new vision of the world; their nonobjective paintings were intended to free man from the shackles of natural forms. But Tatlin and the Constructivists dismissed abstract art as amateurish and useless, advocating instead that art be integrated with the material world and that it serve society; the artist was thus to be an engineer, who united art and life through technology.

Both movements were utopian in outlook, but their ends and methods were too different, and their practitioners too intolerant of one another's art to exhibit side by side. When the fisticuffs between Malevich and Tatlin were broken up, Tatlin and his followers moved their works to another room, tacking a sign over their door "Exhibition of Professional Painters."

Tatlin's Monument to the Third International (shown in the drawing at left) was to house government offices in three revolving units; El Lissitsky's collage (above) shows Tatlin building a scale model. In his 1915 "Yellow, Orange, and Green" (opposite page) Malevich uses geometric forms to create a formless mass.

Theater in the Streets

During the first ten years of the Soviet regime the grand drama of revolution, which had turned all Russia into a stage, provided modernist artists with inspiration on a gigantic scale. Collaborating with leading actors and theater and film directors, they created vast theatrical productions, employing casts of thousands and whole sections of cities to dramatize the events of 1917. They utilized the mass movements of the crowds for histrionic effect the way Sergei Eisenstein did in his dramatic film of 1925, *Battleship Potemkin*. Theirs was truly a mass art, theatricality at its most extravagant, and as such it anticipated Mayakovsky's admonition to his fellow artists: "Comrades, give us a new form of art—an art that will pull the republic out of the mud."

The intention of these demonstrations was both artistic and educational. While celebrating revolutionary anniversaries, the organizers sought to involve as many citizens as possible in the pageantry, to make them feel that they themselves were part of history.

For one such performance—a 1918 re-enactment of the storming of the Winter Palace—the artists requisitioned the palace square, decorating it with Futurist sculptures and decking the surrounding buildings with thousands of yards of bunting bearing abstract designs. They persuaded a battalion commander to contribute his soldiers and equipment, and managed to obtain a number of arc lights that would play across the sky over the square. The palace was duly stormed, the fifty Kerenskys of the puppet government were toppled (a single Kerensky had looked too insignificant against the vast palace facade; he was therefore multiplied fiftyfold). The Red Army swept the White Army away, and the jubilant audience hounded the Whites out of the square. The performance was so realistic that it caused consternation among the authorities when they found out what had been going on. Civil war was, after all, still raging in the provinces, and they feared that the demonstration might have become the beginning of a counterrevolution.

The stage setting reproduced below was designed by the artist Yury Annenkov for a production entitled "The Storming of the Winter Palace," which was mounted in September, 1920, in the huge square adjoining the seat of the former tsarist government. The square had been occupied by Bolsheviks three years earlier. To re-create the scene a cast of 8,000 workers and soldiers was used, and according to contemporary witnesses, 150,000 spectators gathered to watch the massive pageant.

Letting In the Light

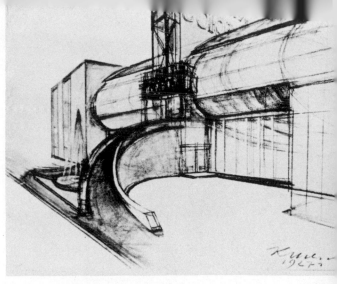

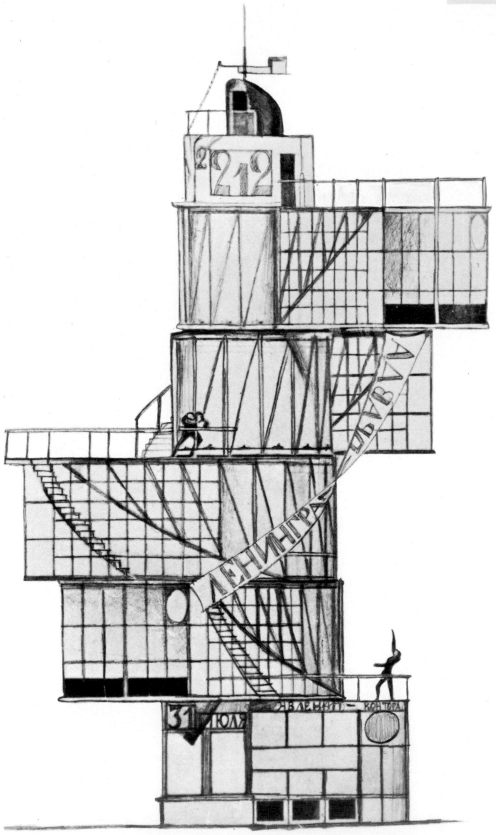

The artistic ferment brewing in Russia from 1910 to 1924 penetrated even the world of architecture. The major inspiration came from the *avant-garde* painters, who were experimenting with architectural concepts in their paintings. The Suprematists' canon of stripping objects to the barest essentials and the Constructivists' doctrine of form following function coincided with the needs of the new communal society envisioned by the socialist revolutionaries.

For the first few years of the Soviet regime, from about 1918 to 1929, the Constructivists and members of other modernist factions—Konstantin Melnikov, Ivan Leonidov, and the brothers Viktor, Leonid, and Alexander Vesnin—were the most influential in formulating plans for the numerous government projects initiated in the wake of the Revolution. Hundreds of designs were made for workers' clubs, dwellings, factories, hospitals, and urban developments.

But few of these projects were ever built. In the decade following the Revolution the innovators came under increasing attack, accused by conservative architects and party politicians of being more interested in form for form's sake than in satisfying the peoples' need for a functional architecture. Gradually the formalists were forced out by architects schooled in the old values, and their spare geometrical forms and imaginative use of concrete and glass gave way to anachronistic imitations of eighteenth-century neoclassicism and of nineteenth-century Muscovite-Romanesque-Byzantine conglomerations.

During his brief career, Konstantin Melnikov was in the forefront of modern architecture. Striving for purity of form and a maximum of light and air in his buildings, he made extensive use of glass and concrete. An early project, the tower opposite (1923) was a plan for a newspaper office; each floor could be electrically rotated. The plan below (1930) was for a glass office, suspended on steel trusses. Neither project was carried out, but the workers' clubs above and at top, opposite, were built in 1928–29. Attacked as a formalist, Melnikov was driven out of the profession in 1936 by more conservative architects.

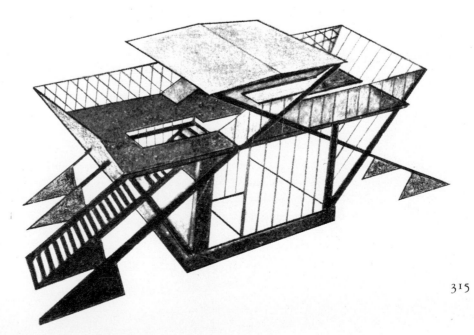

1

2

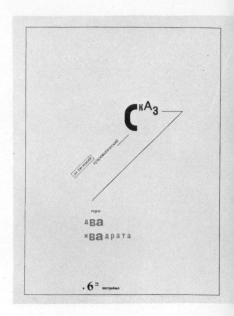

3

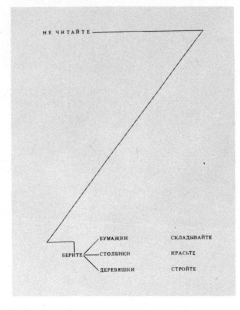

4

5

The Graphic
Frame of Mind

From 1918 to 1921 the Bolsheviks were struggling desperately to maintain power as civil war raged throughout Russia. Their survival depended upon the success of propaganda campaigns directed toward reconciling the populace to the new government and a socialist way of life. The arts most accessible to a largely illiterate audience were called into service: huge rallies were held at which poets read their verse praising the Revolution or advocating self-improvement; propaganda trains rolled across the country carrying speakers and films urging support of the new regime; and the walls of buildings were plastered with agitation-and-propaganda (agit-prop) posters.

By 1922 the danger of political overthrow had subsided, and famine and shortages no longer reigned. The traditional form of propaganda—the printed word—returned when paper and time to write (and to read) again became available. For a brief period, government organizations controlling the arts were largely in the hands of the modernists, who were free to experiment with new ideas in book illustrating, design, and printing. Among the foremost experimenters was El (Lazar) Lissitsky who, having received training both as an engineer and as an architect, finally settled on a career as an artist. His work, in keeping with his training, combines the concepts evolved by both Suprematists and Constructivists.

El Lissitsky's whimsical "Tale of Two Squares," shown here in its entirety, explores the relationships created by the juxtaposition of the most basic abstract forms. Exemplifying Suprematist design, this book was the model for later experiments in typography, such as those of the Bauhaus in Germany. The text is as follows: "1) About Two Squares. El Lissitsky. 2) To all, all Kiddies. 3) El Lissitsky: A Suprematist Tale—about Two Squares in 6 Constructions: Berlin, Scythians, 1922. 4) Do not read: Take—Paper—Fold, Blocks—Color, Pieces of Wood—Construct. 5) Here are—Two Squares. 6) They fly toward Earth—from far away—and 7) and—see Black Chaos. 8) Crash—all is scattered 9) and on the Black was established Red Clearly. 10) Thus it ends—further."

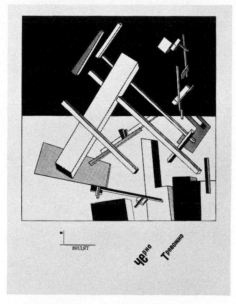

7

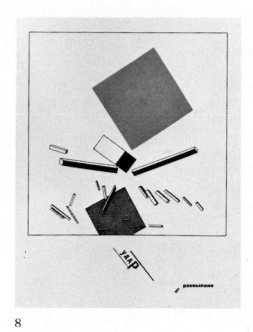

8

OVERLEAF: Posters were the cheapest and most effective means of conveying political and educational messages during the civil war. Both realists and modernists contributed to the art, the modernists using a minimum of detail to convey simple ideas (as in the poster on page 306), while the realists concentrated on stirring emotion. In dealing with political issues, artists either ridiculed the enemies of the people or glorified the proletariat. This poster was done in the latter style in 1921.

VYACHESLAV POLONSKY, *Russky revolyutsionny plakat*

LONG LIVE THE THIRD
COMMUNIST INTERNATIONAL!
EVVIVA IL TERZA
INTERNAZIONALE COMMUNISTA!

12

Soviet Voices

Writing from Fedin to Yevtushenko

The only immediate effect of the Revolution upon Russian literature was the elimination of three redundant characters from the Cyrillic alphabet. Although Lenin was committed to art in the service of society, his policy was one of relative tolerance. Writers were encouraged to glorify the Revolution, but experimentalism in the arts flourished while the government was busy fighting the civil war. Liberal writers promoted art for art's sake, while members of the more conservative Russian Association of Proletarian Writers oriented their work toward the masses, denouncing individualism and effete modernism.

The initial attempts to direct literature along Party lines were made after Lenin's death in 1924. With Stalin's rise to power, all forces, including the literary, were mobilized as tools for economic growth. In 1932 autonomous literary organizations were liquidated and writers were required to join the Union of Soviet Writers, whose avowed purpose was the creation of "artistic writing" to glorify the victories of socialism, to expound the wisdom of the Party, and to "portray Soviet Man and his moral qualities fully and with force."

Acceptance of "socialist realism" led to a monotonous uniformity in Soviet literature. A group of new writers emerged who had been trained in Soviet schools, and older writers either conformed, kept silent, went underground, or

In "1919; The Alarm," a portrayal of a civil war incident painted in 1934–35, just prior to Stalin's purges, Kuzma Petrov-Vodkin anticipates a scene that was to recur frequently in Soviet literature.

emigrated. The Soviets ceased publication of the works of many widely acclaimed writers from other eras and forbade them to be read in schools. Dostoevsky was reviled, Yesenin was labeled "counter-revolutionary." In 1954, the year after Stalin's death, Ilya Ehrenburg condemned the rigidity of Soviet life in his novel *The Thaw,* and thereby gave a name to the entire post-Stalin era in literature. The dominant trend remained socialist realism, but there was a renewed tolerance of divergent points of view.

Since Khrushchev's downfall in 1964, Party policy toward the liberals has varied sharply and unpredictably. In a recent manifestation of the tribulation that has plagued Russian writers and thinkers throughout the country's history—from Avvakum to Pushkin, from Dostoevsky to Mandelshtam, Babel, and Pasternak—Yuly Daniel and Andrei Sinyavsky were tried in 1966 on charges of slandering the State. A year later, in a letter that testified both to the current political atmosphere and the greatness of the Russian literary tradition, Alexander Solzhenitsyn wrote to the Fourth Congress of Soviet Writers, pleading for an end to censorship: "Our literature has lost the leading role it played at the end of the last century and the beginning of this one, and it has lost the brilliance of experimentation that distinguished it in the 1920's. . . . If the world had access to all the uninhibited fruits of our literature, if it were enriched by our own spiritual experience, the whole artistic evolution of the world would move along in a different way, acquiring a new stability and attaining even a new artistic threshold."

Shaping the New Order

Soviet literature of the 1920's is noteworthy for its diverse points of view and artistic methods. The best prose followed pre-Revolutionary tendencies and styles, but its subject was the Revolution or post-Revolutionary reality. Some writers were anticipating the socialist realism of the Stalin era, writing of proletarian heroes.

Konstantin Fedin

From CITIES AND YEARS (1924)

Translated by Michael Scammel

Fedin was at first unable to accept the Revolution fully, but later gave his complete support to the Soviet regime and, in 1959, was named Secretary General of the Writers' Union. In this excerpt from his early Cities and Years, *the first substantial novel to be published in Soviet Russia, he describes Moscow during the civil war years.*

Of course everything in this city was strange—from the church cupolas, resembling beets, to the swan-like curves of the cabbies' droshkies.

In the evenings at sundown it was impossible not to wander over the deserted streets until exhausted.

The peeling pillars of the little houses, the good-natured half-lion-half-dogs by the dust-smothered doors, the long deserted basements, twined with figure-eight railings which looked kindly on the rearing warehouse boxes pierced with innumerable windows. . . .

Can there be found in all the world a city which would keep hundreds of thousands of tons of provisions in palaces, horse fodder in department stores, barrels of cement in manufacturers' apartments, iron ore on main street?

Everything that had managed to be collected in Russia for Moscow and had arrived on its stations was transferred to the center of the city and stowed with the greatest difficulty in restaurants, dance halls and merchants' homes. In the center of the city the loads were moved about, shaken up and, split up into the tiniest portions—in drops, in grains—were moved out to outlying warehouses and elevators where there were more mice than goods and grain.

From morning on, freight trucks waddled elephant-like over the dented and potholed cobbles of the tangled streets and their step caused stone houses to tremble and windowpanes to break.

Circling the Lubiansky Square, from the Myasnitsky Gates and from Pokrovka, down the slope of Theater Way and into the Tretyakov Gap the elephants piled into one another, snarling and jolting the loads on their backs—and to look at them was as if some unknown burnt-out planet were moving into Moscow.

And across Theater Square, along Mokhovaya and farther—along Volkhonka, along Ostozhenka—hastened the elephant-frightened fire victims from the unknown planet—with sacks on their backs, in an endless file—along that part of the streets which the city had formerly yielded to streetcars.

On Ostozhenka near the Crimean Bridge the file poured into a white building and around the building lone figures of fire victims puttered about before the windows. . . .

On the boulevard beside a booth trading in artificial soap and essence of vinegar loomed a glass box with models of human entrails, and tiny letters explained to everyone the purpose of the kidneys and the spleen.

Jumping up a good six feet behind iron railings and facing the military store was a placard addressing the public with columns of figures, and dozens of people were calculating how mighty and how accessible to all was science in the new Russia.

New Russia!

That was she filing into the white building—where until recently high-school uniforms had been properly stored—indefatigable, capturing halls, stairways, attics, boxrooms. And in the commotion, for whole days, the first point was being written in the white house of a joint treaty between mighty sides—Science and Russia. This point was endlessly long, so that a phalanx of typists worked in the office without a break and there was not a corner of the whole house which had not been invaded by the din of Underwoods, as if an iron roof were being repaired.

On the basement floor rotary presses rolled without respite and an artel of printers sweated over thousands, hundreds of thousands of sheets heralding the news of the unprecedented joint treaty.

In corridors and vestibules high spirits blazed with the din of Underwoods and the smell of rotary ink; and people ran about dazed by the figures which measured science, happiness, humanity, Russia.

Fedor Gladkov

From CEMENT (1925)

Translated by A. S. Arthur and C. Ashleigh

Gladkov, born of peasant stock, wrote the prototypical Soviet novel, in which the masses are the true heroes. In the book's final chapter, excerpted below, the main character, Gleb Chumalov, revels in the people's mighty socialist feat of revitalizing a cement factory.

On the landing of the steel-trellised tower stood Gleb, Shidky and Badin, the members of the Factory Committee and Engineer Kleist. But Gleb felt alone amidst the countless crowd below, swelling, swaying, clamoring, covering the ground like a field of sunflowers as far as the eye could reach. They were there—and he was up here.

Right and left in long rows red flags blazed like beacon fires. And the landing itself glowed with red banners floating from the metal cross-bars. The banner of the Party Group was suspended from the railing by Gleb and with its thick folds and fringe fell down towards the other flags among the crowd below. On the other side, where Badin and Shidky were standing, was the banner of the Building Workers' Union. And below the railings, lower down, on a rich expanse of blood-red bunting immense white letters flashed:

WE HAVE CONQUERED ON THE
CIVIL WAR FRONT.
WE SHALL CONQUER ALSO ON THE
ECONOMIC FRONT!

It was swarming with heads and shoulders, swaying and tossing, flashing with red headscarves; or raising dark and pale faces, hats and caps—and everywhere inscribed bannerets waved like red wings. They hid part of the crowd, but behind them were still more masses surging and eddying. On the mountain slope and the rocks, still more crowds and more banners and slogans, like a poppy field. They streamed out of the valley in thousands, higher and higher. In the distance a band was playing a march, and from the depths came the thunderous clamor of the people mingled with the roar of the Diesel engines and the clanging of metal. It was impossible to distinguish the roar of the crowd from the roar of machinery. Brynza was right: machines and people are one. The masses cannot be silent. Their life is different from the life of individuals: they are constantly in strenuous movement, always ready for an irruption. . . .

Gleb grasped tightly the iron railing and could not control the exhausted trembling of his body. His heart was swelling in his breast until he could hardly breathe. From where came this multitude? There were already twenty thousand people here, and still new columns were arriving. There were some marching nearly a mile away along the mountain slope, among the boulders and thickets, pouring themselves into the general mass and spreading higher and higher. In this way the human mass could cover the whole mountain to the very summit. . . .

The works! What strength had been put into it, and what struggle! But here it was—a giant, a beauty! Not long ago it had been a corpse, a devil's mud-heap, a ruin, a warren. And now the Diesels roared. The cables vibrated with electricity, and the pulleys of the ropeway sang. To-morrow the first giant cylinder of the rotary furnaces would begin to revolve, and from this huge smokestack grey clouds of steam and dust would roll.

Wasn't it worth while that all this countless crowd should come here and rejoice in their common victory? He—what was he, Gleb, in this sea of people? No, it was not a sea, but a living mountain: stones resuscitated into flesh. Ah, what power! These were they who with spades, picks and hammers, had cut into the mountains for the ropeway. This had been in spring, on just such a clear sunny day as this. Then the first blood was shed. Now the town had wood to burn

and everything was ready to start the works. How much blood was in this immense army of labor! This blood would last long! The ropeway was working; the steam mill would start soon. The shipyards would open soon. Were there not enough mountain streams to install power-stations!

Yury Olesha

From ENVY (1927)

Translated by Andrew R. MacAndrew

Olesha's ambivalence toward the Revolution caused ambivalence among Soviet critics. First applauded, then reviled, Envy *was finally suppressed and its author imprisoned for his lack of Revolutionary fervor. He was rehabilitated in 1956, four years before his death.*

"It's in there," Ivan said. "Wait. Let's sit down. Here, above this little gully. I've already told you that my dream has been a machine's machine, a universal machine. I thought up a perfect instrument. . . ."

"I don't understand anything about mechanics," Kavalerov said. "I'm afraid of machines."

"And I succeeded. Listen, Kavalerov, I have invented such a machine."

The fence beckoned Kavalerov; yet he felt the odds were that no secret lay behind those commonplace gray boards.

"It can blow up mountains. It can fly. It lifts weights. It will crush ore. It will replace the kitchen stove, the baby carriage, the long-range gun. It is *the* mechanical genius. . . ."

He stood up, placed his hand on Kavalerov's shoulder, and said solemnly:

"But I have forbidden it to do all those things. One fine day I understood that I had been given a supernatural power with which to avenge my era. . . . I have perverted the machine. On purpose. Out of spite."

He laughed happily.

"Try to understand, Kavalerov, what a great satisfaction it was. I gave the most vulgar human sentiments to the greatest technical creation. I dishonored the machine. I avenged my era, the brain that was given me, that lies in my cranium; my brain, that conceived the extraordinary mechanism. To whom could I leave it? To the new world? They are devouring us, like food. They are devouring the nineteenth century, as a boa constrictor devours a rabbit. They swallow us whole and digest us. What they can use, they feed on and assimilate; what is bad for them, they eject. They expectorate our feelings, and feed on our technology. I must avenge our feelings. They won't get my machine, they won't make use of me, they won't feed on my brain. My machine could bring happiness to the new era, all at once, from the very first day of its existence, could bring technology to its Golden Age. But there it is, they won't get it. My machine is a dazzling flash, a sneering tongue stuck out by the dying era at the newborn one. Their mouths will water when they see it. The machine, think of it, their idol, the machine . . . and suddenly. . . . And suddenly the best machine will turn out to be a liar, a sentimental wretch, full of petty-bourgeois traits. It can do everything. But what will it actually do? It will sing our love songs, the silly love songs of the dying century, and gather the flowers of the past era. It will fall in love, become jealous, cry, dream. I did this. I have insulted the machine—the god of these people, of the future. I have even given it the name of a girl who went out of her mind with love and despair. I've called it Ophelia, the most human, the most touching name."

Ivan dragged Kavalerov after him.

He bent down and put his eye to a chink, presenting to Kavalerov his heavy, shiny buttocks that looked very much like dumbbells. . . . It seemed to him that he heard Ivan's voice carrying on a conversation with someone on the other side of the chink. Then Ivan recoiled. And so did Kavalerov, although he was standing a good distance from Ivan. It was as though fear, hiding in the trees opposite, was dangling them both on a single string.

"Who is that whistling?" cried Kavalerov, fear ringing in his voice, as a shrill whistle flew over the suburb. . . .

"I'm afraid of it, I'm afraid of it!" Kavalerov heard Ivan's choking whisper.

Holding on to each other, they rushed downhill . . . . They disappeared into a little street.

"I'm afraid of it," Ivan kept repeating rapidly. "She hates me . . . she's betrayed me . . . she'll kill me. . . ."

Kavalerov regained his senses and became ashamed of his cowardice. He remembered that at the very moment he had seen Ivan begin his headlong flight, something else had come within his range of vision that, in the fright, he hadn't registered.

"Listen," he said, "it's all bunk. It was a boy whistling with two fingers in his mouth. I saw him. A boy appeared on top of the fence and whistled. . . . A boy, that's all."

"Didn't I tell you," said Ivan, "you'd start looking for all sorts of explanations? . . ."

Leonid Leonov

From THE THIEF (1927)

Translated by Hubert Butler

*A novel of wide scope and intricate plot—complicated by a novel-within-a-novel structure—*The Thief *concerns the Dostoevskian underworld of Moscow. It was not reprinted in the Soviet Union until 1959, since literature dealing with criminals was banned by Stalin.*

She was lying on the sofa. Her Chinese dressing gown fell open a little in front as she sat up to put the book she had been reading on the table. Firsov winced, for it was the collection of amateurish stories which he had published before the war. Her dressing gown was rumpled up, and Firsov saw her stockinged legs and a suggestion of lingerie. Dolomanova was never embarrassed in his presence, and this exasperated him, but the intimacy of their friendship permitted them to be casual with each other. Firsov laughed and lowered his eyes in embarrassment.

"Well, how's your film work going?" he asked crossly, offering her a cigarette.

"I'm at it morning, noon, and night, and I'm bored stiff, Firsov!" she cried, suddenly laughing, and supporting herself on her elbows. "Our studio's looking for a bandit, Fedya, a specialist in arson and murder. . . . Will you take it on? You'll get paid: it's not for love. You'd do very well with your beard and all—what do you think? But you're such a queer creature! You're a famous author, aren't you? and yet you never wash or shave. I wish you'd tell me why."

"Don't mind me. Any other remarks you'd like to make? About my ulster, for instance? I don't dress for effect, I dress for decency, and, after all, I didn't invent the fig leaf!" And, with a theatrical gesture, he displayed his torn pockets, which shone with grease and looked as if a dustman had been warming his hands in them for a month.

"There, I'm making fun of you again!" she went on, drawing her black stocking tighter, "but, all the same, I'm very fond of you (that's why I've been studying your prewar work)—or rather, it's not you but your mind I'm so taken up with, so you needn't get conceited, Firsov. . . ."

"Won't you pull down your dressing gown?" said Firsov in a pleading voice, frowning slightly, for the tobacco smoke had crept behind his glasses. "There's no need to expose your knee caps!"

"What's wrong with my knees?" asked Dolomanova sullenly, and in spite of the summer heat a wintry chill seemed to radiate from her eyes. She got up and stood regarding him coldly. He had fallen on his knees before her, his face twitching with passion. With one hand she firmly drew her dressing gown more tightly around her. She was afraid of Firsov's eyes.

"Stand up, Fedya. . . . I like you all the same," she murmured half in alarm, half in annoyance at his humiliating and senseless declaration. "Stand up . . . for you've got a brain, and you're better than all of them."

His glasses were lying on the carpet beside his knees, and, marvellous to relate, remained uninjured to the end of his declaration. For the first time Dolomanova saw Firsov's short-sighted gray eyes; they had a glint of yellow in them and were honest rather than kind, yet they were his only attractive feature.

"Don't I mean anything to you, then? All these last six months I've been swearing I'd never come to you again, and yet here I am. You asked what I had to give you—but haven't I got power, too, of a kind? Yes, and more than all the others have—the power to create, power to embrace the world with my thoughts. . . . and the creative fire that flashes through my body is yours to have, yours alone. I cling to you . . . because life is terrible to me without you. Listen to me, Manka, I implore you."

But his words were like a wave beating against a rock against which many waves have beaten.

"Look here, Firsov, pass me an orange, will you?" she said curtly. "There, on the table—a big one, please."

He staggered up. First of all he put on his spectacles, without which he always felt undressed, and then brought what she asked, looking inexpressibly foolish and humiliated.

"I'm thirsty," he said querulously.

She tore the orange in half and threw one half to Firsov, who turned away in embarrassment to cram it into his mouth and gulp it down.

"Looks like a storm," said Dolomanova. "I love sitting at a window in a storm, and I love to suck oranges, don't you?"

"Oh, I love oranges, too," he replied in the same tone, trying to conceal his mortification. . . .

Boris Pasternak

FRESH PAINT (1922)

Translated by Babette Deutsch

Born in 1890 to a highly cultured family, Pasternak made his debut as a poet in 1914. His most innovative work was done in the 1920's, and the 1934 Soviet Writers' Congress acclaimed him the "greatest poetic master of our times." Yet he refused to compromise his art to Soviet ideology, and so remained an isolated figure. His Nobel Prize winning Doctor Zhivago has yet to be published in Russia.

I should have seen the sign: "Fresh paint,"
  But useless to advise
The careless soul, and memory's stained
  With cheeks, calves, hands, lips, eyes.

More than all failure, all success,
  I loved you, for your skill
In whitening the yellowed world
  As white cosmetics will.

Listen, my dark, my friend: by God,
  All will grow white somehow,
Whiter than madness or lamp shades
  Or bandage on a brow.

THE CAUCASUS LAY SPREAD (1931)

The Caucasus lay spread before our gaze,
An unmade bed, it seemed, with tousled sheets;
The blue ice of the peaks more fathomless
Than the warmed chasms with their harbored heats.

Massed in the mist and out of sorts, it reared
The steady malice of its icy crests
As regularly as the salvos spat
In an engagement from machine-gun nests.

And staring at this beauty with the eyes
Of the brigades whose task it was to seize
The region, how I envied those who had
Palpable obstacles to face like these.

O if we had their luck! If, out of time,
As though it peered through fog, this day of ours,
Our program, were of such substantial stuff,
And frowned down at us as this rough steep lours!

Then day and night our program would march on,
Setting its heel upon my prophecies,
Kneading their downpour with the very sole
Of its straight backbone into verities.

There would be no one I could quarrel with,
And not another hour would I give
To making verses: unbeknown to all,
No poet's life, but poems I would live.

Eduard Bagritsky

MY HONEYED LANGUOR (1919)

Translated by Babette Deutsch

Bagritsky studied to be a surveyor, but poor health made him an invalid and he never practiced his profession. Though he was associated with the Constructivists, his romantic verse—here reminiscent of Rupert Brooke—is far from the modernist spirit of that group.

My honeyed languor comes
                    of silence and of dreams
And boredom long-drawn-out
                    and songs that gauchely yearn;
The cocks embroidered on white towels give me joy,
I like the soot that clings to icons old and stern.

To the hot buzz of flies
                    day after day goes by,
And a meek piety on each its blessing lays;
Beneath the eaves a quail
                    is mumbling sleepily;
The smell of raspberry jam pervades the holidays.

At night the billowing
                    soft goose down wearies me,
The stuffy icon lamp blinking is said to view,
And as he cranes his neck
                    the gay embroidered bird
Commences his long chant
                    of cock-a-doodle-doo.

Here you have granted me
                    a modest refuge, Lord,
Beneath a blissful roof
                    where turmoil cannot grow,
Where clotted days like jam
                    that from a teaspoon drips
In heavy drops
          perpetually flow, flow, flow.

Realists and Rebels

The totalitarian government under Stalin used writers as educators and propagandists. The Party required tendentious socialist realism in writing, but a few works of artistic integrity slipped past the censors, while others were not to be published until after Stalin's death.

Mikhail Sholokhov

From AND QUIET FLOWS THE DON (1929–40)

Translated by Stephen Garry

Sholokhov's earthy epic, which traces the fortunes of a few Don Cossack families through World War I and the Revolution, is rich in the imagery of nature and vivid in its portrayal of the brutality of life on the steppe. It is extremely popular in the Soviet Union.

Aksinia was seventeen when she was given in marriage to Stepan Astakhov. She came from the village of Dubrovka, from the sands on the other side of the Don.

About a year before her marriage she was ploughing in the steppe some five miles from the village. In the night her father, a man of some fifty years, tied her hands and raped her.

"I'll kill you if you breathe a word, but if you keep quiet I'll buy you a plush jacket and gaiters with goloshes. Remember, I'll kill you if you. . . ." he promised her.

Aksinia ran back through the night in her torn petticoat to the village. She flung herself at her mother's feet and sobbed out the whole story. Her mother and elder brother harnessed horses into the wagon, made Aksinia get in with them, and drove to the father. Her brother almost drove the horses to death in the five miles. They found the old man close to the field camp. He was lying in a drunken sleep on his overcoat, with an empty vodka bottle by his side. Before Aksinia's eyes her brother unhooked the swing-tree from the wagon, picked up his father by the feet, curtly asked him a question or two and struck him a blow with the iron-shod swing-tree between the eyes. He and his mother went on beating steadily for an hour and a half. The ageing and always meek mother frenziedly tore at her senseless husband's hair, the brother used his feet. Aksinia lay under the wagon, her head covered, silently shaking. They carried her father home just before dawn. He lay bellowing mournfully, his eyes wandering around the room seeking for Aksinia, who had hidden herself away. Blood and matter ran from his torn ear on to the pillow. Towards evening he died. They told the neighbors he had fallen from the wagon.

[Years pass. Aksinia, brutalized by her husband, falls in love with Gregor, who, in time, rejects her, intending to marry a rich peasant's daughter, the young and innocent Natalia.]

The green, spike-leafed wheat breaks through the ground and grows; within a few weeks a rook can fly into its midst and not be seen. The corn sucks the juices from the earth and comes to ear, the grain swells with the sweet and scented milk; then it flowers and a golden dust covers the ear. The farmer goes out into the steppe and stands gazing, but cannot rejoice. Wherever he looks a herd of cattle has strayed into the corn; they have trodden the laden grain into the glebe. Wherever they have thronged is a circle of crushed wheat: the farmer grows bitter and savage at the sight.

So with Aksinia. Over her feelings, ripened to golden flower, Gregor had trodden with his heavy, raw-hide boots. He had sullied them, burnt them to ash—and that was all.

As she came back from the Melekhovs' sunflower garden Aksinia's spirit grew empty and wild, like a forgotten farmyard overgrown with goose-grass and scrub. She walked along chewing the ends of her kerchief, and a cry swelled her throat. She entered the hut and fell to the floor, choking with tears, with torment, with the dreary emptiness that lashed through her head. But then it passed. The piercing pain was drawn down and exhausted at the bottom of her heart.

The grain trampled by the cattle stands again. With the dew and the sun the trodden stalks rise; at first bowed like a man under a too heavy burden, then erect; . . . and the days shine on them and the winds set them swinging.

At night, as she passionately caressed her husband, Aksinia thought of another, and hatred was mingled with a great love in her heart. The woman mentally planned a new dishonor—yet the old infamy; she was resolved to take Gregor from the happy Natalia who had known neither the bitterness nor the joy of love. She lay thinking over her plans at night, with Stepan's heavy head resting on her right arm. Aksinia lay thinking, but only one thing could she resolve firmly: she would take Gregor from everybody else, she would flood him with love, she would possess him as before she had possessed him.

During the day Aksinia drowned her thoughts in cares and household duties. She met Gregor occasionally, and would turn pale, proudly carrying her beautiful body that yearned so after him, gazing shamelessly, challengingly into the black depths of his eyes.

After each meeting Gregor was seized with yearning for her. He grew angry without cause, and poured out his wrath on Dunia [his sister] and his mother, but most frequently he took his cap, went out into the back yard and chopped away at the stout brushwood until he was bathed in perspiration. It made Pantaleimon [his father] curse:

"The lousy devil, he's chopped up enough for a couple of fences. You wait, my lad! When you're married you can chop away at that! That'll soon take it out of you!"

Ilf and Petrov

From HOW THE SOVIET ROBINSON WAS CREATED (1933)

Translated by Bernard Guilbert Guerney

Ilya Ilf and Yevgeny Petrov began their literary partnership a few years after the Revolution, and wrote a series of satires (printed in Pravda*) lampooning the bureaucracy. The authorities, one critic has written, never dealt them "so much as a slap on the wrist."*

"You understand"—the [magazine] editor was dinning it into [the writer Moldovantzev]—"this thing must be engrossing, fresh, chock-full of adventures. It must, on the whole, turn out to be the Soviet Robinson Crusoe. Done in such a manner that the reader won't be able to tear himself away. . . ."

And, sure enough, the novel was ready by the deadline. Moldovantzev hadn't departed too much from the great original. If it was Robinson they wanted, Robinson they would get.

A Soviet youth suffers a shipwreck. A wave casts him up on an uninhabited island. He is all by his lonesome, defenseless, face to face with the mighty forces of nature. He is surrounded by dangers: wild beasts, lianas, the rainy season looming ahead. But the Soviet Robinson Crusoe, simply brimming over with energy, surmounts all the seemingly insurmountable obstacles. And, three years later, a Soviet expedition finds him—finds him in the full flowering of all his forces. He has conquered nature, has built himself a little house, has ringed the little house with whole truck gardens of green growing things, has successfully gone in for breeding rabbits, sewn a blouse for himself (the kind Leo Tolstoi used to wear) out of monkey tails, and trained a parrot to wake him each morning with the words: "Attention! Off with that blanket—off with that blanket! We're starting the morning workout!"

"Very good!" commented the editor. "And that bit about the rabbits—its simply magnificent. Quite in keeping with the times. But, do you know, the basic idea of the work is not quite clear to me."

"Man's struggle against Nature," Moldovantzev informed him with his usual terseness.

"Yes, but there's nothing Soviet about the novel."

"How's about the parrot? Why, I've made it take the place of a radio. An experienced broadcaster."

"That parrot is good. And that ring of truck gardens is good. Yet one doesn't have any feeling of the obligations of Soviet society. Where, for instance, is the Mestkom, the Local Trade Union Committee? Where is the leading role of the trade union? . . ."

"Where would the Mestkom come from? The island is uninhabited, isn't it?"

"Yes, you're perfectly right—it's uninhabited. But the Mestkom is a must. I'm not an artist of the word, but if I were in your place I would bring in the Mestkom. As a Soviet element."

"But then, the whole story is built on the island's being uninhabited—" At this point Moldovantzev chanced to look into the editor's eyes and stopped short. Those eyes were so vernal, one felt such March bleakness and watered-milk azure there, that the writer decided to compromise. "However, come to think of it," said he, holding up an index finger, "you're right. Of course. How come I didn't figure the thing out right off? *Two* people are saved from the shipwreck: our Robinson and the Chairman of the Mestkom."

"And two other members who have been fired from the Mestkom," said the editor in a chilly tone.

"Oi!" squeaked Moldovantzev.

"Never mind *oi*'ing. Two fired members—and, while you're at it, one very active member, a woman—she'll collect the dues."

"What do you want a dues collector for? Whom is she going to collect dues from?"

"Why, from Robinson,"

"The Chairman can collect from Robinson. It won't hurt the Chairman any."

"That's where you're mistaken, Comrade Moldovantzev. That's absolutely inadmissible. The Chairman of the Mestkom can't make himself small like that and run after Robinson to collect his dues. That's something we're putting up a fight against. He must busy himself with serious work which requires leadership."

"In that case we can save the female dues collector as well," Moldovantzev gave in. "It's all to the good, in fact. She can marry the Chairman, or Robinson himself. It'll make for livelier reading, at that."

"It's not worth while. Don't sink to the paperback level, to unwholesome eroticism. Let her stick to collecting those union dues and putting them away in the fireproof safe—". . .

"It, too, was saved from the sea?" Moldovantzev asked timorously.

"It was."

A silence ensued.

"Was a conference table also cast up by that same wave, by any chance?" the author asked with crafty malice.

"Ab-so-lute-ly! After all, it is necessary to create conditions under which people can work. . . . But, my dear fellow, here's what you must do first and foremost. You must show us the masses. The broad strata of the toilers."

"The wave can't cast up any masses," Moldovantzev turned mulish. "That goes against the story line. Just think of it! A single wave all of a sudden casts up tens of thousands of people! It's enough to make a cat laugh—"

"Incidentally, a modicum of wholesome, hearty, life-loving laughter," the editor put in, "can never hurt."

"No! No wave can do all that."

"Why a wave?" the editor was suddenly puzzled.

"Come, how else would the masses get on the island? For that island is uninhabited, isn't it?"

"Who told you it's uninhabited? You're mixing me all up, somehow. It's all plain. You have an island—it would be even better if it were a peninsula: less trouble that way. And a string of engrossing, fresh, interesting adventures takes place there. And the trade unions carry on their work there—none too arduously, at times. The girl, who is an active political worker, uncovers a series of irregularities—

well, in the area of dues collections, let's say. She is helped along by the broad strata of the toilers. And by the repentant Chairman of the Mestkom. Toward the end you can stage a general meeting. That will prove most effective, precisely from the artistic point of view. Well, that about ties it up."

"But what about Robinson?" babbled Moldovantzev.

"Yes. Good thing you reminded me. This Robinson confuses me. Chuck him out on his ear. An incongruous, utterly unjustified figure of a chronic bellyacher."

"I get it all now," said Moldovantzev in a sepulchral voice. "I'll have it ready tomorrow."

"There, that's the lot. Go ahead and create. By the way, you have a shipwreck at the beginning of your novel. You know, you really don't need any shipwreck. . . . Right? There, that's great! Keep well! . . ."

Valentin Kataev

From LONELY WHITE SAIL (1936)

Translated by Charles Malamuth

The elder brother of the satirist Petrov, Kataev was known primarily as a humorist, but he also wrote seriously about the building of the socialist State. The novel excerpted here, the Soviet Tom Sawyer, *is set in Kataev's native Odessa during the 1905 revolution.*

On that memorable day Gavrik came [early], and the boys immediately went to the city.

Gavrik's face was grey, unusually composed, fixed, his tightly-closed lips blue from the cold. He walked rapidly, unsteadily, his hands deep in the pockets of his wide corduroy pants—he was small, hunched over, ready for anything. . . .

Petya, shivering from the frost, could hardly keep up with his friend. The boys almost ran down the street as devoid of people as if in a dream.

The strained expectation of something or other hung in the ashen air. Footsteps resounded ringingly along the tiles of the sidewalk. Occasionally a window pane of ice stretched over an empty puddle cracked under the heel. Suddenly, somewhere far away, in the center of the city, a light crackling broke out. One might have taken it for a dray carrying a pyramid of empty boxes that suddenly became untied and crashed to the pavement.

Gavrik stopped, listening to the weak noise of the echo.

"What is that?" Petya asked in a whisper. "Boxes?"

"A bomb," said Gavrik dryly, and with assurance. "Somebody got it in the neck." . . .

That day the boys went twice to Malaya Arnautskaya, into the yard with the fountain and the crane.

The first time, having received the "goods," as Gavrik put it, they went to Alexandrov Prospect, which was surrounded by troops. They were allowed to pass without any special difficulty.

Going past several houses, Gavrik dragged Petya into a certain gate. The boys passed through a large deserted yard, past a Cossack tethering post, over empty iron bands and rifle shells, beaten by soldiers' soles into the hard frozen ground.

The boys went into a cellar, and for a long time walked in the damp darkness past wood stores, until they came out in another yard. From that yard it was possible to pass by a narrow opening between two high, dark brick walls into still another yard.

Evidently Gavrik knew all the ins and outs.

The opening was so narrow that Petya, making his way with Gavrik, was forever scraping his schoolbag against the walls. Finally they came out into the third yard, narrow, high, and as dark as a cistern. . . .

The entire yard was covered with broken glass and plaster. The windows of the house surrounding the yard were all shuttered. There seemed to be no one living in it. Everything here was immersed in resonant silence.

But beyond that silence, on the other side of the house, on the unknown street, was not so much heard as sensed the alarming noise of some sort of movement.

Besides that, above, as if from the sky, occasionally loud shots barked, filling the yard with the echoings of a well. Petya pressed himself with his schoolbag to the wall, and, trembling, shut his eyes. Gavrik, however, unhurriedly put two fingers into his mouth and whistled.

Somewhere overhead a shutter clicked and a voice shouted: "Right away!"

In a minute, which seemed an hour to Petya, from the door of the back entrance a red, sweaty man ran out, without an overcoat, his jacket soiled with chalk. . . .

"Give it here, give it here, give it here!" [he] muttered, wiping his wet face with his sleeve.

Paying no attention to Petya himself, he rushed for the schoolbag.

"Give it here! Thanks! Just in time! We haven't a damn thing left!"

He impatiently unfastened the straps, breathing heavily, transferred the little bags from the schoolbag to his pockets, and ran back, managing to cry out:

"Tell Yossif Karlovich to send more right away. Bring whatever you have, or we won't be able to hold out!"

"All right," said Gavrik, "we'll bring it."

Right then a bullet struck under the roof, and the pink powder of brick sprayed the boys.

Retracing their route, they hurried to Malaya Arnautskaya and received there another load of "goods." This time the schoolbag was so heavy that Petya could scarcely carry it.

Now the boy understood quite well what kind of lugs these were. At another time he would have thrown them all away and run home, but on this day, overcome to the very bottom of his soul with the passion for danger, which was much stronger than the passion for play, he wouldn't under any circumstances have consented to desert his pal.

Nor could he refuse to share Gavrik's fame. Otherwise he would be denied the right to tell later about his adventures; the thought of that deprivation at once compelled him to disregard all danger.

Mikhail Bulgakov

From THE MASTER AND MARGARITA (*written* 1928–40)

Translated by Michael Glenny

This Faustian satire centers on Satan and his assistants—one of them a cigar-smoking, pistol-toting black cat—who reign terror on Moscow, its people, and its institutions. Suppressed by Stalin's regime, the book went unpublished until 1967. Bulgakov died in 1940.

Koroviev stopped by the railing and said, "Look, there's the writers' club. You know, Behemoth, that house has a great reputation. Look at it my friend. How lovely to think of so much talent ripening under that roof."

"Like pineapples in a hothouse," said Behemoth, climbing up onto the concrete base of the railings for a better look at the yellow, colonnaded house.

"Quite so," agreed his inseparable companion Koroviev, "and what a delicious thrill one gets, doesn't one, to think that at this moment in that house there may be the future author of a *Don Quixote* or a *Faust* or—who knows?—*Dead Souls?*"

"Frightening thought," said Behemoth. . . .

"Yes," Koroviev went on, wagging a warning finger, "but —but, I say, and I repeat, *but!*—provided those hothouse growths are not attacked by some microorganism, provided they're not nipped in the bud, provided they don't rot! And it can happen with pineapples, you know! Ah, yes, it can happen!"

"By the way," inquired the cat, poking its round head through a gap in the fence, "what are they doing on the veranda?"

"Eating," explained Koroviev. "I should add that this place has a very decent, cheap restaurant. And now that I think of it, like any tourist starting on a long journey I wouldn't mind a snack and large mug of iced beer."

"Nor would I," said Behemoth, and the two rogues set off under the lime trees and up the asphalt path toward the unsuspecting restaurant.

A pale, bored woman in white ankle socks and a white-tasseled beret was sitting on a bentwood chair at the corner entrance to the veranda, where there was an opening in the creeper-grown trellis. In front of her on a plain kitchen table lay a large book like a ledger, in which . . . the woman wrote the names of the people entering the restaurant. She stopped Koroviev and Behemoth.

"Your membership cards?" she said, staring in surprise at Koroviev's pince-nez, at Behemoth's kerosene burner and scraped elbow.

"A thousand apologies, madam, but what membership cards?" asked Koroviev in astonishment.

"Are you writers?" asked the woman in return.

"Indubitably," replied Koroviev with dignity.

"Where are your membership cards?" the woman repeated.

"Dear lady . . ." Koroviev began tenderly.

"I'm not a dear lady," interrupted the woman.

"Oh, what a shame," said Koroviev in a disappointed voice and went on: "Well, if you don't want to be a dear lady, which would have been delightful, you have every right not to be. But look here—if you wanted to make sure that Dostoyevsky was a writer, would you really ask him for his membership card? Why, you only have to take any five pages of one of his novels and you won't need a membership card to convince you that the man's a writer. I don't suppose he ever had a membership card, anyway! What do you think?" said Koroviev, turning to Behemoth.

"I'll bet he never had one," replied the cat. . . .

"You're not Dostoyevsky," said the woman to Koroviev.

"How do you know?"

"Dostoyevsky's dead," said the woman, though not very confidently.

"I protest!" exclaimed Behemoth warmly. "Dostoyevsky is immortal!"

"Your membership cards, please," said the woman.

"This is really all rather funny!" said Koroviev, refusing to give up. "A writer isn't a writer because he has a membership card but because he writes. How do you know what bright ideas may not be swarming in my head? . . ."

At that moment a quiet but authoritative voice said to the woman, "Let them in, Sofia Pavlovna."

The woman with the ledger looked up in astonishment. From behind the trellis foliage emerged the maître d' hôtel's white shirtfront and wedge-shaped beard. He greeted the two ruffians with a welcoming look and even went so far as to beckon them in. Archibald Archibaldovich made his authority felt in this restaurant, and Sofia Pavlovna obediently asked Koroviev, "What is your name?"

"Panayev," was the polite reply. The woman wrote down the name and raised her questioning glance to Behemoth.

"Skabichevsky," squeaked the cat, for some reason pointing to his kerosene burner. Sofia Pavlovna inscribed this name too and pushed the ledger forward for the two visitors to sign. Koroviev wrote "Skabichevsky" opposite the name "Panayev" and Behemoth wrote "Panayev" opposite "Skabichevsky."

Konstantin Simonov

From DAYS AND NIGHTS (1944)

Translated by Joseph Barnes

This semifictionalized eyewitness account of the battle of Stalingrad became a classic among Soviet war novels and is still popular in Russia. Its author, a correspondent at the front, was made editor of the literary magazine New World *in 1954 but was removed from his post two years later for publishing controversial works.*

Saburov was tired, filled with bile, and certainly no less upset than Babchenko about the loss of the warehouse [to the Germans]. He knew the thought of this loss would torment him like a splinter in his mind until the evening, until he could take the building back again. . . .

"Well," Babchenko said, looking at his watch, "it's two o'clock now. That means they're going to sit there until dark. Have you read the command not to retreat one step backward? Or maybe you don't agree with the command?"

"At six o'clock I will begin the attack," Saburov said, trying to control himself, "and by seven I will hold the warehouse."

"Don't tell me that. Have you read the command not to retreat one step?"

"Yes," Saburov said.

"But you gave up the warehouse?"

"Yes."

"Drive them out at once," Babchenko shouted in a voice that was not his own, jumping up from his stool. "Not by seven, but right away."

From his face and gestures, Saburov realized that Babchenko was teetering on the same thin edge of fatigue and nervous exhaustion on which he stood himself. To quarrel with Babchenko at this minute would be useless. . . .

Saburov repeated all the reasons which had made him decide to postpone the attack until night. He added his pledge that he could hold the entire square behind the warehouse under such fire throughout the day that not a single German could be added to those already inside the little building.

"Tell me, have you read the command that we are not to retreat one step backward?" Babchenko asked again, with the same merciless obstinacy.

"I've read it," Saburov said, drawing himself up and keeping his eyes on Babchenko's face with a look as evil and heartless as he saw in the other's eyes. "I've read it, but I just don't want to send men where it isn't necessary to send them when it would be possible to take it all back almost without losses."

"You don't want to? I order you to."

The thought suddenly flashed into Saburov's mind that right away, at this very minute, he must do something with Babchenko, force him to keep quiet, not let him repeat these words, in order to save the lives of many people. He should call Protsenko and report to him that to do as Babchenko wanted was out of the question. Then, whatever might happen, let it happen, let them do what they wanted to him. But habit and discipline flowed back into him and kept him from doing any of this.

"Very good," he said. . . .

Everything that happened after this stayed for a long time in Saburov's memory like a bad dream. They climbed out of the dugout and in a half hour Saburov rounded up all the men who were at hand. . . . Saburov with his thirty soldiers, running from wall to wall, from shell hole to shell hole, opened an assault on the building.

It all ended as he had expected. Ten men remained lying among the ruins. . . .

On the way back still another was killed. An hour after the beginning of this project, Saburov was standing in front of Babchenko behind the low projecting entrance to the building where the lieutenant colonel, taking almost no cover himself, had watched the attack from as close a position as he could find, under fire the entire time.

Saburov saluted and dropped his rifle on the ground with a clatter. His face smeared with blood and mud was so terrifying to look at that Babchenko at first said nothing. Then he said: "Take a rest," . . . and he walked off towards the dugout.

Saburov moved after him. They did not descend into the dugout but sat on their heels by the side of a spur of the wall where the guardhouse was. Both were silent; neither wanted to look the other in the face.

"Blood," Babchenko said. "You wounded?"

Saburov took out of his pocket a dirty, earth-colored handkerchief, spit on it several times, and wiped his face. Then he felt his head.

"No, just bruised and scratched," he said.

"Call up from the company everyone you can get," Babchenko ordered. "I'm going to lead an attack myself."

"How many men?" Saburov asked.

"As many as there are."

"There won't be more than forty," Saburov said.

"As many as there are, I already said," Babchenko repeated.

Saburov sent out an order for more men and also for the mortars to be dragged nearer; they might be able to help. In spite of his stubbornness, Babchenko knew perfectly well that it was his own fault the attack had been unsuccessful, and that the next attack would have no better chances. But after men had died uselessly before his own eyes, and at his command, he considered it essential to try to do what his subordinates had failed to do, to prove at any rate that what he had demanded of them was entirely possible.

While the mortars were being dragged up and the men assembled, Babchenko gave his last command before the attack and then returned to the fragment of wall from which he observed the first attack. He began to examine carefully the stretch of courtyard lying in front of him, checking from just which points it would be easiest and safest to begin the attack. Saburov stood silent beside him. Forty steps away a heavy German shell exploded with a dull thud.

"They've spotted us," Saburov said. "Let's get out of here, Comrade Lieutenant Colonel. . . ."

Babchenko quietly turned to him, looked straight in his eyes, spat between his feet, and took a pinch of tobacco from his pouch and rolled himself a cigarette with firm untrembling fingers.

The next shell exploded right in front of the wall. Several shell splinters buried themselves in the masonry above their heads, sifting dust down on them. Saburov noticed that Babchenko jumped, and this natural, human reflex prompted Saburov in his turn to say the simple, friendly words: "Philip Philipovich, let's get out of here, yes?"

Babchenko remained silent. Then, remembering his cigarette, he took a lighter out of his pocket, snapped it several times, and lit the cigarette turning his back into the wind and bending over low to catch the flame. Maybe if he had not turned he would not have been killed but, turned and crouching, he was struck directly in the head by a piece of a shell exploding five steps away. He sank quietly at Saburov's feet; the body quivered only once, and he was dead. Saburov squatted on his heels beside him, lifted his battered and bloody head, and thought with a cool indifference which surprised him—this was just what should have happened.

The New Inheritors

Since the mid-1950's the heirs to Russia's literary tradition have been more willing to voice independent thoughts and to experiment, in spite of government persecution. A resurgence of poetry has made some writers as popular as film stars, and vast crowds attend their readings.

Ilya Ehrenburg

From THE THAW (1954)

Translated by Manya Harari

For years a maverick follower of the Party line, Ilya Ehrenburg became prominent in the movement to liberalize Soviet literature. This novel was his outcry against the rigidities of Soviet life; but later, in order to appease critics, he wrote a more optimistic sequel.

The visitor was offered the armchair that had lost its stuffing, from which Glasha swept a pile of cardboard, rags, newspapers, and chipped dishes. Saburov was as delighted as a child.

"Thanks, Volodya, for coming. It's a joy to both of us. Just imagine what a coincidence: it's the anniversary of our wedding—two years already. I'd hoped to make it an occasion. . . . It's wonderful to see you. . . . Just think, Glasha, he and I were at school together for ten years. And now he's come. It really is a piece of luck. . . ."

Saburov suggested they should eat at once, but Volodya asked to see his paintings. Saburov protested:

"What's the point? You probably won't like them. Let's drink instead, and talk about old times."

Volodya insisted. It was not so much that he was eager to see the pictures as that he thought Saburov was being modest and would secretly be hurt if he didn't see and praise them. Glasha backed him:

"Indeed he must show them to you, Vladimir Andreyevich. His latest landscapes and the portrait of me—the one in the green blouse—they're simply marvelous. . . ."

He gazed silently at Saburov's landscapes, his expression neither mocking nor approving. Glasha looked in vain for some sign of what he felt about her husband's work. All he said was an occasional curt: "Wait, don't take that away" or "There's a reflection on it" or "Show me some more." Had Saburov improved a lot these last three years, or was Volodya in an unusually receptive mood? He felt crushed. He forgot everything else and it was useless for Saburov to protest: "That's enough, let's have supper."

. . . He was profoundly shaken by Saburov's work: this, after all, was his contemporary, his schoolfellow. And what was so difficult to grasp, he had done that landscape in this slum room, sitting with his cripple, looking out of that small window. How simple it all was and how far beyond his understanding—the full tones, the depths of the dove-grey and blue sky, the clayey heaviness of the soil! Saburov showed him his latest portrait of his wife and again Volodya was overwhelmed. Glasha asked him if it was like her; he didn't answer. He only saw the painting—the ochre of the highlights in the hair, the olive-shadowed face, the green blouse. And gradually, just as in the landscape nature had revealed itself in its poverty and splendor—the melting snow, the blackness of the naked branches, and the light blueness of the sky—the miracle of the northern spring—so now he saw a woman in her ugliness and her beauty. A whole lifetime would not be too much to understand her timid, plain, unnoticeable smile.

Silently he sat down at the table. Silently he drank a glass of vodka, and only then remembered that he must say something. He rose and, with a solemnity which sat oddly on him, proposed:

"To your happiness! To your happiness, Glafira Antonovna! I have seen you in his portrait. I have seen your works, Saburov. To your happiness. That is all."

He emptied his glass. A little later Glasha asked him: "Vladimir Andreyevich, tell me frankly, do you really like it?"

Again he answered nothing but, after thinking a little, said to Saburov: "You know, envy is a rotten feeling, but I envy you."

He drank another glass, and looked again at one of Saburov's landscapes. The earth was the color of bright rust. There were rowan trees, a small grey house, and a very high and empty sky. Volodya looked at it a long time. . . .

"It's magnificently painted. That's a fact."

Saburov protested.

"The trees aren't right. They are and they aren't. I painted it one day in autumn. The weather was extraordinary—the clay was a special color. . . ."

For a long time he talked. . . . Volodya wasn't listening. He might have been looking at the landscape, or he might have been sitting in a daze. Finally he got up:

"I'll go. I don't feel like it a bit, but I'd better go. . . ."

Towards morning, climbing up the slippery street with a wicked wind pushing him, he thought: "Must have sounded silly . . . Saburov lives abominably—in a pinch you might put up with that, but nobody even knows his work. He said I was the first painter who's been to see him. At the union they think he is abnormal. He is, of course—you have to be a schizophrenic to work as he does, not to compromise, to do exactly what you feel. . . . Yes, it does sound silly. All the same it's fact. I do envy him. I can go to Moscow and sweat a little and make up to people a little, and they'll arrange a show for me and I'll get a prize and everybody will say Oh! and Ah!—and I'll still be envious of that madman.

. . . There I go again, thinking about nothing, it's enough to drive you crazy. But if I did go crazy I would still not paint like Saburov. I haven't enough talent and the talent I have had I've thrown away. I'd sit in a mental hospital and I'd paint pedigree hens according to instructions. . . . Is that what you wanted, Vladimir Andreyevich? You did? Well then, you've got it."

Yuly Daniel

From HANDS (1960)

Translated by Stuart Hood, Harold Shukman, and John Richardson

Daniel, a translator of poetry and a writer, whose stories were published abroad under the pseudonym Nikolai Arzhak, was unknown before 1966, when he was tried for "disseminating slander dressed up as literature." He was sentenced to five years hard labor.

So they assigned me to a Special Duties Section—or to put it plainly, the firing squad, the one that carries out executions. You wouldn't say it was a difficult job exactly, but it wasn't easy either. It affects your heart. It's one thing at the front, you understand: there it's either him or you. But here . . . still, you get used to it of course. You follow your man across the yard and you say to yourself: "You've got to do it, Vasily, you've *got* to. If you don't finish him off now, the rat will do in our whole Soviet Republic." . . . Well anyway, that was how I worked for seven months, and then there was this incident. We were ordered to liquidate a group of priests. For counter-revolutionary propaganda. With intent. They'd been subverting their parishioners. . . . Well, that day, Golovchiner and the Lett finished with theirs, and it came to my turn. I'd already had a drink by then. Not that I was afraid, or religious or anything like that. . . . but I sat and drank, and all sorts of foolishness kept passing through my head: how my mother, when she was alive, used to take me to the village church, and how I'd kiss the hand of our parish priest, Father Vasily—he was an old man and he always used to joke with me and call me his namesake . . . Well anyway; I went to fetch the first one and took him out and finished him off. Then I came back and had a smoke, and did the second one. I came back and had a drink and I didn't feel too well, so I said to the chaps: "Wait a minute, I'll be back." I put the Mauser on the table, and went out. I must have had too much to drink, I thought. I'll stick my fingers in my throat and make myself sick, and have a wash, and I'll be all right. I did all that, but I still didn't feel better. All right, I said to myself, to hell with it, I'll finish the job and I'll go and have a sleep. I picked up the Mauser and went for the third one. The third one was young—a big, hefty, good-looking young priest. I led him along the corridor, and I noticed how he lifted the hem of his cassock—it was down to his heels—as he crossed the threshold, and somehow I felt sick, I couldn't understand what was happening to me. We came out into the yard. He stuck his beard in the air and looked at the sky. "Walk on, Father," I said, "don't look back. You prayed for heaven and you'll soon be there." I was just joking to keep my spirits up why, I don't know. It had never happened to me in my life before to talk to the condemned. Well, I let him walk three paces ahead, as we always did, and put the barrel of my gun between his shoulder blades and fired. You know what a Mauser shot is like—a crash like a cannon, and it kicks so that it nearly dislocates your arm. But when I looked—there was my shot priest turning round and walking back at me. It's true of course that every case is different: some people fall flat, others spin round, and a few start pacing, reeling like drunks. But this one was walking towards me with short steps, as though floating in his cassock . . . and I shot him again—this time in the chest. But he tore his cassock open over his chest—he had a hairy, ugly chest—and walked straight on, shouting at the top of his voice: "Shoot at me! Antichrist! Kill me, your Christ!" I lost my head, I fired again and again. But he kept coming on! No wound, no blood, he was walking along and praying aloud: "Lord, you have stopped a bullet armed by evil hands. I accept to die for Your sake! . . . No one can murder a living soul!" and something else of that sort. . . . I don't remember how many times I fired; all I know is I couldn't have missed, I was firing at point blank. There he stood before me, his eyes burning like a wolf's, his chest bare, and a kind of halo round his head—it occurred to me afterwards that he was standing against the sun and the sun was setting. "Your hands," he shouted, "your hands covered with blood! Look at your hands!" I threw the Mauser down and ran into the guard room, knocked someone over in the doorway and ran inside—the chaps were all looking at me as if I were mad, and laughing. I grabbed a rifle from the stack and yelled: "take me this minute to Dzerzhinsky or I'll bayonet the lot of you!" Well, they took the rifle away from me and they led me off quick march. I walked into his study and broke free from the chaps and I said to him, trembling all over and stuttering: "Shoot me, Felix Edmundovich," I said, "I can't kill a priest!" That's what I said, and fell down, and that's all I can remember. I came to myself in hospital. The doctors said: "nervous shock." They looked after me well, I must say. I got treatment, and the place was clean, and the food was good considering the times. They cured me—all but my hands, you see how they won't keep still. I suppose that nervous shock went to my hands. I was sacked from the Cheka of course—those sort of hands are no use to them. Nor of course could I go back to minding a machine. So they made me factory storekeeper. Well, it's a useful job. I can't do any paper work, of course—can't fill any forms, because of my hands. They gave me an assistant for that, a good sensible girl. That's how it is with me now. As for the priest, I discovered afterwards. There wasn't anything divine about it. It was just that, when I went to the washroom, the chaps took the bullets out of the cartridge clip and filled it with blanks. Just for a joke. Oh well, I'm not angry with them—they were young, and it wasn't pleasant for them either, so they thought this up. No, I'm not cross with them. It's just that my hands . . . they're no good for any work.

Yury Bondarev

From SILENCE (1962)

Translated by Elisaveta Fen

One of the most promising writers to emerge during the post-Stalin thaw, Bondarev (born in 1924) wrote two novels about the Second World War before writing Silence. *The book concerns two soldiers who return from war to be disillusioned by Stalinist oppression.*

"Who's there?" shouted Serghey.

"Open up. Hurry!"

Someone was knocking persistently, like a stranger; Serghey heard footsteps splashing about in puddles in the yard; he was surprised that no one had rung the door-bell in the corridor. . . .

"Open up. This is a document check."

Serghey clicked the lock open and stood aside.

The fresh, rain-soaked air burst in. He heard the sound of feet mounting the porch steps. A muffled voice said, "Mamontov, go on ahead," and before he could see the men, their clothes or their faces, Serghey understood that this was not what he had thought it to be. The blinding light of an electric torch struck him across the face, across his eyes, then glided over into the passage, snatching for a moment out of the darkness a wet collar of a raincoat, an epaulette, a varnished peak of a man's cap. One man passed softly into the house while another with the torch stopped beside Serghey.

"Who are you?" he asked. "Your name?" . . .

"I'm asking you, what's your name?" the voice repeated imperiously. "Your surname?"

"Suppose it's Vohmintsev."

"Back to your room, then, Vohmintsev, and turn on the light in the passage. Back to your room!" the imperious voice commanded, and suddenly Serghey heard the alarmed voices of his father and Assia from their rooms. He saw the light go on in the corridor and in the flat. A soldier with a peasant face and wearing a long coat stood on guard with his rifle outside their wide-open door.

Seeing all this, he entered the room, horrified and disbelieving, trying to persuade himself that a terrible mistake had been made, a stupid, flagrant injustice. There he stopped, startled by a voice. It belonged to a slender man of short stature in the uniform of a captain of State Security (drops of rain glistened on his epaulettes), who was holding a piece of paper in his yellowish fingers and saying calmly, in a dull, catarrhal voice: "You're Vohmintsev, Nikolay Grigoryevich? I have an order for your arrest. Get ready."

His father was in his underclothes, a jacket thrown over his shoulders. He looked pitifully defenceless. His face was unshaven like a sick man's and seemed ten years older; his eyebrows quivered as he glanced at the paper, then over the captain's head, meeting Serghey's eyes, uncomprehendingly. He drew in air in two or three shallow gulps, turned round and without a word went into the adjoining room; his gait suddenly becoming unrecognizable—the gait of an old man. The captain followed him, and his nasal voice could be heard, urging: "Be quick please, citizen Vohmintsev. . . ."

"ILLUSTRATION FROM *Babi Yar*," *Yunost*, OCTOBER, 1966

Anatoly Kuznetsov

From BABI YAR (1966)

Translated by Jacob Guralsky

Kuznetsov, who defected to England in 1969, was twelve when the Nazis took Kiev; he heard the machine guns near the ravine called Babi Yar where fifty thousand people were massacred. In telling the story he also reveals anti-Soviet attitudes among native Kievans.

I could not, of course, miss such an event as the deportation of the Jews from Kiev, and ran out into the street.

They came out when it was still dark. Perhaps they hoped to be first to board the train and to find seats. With their wailing children, their old and their sick, the Jewish tenants of the kitchen garden spilled out into the street, weeping and quarreling among themselves. They carried rope-tied bundles, battered wooden suitcases, patched carpetbags and carpentry toolboxes. The old women wore strings of onions around their necks—their provisions for the trip. . . .

Feverishly I scurried from group to group, listening to the talk. The closer I came to Podol, the more people I saw in the streets. They stood watching and sighing at the gates and house entrances.

A great crowd was ascending Glubochitsa toward Lukyanovka, a sea of heads. These were the Jews of Podol on the march. Ah, Podol, Podol! People were talking on all sides. "Where are they taking us? How are we going to get there?" One group could say nothing but, "The ghetto, the ghetto!" A distraught elderly woman approached: "Dear people, this means death!" The old women broke into wailing. It was said that the *Karaim* had passed somewhere (I had never heard the word before, but realized that they must have been some sort of sect)—old men in loose garments reaching to their heels. They had spent the night in their *Karaim* synagogue. In the morning they had come out chanting, "Children, we are going to our deaths! Prepare yourselves! Let us meet death bravely, as Christ did."

Some were indignant. Why should anyone start a panic like that? It was already known, however, that a woman had poisoned her children and herself rather than go. A girl had jumped from a window near the Opera House. Her body lay covered on the sidewalk.

Suddenly there was a great troubled stir. People were chattering on all sides, saying that Melnik Street had been cut off. One could pass through the cordon there, but not return.

This frightened me. Tired and dizzy, I was afraid I would not manage to get out of the crowd and would be driven off with them. I pushed hard against the people, made my way through, and got out. Then I took the long way home through streets that were empty now except for a few late-comers who were almost running to catch up.

When I came home I saw Grandfather in the middle of the yard. He stood there with a finger raised, straining to hear the sound of firing far away.

"D'you know what they're doing?" he said, shaken. "They're shooting them."

I heard it distinctly now: the even ra-ta-ta of a machine gun from Babi Yar.

This was calm, unhurried firing, as on a shooting range. Our Babi Yar adjoined the cemetery. One had only to cross the ravine to get to Lukyanovka.

Grandfather looked puzzled and frightened.

"These shots could be coming from the shooting range," I suggested.

"What shooting range?" he snapped. "The whole of Kurenevka is talking about it. Victor Makedon came back after seeing his wife off. He barely saved himself. Mother of God, Queen of Heaven, what are we coming to!"

We entered the house, but could not sit still, for we heard firing and more firing. Grandfather went to Makedon's house to learn what he could. The place was full of people listening to the young fellow (he had married just before the war) tell how passports had been examined and thrown onto a bonfire. He had managed to shout, "I'm a Russian." Whereupon they had torn his wife from him and led her off to Babi Yar. He had been chased away. . . .

It was cold outside. Yesterday's piercing wind had not abated. I kept running out to hear what people were saying. Grandmother brought me my coat and hat and paused to listen too. It seemed to me she was crying. I turned to look at her more closely. She was crossing herself, facing Babi Yar and muttering "Ahfath! Whoart in Heaven—"

The firing stopped after dark, but resumed in the morning. In Kurenevka it was said that 35,000 had been shot on the first day and that the rest were waiting their turn.

Alexander Solzhenitsyn

From CANCER WARD (1968)

Translated by Nicholas Bethell and David Burg

Hailed by Western critics as the greatest living writer of Russian prose, Solzhenitsyn was imprisoned from 1945 to 1953 for remarks against Stalin. He began writing in 1957, but his recent works, including the one excerpted here, have not been published in Russia.

To Oleg exile was full of laughter and elation, and for that the Kadmins, an old couple he knew, were mainly responsible. The husband, Nikolai Ivanovich, was a gynecologist and his wife was called Elena Alexandrovna. Whatever happened to the exiled Kadmins, they kept saying, "Isn't that fine? Things are so much better than they used to be. How lucky we are to have landed in such a nice part of the world!"

If they managed to get hold of a loaf of white bread—how wonderful! If they found a two-volume edition of Puastovsky in the bookshop—splendid! There was a good movie on at the center that day—marvelous! A dental technician had arrived to provide new dentures—excellent! Another gynecologist had been sent there, a woman, an exile too—very good! Let *her* do the gynecology and the illegal abortions; Nikolai Ivanovich would take care of the general practice. There'd be less money but more peace of mind. And the sunsets over the steppe, orange, pink, flame-red, crimson and purple—superlative! Nikolai Ivanovich, a small, slender man with graying hair, would take his wife by the arm (she was plump and growing heavy, partly through ill-health; he was as quick as she was slow) and they would march off solemnly past the last house of the village to watch the sun go down.

Their life blossomed into steady joy on the day they bought their own tumble-down mud hut with kitchen garden, their last haven, they knew, the roof under which they would live and die. (They decided to die together. When one went, the other would go too: what was there to stay for?) They had no furniture, so they asked Khomratovich, an old man who was also an exile, to fix them an adobe platform in a corner, which became their conjugal bed—beautifully wide and comfortable! Perfect! They stuffed a big, broad sack with straw and sewed it up for a mattress. Next, they ordered a table from Khomratovich, a round one into the bargain. Khomratovich was puzzled. Over sixty years he'd lived in this world, and he'd never seen a round table. Why make it round? "Please!" said Nikolai Ivanovich, rubbing his deft, white gynecologist's hands. "It simply *must* be round!" Their next problem was to get hold of a paraffin lamp. They wanted a glass lamp, not a tin one, with a tall stand, the wick had to have ten strands, not seven, and they insisted on spare globes too. Since no such lamps existed in Ush-Terek, it had to be assembled piecemeal, each part brought by kind people from a long way off. Finally, there stood the lamp, with its homemade shade, on the round table. In Ush-Terek in the year 1954, when the hydrogen bomb was already invented and people were chasing after standard lamps in the capitals, this paraffin lamp on the round homemade table transformed the little clay hovel into a luxurious drawing room of two centuries ago. What a triumph! As the three of them sat round it, Elena Alexandrovna would remark with feeling, "You know, Oleg; life is so good. Apart from childhood, these have been the happiest days of my life."

And obviously she was right. It is not our level of prosperity that makes for happiness but the kinship of heart to heart and the way we look at the world. Both attitudes lie within our power, so that a man is happy so long as he chooses to be happy, and no one can stop him.

Andrei Voznesensky

THE AIRPORT AT NIGHT (1961)

Translated by Henry and Olga Carlisle

Considered by many to be the most talented poet of the Soviet avant-garde, Voznesensky is a master of complex verse forms, "full of invention, fireworks, and humor," as Robert Lowell has said. The poem below is his modern counterpart to Mayakovsky's "Brooklyn Bridge."

My self-portrait, neon alembic, apostle of heaven's door—
Airport!
In their aluminum frames the windows
Gleam like X-ray pictures of the soul.
How frightening it is
                when the sky stands still
in the fiery runways
of fantastic cities!
Twenty-four hours a day
                through your sluice doors
        pour starry destinies,
        porters, whores.
        In the bar, like angels, your alcoholics are fading
            away.
        You speak to them.
They who were beaten down
                you elevate.
You announce an Arrival!

One waits here for boy friends, miracles, bags, careers,
And dazzlingly
        five Caravels
                set down from the skies!
Five carousers wearily lowering their landing gears.
Where is the sixth?
It looks like she's wandered too far,
                wicked storkling,

Little star.
Beneath her the electric cities
                play leap-frog.
Oh, where does she roam
                and sigh and frolic.
Like a cigarette
                burning in the fog?
She doesn't understand the forecast.
The earth is not receiving her.

The forecast is bad, and to await the storm
You retreat like guerillas to the gate areas.
The powerful eye searches other worlds.
The window washers
                make your eyes water,
Sidereal parachutists of the crystal monster.
How sweet and annoying
                to be of the future generation,
Where there'll be no fools
                or gingerbread stations—
Only poets and airports!
The sky moans in its aquarium glass,
Welded to the earth.

Airport—you are the accredited embassy
of ozone and sun!
A hundred generations
                dared not reach for this—
The triumph over mass in construction.
Instead of stone idols
                a glassful of azure
Cools—with no glass.
Around the check-in rows
You are as antimaterial as gas!
Brooklyn Bridge, old fool, grim stone fort,
The monument of this age
is the Airport.

Bella Akhmadulina

GOODBYE (1966)

Adapted by Jean Valentine with Olga Carlisle

A glamorous and beautiful young woman, formerly Yevtushenko's wife, Akhmadulina is widely read and admired. Her verse tends to be traditional, concrete rather than abstract, and always highly personal.

And finally I'll say goodbye.
Don't feel you have to love.
I'm chattering, crazy,
or maybe coming into a crazier kind of
                peace.

How you loved! Your lips just grazing
                over disaster,

tasting nothing. But that doesn't matter.
How you loved! How you destroyed!
Offhandedly, like a great pale curious
                boy.

O coldness of failure, cold certainty,
there's no settling with you. The body
wanders around, sees light; sun and

                moon
shine through the glass pane.

The empty body goes on with its little
                task.
But the hands fall light and slack,
and like a small flock, sideways,
all sounds and smells graze off away.

Iosif Brodsky

THE MONUMENT (c. 1965)

Adapted by W. S. Merwin with Olga Carlisle

Brodsky, born in 1940, was considered by Anna Akhmatova to be the most talented of the young poets. Preferring to remain unpublished in order to write what he pleased, he was tried in 1964 as a "parasite," and given five years hard labor—a sentence later commuted.

Let us set up a monument
in the city, at the end of the long avenue,
or at the center of the big square,
a monument
that will stand out against any background
because it will be
quite well built and very realistic.
Let us set up a monument
that will not disturb anybody.

We will plant flowers
around the pedestal
and with the permission of the city fathers
we will lay out a little garden
where our children
will blink
at the great orange sun
and take the figure perched above them
for a well-known thinker
a composer
or a general.

I guarantee that flowers will appear
every morning
on the pedestal.
Let us set up a monument
that will not disturb anybody.

Even taxi drivers
will admire its majestic silhouette.
The garden will be a place
for rendezvous.
Let us set up a monument,
we will pass under it
          hurrying on our way to work,
foreigners will have their pictures taken
          standing under it,
we will splash it at night with the glare
          of floodlights.

Let us set up a monument to The Lie.

Yevgeny Yevtushenko

THE THIRD MEMORY (1966)

Adapted by Samuel Hazo with Olga Carlisle

Yevtushenko is a political and topical poet whose simple, direct verse and flamboyant personality are extremely popular in Russia. Though a firm believer in communism, he first became famous in the West for his outspoken stand against Stalinism and anti-Semitism.

To everyone comes that time
when anguish clings and clings.
Life then in all its nakedness
becomes pointless as death.

Fearful, weak, suddenly
cold, we shrink, but perseveringly
call out, call out to memory
as we might summon a sister

of mercy. But still the desolation
in the night prevails. The memories
of reason and the heart are not
enough to save what wants

to live within the eyes,
what moves, what makes us speak.
Everything dies. Only
the body's memory survives.

My legs remember being bare
against the coolest grasses.
My feet cannot forget the soft
sting of sand across a road.

My cheek recalls (it was after
a fight) how tenderly a dog
with that kind roughness of his tongue
consoled my rage away.

My brow remembers still
(and guiltily) how silently a kiss
revealed my mother's tenderness
and how in darkness I was blessed.

My fingers keep their memories
of rye, pine needles, rain,
and barely tangible, a sparrow's
shiver or the nervous quiver

down the withers of a horse.
My lips remember lips
of ice and flame, of dawn
and dark, of some lost world

that tastes of oranges and snow.
Then I can whisper, "Life,
forgive my anger at your secrets.
Forgive the guilt that blinded

me until I doubted you.
If you must ask a bitter
price each time you offer
me some relish of the earth,

so be it. Uncertainties,
defeats, the pains of loss—
are these too much to pay
for all that's beautiful in you?"

Despite the tenuous steps toward the liberalizing of Soviet writing and painting in the fifties and sixties, the personal approach of Vasily Sitnikov was still too unorthodox to receive official sanction. The earthy humor of "Man in a Birch Tree" (above), painted c. 1960, is typical of Sitnikov's work. In Russian folklore the birch tree is symbolic of woman.

13

The Popular Imperative

The Arts under the Soviets

Ten years after the Russian Revolution of 1917, at the Fifteenth Convention of the Communist Party, Joseph Stalin and his allies wrested control of the Party from Trotskyites and other factions and redirected Party policy. Now, rather than promoting world-wide communism as Lenin had intended, Russian communists were to concentrate their energies on building socialism at home, as Stalin put it. To create an industrial nation capable of supporting a socialist society, Stalin initiated the first of the Five-Year Plans for industrialization and collectivization.

Thus, a decade after civil war had devastated the economy, famine and violence reigned once more as the country struggled to reach total collectivization of its agricultural resources and a substantial increase in industrial output for the period from 1928 to 1932. The task demanded enormous material and political sacrifices from Soviet citizens, and many rebelled. In the process of collectivizing the land thousands of recalcitrant peasants were executed and millions starved to death, while many of those who supported the new policy gave themselves to it wholeheartedly, and often fanatically.

During this time of social upheaval, Party leaders firmly

In a theatrical extravaganza of flaming flags and banners and posters of socialist heroes, thousands of Soviet citizens sweep through Moscow's Red Square celebrating the anniversary of the Revolution.

enforced the Marxist-Leninist doctrine that the arts must serve society by educating and inspiring the masses. Artists were to give their attentions to studying and emulating the old European and Russian masters rather than experimenting with new forms and styles. Thus they would create for the revolution a cultural tradition in the same way that the tsars of old sought to legitimize their authority by creating links with the country's legendary founders. Simultaneously, a program of "social command" was launched whereby artists and writers were subject to the needs of the Five-Year Plans, becoming, as Stalin said, "engineers of human souls." Works of art had to reveal the spirit of socialism and reflect the Party viewpoint. Each work had to meet the requirements of *partynost* (Party character), *ideynost* (socialist content), and *narodnost* (the ideals and interests of the working masses).

In 1932 artists, architects, and writers were told to form into national unions guided by the Party. Two years later it was decreed that the creative method best suited to the Party's aim was socialist realism. From then on it was the only recognized mode of artistic expression in the U.S.S.R. The national crises gripping the country—collectivization, the purges, World War II, and post-war reconstruction—only served to strengthen the credo of socialist realism; despite the period of relative freedom granted the arts from 1954 to 1964, it continues to prevail.

Icons for the New Religion

Soviet painters and sculptors have created an art that is instructive in nature and admittedly tendentious in its glorification of the masses. Guided by Party doctrine, Soviet artists have returned to the precepts that guided the Academic artists of the eighteenth and nineteenth centuries, except that now the prism through which reality passes, to emerge ennobled, is the prism of socialist realism rather than of Academic pedagogy. In Soviet as in Academic art the result is an emphasis on content and the subordination of form; to convey the socialist message Soviet artists are encouraged to work with forms that have been proved effective in the past. Soviet art thus tends to echo—often quite loudly—the works of other masters and other schools.

The state amply rewards the artist who works in the accepted manner. As a member of an artists' union he belongs to a privileged class, receiving a high salary, expense-paid research trips, and access to artists' resorts. Those who ignore socialist realism and concentrate on personal themes and styles have difficulty getting their work exhibited; when the cultural climate turns particularly cold they are harrassed by the bureaucracy, unable to find jobs or even to obtain artists' materials.

*But for the tractor and the peasant garb, "Mother" (above) might have been an icon
Madonna; the painting is by Pavel Kuznetsov, formerly of Diaghilev's World of Art,
who adapted his art to the demands of the State. "The Defense of Petrograd" (opposite), by Alexander Deineka, symbolically depicts the civil war's opposing factions.*

According to the tenets of socialist realism Soviet artists are encouraged to seek themes arising from the Soviet environment and—while staying within the boundaries of realism—to invent forms that will reflect the activities and human relationships of the Soviet people. Exponents of socialist realism contend that infinite variety is possible within its framework, and indeed the three artists represented here—each of whom made his reputation after the 1917 revolution—have developed individual styles in dealing with the prescribed themes. "Summer" (opposite) is a pastoral scene à la Renoir by Arkady Plastov, whose lyrical paintings, often depicting life on the collective farm, are marked by a delicacy of palette and an impressionistic use of color. On the other hand Yury Pimenov, a student of Kuzma Petrov-Vodkin (one of whose paintings appears on page 320), prefers to deal with factory workers and their surroundings. His painting at right is called "New Moscow" and was done in 1937. In tone and style and in the artist's concern with the poetry of commonplace urban life, the picture is reminiscent of America's Ash Can school of art of nearly thirty years before. In a painting of more recent vintage (above) an artist from the Soviet Republic of Azerbaidzhan, Tair Salakhov, chose an austere approach of sharply contrasting light and shadow in his portrait of composer Kara Karaev.

NOVOSTI

343

Ignored in official art circles, the Soviet Union's modernist painters find recognition among a few Soviet bureaucrats, performers, and intellectuals, who avidly collect their works. As renegades from socialist realism they do not receive financial aid from the State and must seek other means of support, working as laborers or illustrators; some even have themselves declared insane to collect the pension allotted to the mentally ill. Since they are unable to study in any depth the recent experiments in American and European art, their paintings are often amalgamations of poorly assimilated Western styles. Socially ostracized, they tend to turn inward for inspiration, creating intensely personal fantasies. Cut off from government resources, they are forced to steal art supplies or improvise with such materials as shoe polish. The two recent paintings shown here are "Coelacanth" or "Man Fish" (above), by Dmitry Plavinsky, who is highly regarded for his three-dimensional collage techniques; and "Cards on a Marquetry Table" (opposite), one of a series of paintings in which the artist, Vladimir Nemukhin, explores the symbolism of playing cards.

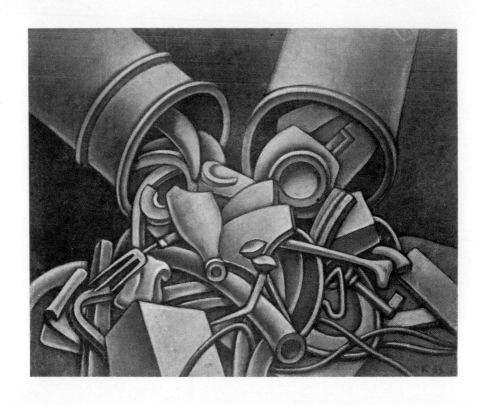

The Impressionistic water color "At the Piano" (opposite) was painted in 1933 by Artur Fonvizin, an early "unofficial" artist. Dmitry Krasnopevtsev, whose "Two Pipes" (1963) appears at top, opposite, believes in a "silent art" in which meaning "is either self-revealed by analogy, or is absent altogether." Oskar Rabin, who painted "Power Lines" (above), has exhibited widely though he is not a member of the Artists' Union.

2. Обложка. 1925.

Since the early 1920's children's art has been a refuge for artists and writers who are not always politically oriented, providing an acceptable outlet for their creativity. The illustrations shown here, which span the Soviet period, represent a stylized approach. Above is the cover for a book called The Circus, written by a noted children's poet, Samuil Marshak, and published in 1925. The illustrator, Vladimir Lebedev (one of whose posters is shown on page 306), later turned to more conventional styles after being attacked as a modernist. At right is a 1969 reworking of folk art motifs for a popular tale about a mistreated orphan girl and her only friend, a cow.

In nearly every square and public building appear sculptures by official artists such as the late Matvei Manizer (shown opposite in his studio). One Party-line sculptor's attempted abstraction, the monument (right) to the first artificial satellite, was marred by the realistic rocket atop the soaring curves. The two collages above, one untitled, the other called "Bleeding Buffalo" (made from a pair of pants), are by unofficial artist Otto Varazi.

Pointing the Way

The body of literature defining socialist realism rests heavily on the works of Lenin (shown exhorting a crowd in the painting above, by Vladimir Serov; Stalin stands behind him). Lenin's and Stalin's theories are excerpted below, along with interpretations by officials and artists: director Sergei Eisenstein; Stalin's enforcer of ideology, Andrei Zhdanov; Premier Khrushchev; and Party Secretary Brezhnev. Khrushchev's remarks at an exhibition including avant-garde painting prompted the letter from a group of artists and the consequent reply by Khrushchev's ideologist, Leonid Ilyichev.

All the culture left by capitalism must be taken and socialism built with it. All science, technology, all knowledge and art must be taken. Without this we shall not be able to build the life of a communist society.

·   ·   ·

Proletarian culture is not something that springs from nowhere, is not an invention of people who call themselves specialists in proletarian culture. This is complete nonsense. Proletarian culture must be a logical development of those funds of knowledge which humanity has worked out under the yokes of capitalist society.

·   ·   ·

In a society based on private property the artist works to produce ware for the market, he needs purchasers. Our revolution has freed the artists from the yoke of these very prosaic conditions. It turned the Soviet Government into their defender and placer of orders. Every artist, everyone that considers himself an artist, has a right to create freely according to his ideals, independent of anything. Only, of course, we communists, we cannot stand with hands folded and let chaos develop in any direction it may. We must guide this process according to a plan and form its results.

Vladimir Lenin, 1919–24

A follower of Lenin cannot be just a specialist in his favorite science or art; he must also be a social and political worker taking a vital interest in the destinies of his country. He must be well acquainted with the laws of social development; he must be able to apply these laws and . . . participate in the political guidance of the country.

Joseph Stalin, 1939

In the second part of *Ivan the Terrible* we committed a misrepresentation of historical facts which made the film worthless and vicious in an ideological sense.

We know Ivan the Terrible was a man with a strong will and firm character. Does that exclude from the characterization of this Tsar the possibility of the existence of certain doubts? It is difficult to think that a man who did such unheard-of and unprecedented things in his time . . . never had doubts about how to act at one time or another. But could it be that these possible doubts overshadowed the historical role of historical Ivan as it was shown in the film? . . . Is it not so that the center of our attention is and must be *Ivan the builder, Ivan the creator of a new, powerful, united Russian power*, Ivan the inexorable destroyer of everything that resisted his progressive undertakings?

The sense of historical truth betrayed me in the second part of *Ivan the Terrible*. The private, unimportant and non-characteristic shut out the principal. . . . A false and mistaken impression was created. . . . The resolution of the Central Committee accusing me of a wrong presentation which disfigures historical truth says that in the film Ivan is presented as "weak-charactered and lacking in will, a kind of Hamlet." This is solidly grounded and just.

Sergei Eisenstein, 1946

What a step backward it is along the highroad of musical development when our formalists, undermining the foundations of true music, compose music which is ugly and false, permeated with idealist sentiment, alien to the broad masses of the people, and created not for the millions of Soviet people, but for chosen individuals and small groups, for an elite. How unlike Glinka, Tchaikovsky, Rimsky-Korsakov, Dargomyzhsky, Mussorgsky, who considered the basis for development of their creative power to be the ability to express in their works the spirit and character of the people. By ignoring the wants of the people and its spirit and creative genius, the formalist trend in music has clearly demonstrated its anti-popular character.

If a certain section of Soviet composers favor the theory that they will be appreciated in fifty or a hundred years' time, and that their descendants, if not their contemporaries, will understand them, then the situation is really terrifying. . . . Such a theory indicates an estrangement from the people. If I, a writer, an artist, a critic, or a Party worker, do not count on being understood by my contemporaries, for whom then do I live and work? . . .

Andrei Zhdanov, 1950

What is this anyway? You think we old fellows don't understand you. And we think we are just wasting money on you. Are you pederasts or normal people? I'll be perfectly straightforward with you: we won't spend a kopeck on your art. Just give me a list of those of you who want to go abroad, to the so-called "free world." We'll give you foreign passports tomorrow, and you can get out. Your prospects here are nil. What is hung here is simply anti-Soviet. It's amoral. Art should ennoble the individual and arouse him to action. And what have you set out here? Who painted this picture? I want to talk to him. What's the good of a picture like this? To cover urinals with?

Nikita Khrushchev at the Manège Gallery, December, 1962

Without the possibility of the existence of different artistic trends, art is doomed. We now see how artists who have followed a single trend which flourished under Stalin, and which did not permit others to work or even to live, are beginning to interpret what you said at the exhibition. . . . We appeal to you to stop this return to past methods which are contrary to the whole spirit of our times.

Letter to Khrushchev, December, 1962; signatories include the writers Simonov and Ehrenburg; artists Konenkov and Favorsky; the composer Shostakovich.

It is said that sometimes at meetings, in discussions of creative questions, it is now considered indecent and old-fashioned to defend the correct Party positions; to do so is to appear to be reactionary, . . . to lay oneself open to the accusation of dogmatism, sectarianism, narrowmindedness, backwardness, Stalinism, etc. . . . It is one thing to combat the consequences of the cult of personality in order to assert the Leninist standards of life . . . and another to deal blows . . . to our society and our ideology. . . . We have full freedom to fight for communism. We do not have and cannot have freedom to fight against communism.

Leonid Ilyichev, December, 1962

The Communist Party is fighting and will continue to fight against abstractionism and against any other formalist distortions in art. We cannot be neutral toward formalism. . . . We call for vivid works of art that truthfully portray the real world in all its diversity of colors. Only such art will give people joy and pleasure. Man will never lose the capacity for artistic talent and will not allow dirty daubs that any donkey could paint with his tail to be foisted on him in the guise of works of art.

Nikita Khrushchev, speech to writers and artists, 1963

The Communist party of the Soviet Union has always manifested and will continue to manifest concern for the development of literature and art. The Party has guided and will continue to guide the activity of creative organizations and institutions, giving them all-round support and assistance . . . we are unfailingly guided by the principle of Party spirit in art and class approach to judging everything that is done in the sphere of culture.

Leonid Brezhnev, speech before the 23rd Party Congress, 1966

The Grand Design

The emergence of socialist realism as the official state doctrine on the arts was the primary cause of the moratorium on modern architecture that held sway in the Soviet Union from the 1930's to the 1950's. Prior to the doctrine's enunciation in 1934, architecture had been divided among the traditionalists, who were oriented toward the styles of the eighteenth and nineteenth centuries; the Constructivists, who delved into experiments in form; and the functionalists, for whom form was strictly subordinate to function. At issue was whether architecture was an art or an engineering science. In theory, the dilemma was resolved by applying to architecture the tenets of socialist realism. Architecture was declared an art, since it combined function and form; and as an art its aim must be to serve the people and illustrate the historical progress made under socialism.

In practice the decree was a victory for the traditionalists. Modernism in Soviet architecture, now timidly gaining ground, was never completely stifled, as can be seen in such monuments to socialist achievement as hydroelectric power stations and factories. But government buildings, which as headquarters of the proletarian regime stand as symbols of the progress of socialism, reflect more the bourgeois spirit of the nineteenth century.

S. FREDERICK STARR

One of the last experimental ventures in architecture before the government's freeze on modernism and nonessential building was the office of the newspaper Pravda *(above) designed by Panteleymon Golosov and built between 1929 and 1935. (Ironically, the propaganda attack on modernism was launched from these offices.) The earlier aesthetic survived somewhat in the clean, dynamic form of the hydroelectric dams, as seen in the design (top) for a dam on the Dnieper, c. 1929. But the 1950's apartment complex at left is more typical of the official design that prevailed from the thirties to the fifties, having an abundance of superfluous details reminiscent of the nineteenth century.*

For the Soviet Union World War II was a disaster akin to that of the Mongol invasions. There were twenty million military and civilian casualties. The land and the economy were devastated. Entire cities—Kiev, Minsk, and Stalingrad (now Volgograd)—were demolished and twenty-five million people left homeless. But the fascists had been turned back, and in the aftermath the heroism and tragedy of the war became the predominant theme in the work of Soviet writers, painters, sculptors, and graphic artists. Architects, faced with the enormous task of rebuilding, also contributed to memorializing the war's heroes. Working with other artists, they dotted the countryside with massive monuments. At Stalingrad, the site of the monuments shown here, a vast architectural complex was constructed that covered the entire top of a hill with gardens, squares, statues, and gigantic friezes like the one shown at the right. (Parts of the hill had been held by the Germans during their murderous, 162-day siege in 1942; the attack reduced the city to rubble, but the Russian army and citizenry—their backs to the Volga—succeeded in surrounding the invaders, forcing them to surrender.) The city itself, which had to be almost totally rebuilt, became a monument, and memorial statues and wall reliefs (above) are numerous there.

OVERLEAF: *In this view of Moscow at sunset, two sharply contrasting styles of Soviet architecture stand on either side of the Moskva River. At right is a hotel built in the early 1950's in a wedding-cake form that might be called Soviet Victorian. At left rises a modern glass and steel office building in the functional design that began appearing in most world capitals during the sixties.*

NOVOSTI

The Show
Goes On

Soviet citizens are great lovers of theatrical spectacle, and as elsewhere the most devoted fans are willing to brave the adversities of bad weather, long queues, and ticket shortages to see their favorite performers. However, in the Soviet Union both the audiences' enthusiasm and the performers' talents are encouraged by the government's ideological support of popular art. Since socialism makes the arts the nation's property and the government's responsibility, the State underwrites many aspects of the performing arts, financing productions and the training of future artists, and regulating ticket prices so that all performances are within reach of the average wage earner.

Like painting, sculpture, and architecture, however, the performing arts are often hamstrung by the dictates of socialist realism. Interpretation of this doctrine in drama, dance, and music is reflected in the perpetual re-creation of nineteenth-century productions, and a passion for historical accuracy in scenery and costumes. Directors follow Stanislavsky's realistic method and are discouraged from seeking new alternatives; choreographers faithfully produce pre-Revolutionary ballets; musicians avoid contemporary pieces; and film makers prefer adapting Dostoevsky's and Gorky's novels to creating original scripts.

The result of this heavy emphasis on ideology in the arts is a profusion of ironic contrasts. Alongside the superb artistry of such performers as cellist Mstislav Rastropovich, violinists David and Igor Oistrakh, pianist Emile Gilels, ballerinas Maya Plisetskaya and Yekaterina Maximova, and soprano Galina Vishnevskaya, there is a reluctance to experiment with new forms. Similarly, the most popular performances in ballet, opera, and dance are fantasies of tsarist splendor recreated for the entertainment of proletarians.

Yet innovative work has been appearing, even if its existence is made precarious by the Soviet bureaucracy. While staying within the framework of socialist realism the directors of such original films as *Ballad of a Soldier* (1959) and *Shadows of Forgotten Ancestors* (1964) have created striking imagery and vivid dramatic effects. And at Moscow's Taganka Theater audiences have witnessed experiments in stagecraft that rival those of the Western *avant-garde*.

Since the days of itinerant showmen, Russians have delighted in the antics of trained animals and puppets. Opposite are shown elephants and their trainer performing at the Moscow Circus; at left, the hands of the famous puppeteer Sergei Obraztsov become a part of his creations.

Under the aegis of a young director, Yury Lyubimov, the Taganka Theater—formerly one of the most sterile in Moscow—has become the liveliest. Its repertoire consists mostly of original dramas rather than nineteenth-century revivals, and includes plays by Bertolt Brecht and Jean Anouilh. Dramatic effects are heightened by the use of experimental lighting and sound, shadows, slide projections, music, dance, puppets, mime, and such vivid images as a chorus of severed heads. At left is a scene from a 1966 production, a satire on American life, using masks and crew-cut wigs. Entertainment in a more orthodox style—though having less political content—is provided by the classical repertoire of the U.S.S.R. State Symphony (shown below) and the folk ballets of the Moiseev dancers, one of whom is caught in mid-leap (opposite).

Map, Genealogy, Acknowledgments, and Index

"Mighty snow-capped mountains border the sea. The endless mountains, forests and valleys, the plateaus and ridges are alive with the creatures of the wild. The corroded and riddled bowels of these great mountains yield copper, silver, zinc, lead, cement, all manner of riches. Oil oozes like dark blood from the earth. . . . Wonderland of riches. From the mountains and sea stretch the steppes, so vast that they seem without limit or boundaries. The waving silken wheat is endless. They have no end, no confine. There is no land so beautiful as ours." In these words a modern Russian writer, Alexander Serafimovich, described his homeland in 1924. The vast Russian plain is all but totally isolated by seas and mountains: the Urals to the east; the Caucasus, the Caspian Sea, and the Black Sea to the south; the Arctic Ocean and the Baltic Sea to the north and west. This plain the Russian people have ruled, in whole or in part, for better than a thousand years, and here their culture has flourished, despite the harsh climate and despite perpetual invasions and constant internal strife. Main features of the land and main centers of culture are shown in the map opposite.

HOUSE OF RYURIK

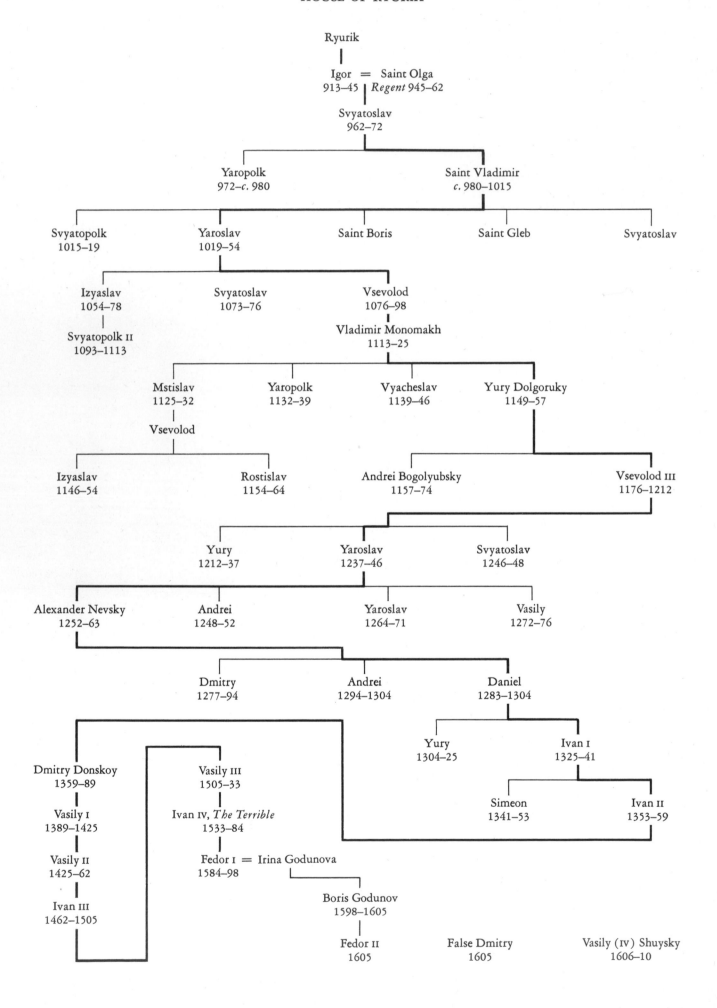

Ryurik

Igor = Saint Olga
913–45 | *Regent* 945–62

Svyatoslav
962–72

Yaropolk
972–*c.* 980

Saint Vladimir
c. 980–1015

Svyatopolk
1015–19

Yaroslav
1019–54

Saint Boris

Saint Gleb

Svyatoslav

Izyaslav
1054–78

Svyatoslav
1073–76

Vsevolod
1076–98

Svyatopolk II
1093–1113

Vladimir Monomakh
1113–25

Mstislav
1125–32

Yaropolk
1132–39

Vyacheslav
1139–46

Yury Dolgoruky
1149–57

Vsevolod

Izyaslav
1146–54

Rostislav
1154–64

Andrei Bogolyubsky
1157–74

Vsevolod III
1176–1212

Yury
1212–37

Yaroslav
1237–46

Svyatoslav
1246–48

Alexander Nevsky
1252–63

Andrei
1248–52

Yaroslav
1264–71

Vasily
1272–76

Dmitry
1277–94

Andrei
1294–1304

Daniel
1283–1304

Yury
1304–25

Ivan I
1325–41

Dmitry Donskoy
1359–89

Vasily III
1505–33

Simeon
1341–53

Ivan II
1353–59

Vasily I
1389–1425

Ivan IV, *The Terrible*
1533–84

Vasily II
1425–62

Fedor I = Irina Godunova
1584–98

Ivan III
1462–1505

Boris Godunov
1598–1605

Fedor II
1605

False Dmitry
1605

Vasily (IV) Shuysky
1606–10

HOUSE OF ROMANOV

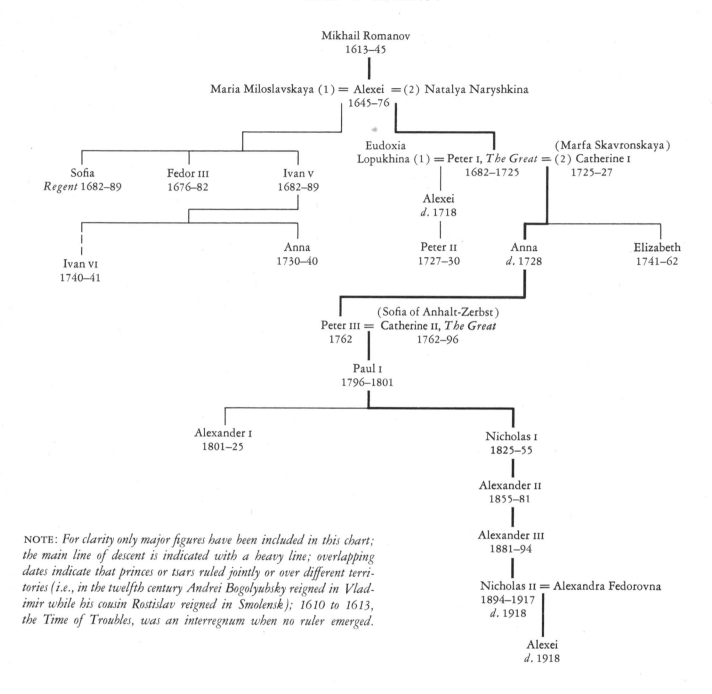

Mikhail Romanov
1613–45

Maria Miloslavskaya (1) = Alexei = (2) Natalya Naryshkina
1645–76

Sofia
Regent 1682–89

Fedor III
1676–82

Ivan V
1682–89

Eudoxia
Lopukhina (1) = Peter I, *The Great* = (2) Catherine I
1682–1725

(Marfa Skavronskaya)
Catherine I
1725–27

Alexei
d. 1718

Ivan VI
1740–41

Anna
1730–40

Peter II
1727–30

Anna
d. 1728

Elizabeth
1741–62

(Sofia of Anhalt-Zerbst)
Peter III = Catherine II, *The Great*
1762   1762–96

Paul I
1796–1801

Alexander I
1801–25

Nicholas I
1825–55

Alexander II
1855–81

Alexander III
1881–94

Nicholas II = Alexandra Fedorovna
1894–1917
d. 1918

Alexei
d. 1918

NOTE: *For clarity only major figures have been included in this chart; the main line of descent is indicated with a heavy line; overlapping dates indicate that princes or tsars ruled jointly or over different territories (i.e., in the twelfth century Andrei Bogolyubsky reigned in Vladimir while his cousin Rostislav reigned in Smolensk); 1610 to 1613, the Time of Troubles, was an interregnum when no ruler emerged.*

UNION OF SOVIET SOCIALIST REPUBLICS
CHAIRMEN OF THE COUNCIL OF PEOPLE'S COMMISSARS

Vladimir Lenin
1917–24

Georgy Malenkov
1953–55

Alexei Rykov
1924–30

Nikolai Bulganin
1955–58

Vyacheslav Molotov
1930–41

Nikita Khrushchev
1958–64

Joseph Stalin
1941–53

Alexei Kosygin
1964–

Acknowledgments

The editors gratefully acknowledge the valuable editorial assistance of Sandra N. Humphrey, Gretchen Maynes, Christine Sutherland, and Elena Whiteside. They are also grateful for the assistance of Herman Ermolaev, Professor of Soviet Literature, Princeton University; to Cal Sacks for the original map; and to the following individuals and institutions for providing pictorial material and supplying information.

À La Vieille Russie, New York
  Mr. Paul Schaffer
  Mr. Peter Schaffer
Art Institute of Chicago
Arts Council of Great Britain
Miss Mila Barsacq, Paris
Mr. S. Beliz, Paris
Bodleian Library, Oxford
  Department of Western Manuscripts
British Museum, London
Mr. Geoffrey Clements, New York
Editions Cercle d'Art, Paris
Mr. and Mrs. Jacques Garvin, New York
Grosvenor Gallery, London
Mr. George Hann, Sewickley, Pennsylvania
Hermitage Museum, Leningrad
Mr. and Mrs. Nikita Lobanov, New York
Mr. H. Lowenkron, New York
Musée de la Ville, Strasbourg
  M. Jean Louis Faure
Museum of Modern Art
  Mr. Richard Tooke
Miss Nadia Nerina, London
Novosti Press Agency, Moscow
  Guenrikh A. Borovik, New York
Mr. Robert J. O'Reilly, New York
Mr. Jerry Rosencrantz, New York
Royal Academy of Arts, London
Miss Janet Schulman, New York
Mrs. L. Slater, Oxford
Mr. A. Kenneth Snowman, London
Society for Cultural Relations with the U.S.S.R.
State Tretyakov Gallery, Moscow
Mrs. Nina Stevens, New York
Victoria and Albert Museum, London
  Metal Works Department
Wartski Jewelers, London

The editors have transliterated Russian names according to System I of J. Thomas Shaw's The Transliteration of Modern Russian for English-Language Publications, with the exception of certain words, such as Bolshoi, Alexei, Fedor, for which there is an accepted English version. In the anthology selections, however, Russian names are reproduced as they appear in the original translation. Dates accompanying each anthology selection are the dates of first publication unless otherwise indicated.

75 "The Coming of the Greek Iconographers," from Medieval Russia's Epics, Chronicles, and Tales, edited and translated by Serge A. Zenkovsky. Copyright © 1963 by Serge A. Zenkovsky. Reprinted by permission of E.P. Dutton & Co., Inc. 130 "Igor's Death and Olga's Revenge," from The Russian Primary Chronicle, edited by Samuel H. Cross. Copyright © 1953 by The Medieval Academy of America. Reprinted by permission of the publishers. 131 "Eulogy to Our Kagan Vladimir," from Medieval Russia's Epics, Chronicles, and Tales, edited and translated by Serge A. Zenkovsky. Copyright © 1963 by Serge A. Zenkovsky. Reprinted by permission of E.P. Dutton & Co., Inc. 132 "The Lay of Igor's Campaign," from A Treasury of Russian Literature, edited and translated by Bernard Guilbert Guerney. Copyright 1943 by The Vanguard Press, Inc. Reprinted by permission of the publishers. 134 "Prince Ingvar Buries the Dead," from Medieval Russia's Epics, Chronicles, and Tales, edited and translated by Serge A. Zenkovsky. Copyright © 1963 by Serge A. Zenkovsky. Reprinted by permission of E.P. Dutton & Co., Inc./"The Capture of Kazan," from Russian Heroic Poetry, edited by N. Kershaw Chadwick. Copyright © 1964 by Cambridge University Press. Reprinted by permission of the publishers. 135 "The Martyrdom of Boris and Gleb," from The Russian Primary Chronicle, edited by Samuel H. Cross. Copyright © 1953 by The Medieval Academy of America. Reprinted by permission of the publishers./"The Life of Saint Theodosius," from A Treasury of Russian Spirituality, edited by G. P. Fedotov. Copyright 1948 by Sheed & Ward Inc., New York. 136 "Marko the Gravedigger Who Was Obeyed by the Dead," from Medieval Russia's Epics, Chronicles, and Tales, edited and translated by Serge A. Zenkovsky. Copyright © 1963 by Serge A. Zenkovsky. Reprinted by permission of E.P. Dutton & Co., Inc. 138 "The Election of Archbishop Mantury" and "Sermon on Omens," from Medieval Russia's Epics, Chronicles, and Tales, edited and translated by Serge A. Zenkovsky. Copyright © 1963 by Serge A. Zenkovsky. Reprinted by permission of E.P. Dutton & Co., Inc. 141 "Ilya of Murom and Nightingale the Robber," from Russian Heroic Poetry, edited

For further reading, the editors recommend the following works. Paperback editions are indicated by an asterisk.

HISTORY

Billington, James H., *The Icon and the Axe*. Knopf, 1966.

Carmichael, Joel, *A Cultural History of Russia*. Weybright and Talley, 1968.

Fedotov, George P., *The Russian Religious Mind*. Harper Torchbooks, 1960.*

Nettl, J. P., *The Soviet Achievement*. Harcourt, Brace, and World, 1968.

Pares, Bernard, *A History of Russia*. Knopf, 1960.

Riasanovsky, Nicholas V., *A History of Russia*. Oxford University Press, 1963.

Riha, Thomas, ed., *Readings in Russian Civilization* (3 vols.). University of Chicago Press, 1964.*

Troyat, Henri, *Daily Life in Russia*. Allen & Unwin, 1961.

Vernadsky, George, *A History of Russia*, Yale University Press, 1929, 1954.

Vucinich, Wayne S., ed., *The Peasant in Nineteenth-Century Russia*. Stanford University Press, 1968.

Ware, Timothy, *The Orthodox Church*. Penguin, 1964.*

ART AND ARCHITECTURE

Bainbridge, Henry Charles, *Peter Carl Fabergé*. Spring Books, 1967.

Gabo, Naum, *Of Divers Arts*. Pantheon Books, 1962.

Gray, Camilla, *The Great Experiment: Russian Art 1863–1922*. Abrams, 1962.

Hamilton, George Heard, *The Art and Architecture of Russia*. Penguin, 1954.

Lazarev, Viktor, *Old Russian Murals and Mosaics*. Phaidon, 1966.

Markov, Vladimir, *Russian Futurism: A History*. University of California Press, 1968.

Miliukov, Paul. *Outlines of Russian Culture* (3 vols.). A. S. Barnes and Co., 1960.*

Onasch, Konrad, *Icons*. A. S. Barnes and Co., 1963.

Rice, Tamara Talbot, *A Concise History of Russian Art*. Praeger, 1963.*

———*Russian Icons*. Spring Books, 1964.

———*The Scythians*. Praeger, 1957.

Ross, Marvin C., *The Art of Karl Fabergé and His Contemporaries*. University of Oklahoma Press, 1965.

Sjeklocha, Paul, *Unofficial Art in the Soviet Union*. University of California Press, 1967.

Voyce, Arthur, *The Art and Architecture of Medieval Russia*. University of Oklahoma Press, 1967.

THE LIVELY ARTS

Bakst, James, *A History of Russian-Soviet Music*. Dodd, Mead and Co., 1966.

Bowers, Faubion, *Broadway U.S.S.R.* Thomas Nelson & Sons, 1959.

Fokin, Mikhail, *Memoirs of a Ballet Master*. Little Brown, 1961.

Freedley, George, and Reeves, John A., *A History of the Theatre*, Crown, 1958.

Haskell, Arnold, *Ballet*. Penguin, 1955.*

———*The Russian Genius in Ballet*. Macmillan, 1963.*

Leyda, Jay, *Kino: A History of Russian and Soviet Film*. Macmillan, 1966.

Nijinsky, Romola, ed., *The Diary of Vaslav Nijinsky*. University of California Press, 1968.*

Roslavleva, Natalia, *Era of the Russian Ballet*. E. P. Dutton & Co., 1966.

Scholes, Percy A., *The Oxford Companion to Music* (9th ed.). Oxford University Press, 1956.

Stanislavsky, Constantin, *My Life in Art*. Meridian, 1956.*

LITERATURE

Alexandrova, Vera, *A History of Soviet Literature, 1917–1962*. Doubleday, 1963.

Carlisle, Olga, *Voices in the Snow*. Random House, 1962.

———*Poets on Street Corners*. Random House, 1968.

Gorky, Maxim, *Reminiscences of Tolstoy, Chekhov, and Andreev*. Hogarth Press, 1968.

Guerney, Bernard Guilbert, *Russian Literature in the Soviet Period*. Random House, Modern Library, 1960.*

Mirsky, D. S., *A History of Russian Literature*. Knopf, 1966.

Segel, Harold B., *The Literature of Eighteenth-Century Russia* (2 vols.). E. P. Dutton & Co., 1967.*

Slonim, Marc, *Soviet Russian Literature*. Oxford University Press, 1964.

Struve, Gleb, *Soviet Russian Literature, 1917–1950*. University of Oklahoma Press, 1951.

Zenkovsky, Serge A., *Medieval Russia's Epics, Chronicles, and Tales*. E. P. Dutton & Co., 1963.*

Index

NOTE: *Page numbers in italic type indicate that the subject is illustrated.*

EXTER, ALEXANDRA, 277, 285

COLLECTIVE FARM GIRL," by Mukhina, *31*

MAGARSHACK, DAVID, translation by, 228–29

MALAMUTH, CHARLES, translation by, 328

MALEVICH, KAZIMIR, 14, 18, 262, 308, 310

"MAN IN A BIRCH TREE," by Sitnikov, *337*

"MAN FISH," by Plavinsky, *345*

MAN WHO LOST HIS SHADOW, THE, by Anderson, 31

MANDELSHTAM, OSIP, 298–99, 321

MANIZER, MATVEI, *350*

MANTURY, ARCHBISHOP, 138

MARKOV, VLADIMIR, translations by, 294–95, 297

"MARRIAGE SONG," 144

MARSHAK, SAMUIL, 348

MARTYRDOM OF BORIS AND GLEB, THE, by Nestor, 135

MARY, VIRGIN, *13*, 15 ff., 69, 70, *72*, 75, *76*, *98*, 99, *100–101*, 102

MASSIN, LEONID, 29, *275*

MASTER AND MARGARITA, THE, by Bulgakov, 329

MATLAW, RALPH E., translation by, 226–27

MAUDE, LOUISE AND AYLMER, translation by, 237–38

MAXIMOVA, YEKATERINA, 360

MAYAKOVSKY, VLADIMIR, 14, 299–301, 308, *308*, 309

MAZEPPA (opera), 15

MELNIKOV, KONSTANTIN, 314, 315

MERCHANT SADKO, THE RICH GUEST OF NOVGOROD, THE, 140–41

MEREZHKOVSKY, DMITRY, 23

MERWIN, W. S., adaptations by, 301, 336

METALWORK, *8, 98, 99, 102, 103, 151, 158–59, 164, 164–65, 169, 265*
  See also SCULPTURE

METHODIUS (missionary), 19, 129

MEYERHOLD, VSEVOLOD, 29

MIDNIGHT SUN (ballet), 29

MIGHTY HANDFULL. See *KUCHKA, THE; specific composers*

MIKHAIL I, TSAR (Romanov), *87*, 103, 159, 161

MINOR, THE by Fonvizin, 212–13

MINSTRELS, 123

MIR ISKUSSTVA. See WORLD OF ART MAGAZINE

MIRELESS, HOPE, translation by, 139

MOISEEV DANCERS, *363*

MONASTERIES AND MONASTICISM, 9, *11*, 19, 21, 42, 44–51, *44–51*, 75, 76, 80, 82, 97, 102, 135, 136, 137, 139

MONGOLS, 10, 11, 20, 33, 52, 58, 69, 134, 137, 138, 356

"MONUMENT, THE," by Brodsky, 336

MONUMENT TO THE THIRD COMMUNIST INTERNATIONAL, 30, *310*

"MOONY THIN DESOLATION, A," by Yesenin, 301

MOROZOVNA, BOYARYNYA, *24–25*, 27

MORRIS, WILLIAM, 258

MOSCOW, 6, 15, 18, 19 ff., 30, 42, 45, 49, 52, *52–62*, 69, 70, 74, 75, 76, 80, 87, 97, 107, 109, 121, 139, 142, 147, 152, 163, 169, 184, 243, 244, 245, 247, 250, 260, *265*, 283, 289, 290, 322, 324, 329, *338, 339, 343, 358–59*, 360, 362

"MOSCOW," by Mandelshtam, 299

MOSCOW ART THEATER, 29, 30, 266, *266–69*, 292, 293

MOSKVIN, IVAN, 266

"MOTHER," by Kuznetsov, *341*

MOTHER (film), 283

MOVIES. See FILM

MUKHINA, VERA, 31

MUSIC, 27–29, 115, *122–23*, 144, 243, *246–49*, 250–51, 270–71, 360, *362–63*
  See also BALLET; *specific works and composers*

MUSSORGSKY, MODEST, 8, 27, 28, 247, 249

"MY HONEYED LANGUOR," by Bagritsky, 325

MYASOEDOV, GRIGORY, 241

MYSTERY (symphony), 29

MYSTERY BOUFFE, by Mayakovsky, 14

N

NABOKOV, VLADIMIR, translation by, 218–19

NAKED KING, THE, by Shvarts, 31

NAKED YEAR, THE, by Pilnyak, 303

NAPOLEON, 23, 54, 181

NARCISSE (ballet), 278

NEEDLEWORK, *100–101*, 116, *116*

NEMIROVICH-DANCHENKO, VLADIMIR, 266

NEMUKHIN, VLADIMIR, 345

NERL, RIVER, 33

NEST OF GENTLEFOLK, A, by Turgenev, 195

NESTER, MASTER, 65

NESTOR (chronicler), 130–31, 135–36

NEVSKY PROSPECT, by Gogol, *189*

NEW JERUSALEM, MONASTERY OF THE, near Moscow, 20

"NEW MOSCOW," by Pimenov, *343*

NICHOLAS, SAINT, *71*

NICHOLAS I, TSAR, 181

NICHOLAS II, TSAR, 104, 168, 169

NIJINSKY, VASLAV, 28, 273, 275, *279, 280–81*

NIKITA, SAINT, *89*

NIKON, ABBOT, 20, 74, 75, 97, 139

"1919; THE ALARM," by Petrov-Vodkin, *320*

NIZHNY-NOVGOROD, Gorky, 107, 115, 283

NOVGOROD, 12, 19, 21, 34, *34, 35, 36*, 37, 42, 70, 76, 85, 107, 138, 140
  See also specific churches

NOVGORODIAN CHRONICLE, 138

NOVODEVICHY MONASTERY, *48–51*

NUTCRACKER, THE (ballet), 30, *252–53*, 253

O

OBLOMOV, by Goncharov, 232–33

OBOLENSKY, DIMITRY, translations by, 294, 297

OBRAZTSOV, SERGEI, 360

ODESSA, 22, 304, 328

OISTRAKH, DAVID, 360

OISTRAKH, IGOR, 360

OLD BELIEVERS, 8, 20, *24–25*, 26, 27, 28, 75, 139

OLESHA, YURY, 323–24